Through Dakota Eyes

Through DAKOTA Eyes

NARRATIVE ACCOUNTS *of the* MINNESOTA INDIAN WAR *of* 1862

Edited by **GARY CLAYTON ANDERSON**
and **ALAN R. WOOLWORTH**

MINNESOTA HISTORICAL SOCIETY PRESS

www.mnhs.org/mhspress

The Minnesota Historical Society Press is a member of
the Association of American University Presses.

Manufactured in the United States of America

10 9 8 7 6 5

International Standard Book Number 0-87351-216-2

♾ The paper used in this publication meets the minimum requirements of the American National Standard for Information Sciences—Permanence for Printed Library Materials, ANSI Z39.48-1984.

Library of Congress Cataloging-in-Publication Data

Anderson, Gary Clayton, 1948–
    Through Dakota Eyes : narrative accounts of the Minnesota Indian War of 1862 / Gary Clayton Anderson and Alan R. Woolworth.
        p.   cm.
    Includes index.
    ISBN 0-87351-215-4 : ISBN 0-87351-216-2 (pbk.)
    1. Dakota Indians—Wars, 1862–1865—Personal narratives.
    2. Dakota Indians—Biography.
    3. Indians of North America—Minnesota—Wars—Personal narratives.
    I. Woolworth, Alan R. (Alan Roland), 1924–   .
    II. Title.
E83.86.A53   1988
973.7—dc19   87-28954
                                                                                CIP

Front cover photographs
(left to right)

John Otherday (photograph by J. E. Whitney) and Big Eagle (both in Minnesota Historical Society Collections), Cecelia Campbell Stay (reversed image; Chippewa County Historical Society, Montevideo, Minnesota).

New material was added to pages 261 and 262 in the fifth impression of this book.

Contents

Illustrations

Maps

Acknowledgments

THE EDITORS wish to acknowledge the contributions of several individuals and organizations who assisted in the compilation of this volume. The "Reminiscence of Thomas A. Robertson" was reprinted with permission from volume 20 of *South Dakota Historical Collections* (1940), a publication of the South Dakota State Historical Society. "A Sketch of the Minnesota Massacre" by Victor Renville was reprinted with permission from volume 5 (1923) of *Collections of the State Historical Society*, a publication of the State Historical Society of North Dakota. The "Statement of Taopi" in Henry B. Whipple, *Lights and Shadows of a Long Episcopate* (1912), was reprinted with permission from Macmillan Publishing Company, New York. "The Sioux Uprising" by Mr. and Mrs. Harry Lawrence in *Minnesota Heritage* was reprinted with permission of T. S. Denison and Company, Inc., Bloomington, Minnesota. The Provincial Archives of Manitoba allowed items in their manuscripts collections to be published.

The Smithsonian Institution, the Newberry Library, the William Hammond Mathers Museum at Indiana University, and the Browns Valley Historical Society in Minnesota gave permission for photographs or artworks in their possession to be used. Carmon Brown, Jean Chesley, Amos Owen, and Joseph J. Martin helped in assembling photographs of the narrators.

Ruth Bauer and Ruby Shields of the Division of Libraries and Archives, Minnesota Historical Society, tracked down documents and answered numerous questions. Mary Burrell and Gloria Haider of the Minnesota Historical Society Press prepared the manuscript for publication, Deborah Swanson proofread the galleys, and Alan Ominsky drew the maps. MHS Press editor Sally Rubinstein has our special thanks for her contributions to the project and for seeing it through to completion.

Introduction

AS THE UNITED STATES riveted its attention on the Second Battle of Bull Run in the Civil War, the Minnesota frontier exploded in violence. Frustrated and provoked by a series of broken promises and by reservation policies that forced cultural change, Dakota Indian warriors began killing white traders and settlers in August 1862. The fighting lasted six weeks and took the lives of nearly five hundred whites, mostly civilians, and an unknown but substantial number of Indians. Twenty-three southwestern Minnesota counties were virtually depopulated.

The conflict left Dakota Indian society fragmented. Most of the six thousand former residents of the reservations were either forced to flee westward to the plains, incarcerated, or executed. Only a few hundred mixed-bloods and their full-blood relatives who had not been found guilty of participating in the fighting were protected by the government. Eventually the survivors—those who had escaped and those who had been imprisoned—settled in North and South Dakota, Nebraska, or Canada or gradually returned to live in Minnesota.

During the thirty-year period after 1862, white Minnesotans published a number of narratives they had written about the conflict. Their stories chronicled the flight of the settlers, detailed the movement of the Minnesota volunteers sent out to engage the Dakota warriors, and glorified the defense of such strategic white strongholds as New Ulm and Fort Ridgely. In 1889 the Minnesota legislature authorized a board of commissioners to assemble the official documents and correspondence of the war, which were published in 1890–93 in two volumes entitled *Minnesota in the Civil and Indian Wars*. None of the published accounts provided much information about what happened within the Indian community, either at the outset of the fighting or throughout the conflict.[1] Yet it is from these sources that authors of state histories have drawn most extensively.

Over the half century following the conflict, newspaper editors and amateur historians occasionally collected the narratives of Dakota people, or the narrators themselves wrote their own accounts, often

1

with the assistance of collaborators — relatives, friends, or interpreters. A handful of these narratives were published in the collections of the Minnesota, South Dakota, and North Dakota historical societies. Others appeared in newspapers and journals, most of which
had limited circulation, and some remained in unpublished form. In
addition, the accounts of Dakota people were recorded as testimony
taken in 1901 at hearings investigating the Sisseton and Wahpeton
claims against the federal government for restoration of their annuities.[2]

In all, sixty-three written Dakota narratives are known to the editors of this volume. (A complete bibliographic listing of the narratives
can be found in the Appendix.) When brought together, the narratives number several hundred printed pages plus dozens of pages in
manuscript. They vary considerably in content and in scope. From
the sixty-three narratives, the editors selected all or parts of thirty-six
for inclusion in this volume. In making the selections, the editors
chose narratives by persons who were present in the Dakota reservation community at the onset of the conflict, those determined to be the
most detailed and informative, and those that contribute to a better
understanding of the events and circumstances of the period and of
the Dakota people's experiences.

Limiting the number to be included in this collection became
necessary for several reasons. Some of the narratives not chosen contain the same information that is given in greater detail elsewhere.
Others are fragmentary or incomplete. The problem of selection is illustrated by the mass of testimony — nearly eight hundred pages —
recorded in hearings before the United States Court of Claims. Much
of the testimony is in the form of questions and short answers and cannot be effectively presented as narratives. Occasionally, however,
witnesses were asked to describe in their own words the events of the
conflict, and they responded with rather long answers that constitute
readable accounts. These have been included in this volume, for they
provide crucial and often overlooked information.

In preparing the thirty-six narratives for publication, the editors
followed certain guidelines. Only material that covered events during
periods well before or after the conflict has been omitted. Where such
omissions occur within the narrative texts, they are indicated by ellipses. In the case of the court testimony, the deletion of questions or
fragmentary answers is also indicated by ellipses. In the narrative
texts the editors have added corrections, missing words, explanatory

phrases, and punctuation within brackets. Where identification of persons or events seemed necessary, the editors have provided explanations in the reference notes to each chapter. Consideration was given to the problems created by the changing nature of language — both English and Dakota. Some terms that were in common use a hundred years ago are now judged to be offensive. Nonetheless, such terms as used by narrators or translators remain unchanged in the narratives. The effort has been to leave the narratives largely as they were originally produced, without alterations to context, interpretations, or idiosyncrasies.

Preceding each narrative a brief biographical sketch introduces the narrator, explains his or her place in the reservation community of 1862, and identifies any collaborator who assisted in producing the narrative. Dakota names can be transliterated into English using a variety of spellings and styles. Dakota, much like English, is a living language that historically has gone through many changes. Linguists who study the Siouan language today, however, generally work from the perspective of Lakota, the language used by the western groups of Dakota people, because most twentieth-century work of lexicographic nature has been in Lakota. But among the men and women who left narratives were Dakota speakers who assisted missionaries Stephen R. Riggs, Samuel W. Pond, and Thomas S. Williamson in putting together dictionaries and grammars of their own language. Although archaic by modern standards, Riggs's lexicon with its spelling formulations is still legitimate and historically appropriate in relation to Dakota-speaking people, and it has been adopted in the introductory and biographical material.[3]

There are several facts that should be kept foremost in readers' minds as they evaluate the narratives. First, a good number of the narrators originally gave their accounts orally to collaborators, who prepared transcriptions, translations, or edited versions. It is fair to assume that such narratives closely resemble but do not faithfully duplicate the original oral account. Obviously, collaborators could easily influence both the tone and the content of the narratives, for opportunities to incorporate their biases abounded. Second, even forty or fifty years after 1862 anti-Indian feeling was still so intense in Minnesota, and racism was so pervasive in American society, that Dakota narrators undoubtedly felt constrained in what they could say. Surely the narrators knew that the largest part of their audience held no sympathy for the Dakota Indians.

Some of the selected narratives cover the entire period from early August 1862 through the summer of 1863; others deal with a single event related to the conflict. The editors found it extremely difficult to integrate such diverse narratives and successfully maintain the flow of the story being told. Therefore the decision was made to present the material chronologically, with each of the ten chapters presenting major events of the conflict in sequence. This required that the longer narratives be broken up among several chapters. At the end of each narrative segment, however, there appears the number of the page where the narrative continues. This format allows readers either to compare the views of different narrators within a chapter or to read an entire narrative without excessive interruption.

As a group the narratives offer a unique spectrum of views of the 1862 conflict, one far different from that presented by Euro-Americans and one that parallels in part the factionalism that existed in the Dakota community. While the numbers do not exactly reflect the political factions, they illustrate the various perspectives held by Dakota people. Seven of the narrators—Big Eagle, Robert Hakewaste, Little Crow, White Spider, George Quinn, Lightning Blanket, and Wowinape—actively participated in the fighting or supported the "war party." Five more—Star, Light Face, Iron Hoop, Little Fish, and Little Wheat—might be added to that group, for evidence indicates that they vacillated over the conflict and opposed the fighting only after it had failed. A few narrators were at times at least sympathetic with some of the leading Dakota participants in the struggle. Among them were Thomas Robertson, Charles Crawford, and Antoine J. Campbell. Four represent those Dakotas who did not support the war party and, instead, began to build a "peace party." Paul Mazakutemani, Taopi, Wabasha, and Lorenzo Lawrence fit this description. And some, such as Standing Buffalo, were caught between the two camps and tried simply to avoid the destructiveness of the conflict.

In order to present the broadest possible range of perspectives on the conflict, the editors sought and found narratives that provide information about the entire Dakota community. Among the narrators are men, women, young people, elders, full-bloods, and those people who through marriage or blood relationship were an intrinsic part of the diverse reservation population. One example of the latter is Joseph Godfrey, the son of a French-Canadian man and a black woman who was raised in the family of a mixed-blood fur trader. He married a

Dakota woman and at the time of the attack on the Redwood Agency, they lived on the reservation some twenty miles below the agency. Taken together, the narratives relate in graphic detail what happened in the Indian camps, providing fascinating new insights into the conflict.

Prominently represented in the narratives are the mixed-bloods, or, as they were frequently referred to in the 1860s, the "breeds." Some were the children, grandchildren, or even great-great-grandchildren of French voyageurs and Dakota women and can be called Franco-Dakota people. Others had English or Scottish ancestors and can be characterized as Anglo-Dakota people. In 1862 their numbers were significant, comprising roughly 15 percent of the Dakota reservation population. Some of the mixed-bloods identified closely with the tribal group and had substantial influence in Dakota councils. Many of the others who became entangled in the conflict were made captives by the Indian warriors. All were able to watch closely the events surounding the struggle; their narratives provide informative assessments of them.

The viewpoints of mixed-bloods become even more interesting when subjected to the passage of time, as represented by the narrative of Samuel J. Brown. Like other Anglo- and Franco-Dakota people, Brown grew up in close association with the traditional lifestyle, spoke the Dakota language in the home, and easily identified with Dakota relatives. The son of a white father (who was once agent to the Dakotas) and a Franco-Dakota mother, Brown was seventeen years old, a student in a boarding school, and vacationing at his parents' house near the reservation in August 1862. He was among the family members taken captive by the Dakotas. More than thirty years later, a Mankato newspaper published Brown's extensive narrative, which was based on a journal he had kept during the conflict. It revealed a man who thought and wrote as a non-Indian vehemently opposed to the Dakota warriors. In 1897, the year his narrative was published, strong prejudice against people of color openly existed in America. It was the era when Herbert Spencer's doctrine of Social Darwinism and the survival of the fittest reigned supreme and when newspaper editors wrote of the "White Man's Burden." Brown's condemning prose fit into the context of the times, when all nonwhites who resisted the so-called benefits of western cultures, whatever their justification, were quickly marked as uncivilized savages. In addition, Brown gave his narrative to a newspaper editor who was undoubtedly well versed in the rhetoric of the day. Whether the editor took editorial license with Brown's manuscript is open to speculation.

The assimilationist views expressed by Brown can also be found in the narrative of Cecelia Campbell Stay, who was a thirteen-year-old Anglo-Dakota girl at the conflict's beginning. Both of these narrators were "white" in their sympathies, and their narratives are similar in the language used and views expressed. They are not unique; they are representative of many of the reservation people who were attempting to adjust to a Euro-American life-style in 1862. According to the annual reports of Indian agents, schoolteachers, and missionaries working on the reservation, perhaps as many as one-fourth of the Dakota people at some time held similar views. Among them were some people who had abandoned much of the Dakota way of life, moved from their villages onto farms, and adopted the whites' clothing. A goodly number had converted to Christianity.

Also among the narratives are those of mixed-bloods who had rejected the acculturation program of the government and the missionaries. They often wore long hair, leggings, and breechcloths — the visible symbols of their Indian life-style. Two examples are the accounts of Gabriel Renville and George Quinn. Renville, the son of a French-Canadian fur trader who was killed by an Ojibway raiding party in 1833, was raised as a Dakota by his stepfather, Joseph Akipa Renville. Quinn, who called himself "half white man and half Indian," was brought up "among the Indians as one of them." Neither Renville nor Quinn spoke English; both, however, learned from missionaries how to read and write the Dakota language and each wrote or spoke his narrative in Dakota. When the conflict began in 1862, Renville opposed the Dakota warriors and helped to organize a soldiers' lodge for the peace party. After the war he became the leader of the Sisseton Reservation community in South Dakota and lived there until his death in 1892. Quinn elected to join in the struggle against whites and participated in the fighting. He was captured by white soldiers, convicted by the military tribunal, and sentenced to be hanged. After receiving a reprieve, he was imprisoned until 1866. He eventually returned to Minnesota and died at Morton in 1915.

What is clearly demonstrated by the narratives, whether of mixed-bloods or full-bloods, is the complexity of Dakota society in 1862. It becomes obvious that the degree of Indian or white blood did not necessarily determine an individual's loyalties during the conflict.

Both mixed-bloods and full-bloods are represented in the war party and in the peace party and in between, torn by opposing loyalties; within each group the entire range of cultural responses and political and religious views can be found. As documents that are also barometers of sociocultural change, these narratives provide new material for ethnologists, cultural anthropologists, and other scholars of Dakota culture.[4]

Reading the narratives carefully will quickly reveal that some accounts do not always conform to the views of and arguments made by historians, and at times the narratives themselves present contradictory evidence. It is the nature of eyewitness accounts that there are disagreements on details. No two people ever remember a single event in identical ways, especially with the passage of time. (It can also be noted that discrepancies are apparent in written accounts produced by whites.) By presenting the events of 1862 as viewed by many pairs of eyes, we can make deeper and broader perspectives available to readers.

Several of the narratives fall into the category of oral tradition. Note, for example, the accounts of White Spider, Little Crow's half brother, and Wowinape, who memorized Little Crow's speech, and Esther Wakeman, who told her story to her daughter. Other accounts also were handed down through more than one generation or were recorded several decades after the events. These include the narratives collected from Good Star Woman, Frank Jetty, George Crooks, and Joseph Coursolle. Having a story pass down through generations of consummate storytellers does not lessen its value. Indeed, that a family holds to a story in all its detail argues strongly in favor of the overall accuracy of the account. In some of the narratives there is, too, a blending of Indian oral history and white written history that is unusual in bicultural literature. The instances of this are especially apparent in the Sisseton and Wahpeton claims testimony — a result of the direct questioning of the witnesses in a courtroom situation.

The oral history accounts published in this volume represent only a few of the stories that are to be found still circulating in the Dakota community today. Recently Dakota leaders have revealed the existence of additional accounts, including yet another left by Wowinape, Little Crow's son. The editors hope that the Dakota people will see this volume as a starting point and that in the future more accounts will be collected and published. Making available such information will lead eventually to a more balanced assessment of the

Dakota conflict and what happened to the people — Indian and white — who were suddenly caught up in it.

When first encountered by Europeans in the 1650s, the Dakota Indians inhabited most of present-day Minnesota and parts of eastern South Dakota and North Dakota. Although oral tradition is not exact on the point, supposedly seven major divisions, or tribal groups, existed at that time. The eastern Sioux or Dakota included the Mdewakanton, Sisseton, Wahpeton, and Wahpekute bands. They were joined on the west by the Yanktons and Yanktonais, and finally by the Tetons, the most western of the tribal groups. The Mdewakantons occupied the Mississippi River valley between present-day Prairie du Chien, Wisconsin, and the Falls of St. Anthony in what is now Minneapolis. The Sissetons, Wahpetons, and Wahpekutes often visited or camped in the valley but were more likely to stay in the Minnesota and Blue Earth river valleys.

Although heavily involved in trade with Europeans, the Dakotas who lived in what would become Minnesota suffered little from contact with Euro-Americans until the 1820s, when their game herds began showing signs of depletion. Economic problems soon were complicated by the encroachment of white settlers who pressured the eastern Sioux for their lands. By the Treaty of 1837, the Treaty of Traverse des Sioux, and the Treaty of Mendota (both signed in 1851), the Dakota Indians relinquished claims to land in Minnesota. According to the terms set in 1851, they accepted settlement on reservations. The reserves lay along the Minnesota River above New Ulm, being a strip twenty miles wide and extending up the river 140 miles to Big Stone Lake. The boundary between the upper and lower reservations was just south of the Yellow Medicine River. In an agreement negotiated in 1858 the Dakotas gave up the ten-mile strip north of the Minnesota River. At that time, the four Dakota tribes numbered some six thousand persons.

The Redwood, or Lower Sioux, Agency, headquarters for the eastern reservation, comprised an impressive array of buildings and well-tended fields in 1862. A stone warehouse, built in 1861 to store food supplies and farming equipment, dominated the agency grounds. The government had also built houses for the agent, the superintendent of farming, the interpreter, a physician, a carpenter, and a blacksmith. A boarding school, mess hall, shops, sawmill, and stables were also constructed at government expense, giving the agency the appearance of a well-ordered village. By 1861 traders Louis Robert, William H. Forbes, François La Bathe, and Nathan and Andrew J. Myrick had built four stores. In all, the agency was home to well over a hundred persons.

The federal government provided cash annuities and allotments of goods in the treaties, but the Indians and their Franco- and Anglo-Dakota relatives found it difficult to adjust to their new roles as government wards. By 1855, many of the eastern Dakota people had finally settled on the reservation. There they were furnished with some food and were instructed in Euro-American farming methods. Five years later, perhaps one-fourth of the Dakotas had tried farming and a few had turned to practicing Christianity.

Nevertheless, the majority of Indians retained a tribal affiliation. Of the nine Mdewakanton bands, those led by Big Eagle, Little Crow, Mankato, and Traveling Hail settled within a few miles of the Redwood Agency. The Indians who followed Wakute and Wabasha took up residence a few miles below the others, while the band under Shakopee, or Little Six, settled at two locations above the agency, one on the Redwood River and the second on Rice Creek. The Wahpekutes under Red Legs generally lived at the southeastern border of the reserve, not far from the ethnically German town of New Ulm. Of all the Mdewakanton and Wahpekute bands, Shakopee's initially had the largest population, with more than four hundred people. Most of the others ranged in size from about one hundred to three hundred. The farmer band, under Taopi, increased in size every year as more Indians became farmers. By 1862 it nearly equaled Shakopee's band in size, but its members were settled on individual farms along the roads leading to the agency.

Farther up the Minnesota River, a second agency had been built for the Sisseton and Wahpeton tribes near the mouth of the Yellow Medicine River. The Yellow Medicine, or Upper Sioux, Agency served about four thousand Indians, most of whom lived outside the boundary of the reserve in what was then Dakota Territory. The Yellow Medicine Agency was not as well developed as the Redwood Agency, yet Thomas J. Galbraith, the new Indian agent appointed in 1861 by President Abraham Lincoln, was in the process of moving his headquarters there in 1862. The staff at the Yellow Medicine Agency was similar in size to that at the Redwood Agency, and several new buildings, including a hotel, had recently been completed.

The government had not been as successful in the acculturation of

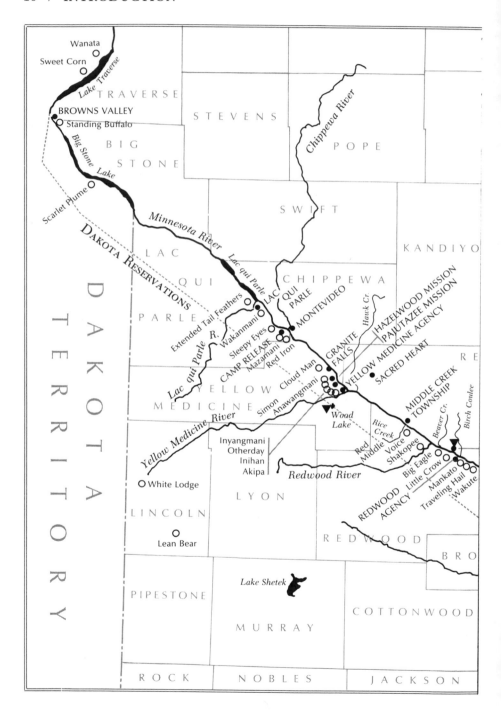

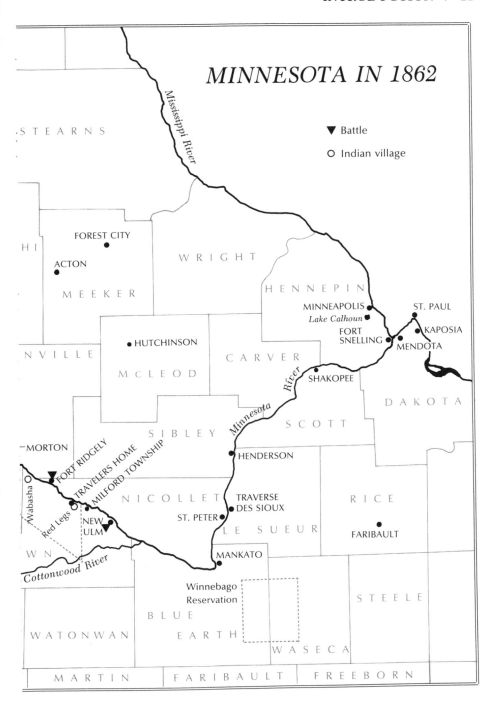

MINNESOTA IN 1862

▼ Battle
O Indian village

STEARNS

Mississippi River

HI

FOREST CITY

ACTON

MEEKER

WRIGHT

HENNEPIN

MINNEAPOLIS
Lake Calhoun

ST. PAUL

KAPOSIA

FORT
SNELLING

MENDOTA

HUTCHINSON

NVILLE

CARVER

McLEOD

River

SHAKOPEE

Minnesota

DAKOTA

MORTON

FORT RIDGELY

TRAVELERS HOME

MILFORD TOWNSHIP

SIBLEY

SCOTT

HENDERSON

Wabasha

Red Legs

NEW
ULM

NICOLLET

ST. PETER

TRAVERSE
DES SIOUX

RICE

LE SUEUR

FARIBAULT

W N

Cottonwood River

MANKATO

Winnebago
Reservation

BLUE

EARTH

STEELE

WATONWAN

WASECA

MARTIN

FARIBAULT

FREEBORN

the Sissetons and Wahpetons as it had been with the Mdewakantons
and Wahpekutes, but by 1862 Galbraith had begun the process of sur-
veying the reservation and selecting individual farms for Indians. He
received assistance in this effort from the two missionaries who lived
northwest of the agency. Two miles away the Reverend Thomas S.
Williamson in 1853 had founded the Pajutazee Mission, and the Reverend Stephen R. Riggs operated the Hazelwood Mission three miles
farther on. These two men had been working among the eastern Sioux
since the 1830s and had a following of Christian Indian farmers.

Among the many people in the reservation community were the
Franco- and Anglo-Dakotas. Those allied to the Mdewakantons and
Wahpekutes were the largest in number, since these people had been
in prolonged contact with Euro-Americans. Officials of the United
States Office of Indian Affairs conducted a census in 1855–56 that
showed about 650 mixed-bloods of Mdewakanton descent in Minnesota. Some of the group had merged with the white population of
eastern Minnesota, but most were living on the reservation. After
1856 the developing farm programs on the reservation provided an in-
centive for others to join them. Many also worked on the reservation,
being employed by the traders as clerks or the government as interpreters. Juggling two distinct cultures at the same time — occasionally
serving one and then the other — repeatedly placed the Franco- and
Anglo-Dakota people at the centers of controversies.

In 1862 many Dakota Indians who continued to live by the hunt
began feuding with traders over the issue of past payments for debt.
Funds from the 1858 treaty, it was believed by the Dakotas, had paid
all past debts owed by individual Indians. Traders, on the other hand,
argued that Indians had received credit after the treaty. By the spring
of 1862, traders and their Indian customers were on the verge of a vio-
lent break. Many of the mixed-bloods were caught squarely between
the two groups.

The conflict over traders' debts was only one of several important
issues creating unrest. Indian agents as early as 1860 had adopted the
practice of handing out annuity money and food only to Indians who
showed some inclination to become farmers. Thus many Dakotas had
cut their hair and donned white-man's clothing. Those who refused
to make such a change continued to hunt on lands increasingly occupied by white homesteaders whom they viewed as intruders. Consequently, to a majority of the reservation Indians, all farmers,
regardless of racial or ethnic origin, became threats to their existence.

In addition, after the American Civil War broke out, Congress simply had other seemingly more pressing concerns than making the annual appropriation of funds to feed and house Indians. While the money rightfully belonged to the Dakota people and treaties existed that spelled out these financial obligations, the enabling legislation was simply delayed, and food contracts could not be let until the funds had actually been appropriated.

By late summer in 1862, the system of supply appeared to be breaking down as annuities were months late in arriving at the agencies. Frustrated and angry Indians could be found throughout the two reservations. The bitter resentment finally erupted on August 17, 1862, when four Indian hunters turned on a group of white settlers near Acton in Meeker County, killing several people in apparent retaliation for an insult. Returning quickly to the Redwood Agency, they told their story to a group of Mdewakantons who had for some time been resisting the farmer movement. These men sympathized with those involved in the attack and soon agreed to begin a war rather than surrender the guilty hunters. They then sought the support of Little Crow, the most influential of the Mdewakantons.

The angry band of Mdewakantons who turned to Little Crow in the early hours of August 18 had some years earlier formed a soldiers' lodge, or hunting committee, to promote their views. This lodge had traditionally been used to control the village hunt, its primary duties being to assign tasks to individual hunters and to make sure that game herds were not spooked prematurely by anxious hunters. The lodge, however, had increasingly become an instrument for resisting government acculturation and a forum for voicing discontent with the reservation system (see Big Eagle's narrative, for example). Unlike the more conventional tribal council, the lodge was dominated by hunters, and it refused admittance to farmer Indians. When faced with the full force of about a hundred members of the soldiers' lodge, Little Crow reluctantly agreed to join the war.

Once the fateful decision had been made, the soldiers planned an assault on the Redwood Agency. The attack began at seven o'clock in the morning on August 18. It resulted in the killing of nearly two dozen people, most of whom were either traders or government employees. Dakota narratives telling of these events show beyond a doubt that the war was as much a surprise to many Dakota people, especially farmer Indians and mixed-bloods, as it was to the whites at the agency. Indeed, several Franco- and Anglo-Dakota people fled with the whites to Fort Ridgely and New Ulm. Indians, especially those who had joined the farmer movement, were as fearful for their future as were the whites.

After the traders' stores and the agency buildings had been over-run, the war became general, with Indian warriors fanning out in all directions to raid white settlements. Many groups of fleeing settlers, frequently Germans or Scandinavians, were intercepted, and about four hundred civilians lost their lives in the first four days of fighting. Although few Indian accounts of the killing were recorded, those that are available indicate that the warriors' success in the first few days induced many recruits to join the cause. Evidence collected by the military tribunal after the war shows that as many as twenty Franco- and Anglo-Dakota men joined the war effort.

By the evening of August 18, rumors of the fighting reached the Sissetons and Wahpetons at the Yellow Medicine Agency. The Indians near the agency who were Christians and farmers were reluctant to get involved in the war. But their numbers were too few to safeguard the white missionaries, government workers, and traders and their Franco- and Anglo-Dakota employees. Escaping to safety was the reasonable option, and many Sissetons and Wahpetons protected the white refugees as they crossed the Minnesota River bound for the eastern settlements. A few outlying communities, attacked several days after the war began, were not as fortunate. Settlers living as far south as Jackson County on the Iowa border and as far west as Lake Shetek in Murray County were set upon by war parties and suffered losses.

After clearing the countryside of white settlers, the leaders of the Mdewakanton soldiers' lodge organized attacks on Fort Ridgely on August 20 and 22 and on New Ulm on August 19 and 23. While both the fort and the town were poorly prepared for war, the Indians failed in the end to overrun either. Nevertheless, the fighting at each place became desperate at times, and both the fort and the town were near-ly burned to the ground. The failure of the Dakotas to take these strongholds made it necessary for them to evacuate their camp near Little Crow's village. The flight up the Minnesota River valley toward Lake Traverse was a turning point in the war.

The largest number of narratives left by full- and mixed-blood participants begin with the exodus from the area around the Redwood Agency. One reason for this is the development of the peace party, a group of Indians who planned strategy aimed at negotiating with the whites and ending the fighting. The peace party grew stronger as it became increasingly obvious that the Dakotas could not win the war. The group attracted the Sisseton and Wahpeton farmers and most of the Franco- and Anglo-Dakota families who had been unable to resist the initial organizational advantage of the soldiers' lodge. The narratives left by those who sympathized with the advocates of peace provide a wealth of information regarding the intratribal social and political discord that strengthened as the war's unpopularity spread among the Indians.

The struggle within the Dakota community reached a climax by mid-September when an army of more than a thousand men under the command of Colonel Henry H. Sibley marched up the Minnesota River valley and threatened to crush the Indians. The peace party opened negotiations with Sibley and also worked to gain control of more than a hundred white captives, mostly women and children, who were in the hands of the war party members. At times it seemed as if open warfare would break out within the Indian camps.

On September 23, when Sibley's army defeated a much smaller Indian contingent at the battle of Wood Lake, many Dakotas were forced to flee to the plains. The peace party, meanwhile, formed its own conclave, called Camp Release, and secured there a majority of the captives. By September 26 the fighting in Minnesota had ended, and Colonel Sibley turned to collecting information in order to determine who among the Indian participants should be punished. He was aided in this exercise by the surrender of many of the members of the war party. During October and November, nearly four hundred full-bloods and mixed-bloods were tried by a military tribunal, and 303 were sentenced to be hanged.

At this point, President Lincoln ordered that the trial transcripts of the condemned Indians be examined. Careful review found many errors, and Lincoln's assistants determined that evidence to warrant a death penalty was sufficient in only thirty-nine cases. On December 26, thirty-eight Dakota men (one received a reprieve) were hanged en masse at Mankato. While preparations were being made for the executions, the fate of the other Indians taken prisoner on the upper Minnesota River was settled. In the spring of 1863, the men who had been judged guilty were placed in a prison camp at Davenport, Iowa. The dependents of these men and of those executed, along with Dakota men who had been found innocent — a group of more than a thousand people — were all moved to a reservation on Crow Creek in southeastern Dakota Territory.

Those Indians who escaped capture spent the winter months of 1862–63 on the northern Dakota plains near Devils Lake. The Mdewakantons among them, perhaps five hundred people, unsuccessfully tried to form a union with other Plains Indian groups in order to continue the war. By spring news reached the Indians that the newly promoted General Sibley was planning an expedition against them. Sibley mounted a campaign in June and July, reaching Devils Lake and eventually marching as far west as the Missouri River. He found few Indians willing to fight. Indeed, by this time, the majority were tired of war and ready for peace. Many eventually negotiated a truce and settled on reservations in North and South Dakota where many of their descendants live today. Others remained in Canada or fled farther west where they were integrated into western tribes.

NOTES

1. For information on the Dakota War of 1862, see Minnesota Board of Commissioners on Publication of History of Minnesota in Civil and Indian Wars, *Minnesota in the Civil and Indian Wars, 1861–1865*, 2 vols. (St. Paul: The Board, 1890–93); William Watts Folwell, *A History of Minnesota*, 4 vols., rev. ed. (St. Paul: Minnesota Historical Society, 1956–69); Isaac V. D. Heard, *History of the Sioux War and Massacres of 1862 and 1863* (New York: Harper and Brothers, 1864); Charles S. Bryant and Abel B. Murch, *A History of the Great Massacre by the Sioux Indians, in Minnesota, Including the Personal Narratives of Many Who Escaped* (Cincinnati: Rickey and Carroll, 1864); Harriet E. Bishop, *Dakota War Whoop: Or, Indian Massacres and War in Minnesota of 1862-3* (St. Paul: D. D. Merrill, 1863; Minneapolis: Ross and Haines, 1970); Lucius F. Hubbard and Return I. Holcombe, *Minnesota as a State, 1858–1870*, vol. 3 of *Minnesota in Three Centuries, 1655–1908*, ed. by Lucius F. Hubbard, William P. Murray, James H. Baker, and Warren Upham (New York: Publishing Society of Minnesota, 1908); Kenneth Carley, *The Sioux Uprising of 1862*, 2d ed. (St. Paul: Minnesota Historical Society, 1976); Daniel Buck, *Indian Outbreaks* (1904; reprint, Minneapolis: Ross and Haines, 1965); Oscar Garrett Wall, *Recollections of the Sioux Massacre: An Authentic History of the Yellow Medicine Incident, of the Fate of Marsh and His Men, of the Siege and Battles of Fort Ridgely, and of Other Important Battles and Experiences, Together with a Historical Sketch of the Sibley Expedition of 1863* (Lake City, Minn.: Home Printery, 1908); Robert Huhn Jones, *The Civil War in the Northwest: Nebraska, Wisconsin, Iowa, Minnesota, and the Dakotas* (Norman: University of Oklahoma Press, 1960); Louis H. Roddis, *The Indian Wars of Minnesota* (Cedar Rapids, Iowa: Torch Press, 1956). Some of the Dakota narratives that are included in this volume have been used in Gary Clayton Anderson, *Kinsmen of Another Kind: Dakota-White Relations in the Upper Mississippi Valley, 1650–1862* (Lincoln: University of Nebraska Press, 1984) and *Little Crow, Spokesman for the Sioux* (St. Paul: Minnesota Historical Society Press, 1986).

2. See Folwell, *History of Minnesota*, 2:418–37, for a full discussion of the Sisseton and Wahpeton claims.

3. Stephen R. Riggs, *A Dakota-English Dictionary*, Contributions to North American Ethnology, vol. 7, ed. James Owen Dorsey (Washington, D.C.: Government Printing Office, 1890).

4. For a discussion of American Indian autobiography and sociocultural change, see H. David Brumble III, "Sam Blowsnake's Confessions: *Crashing Thunder* and the History of American Indian Autobiography," *Canadian Review of American Studies* 16 (Fall 1985): 271–82, and *An Annotated Bibliography of American Indian and Eskimo Autobiographies* (Lincoln: University of Nebraska Press, 1981); R. D. Theisz, "The Critical Collaboration: Introduction as a Gateway to the Study of Native American Bi-Autobiography," *American Indian Culture and Research Journal* 5 (1981): 65–80; Allen G. Pastron, "An Annotated Bibliography of Native American Autobiographies and Life Histories," in *The Crisis in North American Archaeology*, ed. Allen G. Pastron, Patrick S. Hallinan, and C. William Clewlow, Jr. (Berkeley: The Kroeber Anthropological Society Special Publication no. 3, 1973), 144–63; Stanley Brandes, "Ethnographic Autobiographies in American Anthropology," in *Crisis in Anthropology: View from Spring Hill, 1980*, ed. E. Adamson Hoebel, Richard Currier, and Susan Kaiser (New York: Garland Publishing Co., 1982), 187–202. See also Beatrice Medicine, "The Role of Women in Native American Societies," *Indian Historian* 8 (Summer 1975): 50–53; Rayna Green, *Native American Women: A Contextual Bibliography* (Bloomington: Indiana University Press, 1983), 1–17.

CHAPTER **I**

Causes of the
Dakota War of 1862

HISTORIANS have assessed the causes of the Dakota War in numerous publications, but most of these works have been based on the materials left by white observers. As early as 1863 a history of the war written by Isaac V. D. Heard reviewed a wide range of factors leading to the war. Since the 1851 treaties, resentment had grown among the Indians over confinement to a prairie reservation and loss of good hunting grounds. Despite negotiators' promises and treaty terms, the Indians had seen all their money diverted into white men's pockets to pay inflated traders' debts or through outright fraud. A new way of life was being forced on the Indians at the Minnesota River reservations as land was allotted, the band structure broken up, clothing and hair styles changed, and farming substituted for hunting as an occupation. Government agents punished warriors who mounted forays against such traditional Dakota enemies as the Ojibway despite the fact that the Americans were fighting each other in the Civil War. Finally the power and influence of shamans, or medicine men, were disparaged by whites who offered Christianity.

Added to the problems growing out of cultural conflict was the failure of reservation administrators to meet the obligations incurred in government treaties. Too few schools were built or teachers provided, and instruction in farming was insufficient. Goods intended for allotments turned up for sale at exorbitant prices in traders' stores where desperate Indians purchased them on credit, thereby creating yet another trader's claim against annuities. A corrupt Office of Indian Affairs did nothing; on the contrary, by allowing inflated claims to be assessed against the annuities earmarked for a whole band, the Office made matters worse. Indian officials failed to investigate charges of illegal sales of liquor or mistreatment of Indian women by white men. Indian superintendents encouraged an unequal distribution of goods where farmers received extra amounts and hunters, who found less

19

and less game each year, often received nothing or one modest outlay a year.

By the summer of 1862 when the patience of many Dakotas was wearing thin, the situation worsened. The fall harvest in 1861 was poor due to an infestation of cut worms. The subsequent winter was unusually severe. In late spring as they assembled to receive their annuities, the Indians were starving; only roots sustained many of them. The goods and money were late. Officials of the Office of Indian Affairs, hard pressed for cash, debated whether or not to send the funds in paper or gold, the former being less expensive. At this point, the traders cut off all credit. By late July the ripening crops of corn and vegetables promised a rich harvest, but rumors circulated that there might be no annuities at all that year. The warriors assessed their situation and discussed in the soldiers' lodge the fact that many able-bodied white men had left Minnesota to join the Union Army, which had suffered defeats that summer. They argued that the time was right for the Dakotas to take action to reclaim their ancestral lands. Support might even be expected from Canada or Great Britain, an old ally of the Dakota people and oftentimes an adversary of the Americans. And finally, the warriors had before them the example of Inkpaduta, a Wahpekute leader whose band had killed two dozen or more whites in 1857 and had never been punished.

The tension increased. At the Yellow Medicine Agency the warriors broke into a warehouse on August 4 to get food. Only a detachment of Minnesota militia threatening to use a cannon restored order. Two weeks later, with discontent still rampant and the militia gone, the war began. In retrospect, given the many problems on the reservations by late summer, it should not seem surprising that white historians and Indians alike stress a variety of elements when searching for the causes of the war. This can be seen in the three excerpts that follow, each of which provides a different viewpoint.

The first narrative, covering the period just preceding the fighting, is provided by Big Eagle, a full-blood who was a band leader and had been a candidate for Mdewakanton spokesman. Big Eagle mentions such traditional causes as broken treaties and the abuses by traders, but he also states that acculturation programs caused tremendous friction and that social relationships between Indians and whites accordingly suffered. Wabasha, also a full-blood and a band leader, emphasizes the difficulties in negotiating with the federal government. The third narrative is by Robert Hakewaste, a full-blood and a leader; it gives a first-hand look at the troubles at the agencies. These narratives especially reveal the growing ethnic friction in the upper Minnesota River valley and how the problems of the 1850s were contributing factors leading to the outbreak of war.

Narrative 1
BIG EAGLE'S ACCOUNT

JEROME BIG EAGLE or Wamditanka was born in 1827 at Black Dog's village, located a few miles above Mendota on the south bank of the Minnesota River. He succeeded Grey Iron, his father, as chief in 1857 and the following year joined the farmer band of Mdewakantons at the Redwood Agency. He was an unsuccessful candidate for speaker of the Mdewakanton tribe in spring 1862, and when the war broke out several months later, he reluctantly joined the warriors, leading his band at the second battles of New Ulm and Fort Ridgely and in the fighting at Birch Coulee and Wood Lake.

After surrendering in September, Big Eagle was tried by the military commission and given the death sentence. He received a reprieve and was sent to the prison camp at Davenport, Iowa, where he was pardoned by President Lincoln in late 1864. Soon thereafter, he joined his band at the Crow Creek Reservation and moved to the Santee Reservation in 1866.

Distressed over his loss of leadership and angry at being subject to an Indian agent's control, he moved his family from Santee in spring 1869, finally settling near Birch Coulee. While visiting at Flandreau, South Dakota, in June 1894, he met newspaper reporter Return I. Holcombe, who interviewed him regarding his role in the war. Nancy McClure Huggan (whose narrative is included in this collection) and the Reverend John Eastman, her son-in-law, served as translators. Holcombe's narrative was published in a St. Paul newspaper and by the Minnesota Historical Society. Big Eagle spent his last years quietly near Granite Falls, where he died on January 5, 1906.[1]

Narrative Source: Jerome Big Eagle, "A Sioux Story of the War," *Collections of the Minnesota Historical Society* 6 (1894): 382–400.

BIG EAGLE wearing the eagle feathers he won in battle with the Ojibway, 1863-64, in Davenport, Iowa

I WAS BORN in the Indian village of my father near Mendota, in 1827, and am now sixty-seven years old. My father was Grey Iron, a sub-chief of the Midawa-xanton Sioux. When he died I succeeded him as chief of the band and adopted the name of his father, Wambde-tonka, which, as is commonly called, means the Big Eagle. When I was a young man I often went with war parties against the Chippe-was and other enemies of my nation, and the six feathers shown in the head-dress of my picture in the Historical society at St. Paul stand for six Chippewa scalps that I took when on the warpath. By the terms of the treaties of Traverse des Sioux and Mendota in 1851, the Sioux sold all of their lands in Minnesota, except a strip ten miles wide on each side of the Minnesota river from near Fort Ridgely to the Big Stone lake. The Medawakantons and Wacoutas [Wahpekutes] had their reservation up to the Yellow Medicine. In 1858 the ten miles of this strip belonging to the Medawakanton and Wacouta [Wahpekute] bands, and lying north of the river were sold, mainly through the in-fluence of Little Crow. That year, with some other chiefs, I went to Washington on business connected with the treaty. The selling of that strip north of the Minnesota caused great dissatisfaction among the Sioux, and Little Crow was always blamed for the part he took in the sale.[2] It caused us all to move to the south side of the river, where there was but very little game, and many of our people, under the treaty, were induced to give up the old life and go to work like white men, which was very distasteful to many.

Of the causes that led to the outbreak of August, 1862, much has been said. Of course it [going to war] was wrong, as we all know now, but there were not many Christians among the Indians then, and they did not understand things as they should. There was great dissatisfac-tion among the Indians over many things the whites did. The whites would not let them go to war against their enemies. This was right, but the Indians did not then know it. Then the whites were always trying to make the Indians give up their life and live like white men — go to farming, work hard and do as they did — and the Indians did not know how to do that, and did not want to anyway. It seemed too sud-den to make such a change. If the Indians had tried to make the whites live like them, the whites would have resisted, and it was the same way with many Indians. The Indians wanted to live as they did before the treaty of Traverse des Sioux — go where they pleased and when they pleased; hunt game wherever they could find it, sell their furs to the traders and live as they could.

Then the Indians did not think the traders had done right. The Indians bought goods of them on credit, and when the government payments came the traders were on hand with their books, which showed that the Indians owed so much and so much, and as the Indians kept no books they could not deny their accounts, but had to pay them, and sometimes the traders got all their money. I do not say that the traders always cheated and lied about these accounts. I know many of them were honest men and kind and accommodating, but since I have been a citizen I know that many white men, when they go to pay their accounts, often think them too large and refuse to pay them, and they go to law about them and there is much bad feeling. The Indians could not go to law, but there was always trouble over their credits. Under the treaty of Traverse des Sioux [1851] the Indians had to pay a very large sum of money to the traders for old debts, some of which ran back fifteen years, and many of those who had got the goods were dead and others were not present, and the traders' books had to be received as to the amounts, and the money was taken from the tribe to pay them. Of course the traders often were of great service to the Indians in letting them have goods on credit, but the Indians seemed to think the traders ought not to be too hard on them about the payments, but do as the Indians did among one another, and put off the payment until they were better able to make it.

Then many of the white men often abused the Indians and treated them unkindly. Perhaps they had excuse, but the Indians did not think so. Many of the whites always seemed to say by their manner when they saw an Indian, "I am much better than you," and the Indians did not like this. There was excuse for this, but the Dakotas did not believe there were better men in the world than they. Then some of the white men abused the Indian women in a certain way and disgraced them, and surely there was no excuse for that.

All these things made many Indians dislike the whites. Then a little while before the outbreak there was trouble among the Indians themselves. Some of the Indians took a sensible course and began to live like white men. The government built them houses, furnished them tools, seed, etc., and taught them to farm. At the two agencies, Yellow Medicine and Redwood, there were several hundred acres of land in cultivation that summer. Others staid in their tepees. There was a white man's party and an Indian party. We had politics among us and there was much feeling. A new chief speaker for the tribe was to be elected. There were three candidates — Little Crow, myself and

Wa-sui-hi-ya-ye-dan ("Traveling Hail"). After an exciting contest Traveling Hail was elected.[3] Little Crow felt sore over his defeat. Many of our tribe believed him responsible for the sale of the north ten-mile strip, and I think this was why he was defeated. I did not care much about it. Many whites think that Little Crow was the principal chief of the Dakotas at this time, but he was not. Wabasha was the principal chief, and he was of the white man's party; so was I; so was old Shakopee, whose band was very large. Many think if old Shakopee had lived there would have been no war, for he was for the white men and had great influence. But he died that summer, and was succeeded by his son, whose real name was Ea-to-ka ("Another Language"), but when he became chief he took his father's name, and was afterwards called "Little Shakopee," or "Little Six," for in the Sioux language "Shakopee" means six. This Shakopee was against the white men. He took part in the outbreak, murdering women and children, but I never saw him in a battle, and he was caught in Manitoba and hanged in 1864. My brother, Medicine Bottle, was hanged with him.[4]

As the summer advanced, there was great trouble among the Sioux—troubles among themselves, troubles with the whites, and one thing and another. The war with the South was going on then, and a great many men had left the state and gone down there to fight. A few weeks before the outbreak the president [Abraham Lincoln] called for many more men, and a great many of the white men of Minnesota and some half-breeds enlisted and went to Fort Snelling to be sent South. We understood that the South was getting the best of the fight, and it was said that the North would be whipped. The year before the new president had turned out Maj. [Joseph R.] Brown and Maj. [William J.] Cullen, the Indian agents, and put in their places Maj. [Thomas J.] Galbraith and Mr. Clark Thompson, and they had turned out the men under them and put in others of their own party. There were a great many changes. An Indian named Shonka-sha ("White Dog"), who had been hired to teach the Indians to farm, was removed and another Indian named Ta-opi ("The Wounded Man"), a son of old Betsy, of St. Paul, put in his place. Nearly all of the men who were turned out were dissatisfied, and the most of the Indians did not like the new men. At last Maj. Galbraith went to work about the agencies and recruited a company of soldiers to go South. His men were nearly all half-breeds. This was the company called the Renville Rangers, for they were mostly from Renville county. The Indians now thought the whites must be pretty hard up for men to fight the South, or they would not come so far out on the frontier and take half-breeds or anything to help them.

It began to be whispered about that now would be a good time to go to war with the whites and get back the lands. It was believed that the men who had enlisted last had all left the state, and that before help could be sent the Indians could clean out the country, and that the Winnebagoes, and even the Chippewas, would assist the Sioux.[5] It was also thought that a war with the whites would cause the Sioux to forget the troubles among themselves and enable many of them to pay off some old scores. Though I took part in the war, I was against it. I knew there was no good cause for it, and I had been to Washington and knew the power of the whites and that they would finally conquer us. We might succeed for a time, but we would be overpowered and defeated at last. I said all this and many more things to my people, but many of my own bands were against me, and some of the other chiefs put words in their mouths to say to me. When the outbreak came Little Crow told some of my band that if I refused to lead them to shoot me as a traitor who would not stand up for his nation, and then select another leader in my place.

But after the first talk of war the counsels of the peace Indians prevailed, and many of us thought the danger had all blown over. The time of the government payment was near at hand, and this may have had something to do with it. There was another thing that helped to stop the war talk. The crops that had been put in by the "farmer" Indians were looking well, and there seemed to be a good prospect for a plentiful supply of provisions for them the coming winter without having to depend on the game of the country or without going far out to the west on the plains for buffalo. It seemed as if the white men's way was certainly the best. Many of the Indians had been short of provisions that summer and had exhausted their credits and were in bad condition. "Now," said the farmer Indians, "if you had worked last season you would not be starving now and begging for food." The "farmers" were favored by the government in every way. They had houses built for them, some of them even had brick houses, and they were not allowed to suffer. The other Indians did not like this. They were envious of them and jealous, and disliked them because they were favored. They called them "farmers," as if it was disgraceful to be a farmer. They called them "cut-hairs," because they had given up the Indian fashion of wearing the hair, and "breeches men," because they wore pantaloons, and "Dutchmen," because so many of the settlers on the north side of the river and elsewhere in the country were Germans. I have heard that there was a secret organization of the Indians called the "Soldiers' Lodge," whose object was to declare war against the whites, but I knew nothing of it.

At last the time for the payment came and the Indians came in to the agencies to get their money. But the paymaster did not come, and week after week went by and still he did not come. The payment was to be in gold. Somebody told the Indians that the payment would never be made. The government was in a great war, and gold was scarce, and paper money had taken its place, and it was said the gold could not be had to pay us. Then the trouble began again and the war talk started up. Many of the Indians who had gathered about the agencies were out of provisions and were easily made angry. Still, most of us thought the trouble would pass, and we said nothing about it. I thought there might be trouble, but I had no idea there would be such a war. Little Crow and other chiefs did not think so. But it seems some of the tribe were getting ready for it.

Continued on page 35.

Narrative 2
WABASHA'S STATEMENT

JOSEPH WABASHA or Wabasha III was born in about 1800 near present-day Winona, Minnesota. Wabasha II, his father, had been the hereditary leader of the Mdewakanton tribe, and when he died in 1836, his son was elevated to the chieftainship. A rival of Little Crow's, Wabasha opposed the 1851 Treaty of Mendota and reluctantly participated in the Treaty of 1858, in which the Mdewakantons gave up claims to land in Minnesota. Nevertheless, he moved his band to the reservation in 1853 and encouraged his people to become farmers and Christians. He had his hair cut in 1859 by Joseph Brown, the Indian agent.

Wabasha led opposition to the war and quietly organized a peace party; however, he was present at the battles at Fort Ridgely, New Ulm, Birch Coulee, and Wood Lake. He was on hand at Camp Release when many of the white captives were turned over to Colonel Sibley. In May 1863, his band was removed to the Crow Creek Reser-

vation and three years later, to the Santee Reservation. Although friendly to whites, Wabasha testified before the Indian Peace Commission on June 15, 1868, on board the steamer Deer Lodge near Fort Rice, Dakota Territory, about the wrongs done to the Dakota people. The interpreter's name is not given. Wabasha died at Santee on April 23, 1876. A portrait bust of him was placed in the Minnesota State Capitol in 1986.[6]

Narrative Source: Papers Relating to Talks and Councils Held with the Indians in Dakota and Montana Territories in the Years 1866–1869 (Washington, D.C.: Government Printing Office, 1910), 90–91.

I WENT to Washington the first time as I have stated above [1837]. I went again a second time [1858] before [after?] our removal to Red Wood.[7] I went for this purpose; I had then sold our lands from east to west, from sunrise to sunset; I went to secure a reservation for my people. The Great Father put a garrison of soldiers near our country at Red Wood [Fort Ridgely], and before going to Washington I col-

WABASHA in 1858 in Washington, D.C.

lected the chief men of the tribe and took them to the fort; some of
them failed to come. I spent half a day in hunting them up, and getting their signatures to a letter that they wished to write to the President [Franklin Pierce].[8] The soldiers were put there to take good care
of us and see that we were not interfered with by the whites. I told
the commandant at the fort that I wished him to write a nice letter
for us. I told him that I had always been brought up as an Indian, had
worn a blanket and feather, painted my face and carried a gun. I
wished him now to write to the Great Father that I had determined
to leave off these things. I said write that I am determined to leave the
war path, and to leave off drinking whisky, and give up plundering
and thieving, and I want you to give me your ways. I know that your
ways are good, and that your people obtain land and hold it, they
plant corn and raise domestic animals. I wish you to give my people
land where we may do the same. If we are left without a country, we
will be obliged to go out on the plains. We would be in danger of
perishing by cold and starvation; and then there are other tribes that
live there that are likely to make war on us. I wish, therefore, the
Great Father to give us land on the Minnesota River, and to help us
to live like whites. I took this letter and carried it to Washington. After
a few days I had an interview with the President. He shook hands
with me, and told me to tell him all that I wanted. I said, my Father,
all that I wish is written in this letter, and I handed him the letter.
(Little Crow and Little Six were the only chiefs that did not sign the
letter.) A few days afterwards, I was called to the Interior Department to attend to our business. I was told that our request had been
granted, and that a reservation had been appropriated for us at Red
Wood on the Minnesota River, and that each head of a family should
have assigned to him 100 acres of land; 80 of prairie and 20 of timber.
When I saw our Great Father, I spoke to him about what was my
chief desire, which was to have land. The traders were constantly following me for other purposes, and opposing me bitterly; but I paid
no attention to them — I shut my ears against them. I only desired to
get a title to lands and fix my people so that they could live. I made
a treaty at this time, and lands were given to us at Red Wood, on both
sides of the Minnesota River.[9] I went home, and lived upon the land,
and built houses there. The Great Father told me, before leaving, that
he wished us to be well off, but that the whites would endeavor to get
this land from us, and that the traders were like rats; that they would
use all their endeavors to steal our substance, and that if we were

wise, we would never sign a paper for anyone. If we did so, he said, we would never see 10 cents for all our property. I remembered the words of our Great Father and I knew that they were true. I was, consequently, always afraid of the traders.

Two years after this, when we had gathered our corn, we all went out on the fall hunt for furs. After we had been out some time the traders, the most active of whom was Mr. [Nathan?] Myrick, sent out for the chief to come in to sign papers for him in reference to selling the land on the north side of the Minnesota River [1858]. I refused to go in. The others, I am told, went home and signed some papers and received for doing so, horses, guns, blankets, and other articles. They told me this after I came home. I always refused to sign papers for the traders, and they therefore hated me. By the result of this paper signed without my consent or knowledge, the traders obtained possession of all the money coming from the sale of the land on the north side of the Minnesota River, and also half of our annuity for the year 1862.[10] When this became known to the young men of the tribe, they felt very angry. The tribe then assembled a council of soldiers near Wakutes' house, and invited me to attend. I did attend. In that council it was determined that they would not submit to having half of their annuity taken from them, and it was ordered that all Indians should draw their annuity in full from the disbursing officer, and refuse to pay the credits to the traders for that year. I made a speech in council and told the Indians that I thought it was proper that they should obtain their whole annuities and refuse to pay the traders, and that I did not want the half-breeds to be admitted to our councils; that they had always been the tools of the traders, and aided them to deceive the Indians. After this council I thought about this matter a great deal, but heard nothing about it further until early one morning, as I was making a fire, an Indian on horseback rode up to my house and said that the Indians were fighting the traders. I asked him the cause of this sudden outbreak. He said that some of Little Six's band had killed some whites in the big woods and had come back determined to kill all the traders, and that fighting had already commenced. I got on my horse and rode up to the store. I saw that the traders were already killed. I then went to Mr. [Philander] Prescott's house; he was an Indian farmer and a half-breed.[11] I told him to write me a letter to the fort, for that I would have no part in this matter. I was determined to fly to the whites. Mr. Prescott was very much frightened and did not write the letter well. I then went home and sent word to Wa ku ta [Wakute] and Hu sha sha [Red Legs], who had not yet heard of the outbreak. I then wished to go to the fort, but found it impossible for I was afraid of the Indians.

Narrative 3
ROBERT HAKEWASTE'S TESTIMONY

ROBERT HAKEWASTE or Good Fifth Son was born in 1828 at the Dakota village of Kaposia on the Mississippi River opposite the present-day city of South St. Paul. He had married and was an important member of Little Crow's band when the war broke out in 1862. Although present at the second battles of New Ulm and Fort Ridgely and at the fighting at Birch Coulee and Wood Lake, he was not an active participant. He was not tried by the military commission. In the spring of 1863 he moved to the Crow Creek Reservation.

Three years later, Hakewaste left Crow Creek for the Santee Reservation, by which time he had become an active leader of his people. In 1880 he journeyed to Washington, D.C., as a tribal delegate, and in 1882 he signed an agreement with the United States government. On September 26, 1901, at Santee Agency, Nebraska, he testified at length before a United States commission on the causes of the Dakota War, the treatment of white captives, and some of the battles. Dr. Charles A. Eastman was the interpreter. The date of Hakewaste's death is not known.[12]

Narrative Source: Robert Hakewaste, "Evidence for the Defendants," The Sisseton and Wahpeton Bands of Dakota or Sioux Indians v. the United States, 1901–07, U.S. Court of Claims no. 22524, part 2, p. 358–59.

THERE were several of us [who] went over to Yellow Medicine Agency [during the first week of August 1862] because we had no food. We went over to see the agent. Our agent [Thomas J. Galbraith] was up there at the time, and all at once we noticed that there was a disturbance up there among the people, evidently on account of something up there. There were some soldiers with an officer [Lieutenant Timothy J. Sheehan and 101 men of the Fifth Minnesota Volunteers] and a big gun or cannon up on the hill, and we noticed some men— Indians—coming along the river bottom, many on horseback and many on foot. Some of them had no garments on. We were told that they were coming to fight. We went there because we wanted some food, and we understood they were in a starving condition, and they had no food among the Indians, and we heard we were going to receive some food [from Galbraith], and the soldiers had quieted the disturbance, and, as the agent promised us to receive some food down there [at the Redwood Agency], we came away. . . .

When we came back [to the Redwood Agency] they didn't give us food as they promised—the agent did not give us food as he promised—and also at that time there was a soldiers' lodge formed that was to secure from those people who tried to get credit, because the traders were going to give credit for the money that we had—our trust money—and they were going to receive a payment from the Government if we took the trade, and this soldiers' lodge was formed to guard against that—anyone who was going to take credit from these traders—and when this was known the traders told us that, because of this soldiers' lodge and preventing credit, they were not going to give us any credit and we were going to eat grass. We were in a starving condition and desperate state of mind. During this time there were four Indians going off hunting. They had known of all this excitement up above [at Yellow Medicine] and below them [at the Redwood Agency], and influenced by that, I presume, committed the murder[s] [at Acton].

NOTES

1. Jerome Big Eagle, "A Sioux Story of the War," recorded by Return I. Holcombe, *St. Paul Pioneer Press*, July 1, 1894, p. 15, also published as Jerome Big Eagle, "A Sioux Story of the War," *Collections of the Minnesota Historical Society* 6 (1894): 382–400 (hereafter *Minnesota Collections*), reprinted as "Chief Big Eagle's Story," *Minnesota History* 38 (September 1962): 129–43. See also Original Transcripts of the Records of Trials of Certain Sioux Indians Charged with Barbarities in the State of Minnesota, case no. 34, Senate Records 37A-F2, National Archives, Record Group 46, Washington, D.C. (hereafter Transcripts of Trials of Sioux Indians, NARG 46) (microfilm copy in Division of Libraries and Archives, Minnesota Historical Society).

2. For information on Little Crow's role in the 1858 treaty, see Anderson, *Little Crow*, 101–4, 106, 110–12.

3. Passing Hail or Traveling Hail or Wasuhiyahidan was a leader of a Mdewakanton band. He was reared as a Dakota at the Lake Calhoun village. He moved with his band to Oak Grove (present-day Bloomington) in 1839 and to the reservation in 1853. He was a member of the delegation to Washington, D.C., where he opposed but

signed the Treaty of 1858. He encouraged farming among his people and was elected speaker for the Mdewakanton and Wahpekute bands in the summer of 1862, defeating Little Crow and Big Eagle. He spent the winter of 1862–63 in the Dakota camp at Fort Snelling and moved with his band to the Crow Creek Reservation. When a federal commission investigated reservation conditions, he testified on September 5, 1865. In spring 1866 he moved with his band to the Santee Reservation where he died in 1866. Charles J. Kappler, comp. and ed., *Indian Affairs. Laws and Treaties* (Washington, D.C.: Government Printing Office, 1904), 2:784; U.S. Congress, Joint special committee to inquire into the condition of the Indian tribes, *Report* (Washington, D.C.: Government Printing Office, 1867), 406–7; U.S. Office of Indian Affairs, *Report, 1859*, 100, *1860*, 68, *1863*, 314; George Quinn, "Account of George Quinn," ed. Kenneth Carley, *Minnesota History* 38 (September 1962): 147.

4. Little Six and Medicine Bottle were kidnapped while in Canada by American troops and returned to Minnesota for trial. Big Eagle erred in stating that they were hanged in 1864, the actual date being November 11, 1865. For information on the kidnapping and the trial, see the Edwin A. C. Hatch Papers, Division of Libraries and Archives, Minnesota Historical Society, St. Paul; Proceedings of Military Commission for the 1863–64 Trial of Little Six [Shakopee], handwritten transcript, U.S. Army Military Commission, Sioux War Trials, 1862–65, United States Senate Records, NARG 46; Alan R. Woolworth, "A Disgraceful Proceeding," *The Beaver*, Spring 1969, p. 54–59.

5. The Winnebagos were moved by the government from Iowa to Minnesota and settled on the Long Prairie Reservation in Todd County in 1848 and resettled on one in Blue Earth and Waseca counties in 1855. Ojibway Indians lived in scattered villages across the northern portion of Minnesota.

6. Charles C. Willson, "The Successive Chiefs Named Wabasha," *Minnesota Collections* 12 (1908): 511–12; Thomas Hughes, *Indian Chiefs of Southern Minnesota, Containing Sketches of the Prominent Chieftains of the Dakota and Winnebago Tribes from 1825 to 1865* (Mankato: Free Press Co., 1927; Minneapolis: Ross and Haines, 1969), 10–11.

7. The interpreter probably misunderstood Wabasha at this point as there is no evidence that Wabasha visited Washington, D.C., at any time other than 1837 and 1858.

8. This letter requested permission for the eastern Sioux to present their grievances to the president in Washington, D.C.; see Anderson, *Little Crow*, 93.

9. Wabasha refers here to the 1858 treaty that contained articles calling for the allotment of land. It did not, however, give the Sioux title to land on both sides of the Minnesota River as Wabasha states. Land title was restricted to the south side of the river. See Kappler, comp. and ed., *Indian Treaties*, 2:781–85.

10. Traders claimed that credit had been extended to the Indians after the 1858 treaty and that the Dakotas would have to pay these bills before receiving more goods. Little Crow played a major role in convincing various subchiefs to agree to using money obtained from the 1858 treaty to pay the delinquent charges; see Anderson, *Little Crow*, 111–13.

11. Prescott spent more than forty years trading with the eastern Sioux and working for them as a farm instructor. He had married a daughter of the Mdewakanton subchief Cloud Man, but he was not a "half-breed" as Wabasha suggests; see Philander Prescott, *The Recollections of Philander Prescott, Frontiersman of the Old Northwest, 1819–1862*, ed. Donald D. Parker (Lincoln: University of Nebraska Press, 1966).

12. Kappler, comp. and ed., *Indian Treaties*, 2:1067.

CHAPTER II

The War Begins

AS THE TENSION escalated in early August 1862, several small hunting and war parties left the reservations. These groups were dominated by young men, some of whom were angry over the way whites had treated their people and the failure of traders to assist the Indians. One war party tried to vent its discontent by striking the Ojibway; the hunting parties, on the other hand, headed for the Big Woods, some thirty miles east of the Redwood Agency. One of these parties from Shakopee's village on Rice Creek met and quarreled with Robinson Jones, a settler, near the small community of Acton. The impassioned warriors turned on Jones, killing him and several members of his family and creating the spark that ignited the war.

After the incident at Acton, the Dakota hunters responsible hurried back to the Rice Creek village where they told a hastily formed council of their actions. The soldiers' lodge at Rice Creek called an emergency meeting at which the events of the past few weeks were discussed in the context of the killings at Acton. Many soldiers concluded that those who committed the murders would be severely dealt with, the whites demanding their lives, and sometime after midnight a consensus evolved that endorsed going to war against the whites. The small Rice Creek village represented only a fraction of the Dakota people; therefore, the Mdewakanton soldiers attempted to seek allies at nearby villages, hoping especially to secure the support of Little Crow.

Two of the following excerpts describe the killings at Acton. The first narrative comes from Big Eagle; the second is a recollection of the event by Good Star Woman. While these accounts fail to provide fresh insights into the Acton incident, they emphasize the starving condition of the Indians involved in the killing and their fear that taking food from whites would result in punishment. Both narratives also point to the dare that prompted the violence, and the second stresses that the perpetrators were not from the Redwood Agency. In the aftermath, some Mdewakantons were quick to argue that Wahpetons were responsible for the war. The third selection deals with the final debate regarding the proposed war that occurred when the members of the soldiers' lodge reached Little Crow's village. No fewer than three accounts (one of which is reproduced here) of this discussion have survived, all of which emphasize the initial reticence of Little Crow to join the fighting.

Narrative 1
BIG EAGLE'S ACCOUNT

For biographical information on Big Eagle, see Chapter I, Narrative 1.

YOU KNOW how the war started — by the killing of some white people near Acton, in Meeker county. I will tell you how this was done, as it was told me by all of the four young men who did the killing. These young fellows all belonged to Shakopee's band. Their names were Sungigidan ("Brown Wing"), Ka-om-de-i-ye-ye-dan ("Breaking Up"), Nagi-wi-cak-te ("Killing Ghost"), and Pa-zo-i-yo-pa ("Runs against Something when Crawling"). I do not think their names have ever before been printed. One of them is yet living. They told me they did not go out to kill white people. They said they went over into the Big Woods to hunt; that on Sunday, Aug. 17, they came to a settler's fence, and here they found a hen's nest with some eggs in it. One of them took the eggs, when another said: "Don't take them, for they belong to a white man and we may get into trouble." The other was angry, for he was very hungry and wanted to eat the eggs, and he dashed them to the ground and replied: "You are a coward. You are afraid of the white man. You are afraid to take even an egg from him, though you are half-starved. Yes, you are a coward, and I will tell everybody so." The other replied: "I am not a coward. I am not afraid of the white man, and to show you that I am not I will go to the house and shoot him. Are you brave enough to go with me?" The one who had called him a coward said: "Yes, I will go with you, and we will see who is the braver of us two." Their two companions then said: "We will go with you, and we will be brave, too." They all went to the house of the white man (Mr. Robinson Jones), but he got alarmed and went to another house (that of his son-in-law, Howard Baker), where were some other white men and women. The four Indians followed them and killed three men and two women (Jones, Baker, a Mr. Webster, Mrs. Jones and a girl of fourteen). Then they hitched up a team belonging to another settler and drove to Shakopee's camp [(]six miles above Redwood agency) [the Rice Creek village], which they reached late that night and told what they had done, as I have related.

The tale told by the young men created the greatest excitement. Everybody was waked up and heard it. Shakopee took the young men to Little Crow's house (two miles above the agency), and he sat up in bed and listened to their story. He said war was now declared. Blood had been shed, the payment would be stopped, and the whites would take a dreadful vengeance because women had been killed. Wabasha, Wacouta, myself and others still talked for peace, but nobody would listen to us, and soon the cry was "Kill the whites and kill all these cuthairs who will not join us." A council was held and war was declared. Parties formed and dashed away in the darkness to kill settlers. The women began to run bullets and the men to clean their guns.

Continued on page 55.

Narrative 2
GOOD STAR WOMAN'S RECOLLECTIONS

GOOD STAR WOMAN or Wicahpewastewin was also known as Dorine Blacksmith. She was born in 1854 near the Yellow Medicine Agency. Her father, Hepi Wakandisapa or Black Lightning, was a Franco-Dakota; her mother, Archargowe, was a Dakota. Both belonged to the Mdewakanton tribe and were willing to adopt the ways of the whites. During the war they tried to avoid violence, and by the fall of 1862 they were living in the camp at Fort Snelling. In May 1863 they were removed to the Crow Creek Reservation, where her father learned the blacksmith trade and adopted the name Joseph Blacksmith. Four years later they joined other Sioux at the Santee Reservation in Nebraska Territory and in 1869 moved to the Sisseton Reservation in eastern Dakota Territory. Good Star Woman married and after rearing her children lived with two daughters near Red Wing, Minnesota.

GOOD STAR WOMAN, seated, with her family in about 1930

In the 1930s ethnologist Frances Densmore visited her and wrote down Good Star Woman's war narrative. Good Star Woman spoke in Dakota, and her daughter translated. Her story was based on the vivid impressions made on the mind of an eight-year-old girl by the dramatic events of the war, which remained with her more than seventy years afterward. Her narrative emphasizes the Indian-white hostilities prior to the war and how the conflict affected her family. It is one of the few accounts left by a Dakota woman. It is probable that she lived near Red Wing for the remainder of her life, but her place and date of death are unknown.

Narrative Source: Frances Densmore, "A Sioux Woman's Account of the Uprising in Minnesota," 1934, typescript, Frances Densmore Papers, Division of Libraries and Archives, Minnesota Historical Society.

HUNTING and trapping were the principal industries of the Sioux and they took the hides to the trader. Sometimes he went to the Indians in their hunting camps, taking pork, coffee and other commodities which he gave to the Indians in exchange for hides. He packed the furs on his sled and went on to the next camp. So far as the Indians knew, there was no account kept when the trader collected the hides nor when they took the hides to his store. They only knew that they "owed a lot to the trader."

After a while two traders called the Indians to a council. Good Star Woman's father did not go and when the men came back he said "What did they want to tell you?" They replied, "The trader said he wanted everybody who owed him anything to sign a paper and then he would collect the money from the Government. He didn't show us any papers, he just wanted us to sign. He said the Government would allow each Indian twenty dollars a year, and what he owed the trader would be taken out of that. Then we won't have to go hunting any more."

The trader also told the Indians that if they didn't sign the paper they could get nothing at his store, saying, "If you have to eat grass, go ahead and *eat* grass but don't come around here asking for food."

From that time the Indians and the trader were unfriendly but the trouble did not begin right away.

The trouble at Birch Coulee started with four young Sioux, two from near Birch Coulee and two belonging to the Pezutazizi (yellow medicine) group living near Granite Falls. They went hunting to get some meat, perhaps staying two or three nights. On the way home they came to the farm of a white man and one said "Let's ask this man for water, so we can cook some supper. I'm hungry." A hen flew up and left some eggs, hidden in the grass. One Indian said he was going to take the eggs. Another said, "Let them alone, they belong to this farmer." The first Indian said, "That is nothing. You are just afraid of this white man." So he stepped on the eggs and broke them. The farmer did not see this as it happened some distance from the house.

The Indians were still hungry, so two of them took a pail and went toward the house to get water, to cook some of the meat they had brought. The farmer saw them and motioned them to go away, then he went into the house, got his gun and threatened them but did not shoot. The Indian who had advised leaving the eggs alone turned to the other and said, "You called me a coward. Shoot this man. If you don't I'll kill you right here." So the Indian shot the farmer and his wife. Some white men chased them toward Birch Coulee.

That night some Indians who had been hunting came home and found what had happened. This was late at night, but they talked it over and the head men got together and said the trouble must not go any further. But the Indians who had been told to eat grass got angry and the attack on the trader[s] followed in a short time.

Continued on page 52.

Narrative 3
LITTLE CROW'S SPEECH

LITTLE CROW or Taoyateduta or His Red Nation was born at Kaposia in about 1810 to Big Thunder and Miniokadawin or Woman Planting in Water. He received a customary Dakota education and as a young man went on trading expeditions to the western Dakota bands. He married four daughters of the Wahpeton leader, Inyangmani. In 1846 he succeeded his father as leader of a Mdewakanton band but sustained gunshot wounds to both wrists in defeating his half brother for the position. He was a negotiator and signer of the Treaty of Mendota in 1851 and the Treaty of 1858. He also made a trip to Washington, D.C., in 1854 to campaign for well-defined boundary lines for the Dakota reservations. In the 1850s he was recognized as the spokesman for all the Mdewakanton bands. By the 1860s he had accepted some of the white man's ways but refused to adopt anything that would compromise his Dakota religious beliefs.

In 1862 Little Crow was living in a wood-frame house in the center of his village, located two miles northwest of the Redwood Agency. Nevertheless, oral accounts of his life, provided by family members, suggest that the members of the soldiers' lodge confronted Little Crow at his tepee, which was adjacent to the house. When the Rice Creek delegation arrived, Little Crow was resting from an early morning hunt. He reacted strongly with an impassioned speech to the news of the Acton affair. His young son, Wowinape, stood beside him and memorized his father's words.[1] On three separate occasions, Wowinape described the confrontation to Hanford L. Gordon, an attorney. With the aid of the Reverend Stephen Riggs, Gordon translated Little Crow's speech and included it in two books published in 1891 and 1910.

Thus in 1862 the warriors perceived Little Crow to be the most able, experienced, and committed to Dakota ways of the Mdewakanton leaders and coerced him to command the warriors. Six weeks later, after the battle of Wood Lake, he and a few loyal followers fled to the Dakota plains where they spent the winter and spring attempting to form alliances with other Sioux bands or other Indian tribal groups or with the British in Canada. Failing in these efforts, Little Crow returned to Minnesota where he was shot and killed by a white farmer, Nathan Lamson, near Hutchinson on July 3, 1863.[2]

Narrative Sources: H[anford] L. Gordon, *The Feast of the Virgins and Other Poems* (Chicago: Laird & Lee, 1891), 343–44, and *Indian Legends and Other Poems* (Salem, Mass.: Salem Press Co., 1910), 381–83.

[Little Crow listened to the appeals and threats of the young men. He blackened his face as a sign of mourning and covered his head. Finally one man brazenly accused him of cowardice. Little Crow responded by dashing the taunter's eagle-feather headdress to the ground and delivered a powerful speech.]

TA-O-YA-TE-DU-TA is not a coward, and he is not a fool! When did he run away from his enemies? When did he leave his braves behind him on the war-path and turn back to his *teepees?* When he ran away from your enemies, he walked behind on your trail with his face to the Ojibways and covered your backs as a she-bear covers her cubs! Is *Ta-o-ya-te-du-ta* without scalps? Look at his war-feathers! Behold the scalp-locks of your enemies hanging there on his lodge-poles! Do they call him a coward? *Ta-o-ya-te-du-ta* is not a coward, and he is not a fool. Braves, you are like little children; you know not what you are doing.

You are full of the white man's *devil-water* (rum). You are like dogs in the Hot Moon when they run mad and snap at their own shadows. We are only little herds of buffaloes left scattered; the great herds that once covered the prairies are no more. See! — the white men are like the locusts when they fly so thick that the whole sky is a snow-storm. You may kill one — two — ten; yes, as many as the leaves in the forest yonder, and their brothers will not miss them. Kill one — two — ten, and ten times ten will come to kill you. Count your fingers all day long and white men with guns in their hands will come faster than you can count.

LITTLE CROW, sketch by Frank B. Mayer, 1851

Yes; they fight among themselves—away off. Do you hear the thunder of their big guns? No; it would take you two moons to run down to where they are fighting, and all the way your path would be among white soldiers as thick as tamaracks in the swamps of the Ojibways. Yes; they fight among themselves, but if you strike at them they will all turn on you and devour you and your women and little children just as the locusts in their time fall on the trees and devour all the leaves in one day. You are fools. You cannot see the face of your chief; your eyes are full of smoke. You cannot hear his voice; your ears are full of roaring waters. Braves, you are little children — you are fools. You will die like the rabbits when the hungry wolves hunt them in the Hard Moon (January). *Ta-o-ya-te-du-ta* is not a coward: he will die with you.

NOTES

1. For more on Wowinape, see his narrative in Chapter X, p. 279, below.
2. See Anderson, *Little Crow*.

CHAPTER III

Attack on the Redwood Agency

THE EVENTS at the Redwood Agency on August 18, 1862, have been chronicled by several white historians. The information used to develop these histories was drawn largely from the missionaries, traders, and laborers who survived the assault. Other accounts, however, have been left by Dakota full- and mixed-bloods. These narratives emphasize the confusion and fear that gripped large numbers of full- and mixed-bloods, as well as whites, when the killing commenced; they also reveal the tendency of the Dakotas to protect their relatives.

Seven such accounts of the attack are known to exist. The most detailed description is the one by Cecelia Campbell Stay and is published here for the first time. Stay recalls the Acton incident as well as the way mixed-bloods were initially treated by the victorious warriors. A second narrative is provided by Good Star Woman, who lived a few miles west of the agency with her family. Her people were as stunned by the war as were the whites at the agency. A third account was given orally by Esther Wakeman, Little Crow's sister-in-law; it suggests that Little Crow did his best to prevent war and joined the fighting reluctantly.

The four other accounts are by Big Eagle, who left a complete narrative of the war; Joe Coursolle, a mixed-blood who was a teamster and fur trader; White Spider, also known as John Wakeman, Little Crow's younger half brother; and finally, Taopi, a farmer Indian. Coursolle's account clearly has been embellished by F. J. Patten, the collaborator who wrote down the story. Even so, it provides information about those Indians who did not join the warriors. White Spider's assessment was recorded thirty-five years after the war and represents an attempt to clear Little Crow's name. Taopi's brief description shows that farmer Indians tried to stop the killing but failed.

Narrative 1
CECELIA CAMPBELL STAY'S ACCOUNT

CECELIA CAMPBELL STAY, usually called Celia, was born in St. Paul to Antoine Joseph and Mary Ann Dalton Campbell on October 10, 1848. The mixed-blood Campbell family lived at Traverse des Sioux, 1851–55, and at the Redwood Agency, 1855–62. Held captive during the war, they were freed at Camp Release in late September 1862.

Celia was aware of the tumultuous events taking place around her and often reminisced about the war in later years. She also produced three accounts between 1882 and 1924, parts of which are included in this collection. They are in English and are filled with vivid details concerning her family and neighbors. Her narrative of the war's beginning and the killing of white employees and traders at the agency is the most informative of any account known to exist.

In October 1866 she married Joseph Charron, a French-Canadian farmer, at St. Peter; they had five children. After Charron's death in 1879 she married Francis Stay, a French-Canadian hunter and farmer, in April 1880 and lived with him until his death in 1926. Five children were born to this marriage also. She died at Montevideo on August 9, 1935.[1]

Narrative Source: Cecelia Campbell Stay, "The Massacre at the Lower Sioux Agency, August 18, 1862," typescript, 1882, Provincial Archives of Manitoba, Winnipeg, Manitoba (paragraphing added by the editors).

LOWER SIOUX AGENCY was a neat little village built on the top of the hill 12 miles west of Fort Ridgeley[.] I should judge that was the direction. A belt of timber [was] on one side facing the river [and] on the other[,] prairie. The [Indian] Department buildings were all commodious and painted white[;] there were four of them, first was a boarding house with four rooms with old Joe and wife, German cooks and hired girls, hired men boarded there.[2] I had a brother also named Joe about three years old[;] this old couple [Old Joe and his wife] took a liking to him, perhaps it was the name being the same or because they were childless. Any way every time we went there on errands they give my brother buns or bread which we were very fond of[;] there was so much lard worked in [it] made the crust sweet and easy to chew.

Opposite and a little below was John Nairn's carpenter shop[;] a few yards up the road was a warehouse or granary combined, next the house we lived in, further up another where the carpenters family lived in one end of the house, Robertson's in the other end, opposite was Dr. [Jared W.] Daniel[s]'s cottage just built, next going down the road again was the other and last white house where the doctor [Philander Humphrey] lived, back of them was a hewed log stable, a ravine ran along ending just north of the boarding house, there was two root houses and an ice house on its north side and a fine spring enclosed, to the north was LaBathe's store and kitchen[,] all log cabins[,] next Myrick's new fram[e] store & kitchen stables and ice house[;] across from that ravine a few rods was Captain Louis Robert's store[,] a log one and a new frame one, log kitchen and stables, going east of there a road took past Robinettes log house[,] that is they lived there [at the] time of the outbreak, then Petit Jeanis (John Genois) boarding house[,] all men, opposite was Major Forbest [Forbes's] store and new kitchen[;] this [the traders' stores] was the scene of slaughter in the outbreak. . . .

Now I will speak of-the-never-to-be-forgotten day August 18th, 1862[;] on Monday I got up for breakfast[,] ready [readied] and set the table, by that time my brothers and sisters were running [and] playing around the house[;] I told them to wake mother up, waited awhile and then called her myself, seeing she did not get up I went and stood at the door and saw something dark moving along the ground as far as I could see[;] it was shaped like a boa constrictor[;] my eyes were rivetted on the object [but I] could not make it out until it got to the fork of the roads[;] then, I saw it was Indian heads I had seen moving in a steady column, one man was on a white horse trying to intercerpt them crossing and recrossing the road [a]head of them. It was Chatenchun, I found out it was not his brother living at Hastings (Marpiyawakunza)[.][3] I will tell you more of this one later[.] Grandmother [Margaret Campbell] was eating breakfast next door[.] She came out looking and said "I wonder what there is such a crowd for[.] You go and ask them[,] probably they are distributing food and rations and goods today[" ,] so the hunchback woman Mazampason went and met some Indians going through the fence adjoining the house[.] They turned back[;] some said it was a war party of Chippewas, some said it was for (Wapaminipi) distributing provisions and goods. Then this man on the grey and white horse cam[e] opposite the house and shouted to us wanting to know if father was at home or

CECELIA CAMPBELL STAY at about age seventeen

where? They told him at Mysick's [Myrick's] store where he was clerk-ing. [The man wanted to know] if he [father] only had his team home to take us off.

Grandmother sat by on the banking of the house bewailing the ab-sence of her sons, father and Uncle Baptiste. Uncle Hippolite sat by Grandmother[,] a sixteen shooter loaded by his side[,] a doubled bar-relled shot gun across his knees;[4] he said "he would defend with his life." Woe to the Indian that would have offered harm to us that day. Here we saw father and Uncle Baptists [*sic*] coming surrounded by eight of our brave friendly Indians, they had just saved father's life. Poor Grandmother's heart was full[;] she began to question father but his [head?] had been full to overflowing[;] he could not speak for some time. He said "they had got up early to have a reasonable start for New Ulm after some loads.["] Andrew Myrick was not an early riser[,] always slept late, did not get up after several summonses. Father went himself and told Andrew to get up[;] they were ready [and] awaiting orders on bills which they could not go without. Father then went out and sat on a dry good[s] box turned upside down to the right of the front door outside, he had been waiting so long[;] he was very impatient to start the long trip before it got too hot, he was cutting the weeds around him with the crack of his whip when he saw the Indians coming. One came to him making a war speech which he understood was against the Chippewas[.] I don't remember the words, he shook hands with him and went in the store. Uncle Baptist was inside with George Washington Divol[l] who as usual was fooling [around?], he told Uncle [to] light the pipe and red pipestone which always lay on the counter; it had a long flat stem[.] Regular Indians make a bag of KninickKinnick and tobacco mixed[. The bag] stood by it, so Uncle was filling the pipe when this Indian steps in. Father heard two shots fired. Uncle came out[;] all color fled from his countenance. "Brother," he said, "Divol and Lind [James Lynd] are killed." James Lind was standing at the East door facing the flagpole. It was a curious fact[;] father said [that] Lind was laboring under some presentiment that morning; he was so quiet and left his writing to stand the same place he stood when shot, whether the Indians killed both of these men or whether there was an Indian to each man I cannot tell at this late date.[5]

I was not quite fourteen years of age when this happened and remembered every word and act and day in different camps for years[.] Data gradually [has] left my memory[;] by and by everything may be forgotten so I rewrite my narrative before it is too late. If I had been at the scene of murder and plunder I would never forget unless imbelcility [sic] set in. Even if some sinner deserved the death[,] it was yet slaughter[,] for assuredly God's wrath was meted out to many as well as too many innocents [who] suffered for those very sins [that] the earth itself could not contain any longer.

The[n] Uncle Baptiste came out and telling father Divol and Lind were killed father said "let's go back in[.]" He meant to go in and close up the store and get the guns and ammunition to defend themselves

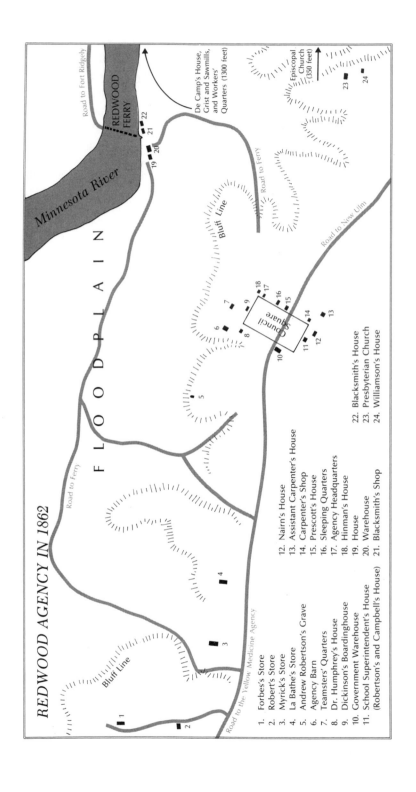

REDWOOD AGENCY IN 1862

Minnesota River

Road to Fort Ridgely

REDWOOD FERRY

De Camp's House, Grist and Sawmills, and Workers' Quarters (1300 feet)

Episcopal Church (350 feet)

Road to Ferry

Bluff Line

F L O O D P L A I N

Road to Ferry

Bluff Line

Road to New Ulm

Council Square

Road to the Yellow Medicine Agency

1. Forbes's Store
2. Robert's Store
3. Myrick's Store
4. La Bathe's Store
5. Andrew Robertson's Grave
6. Agency Barn
7. Teamsters' Quarters
8. Dr. Humphrey's House
9. Dickinson's Boardinghouse
10. Government Warehouse
11. School Superintendent's House
    (Robertson's and Campbell's House)
12. Nairn's House
13. Assistant Carpenter's House
14. Carpenter's Shop
15. Prescott's House
16. Sleeping Quarters
17. Agency Headquarters
18. Hinman's House
19. House
20. Warehouse
21. Blacksmith's Shop
22. Blacksmith's House
23. Presbyterian Church
24. Williamson's House

when the Indians divined his purpose. "Grab him, grab him,["] they said and they came behind him [and] caught his hands [and] held [them] back of him[;] then [in] the struggle [they] began to get loose; an Indian levelled his gun at father's breast and told him now was the time to revenge himself for being thrashed once for stealing whiskey and another time [for coming] to the house drunk singing and tramping around[,] looking through the windows[,] keeping us awake and breaking the lights [panes of glass] out of a window in the next house[.] Father remembered this in his speech that day, but for those eight friendly Indians coming in the nick of time father would have died then and I would not have been there either to tell what happened. Iron Elk and his nephew chattan [*sic*] and six others— Hasuheyaryadan, Grey Eagle I think was one[,] and Chattans brothers Chaska and Ha-Pan might be the others[,] besides two more than [that] one would lie with him if they hurt that man, these eight were related by blood to Grandfather Scott Campbell[;] they got around the brothers and brought them to us, they shifted place so no stray bullet could hit but an Indian and that meant "war to the knife".[6] Passing Hail had the bravest warriors that ever lived and they took side with the white people. Does history mention this fact? Are their names on the Camp Release monument? Father in his struggle that morning struggled away from the building to give Mysick a chance to shoot the Indians holding him but not a move could be see[n] at the blind hung at the window: Myrick was a splendid shot having a sixteen shooter by his bed always, father's doubled barrelled gun was also loaded and standing in his room, once free they had everything to defend themselves upstairs. All they heard of him [Myrick] was when he stamped his books [boots] on after calling him. The Indians called spunky [Myrick?] "Wachinco". Late in the day we heard he was killed when they spoke of burning the building, he got off through the roof by a trapdoor and slid off a lean-to towards their spring[;] they shot him. Little Billy Findley [fled?], old man Fritz his German cook was also killed[,] poor harmless old man, I never knew any other name for him or relatives.

In the afternoon father and brothers took spades and went to bury the dead and they were forbidden[;] whether he had time to cover any I never asked him. Francis Giard, a French Canadian we had hired at 18 years of age during [the] Inkpaduta trouble in 1857 (Fall.) [*sic*] working for us 1858, 59, 60 and 61) until that year 62[; he] was at Mrs. [*sic*] Forbes' store sitting outside when the Indians shot Antoine Young

(Dion)[,] brother to Demas Dion of Traverse des Sioux[;] he was married to a Miss Crat of Wabashan. I think I am correct[;] I would not innocently give you an impression I would or could write falsehoods for I mean to tell you the solemn truth and nothing but the truth. I can't say who else was shot just there when young [sic] was killed but Giard went in the store where Joseph Belland was killed and fell across Giards [Belland's?] legs[;] he feigned death until they were going to burn the building when he jumped up and scared the plunderers, one big black-eyed fellow came[,] raised his tomahawk[,] and Giard told him "Ho Coda (yes Comrade) strike me here,["] pointing to his forehead, the Indian said "he was too brave to kill." He wanted him to hitch up a yoke of oxen to a wagon loaded with plunder[;] the poor oxen were wild with terror[;] first we say [saw] of him he was coming on a jump hanging [on] to their rope for dear life, he tied them outside (instead of letting them go on) and came in the house. Mother asked him many questions, between our folks and Iron Elk (one of father's saviours) [we] prevailed in spite of him [his objections] to save himself because we were not safe ourselves, if any tried to hurt him Uncle Hippolite was around[;] he would kill some of them and they [then] it would be war between our defenders and the hostiles[, the latter] being more numerous[,] we had but a short stand to make before we would all be killed. Iron Elk looked in and told mother to tell Giard to go upstairs[;] he very reluctantly obeyed. The Indian wanting Giard came asking for him, Iron Elk said "he must have gone on because there was no Frenchman there,["] but he [the Indian] opened the door to go upstairs[.] Iron Elk ordered him out telling him not to scare the women and children. Uncle spoke rough and he went out and stood opposite the house watching very intently[;] as soon as he was gone and [it was] safe, Iron Elk spread his blanket the length of his arms thus shielding Giard while he passed between the two houses, telling him to make for the cornfield back [of the house and] then the river, he followed the bluff until he came to Jean (John) Grnois [Genois] and the boy Lefevre sitting on a log alongside a path[.] Petit Jean as we called him was laughingly recounting how he run down the hill; he could not believe they were killing all alike, he was coming to us[.] After [a]while Giard told him we were not sure of our lives and made him leave to save himself, they crossed the river[,] travelled nights, hid day times, got separated the first time they hid[,] arrived to safety very sore footed after several days of untold hardship.

Through the day there were many Indians gathered in front of the house[.] All had guns [and] stood in a single row looking daggers. Uncle Hypolite asked them what they were doing[,] if they came to scare women and children or did they not know they were men, so they left and bothered us no more with the sight of their unsightly hideousness. Iron Elk stood by us, so did his nephew, his sister Blue eyes, son Chattan. This one then went to hunt up a horse team and wagon to take us to the fort. He only found an ox team and red river cart going to Fort Ridgely[.] [With] this [traveling] was out of the question[;] there was no alternative but to stay. Tim[e] was passing[;] it must have been along about two o'clock P.M.[;] not a mouthful had some os [of] us [to] eat. Mother[,] who had so hurriedly got up on hearing of bloodshed[,] commenced to fry saleratus, bread, [and] prepare for a move some where which Omnipotent Providence only knew. There came the hue and cry "the soldiers [Captain John Marsh's command] are coming, poor unfortunate little band of heroes" just a mouthful for the lion's mouth as mother said. ["]Let's go and see how many there are" so we ran to the hill and saw a handful of glistening bayonets just passing David's [sic] Faribault's house across the river[.] Mother burst out with "poor soldiers[,"] "what foolish soldiers," "they'll all be killed[,]" come we must get away out of earshot[;] I don't want to hear a shot that kills them. The cart was packed full and we started a foot for the "Little Chief's["] house or (passing hail) [sic] village. Wasuheyayedan, how we hurried to get out [of] there[.] None knew or can imagine but we who trotted that distance[.] I should judge it was four miles to his house[.] When we had made about two miles we heard the first volley [of the attack on Marsh.] Mother dropped as tho she was dead with her baby Stella on her back, she had fainted[.] We gathered around her until she got up, we came to the Chief's house long before sundown, Father came after awhile and told us there was no horse team to be got and how they refused to let him bury the dead. Just as the sun was going down in all his glory Louis Boucier[,] a half breed[,] came up with a wounded shoulder, his shirt pulled down off that arm, father gave him a sound scolding for his shameful participation in that awful butchery of brave soldiers, we heard he was killed by hostile Indians not long after.

Another incident I want to bring before my readers is that same day, [I] shall name our family first for we lived at that house, where some taken prisoners were congregated. There was Grandmother Mrs. Margaret Scott Campbell [Campbell], Uncle Hypolite [and his] wife Yuratwin (a cousin of Standing Buffalo) and two children John

& Theresa, Uncle Baptiste, Uncle Scott, father, A. J. Campbell, mother, sister Emily 15 years old, myself (Celia), 13 and Mary 9, Joseph 7, Martha 5, Willie 2, Stella about 7 weeks old, all those who were fleeing fugitives [and were] brought back to us were Mrs. Antoine Findly and step-son Billy Findly, Louis Martin [and his] wife and three children. Mrs. Matilda Vanosse [with] one child on her back, as far as we could see her come, she would fall in a fit, the Indian called Wamonousa (Thief) would help her up and come a little ways and she would have another fit, they thought at first it was a drunken man, as soon as they thought of her Uncle Scott went, met them and between them they got her to the house, at the door as soon as they let her go she fell full length on the floor, in another fit, you may be sure what an impression that incident[,] of all on that day[,] left indelibly on my memory[,] not only me but [on] all who survived that incident. Mrs. Findly never left us during the seven weeks of our captivity until [she was] safe back to Traverse des Sioux [and] out of danger. August 19th 1862 on Thursday [Tuesday] we had orders to rendezvous at little Crow's village, a little further up, the team went back and forth moving, at last we followed it back on foot over there.

Continued on page 135.

Narrative 2

GOOD STAR WOMAN'S RECOLLECTIONS

For biographical information on Good Star Woman, see Chapter II, Narrative 2.

THE FAMILY of Good Star Woman lived near the trading post. Her father had a sister who had raised more corn than she needed, so she told them to come over and eat it. She lived a few miles toward the west and they moved over to her place. That was in August, 1862. Early the next morning the mother of Good Star Woman said "I'll go and get some wood, and in the afternoon we will pick our corn." The little girl went with her mother. It was the custom of the Sioux women to carry wood on their backs, the pack being carried by a strap across the chest or forehead. In preparing to carry wood, a woman laid the ends of the long carrying strap, parallel, on the ground, then laid the wood across the straps, leaving enough of the lengths to tie upward over the wood, while the loop, or middle portion, was ready to be placed across the woman's head or shoulders.

Good Star Woman's mother had laid only a few sticks on her carrying strap when she heard shots. "Hurry," she cried, "The Chippewa must be here," and they ran back to the camp. There they heard more shots and everyone thought it must be the Chippewa as they had had raids of the Chippewa and were always looking for them.

When they returned to the camp it was still very early and the little children were in bed. An Indian came riding into the camp, so frightened that he could not tell them what was the trouble. They kept saying "Tell us, what is the trouble." At last he said "The Sioux are killing the whites." This was taking place four or five miles away but they could hear the guns. The children wakened and began to cry.

Later they learned that one of the traders was standing on the steps of his store when the trouble took place. He had been there many years and could speak Sioux fluently and he said to the Indians, "Why are you fellows coming here? Are you jealous of me?" One of the Indians said "*I'm* the one," and shot him.

The two Indians who killed the white farmer [at Acton] were shot in punishment by their own people. One of them was sitting at the end of his wigwam, opposite the door, when an Indian came in and said, "You were the cause of all this suffering, making the women and children suffer so much," and he shot him dead. The other went out of his tent and was walking along when someone shot him in the back. One of the leaders said, "This is what we ought to have done in the beginning and then this suffering would not have come, the women crying and the little children having to walk so far." Every morning they could hear the women crying, and as they went from place to place the little children had to walk and they cried from weariness and fright.[7]

Continued on page 263.

Narrative 3
ESTHER WAKEMAN'S REMINISCENCES

ESTHER WAKEMAN, also known as Mahpiyatowin or Blue Sky Woman, was the daughter of Wakianheida or Going Higher. She was born in 1845 at the Mdewakanton village near Oak Grove (present-

day Bloomington). She married White Spider, a half brother of Little Crow's, in 1851 and moved to the reservation in 1853. Her husband was a clerk for William H. Forbes at the time of the war. They had nine children.

Esther witnessed the family side of Little Crow's actions in the war and kept repeating her account to her children. She fled with Little Crow and his followers to the northern plains of Dakota Territory, wintered at Devils Lake, and moved on to Canada in the spring. Ultimately, to avoid starvation, she and her family surrendered to American authorities at Pembina, Dakota Territory, in January 1864. While her husband was imprisoned at Davenport, Iowa, for a two-year term, she and her children were sent to the Crow Creek Reservation. They were reunited at the Santee Reservation, but the family moved again four years later to the Sisseton Reservation. Finally Esther and John Wakeman returned to Minnesota and settled near Morton in 1885. Esther died at an unknown date but had passed on to her daughter, Elizabeth (Mrs. Harry Lawrence), her story of the war, which was published in 1960.[8]

Narrative Source: Mr. and Mrs. Harry Lawrence, "The Indian Nations of Minnesota: The Sioux Uprising," in *Minnesota Heritage: A Panoramic Narrative of the Historical Development of the North Star State*, ed. Lawrence M. Brings (Minneapolis: T. S. Denison and Co., 1960), 80–82.

I WAS seventeen and had two children [at the time of the war]. . . . My brother and my husband worked at the agency.

On that fateful morning in August, 1862, Little Crow had gone hunting to get some fresh meat for breakfast. I went to the corn field to chase the crows away from the corn. I heard voices and I climbed up on the protection that had been built to protect the corn.

Men were coming from the direction of Redwood. I heard one of them say, "If we do this, we will not have to worry for at least two years." I jumped down from the protection so that I would not be seen, and a little later I heard shooting.

Frightened, I ran to the house. Little Crow had just come back from hunting. He had some catfish and ducks. When I told him of the shooting, he did not say a word.

I was worried about my husband and brothers, so I ran to the agency. Two men were coming from the agency, supporting my brother between them. I was told that they had been eating breakfast when Ta-wa-su-ota suddenly appeared in the room and shot the storekeeper. My brother who was sitting next to the storekeeper became covered with blood and fainted.[9]

I continued to the agency and ran through the rooms. The place had been ransacked. It was horrible. Someone spoke to me: I turned my head and saw a white man hiding. He said, "Don't speak to me." Ta-wa-su-ota appeared in the doorway and shot at him. He escaped through the window.

I could not find my husband. When I saw him again, he told me he had escorted two white women to a ravine and told them to follow it, traveling by night only to New Ulm. One of them offered him her wedding ring.[10] He answered, "No, no! I don't want your ring. Just look at my face and if anything happens, remember it."

Like a destructive storm, the war struck suddenly and spread rapidly. Everything was confusion. It was difficult to know who was friend and who was foe.

Little Crow divided some white women and children who found it difficult to escape among his friends to protect them from the renegades. The Indians raided farms to get food for the refugees. One day a large group of soldiers attacked them and they were forced to fight.

Little Crow wanted to make peace, but the majority of the people wanted him to lead them in a war. At a council meeting, they threatened him and called him a coward until he in anger agreed to lead them in war.

During the war, my husband and I fled to Canada. When we returned we were imprisoned for three years. Our treatment was terrible. All the food was mixed in one big pot and it wasn't fit to eat. Three of my brothers died of smallpox while in prison.

Narrative 4
BIG EAGLE'S ACCOUNT

For biographical information on Big Eagle, see Chapter I, Narrative 1.

AT THIS TIME my village was up on Crow creek, near Little Crow's. I did not have a very large band—not more than thirty or forty fighting men. Most of them were not for the war at first, but nearly all got into it at last. A great many members of the other bands were like my men; they took no part in the first movements, but afterward did. The next morning, when the force started down to attack the agency, I went along. I did not lead my band, and I took no part in the killing. I went to save the lives of two particular friends if I could. I think others went for the same reason, for nearly every Indian had a friend that he did not want killed; of course he did not care about anybody's else [sic] friend. The killing was nearly all done when I got there. Little Crow was on the ground directing operations. The day before, he had attended church there [the Episcopal mission] and listened closely to the sermon and had shaken hands with everybody. So many Indians have lied about their saving the lives of white people that I dislike to speak of what I did. But I did save the life of George H. Spencer at the time of the massacre.[11] I know that his friend, Chaska, has always had the credit of that, but Spencer would have been a dead man in spite of Chaska if it had not been for me. I asked Spencer about this once, but he said he was wounded at the time and so excited that he could not remember what I did. Once after that I kept a half-breed family from being murdered; these are all the people whose lives I claim to have saved. I was never present when the white people were willfully murdered. I saw all the dead bodies at the agency. Mr. Andrew Myrick, a trader, with an Indian wife, had refused some hungry Indians credit a short time before when they asked him for some provisions. He said to them: "Go and eat grass." Now he was lying on the ground dead, with his mouth stuffed full of grass, and the Indians were saying tauntingly: "Myrick is eating grass himself."

When I returned to my village that day I found that many of my band had changed their minds about the war, and wanted to go into it. All the other villages were the same way. I was still of the belief that it was not best, but I thought I must go with my band and my nation, and I said to my men that I would lead them into the war, and we would all act like brave Dakotas and do the best we could. All my men were with me; none had gone off on raids, but we did not have guns for all at first.

Continued on page 93.

Narrative 5
JOSEPH COURSOLLE'S STORY

JOSEPH COURSOLLE or Joe Gabbro was known as Hinhankaga or The Owl to the Dakota Indians. Born near present-day Devils Lake, North Dakota, in about 1833, he was the son of Pierre Coursolle, a French-Canadian fur trader, and Base-deche-xmiou, a Sisseton Dakota. After his parents' death in the early 1840s, he was reared and educated by Henry H. Sibley at Mendota. By 1850 he was a blacksmith at Mendota. He married Jane Killkool, a white woman, two years later and had a family of at least eight children. Between 1856 and 1860, they lived at Traverse des Sioux where he was a teamster and fur trader, but by the time of the war, they were living in the mixed-blood community at the Redwood Agency.

Fleeing the fighting, most of the family escaped to Fort Ridgely where Coursolle enlisted in Captain Joseph Anderson's company of mounted militia, a unit that fought at Birch Coulee. Subsequently Coursolle worked as a guide and scout for General Sibley, continuing with Sibley's command into the summer of 1863. By 1870 Coursolle and his family were living at Traverse des Sioux and five years later they moved to Santee, Nebraska, where he died in about 1893.

Coursolle's oral account of the war was passed to his son and grandson, Clem Felix, who told the story to F. J. Patten. It was probably Patten who added the romantic touches to the narrative and inexplicably transformed Coursolle's wife Jane into a Franco-Dakota named Marie.[12]

Narrative Source: "The Ordeal of Hinhankaga," as told by Clem Felix to F. J. Patten, typescript, ca. 1962, Division of Libraries and Archives, Minnesota Historical Society.

DURING the whole of the night — I shall never forget the date, August 18, 1862, — a strange foreboding kept sleep away. Marie, my fair-skinned French-Sioux wife, lay still beside me but I knew that she, too, was awake. Cistina Joe (Little Joe) my son, nine days old, kicked in his crib. My slender, black-eyed girls, Elizabeth, six, and Minnie, four, breathed quietly. Duta, my red setter, rumbled low growls outside the open door. Something was out of place, but what could it be?

The night was hot and sticky. From the village of Little Crow, two miles up the valley, I could hear tom-toms throbbing. But that often happened and this familiar sound could not have put that anxious feeling in my stomach.

Suddenly a light hand touched my shoulder. "Sh-h-h, Hinhankaga, be still. I am a friend." I had heard no one enter the room. Why Duta had not challenged her I do not know. "Sh-h-h," she continued, whispering in Sioux, "big trouble coming. Tomorrow warriors kill all whites. Go, now, before too late. Tell no one I warned you or I, too, will die." Then she slipped away as silently as she had come.

In spite of the heat, shivers ran up my back. "Does she speak true?" I thought. "The Indians are angry. The gold annuity payment is late. There is hunger in the lodges. I have heard the men asking for food at Trader Merrick's [Myrick's] store, promising to pay when the money comes. But they have been my friends for years. My French father married a Sioux woman. I am as much Indian as white. Surely they will not kill. Still, if there be no danger why have I been warned? No, I must take no risk. We will go at once to Fort Ridgely where the white soldiers live.["]

Daylight was growing and Cistina Joe was awake. We shook Elizabeth and Minnie and they quickly dressed. I carried baby Joe and Marie carried food in a blanket. Duta we shut in the cabin so he could not betray us to the warriors by his barking.

Quickly we ran down the path to my dug-out canoe at the river. The canoe was too small to carry all and I worried about leaving Elizabeth and Minnie for a second crossing but there was nothing else I could do.

All was still and a few strokes carried Cistina and Marie to the north shore. Just as we landed my heart jumped into my throat as I heard the scuffing of moccasins coming down the trail.

"Elizabeth and Minnie," I called softly across the narrow river. "Quick! Hide in the bushes!" Marie carried the baby and we crawled into a plum thicket.

Four Indians came down the path, single file. I did not know them. They were from a village farther up the valley. I was thankful when they passed the hiding girls, turned to the right and trotted down the river trail.

When they were gone I listened but heard no others coming. But soon rifle shots exploded at the Agency and war whoops filled the air.

Believing Minnie and Elizabeth to be safe I waited until all seemed clear, then paddled the canoe again across the river.

Elizabeth and Minnie were gone! My heart turned to stone. How frightened they must be! I must find them!

Up and down the river bank I ran but no trace of them could I find. Perhaps friendly Indians from the Agency had taken them to their lodge. Up the bluff I crawled through the brush and trees. Duta caught my scent and came bounding to me leaping and barking with joy. "Oh," I thought, "the Indians will hear him and find me. Then they will kill me and Elizabeth and Minnie will have no one to save them."

I was forced to do the cruelest task of my life. I slipped off my belt and pulled it tight around Duta's neck. Tears ran from my eyes as I felt him struggle for breath. Finally he was dead. I knelt down, took his head in my lap and whispered, "Forgive me Duta, forgive me."

I searched for hours. Our cabin was gone. Smoke still came from its ashes. Other buildings at the Agency were burned. I saw many dead men, scalped and tomahawked with brains oozing out of their skulls. I saw Andrew Merrick [Myrick] dead, his mouth stuffed with grass. The Agency ruins were deserted. There was no one there to give me word of my little girls. How I dreaded to go back and tell Marie.

"Are they dead?" she whispered as she saw me coming alone. "I don't know. I couldn't find them. But I saw no bodies of women or girls so I think they are alive."

"No one came while you were away," said Marie, "but there were many gun shots and much yelling down the river. I think there was a battle and the Indians won."

"I'll never give up until I find them," I said. "But first I must get you and Cistina Joe to the Fort." There was still yelling but no shooting down the river so I said, "If there was a battle and the Indians won, now is the time to go — while they are scalping the dead and celebrating their victory."

The battle noise Marie heard down the river, I learned later, was the ambush of Captain Marsh's company at the ferry crossing to the Agency.

We started down the government road to Fort Ridgely keeping out of sight in the brush and trees. Soon an army ambulance came up behind us, the horses running at top speed. I stepped into the road and the driver whoaed the team to a halt. In the ambulance was a wounded soldier. Marie climbed in with Cistina Joe and I ran behind as the horses again broke into a gallop. When my wind played out I jumped in too. No Indians appeared and we reached Fort Ridgely without mishap. It was comforting to feel the safety of the Fort but how our hearts ached for Minnie and Elizabeth.

I went with Marie and Cistina Joe to the barracks reserved for women. There Marie met many women with more reason for crying than she — women who had seen their husbands and their boys tomahawked and scalped. I stayed with her until she was given her place to sleep on a mattress on the floor.

Marie and I were worried about Cistina Joe. His body was hot and his face was flushed.

Continued on page 158.

Narrative 6
WHITE SPIDER'S INTERVIEW

WHITE SPIDER or Unktomiska was also known as John C. Wakeman and Big Thunder or Wakantonka. The son of Big Thunder and Gray Chin Woman (Wikusauwin), he was born near Kaposia (present-day South St. Paul) in July 1831. He grew up near the Dakota village with Little Crow, his half brother. By fall 1853, the Kaposia band had moved to the reservation on the upper Minnesota River where White Spider married Blue Sky Woman (Mahpiyatowin) in 1851. Although he was present at many battles during the war, he always claimed that he spent most of his time saving whites. Following the defeat at Wood Lake, he fled with Little Crow to the Dakota plains near Devils Lake and eventually to Canada. He and his family surrendered at Pembina, Dakota Territory, in January 1864.

While his family was sent to the Crow Creek Reservation, he received a prison term and remained interned at Davenport, Iowa, until 1866. Four years later, he and his family joined the Dakota settlement at Flandreau, Dakota Territory, where he farmed and was a mail carrier. In about 1882, the Wakemans moved to Gray Cloud Island below St. Paul and in 1885 to Morton, Minnesota. He told his story of the war to Edward A. Bromley and Return I. Holcombe in 1897 for newspaper publication. He spoke some English and was assisted by Mary Whipple, a bilingual teacher at Morton. He died at Morton on April 23, 1902.[13]

Narrative Source: Edward A. Bromley, "The Story of the Sioux Outbreak," Minneapolis Sunday Times, August 15, 1897, p. 16.

WHITE SPIDER *at Fort Snelling in 1864*

THEN, in 1862, Little Crow went out on a hunt for a month and a half. Then, on the 18th of August, 1862, about 7 o'clock, the massacre commenced at Redwood agency.

Then the first person that commenced thinking what could be done to save some lives was John Wakeman (Big Thunder.) And I met Little Crow and he said: "Go and gather up what white women and children you can. This state of things won't last very long. The Indians will have to go pretty soon, and then the captives will perish; so, go quick," he said. So I took with me his strong young men, and I took a staff in my hand, and with my hand I took the captive women and children and saved them. That was my work. I had no moccasins on my feet, but I went a long way. I went seven miles. I took Miss West and another woman and two children and they were saved.[14] Then that night, the 18th of August, 1862, we gathered the rest of the white women and children together in Little Crow's home, and I stood guard over them. Those that still live remember that, I think.

Then Little Crow kept a good many of the captives in his own home, and treated them the same as he treated his own children, and had them eat with him. And early one day, about 7 o'clock, he come to my home and said: "My brother, I feel bad this morning. The captives at my house this morning are crying and I feel very sorry. I have heard that God will have pity on poor captives, and, my brother, I have heard that God will be hard on those who are hard on captives. My brother, the captives in my house have nothing to eat, and so they are crying. I think you could find some flour where the Indians first commenced fighting. So take seven young men and see if you can bring me some to comfort these people. It won't be a great while," he said. I agreed with what Little Crow said and rose up quickly and brought some flour for the captives. While I was on the way I met the guards, and I had a hard time with them, but I thought I was doing the work of God and I went through.

Then General [Colonel] Sibley sent a letter to Little Crow and said: "If you are there, Little Crow, the president says return to him the captives. And I am at the head of the army, and the best thing you can do is to make peace with me."[15] Then Little Crow set himself to work to make peace, and there was a great commotion and much opposition, and it was proclaimed that he who should make peace would be trampled to death. And they said to Little Crow, "Answer; I am a man." So Little Crow turned and said to Passing Hail (Wasuhiyayidon): "You answer this letter." But the nation replied: "No, you answer it for us yourself." But Little Crow answered them: "Last June you rejected me from being leader and this war is not my work." But the nation was determined and so pressed him to answer the letter as they wanted. Then some of them deceived him and went and sent a letter secretly desiring peace, and so they dissembled.

Now, the massacre was not got up by Little Crow, because I was with him and tell what I know.

And the president of the United States, who was all wisdom, I am assured, will now look with pity on those who had mercy on the captives and sought to save them. I am now very poor. When there was an appropriation to reward those who had assisted the captives I received nothing by reason of the jealousy of the Indians.

Among the white men who know some of my conduct, I can refer to S. D. Hinman, who knows of some things; and also to John P. Williamson, who knows some also.[16] Then Little Crow is my older brother. We had the same father, but we had different mothers. And I have taken the name of my father, Big Thunder (Wakinyan-tanka), and I subscribe my English name.

> — John Wakeman.
> Birch Cooley, Minn.

And I now live near Redwood.

Narrative 7
TAOPI'S STATEMENT

TAOPI, meaning Wounded Man, was born in about 1820 at Kaposia to Iron Sword and Berry Picker (Azayamankawin) who was also known as Old Bets or Betsy. Although he fought the Ojibway in several battles in his youth, in 1858 he joined the farmer band at the Redwood Agency, becoming its head chief three years later. At this time, he also converted to Christianity.

During the war, he and other Dakotas formed a camp to oppose the conflict and to aid white captives whom they surrendered at Camp Release in late September. At that time he made his statement about the war; the translator and transcriber are unknown. He testified before the military commission at the trials of the Dakota Indians, and the following year he served as a scout for General Sibley. Returning to Minnesota, he settled with his family near Faribault, where he died on February 19, 1869.[17]

Narrative Source: "Statement of Taopi, Chief of the Farmer Indians," in Henry B. Whipple, *Lights and Shadows of a Long Episcopate* (New York: Macmillan, 1912), 111–13.

ON THE MORNING of the 18th of August, 1862, I was preparing to go down to the Mission House, the residence of our minister, the Rev. Mr. Hinman. He had promised to go with me to assist in laying out our burial lot near the new church. My child had been buried but a few days before. As I was about starting, an old man (Tah-e-mi-na) came to my house and said, "All the upper bands are armed and coming down the road." I asked, "For what purpose are they coming?" He said, "I don't know." The old man had hardly gone out when Ta-

TAOPI
in St. Paul
in 1862

te-campi came running to my house and said, "They are killing the traders." I said, "What do you mean?" He said, "The Rice Creek Indians [Shakopee's band] have murdered the whites on the other side of the Minnesota River, and now they are killing the traders." I said, "This is awful work."

As soon as he was gone I heard the report of guns. I went up to the top of my house and from there I could hear the shouts of the Indians, and see them plundering the stores. The men of my band now began to assemble at my house. We counselled, but we could do nothing to resist the hostile Indians because we were so few and they were between us and the settlements. I told them not only to keep out of the disturbance but also not to go near the plunderers. Some of them obeyed me. I sent Good Thunder with a message to Wabasha, but he could not reach his house on account of the hostile Indians.[18] The hostile Indians soon came to our village and commanded us to take off our citizen's clothing and put on blankets and leggings. They said they would kill all of us "bad talkers." We took our guns and were prepared to defend ourselves. We did not know what to do. I wanted to take my wagon and go to the whites, but I could not.

Good Thunder came back and brought news that nearly a whole company of soldiers from the fort had been killed at the Ferry. Good Thunder and Wa-ha-can-ka-ma-za and myself went into my cornfield to talk over the matter. We wanted to escape to the fort that night, but could not because we were watched. We determined to go to the whites at the first opportunity. I proposed to take two white girls who had been taken prisoners at Redwood, and take them to within a short distance of the fort, and then send them in with a letter stating that we were ready to cooperate with the whites in any way they might direct. We were ready, but the girls were afraid to go.

Continued on page 255.

NOTES

1. "Pioneer Lady Passes Here at Age of 86," *Montevideo American*, August 16, 1935, p. 1, 4.

2. Joseph C. and Emily Dickinson moved to Minnesota from Maine. By 1860 they operated a hotel at Henderson, and by 1861 they were running a boardinghouse for agency workers at the Redwood Agency. Escaping on August 18, thirty-four-year-old Joseph, thirty-year-old Emily, and their son and daughter sought refuge at Fort Ridgely. Cecelia Campbell was mistaken when she said they were childless. Joseph fought to defend the fort and accompanied the burial party to Birch Coulee where he was killed on September 2; U.S. Census, 1860, Henderson, Sibley County, roll 574, p. 751, microfilm in Division of Libraries and Archives, Minnesota Historical Society; Marion P. Satterlee, *A Detailed Account of the Massacre by the Dakota Indians of Minnesota in 1862* (Minneapolis: The Author, 1923), 65, 98; Board of Commissioners, *Minnesota in the Civil and Indian Wars*, 1:818, 189; Joseph R. Brown, "Official Report [Battle of Birch Coulee]," September 4, 1862, in Bishop, *Dakota War Whoop*, 188.

3. General Sibley recommended Chatanchun or Downy Hawk Feathers for an award of fifty dollars in 1866 for unspecified deeds during the Dakota War; the editors have found no further information on him. See U.S. Office of Indian Affairs, *Report, 1866*, 239.

4. Hypolite (Paul) Campbell was born in 1828 and Baptiste Campbell in 1831, both at Mendota. They were younger brothers of Antoine Joseph Campbell. Baptiste was tried and convicted for participation in the war and hanged at Mankato, December 26, 1862. Hypolite, too, was involved in the war and fled to Fort Garry, Manitoba, where he opened a blacksmith shop; J. Fletcher Williams, *A History of the City of*

Saint Paul to 1875 (St. Paul: Minnesota Historical Society, 1876; reprint, Minnesota Historical Society Press, Borealis Books, 1983), 135; M[arion] P. Satterlee, *The Court Proceedings in the Trial of Dakota Indians following the Massacre in Minnesota in August 1862* (Minneapolis: Satterlee Printing Co., 1927), 46–48; Transcripts of Trials of Sioux Indians, case no. 138, Senate Records 37A-F2; *St. Peter Tribune*, May 10, 1865, p. 3. The sixteen shooter was a Henry rifle.

5. George Washington Divoll, a Vermont native, was thirty-six years old and employed as an Indian trader by the Myrick brothers; U.S. Census, 1860, Redwood Township, Brown County, roll 567, p. 250. James W. Lynd was born in Maryland in 1830. He moved to Minnesota Territory in about 1853, edited the *Henderson Democrat* for Joseph R. Brown in 1859, and served as a state senator in 1861. He is remembered for his ethnological study of the Eastern Dakotas; the manuscript for it was partially destroyed after his death; S[tephen] R. Riggs, "Memoir of Hon. Jas. W. Lynd," *Minnesota Collections* 3 (1880): 107–14.

6. Iron Elk or Hahakamaza was a leader in Cloud Man's band of Mdewakantons. He signed the Treaty of Mendota in 1851 and the Treaty of 1858. He was tried by the military commission, convicted, and sentenced to be hanged for being at the battles at Fort Ridgely, New Ulm, and Wood Lake. He may also have been active in the warriors' soldiers' lodge. His sentence was remitted, and he was sent to the prison camp at Davenport in 1863. He was pardoned in 1866 and taken to the Santee Reservation. He signed the Treaty of 1882, and in that same year he testified in a lawsuit regarding the misconduct of the Reverend Samuel D. Hinman. He was still living in 1893; the date of his death is not known. See Kappler, comp. and ed., *Indian Treaties*, 2:592, 784, 1067; Satterlee, *Court Proceedings*, 34; Hinman v. Hare, New York Supreme Court (1883), 585–86, bound testimony in library of the Minnesota Historical Society; Transcripts of Trials of Sioux Indians, case no. 113, Senate Records 37A-F2; Santee Sioux Annuity Rolls, 1892–1899, Records of the Bureau of Indian Affairs, NARG 75 (microfilm copy in Division of Libraries and Archives, Minnesota Historical Society).

7. There were four Dakota men involved in the incident at Acton. Various rumors and stories circulated about their fate. Louis Mazawakinyana testified that all four were dead by 1901; "Evidence for the Claimants," *The Sisseton and Wahpeton Bands of Dakota or Sioux Indians v. the United States*, 1901–07, U.S. Court of Claims no. 22524, part 1, p. 183, bound testimony in library of the Minnesota Historical Society.

8. *St. Paul Pioneer Press*, October 24, 1897, p. 11; *Morton Enterprise*, April 25, 1902, p. 1; Mrs. Harry Lawrence, Interview, April 27, 1965, Division of Libraries and Archives, Minnesota Historical Society.

9. Tawasuota or Many Hails is credited with firing the first shot against the traders at the Redwood Agency. He is said to have sought out and killed James W. Lynd for refusing him credit. Many Hails admitted his guilt to Louis Mazawakinyana some forty years later. He fled to the Swift Current River area near Prince Albert, Alberta, where he was still living in 1900; Louis Mazawakinyana, "Evidence for the Claimants," *Sisseton and Wahpeton Bands . . . v. the United States*, U.S. Court of Claims no. 22524, part 1, p. 183; Hubbard and Holcombe, *Minnesota as a State*, 312–13.

10. John Nairn, the government carpenter at the Redwood Agency, his wife, and their four children escaped to Fort Ridgely. Mrs. Nairn offered White Spider her wedding ring; *St. Paul Pioneer Press*, October 24, 1897, p. 11; Satterlee, *Detailed Account*, 100.

11. George H. Spencer was born in Kentucky on December 20, 1831. He entered the fur trade in St. Paul in 1851 and was working at William Forbes's post on Big Stone Lake in 1860–62. Spencer was at the Redwood Agency buying goods when the war broke out; he received three gunshot wounds. After the war he worked as a bookkeeper in St. Paul, was an Indian agent at Crow Creek in 1881, and moved to Montana in 1887, where he died on May 31, 1892; Warren Upham and Rose B. Dunlap, *Minnesota*

REDWOOD AGENCY ATTACKED / 67

Biographies, Minnesota Collections, vol. 14 (St. Paul: Minnesota Historical Society, 1912), 727; T. M. Newson, *Pen Pictures of St. Paul, Minnesota, and Biographical Sketches of Old Settlers* (St. Paul: The Author, 1886), 284–87; Bishop, *Dakota War Whoop*, 55–60, 170, 206–8, 233–39, 420–25.

12. J. Wesley Bond, *Minnesota and Its Resources* (Chicago: Keen and Lee, 1856), 269, 306–7; Patricia C. Harpole and Mary D. Nagle, eds., *Minnesota Territorial Census, 1850* (St. Paul: Minnesota Historical Society, 1972), 11; U.S. Census, 1857, Traverse des Sioux, Nicollet County, Minnesota Territory, p. 294, 1860, roll 572, p. 535, 1870, roll 8, p. 6; Roll of Mixed-Blood Claimants, 1856, Records of the Bureau of Indian Affairs, NARG 75 (microfilm copy in Division of Libraries and Archives, Minnesota Historical Society).

13. *St. Paul Pioneer Press*, October 24, 1897, p. 11.

14. Emily J. West was born in 1810 and moved to Minnesota Territory in 1856 to work as an Episcopal missionary and teacher. In October 1860 she went to the Redwood Agency with the Reverend Samuel D. Hinman and remained there until August 18, 1862, when she fled to Fort Ridgely. Later she worked in Episcopal missions at Santee, Nebraska, to about 1878. She died at her farm near Herrick, Nebraska, November 1, 1899; George C. Tanner, *Fifty Years of Church Work in the Diocese of Minnesota, 1857-1907* ([St. Paul]: Committee of Publication, 1909), 83–86, 387, 393–95; *Iapi Oaye (The Word Carrier)* 28 (November 1899): 35.

15. Sibley to Little Crow, September 8, 1862, in Adjutant General of Minnesota, *Annual Report, 1862*, 444–45.

Henry Hastings Sibley was born on February 20, 1811, in Detroit, Michigan. He joined the American Fur Company in 1834, settled in Minnesota the following year, and was active in the fur trade for almost thirty years. He was a delegate to Congress, 1849–53, where he campaigned for the creation of Minnesota Territory. When Minnesota became a state, he worked on drafting the state constitution and served as the first governor, 1858–60. He was commissioned a colonel on August 19, 1862, a brigadier general on September 29, and breveted a major general on November 29, 1865. After his military expeditions, 1863–66, he returned to civilian life as president of the St. Paul Gas Company. He also served on the University of Minnesota board of regents, 1851–60 and 1869–91, and was a founder of the Minnesota Historical Society, of which he was its president, 1879–91. He died in St. Paul on February 18, 1891. See Upham and Dunlap, *Minnesota Biographies*, 702–3; J. Fletcher Williams, "Henry Hastings Sibley: A Memoir," *Minnesota Collections* 6 (1894): 257–310; Nathaniel West, *Ancestry, Life, and Times of Hon. Henry Hastings Sibley* (St. Paul: Pioneer Press Publishing Co., 1889).

16. Samuel D. Hinman, Episcopal missionary to the Dakotas, was ordained a deacon by Bishop Henry B. Whipple on September 20, 1860, at Faribault and was assigned to a mission at the Redwood Agency. He fled to Fort Ridgely on August 18, 1862. After a winter spent in mission work in the Dakota camp at Fort Snelling, he moved with the Dakotas to the Crow Creek Reservation in the spring of 1863. He worked among the Santee Dakotas at the Santee Reservation until 1878 when he was removed because of misconduct. He moved to the Birch Coulee mission at Morton in the spring of 1886, where he married his second wife, Mary Myrick, the mixed-blood daughter of Andrew Myrick. He died on March 24, 1890; Franklyn Curtiss-Wedge, *The History of Redwood County, Minnesota* (Chicago: H. C. Cooper, Jr., and Co., 1916), 1:428; Tanner, *Fifty Years of Church Work*, 387, 393–401; Hinman v. Hare, New York Supreme Court (1883); *Redwood Gazette* (Redwood Falls), May 26, 1987.

John P. Williamson, son of Dr. Thomas S. Williamson, was the pastor of the Presbyterian church at the Redwood Agency. He was on a trip to Ohio when the war broke out. He spent the rest of his life as a missionary to the Dakotas; Winifred W. Barton, *John P. Williamson: A Brother to the Sioux* (New York: Fleming H. Revell, 1919).

17. Mark F. Diedrich, "Christian Taopi: Farmer Chief of the Mdewakanton Dakota," *Minnesota Archaeologist* 40 (June 1981): 65–77.

18. Andrew Good Thunder, born in 1815 at Mendota, was a Mdewakanton. Reared as a Dakota, he converted to Christianity at the Episcopal mission at the Redwood Agency in about 1861 along with his wife Snana. During the war he aided white captives and was awarded $250 in 1866. He lived on the Santee Reservation and with the Dakota colony at Flandreau, Dakota Territory, prior to returning to Minnesota in about 1883. He was a prominent member of the Episcopal church at Morton until his death in 1901; Tanner, *Fifty Years of Church Work*, 387, 404–6; *Redwood Falls Reveille*, February 27, 1901. See also Snana's narrative in Chapter VI, p. 141, below.

CHAPTER **IV**

The War Becomes General

AFTER the attack at the Redwood Agency on August 18, mass confusion reigned everywhere. Many warriors, in a spontaneous display of celebration, turned to pillaging the stores and houses near the agency, continuing until word reached them that a small company of militia had arrived at the far side of the river. Alerted by the refugees arriving at Fort Ridgely, Captain John Marsh, the commandant, led forty-six soldiers on a reconnaissance mission toward the Redwood Ferry, unaware of the calamity that awaited them. As the column prepared to cross the Minnesota River, warriors ambushed the soldiers, killing twenty-three of them in a few minutes.

The successful ambush of Marsh's command prompted many young Dakota men who had remained neutral to join the war effort, and the fighting was carried into the countryside. White settlers east and south of the agency were attacked while doing their farm chores. The Dakota warriors almost always killed the men and carried women and children into captivity. On occasion, however, the warriors did not spare even the women and children. It was during the next three days of raiding that most of the white civilians lost their lives.

Five accounts of the expansion of the conflict into the countryside have survived. Samuel J. Brown, a mixed-blood, left an extensive narrative. He fled his home with his family and several whites on August 19. Indians captured the party shortly thereafter and conveyed them to Little Crow's newly formed camp. Brown vividly described the warriors whom his family encountered, the near destruction of his party, and the general disorder at the camp.

Brown's account is well supplemented by the narrative of Joseph Godfrey, a black who lived among the Dakotas and witnessed several incidents of warriors killing white settlers. Nancy McClure, a mixed-blood married to another mixed-blood, David Faribault, recorded her memories of events that occurred near Little Crow's camp. McClure's account conveys how difficult the war became for mixed-bloods who were captives.

Finally, two Dakota warriors' accounts provide information on the period following the attack on the agency. The narratives were dictated by Big Eagle and George Quinn, neither of whom had any part in starting the war or killing the traders but who came to support the war effort by the afternoon of August 18. Quinn, a nineteen-year-old mixed-blood, fought alongside the Indians. Big Eagle recalls the destruction of Marsh's command, the fullest narrative from a Dakota eyewitness.

Narrative 1
SAMUEL J. BROWN'S RECOLLECTIONS

SAMUEL J. BROWN was born March 7, 1845, at a trading post on the east side of the Coteau des Prairies (later part of the Sisseton Reservation in northeast South Dakota). His father was Joseph R. Brown, the noted frontiersman and Indian agent for the Dakotas, and his mother was Susan Frenier Brown, a mixed-blood Dakota. He was educated at St. Paul, Henderson, and Faribault. On vacation from school when the war broke out, he happened to be at his home along the north bank of the Minnesota River about eight miles east of the Yellow Medicine Agency.

Sam and his family, with the exception of his father who was away on business, were captured near the family farm. After staying in Little Crow's house for a few days, the family was rescued by Aki-pa, Susan Brown's stepfather. The family later became a part of the band of refugees at Camp Release, which was finally surrounded by troops commanded by Colonel Sibley on September 26, 1862. Sibley recruited young Brown for the scout unit, in which he served until becoming partially paralyzed as a result of being caught in a late winter storm while on a mission in April 1866.

After the war Samuel Brown moved with his family to Browns Valley, Minnesota. He married Phoebe Robinson in 1877, and they had three children. Phoebe died in 1910, but Samuel survived until August 29, 1925. Drawing on a diary he kept during the war, he composed several accounts of the war, including the classic "In Captivity," of which the middle section is reproduced in this volume.[1]

Narrative Source: Samuel J. Brown, "In Captivity: The Experience, Privations and Dangers of Sam'l J. Brown, and Others, while Prisoners of the Hos-

tile Sioux, during the Massacre and War of 1862," *Mankato Weekly Review*, April 6, 13, 20, 27, May 4, 11, 1897.

ON MONDAY, the 18th of August, I went to Yellow Medicine with my sister Nellie [Ellen], to get some washing done. On the way an Indian named Little Dog came out of his house, as we passed by, and beckoned to us to stop.[2] We did so and he approached us and as he came up we could see that he was troubled. He told us breathlessly that the lower bands had broken out and killed everybody at the agency, and were slaughtering the whites in the vicinity of Beaver Creek, and that they were killing everybody without mercy and without regard to age or sex, and intended to sweep the country as far as St. Paul. He begged us to turn back, tell mother, and get out of the country. He said that he warned us at the risk of his life. Little Dog was a "farmer" Indian, one of that band of Sioux braves who had their hair cut, their scalp locks taken from them by Uncle Sam in 1858, who discarded the Indian dress for that of the white man — the breech cloth for the pantaloon — who lived in a brick house instead of a skin tepee, drove oxen instead of horses, and depended for his subsistance upon the plow and hoe instead of the bow and arrow. As Little Dog has attributed his present prosperous condition with this change to my

SAMUEL J.
BROWN
in 1866

father when he was Indian agent from 1857 to 1861 he naturally had a warm spot for his family. But the Indian [Little Dog] was an inveterate liar. Indeed he was regarded as one of the greatest liars in the country, and besides, "Indian scares" had become so frequent that we paid no attention to the warning and drove on. This was about noon, and as we were passing the agency headquarters, one and a half or two miles further on, George Gleason, the government clerk there, came out to our carriage and chatted with us. He said he was going away that afternoon with Mrs. Wakefield—wife of the agency physician—he to visit his people in the east, and she to visit with friends at Shakopee, Minn.[3] He promised that when he got back he and Hon. James W. Lynd would visit with us at our home, and spend the fall hunting, fishing, horseback riding, etc. About three miles further on we arrived at the washerwoman's—near Dr. Williamson's old mission station. As we were coming away an old Indian woman ran up and told us (in a whisper) that we had better be getting away, as there would soon be trouble. We drove rapidly to the agency and stopped at John Fadden's for dinner.[4] We there asked an Indian woman, who was doing washing at the hotel, if she had heard any news, and if there was any trouble among the Indians. She said she had not, but when we told her what we had heard she said that all this talk grew out of the report that the Missouri Indians were coming over on a horse stealing expedition, and that the people were excited over it.

We left the agency at about half-past three. George Gleason and Mrs. Wakefield had just left. When we reached home that evening we told all we had heard. My brother Angus and brother-in-law, Charles Blair, pooh-poohed the idea of trouble with the Indians, but mother was scared. After we had all gone to bed she locked and bolted the outside doors and then retired.

About four o'clock the next morning, Tuesday, August 19th, while lying half awake in my bed. I heard someone outside, directly under my room window. (I was up in a back room in the third story.) I heard someone outside calling in a loud voice a number of times for "Brown! Brown! Brown!" But I was tired from the trip to Yellow Medicine the day before and was sleepy and therefore did not feel disposed to answer the call. An ox train from Forest City on the way to the agency had camped the evening before on the hill just back of the house, and as I kept a ferry I thought the voice came from one of the teamsters, who wanted to cross on the ferry. I lay abed perfectly still, half awake, and listening, when Charles Blair, who was occupying a room adjoining mine, raised the window and called out: "What do you want this time of night," and the answer came: "For God's sake hurry, Indians are burning everybody at the agency. The Yanktonnais are burning the stores and killing everybody. I have barely escaped with my life—for God's sake hurry."

This brought me into awakefulness. I lost no time in getting into my clothes and hastening down stairs. I do not know how I got down two flights of stairs, but think I slid down most of the way on the banisters, for I was very soon at the bottom, and in the dining room, listening to the particulars of the attack on the stores—of the burning, plundering and killing—from the lips of old Peter Rouilliard [sic], an old Canadian Frenchman, who had lived with the Indians for many years.

We became very much alarmed. Mother told me to awake Lonsman, the hired man, and send him at once for the horses. I rushed to Lousman's [sic] room, but found it locked, and I pounded and kicked, and finally I succeeded in waking him and getting him out of bed. He immediately started for the horses (they were running loose on the prairie) and after chasing them around a bit and failing to catch them he went to the cattle yard, where we had over 100 head of oxen and cows, and yoked three pair of oxen and hurried[ly] hitched them to three lumber wagons. By this time five or six families, neighbors of ours arrived, two Ingalls girls, Charles Holmes, Leopold Wohler and his wife, Garvie's cook and two or three others whose names I cannot now recall.[5] We gave them two of the teams and kept one for ourselves. All got into the wagons and started for Fort Ridgeley, thirty-five miles below us. We started up the hill back of the house and then took the Ridgley road. My brother Angus and brother-in-law, Charles Blair, caught a horse apiece and remained behind intending that should any Indians be seen approaching the house to mount and gallop after us. We had gone but a mile or so, however, when they caught up to us—concluding it was not safe to stay. They had ridden out to the teams camped back of the house on the Forest City road and told the men to unload their teams and hurry back—that the Indians were killing the whites and they would surely be killed if discovered. There were two teams and both were loaded with flour for the agency. (The drivers made good their escape.)

We jogged along pretty fast—the oxen being kept on a trot—and calculated that we would reach the Fort about noon or [a] little after. When we had gone about six miles we saw some people a mile or two to the right of us, near the timber on the brow of the hill, but supposed they were white men working on their farms. (The Yanktonnais whom we were afraid of lived above us.) These people were running back and forth. They soon began to run towards us, or rather to scatter out toward the road ahead of us. Very soon an Indian half-naked and on horseback popped up before us from behind a knoll, and began to beckon the others toward him, and before we knew it we were surrounded.

Mother at once grasped the situation. Little Dog had told the truth. We were in the midst of the murdering Indians. She knew that to save us she must speak and make herself known. She must do so quickly or we would be killed. So she stood up in the wagon, and waving her shawl she cried in a loud voice that she was a Sisseton — a relative of Waanatan, Scarlet Plume, Sweetcorn, Ah-kee-pah [Akipa] and the friend of Standing Buffalo, that she had come down this way for protection and hoped to get it.[6] We immediately saw swarms of Indians around us. They were popping out of the grass on every side and in every direction — every blade of which seemed to have suddenly turned into an Indian, all running towards us; some with blackened faces and bloody hands, came up and demanded that we be killed. The awful Cut Nose, the terrible Shakopee or Little Six, and the imprudent Dowanniye, three of the worst among the lower Sioux, came to us first, shaking their bloody tomahawks menacingly in our faces.[7] They were the most savage looking of the lot — perfect man-eaters in appearance. We had brought along two shot guns, but no ammunition. The barrels were empty and we were completely in the power of the Indians. But there happened to be one in the crowd that took our part. He rushed up to our wagon with gun in one hand and uplifted tomahawk in the other intending to massacre us, when he happened to recognize my mother. This Indian had once (the winter before) come to our house when he was freezing, and mother took him in and warmed him. He told the other Indians of this and said he remembered it and would show his appreciation of the kind act by protecting us. Upon recognizing mother he jumped into our wagon and shouted at the top of his voice: "This woman," pointing to mother, "saved my life last winter, and I shall save her's now," and in an impassioned speech declared that not a hair on our heads should be molested. The others then withdrew sullenly, saying "they would kill the white men anyway." There were five of these white men besides Blair and Lonsman, and each Indian had selected his victim — the

particular one he was to shoot. But mother knew the Indians too well
to allow any killing to be done. Besides her desire to save the lives of
these white men, she knew that if they once got to killing and scalping
in her presence their savage natures would become uncontrolable and
we would all meet the same fate. So she begged that their lives be
spared. She begged them not to kill these unoffending white men who
had come to her for protection. When she saw that they were not disposed to turn from their purpose she angrily demanded that their lives
be spared — telling them plainly and eloquently that unless they did
so the vengeance of the upper Sioux would fall upon them. "Save
them, save them, what do you mean?" says Cut Nose, with bloody
hands and face and arms. "Save them," he replied, "are you not grateful that your own life is spared?"

"Remember what I say, if you harm any of these friends of mine,
you will have to answer to Scarlet Plume, Ah-kee-pah, Standing Buffalo and the whole Sisseton and Wahpeton tribe," continued mother,
and then appealed to her friend for help. Whereupon he with Cut
Nose, Shakopee (or Little Six), Dowanniye, and all the other Indians,
repaired to a mound close by and held a council. They soon came running back to the wagons where we were all huddled together (twenty-
six of us) and informed us that mother and her family, including Blair
and Lonsman, could all liye [live] but the rest must die. They had
vowed at the commencement of the outbreak, the day before, they
said, to spare no white man, and should they spare these, Little Crow
and the Soldiers' Lodge would have them (the warriors) all shot.
Mother again pleaded and then argued and at last threatened, and all
went to the mound again to talk the matter over. After much bitter
wrangling, and mainly through the persuasive eloquence of our
friend, they reluctantly decided to accede to the wishes of my mother,
that is, to spare the lives of the white men and let them go. Holmes,
Wohler and Garvie's cook and one other, were ordered to start off at
once across the prairie in the direction of the big woods, while old Peter Rouillard was ordered back to his Indian wife at Yellow Medicine.
The three women — Mrs. Wohler, Misses Jennie and Amanda
Ingalls — were ordered to remain still in their wagon. Then all the
men ran off — four in one direction and one in another. Immediately
one of the four (Mr. Wohler) turned and ran back to get his boots. Cut
Nose ran up to him, while mother was screaming for help, and cocked
his gun and threatened to shoot him if he did not hurry off. Leopold
picked up one boot and started off, but turned again and ran back for

the other, when in the midst of mother's screaming, the Indians again drove him away. But this was not all. Leopold went a little ways and returned the third time. It so happened that in the excitement he had not offered to kiss his wife good-bye. Cut Nose was leading her off when Leopold ran up, bareing his breast, saying: "Shoot me, but I shall first kiss my wife." Mr. Wohler was but recently married and was desperately in earnest. This act completely paralyzed the Indians, for they stood like statues while Wohler embraced his pretty young wife and showered her with kisses, then broke loose and ran away. With the exception of Blair and Lonsman the men were now all gone. Lousman [sic], the Indians said, must stay and drive the oxen and do chores for my mother, while Blair would be attended to later on. The white women — Mrs. Wohler and the two Misses Ingalls — were then parcelled out among the Indians and ordered to follow them. One beautiful young girl of about 17 years of age refused to alight from the wagon when ordered to do so. Cut Nose had told her he wanted her for his wife, and to get out of the wagon and follow him. She screamed and resisted, when he drew his knife and grabbed her by the hair and threatened to scalp her and frightened her so that she got out and he led her away. Presently the Indians came back with the women and ordered them all to get into one of the wagons — our family and Lonsman and Blair, sixteen in all, being in the other — and started, for we knew not where, the Indians ordering us to follow them.

One hideous looking fellow — Dowanniye by name — who was on horseback, rode up to our wagon and snatched my sister's hat from her head and placed it upon his own and then commenced singing the war song. He was very merry. He would shout and yell at the top of his voice and say that the Indians would have a good time now, and that if they got killed it would be all right; that the whites were trying to starve them to death to get rid of them and were delaying the payment for that purpose; that he preferred to be shot and to die as becomes a Sioux rather than to be starved to death. He jerked off Lonsman's vest and put it on inside out, Lonsman got very angry at this, and demanded its return. He wanted it back he said, because there was a twenty dollar gold piece in one of the pockets — all the money he had in the world — and the Indian might lose it. He was making a great fuss over this, when Blair ordered him to shut up or he would throw him out of the wagon. Lonsman quieted down and muttering something about "making that Indian pay for this some day."

Shakopee or Little Six, who was also on horseback, would now and then galop [sic] ahead and then suddenly turn and with a whoop and a yell dash toward us and cock his gun and eye us fiercely. Mother did not like this. She told him that she wanted none of his foolishness around her, and that he must either shoot and kill or stop his antics. He would reply that we were his prisoners and should not talk so much, and then commenced singing the war song. He would shake his tomahawk at Blair and Lonsman and then repeat the war song that got so familiar afterwards, viz:

"Iaxica-canze-maye-ca-e,
Niyake-bawahunhun-we."

The English of which is: "The Dutch [Germans] have made me so angry, I will butcher them alive." When he saw that mother was not afraid of him he quit his fooling.

We had proceeded but a little ways when we came upon four dead bodies—three men and one woman—all horribly mutilated. Our captors had committed the murders. The men had been mowing, and the woman had been raking hay. Their scythes and pitchforks lay near—the woman had a pitchfork sticking in her person, and one of the men had a scythe sticking into his body. Cut Nose gleefully told that he had killed this man and described how he did it. The man was mowing, he said, and he went up to him in a friendly manner and offered his hand, and as the white man threw down his scythe and reached out his hand the Indian drew his knife and like a flash plunged it into the white man's breast, just under the chin, whereupon the white man grasped him around the waist and both struggled for the mastery, when they fell—the white man on top. In working the knife into his breast the Indian got his thumb into the white man's mouth and "got bit." The knife in the hands of the Indian soon touched a vital spot and the white man rolled off, dead. Cut Nose held up his bitten thumb. It was bitten and chewed, and was lacerated most horribly.

This fiend in human shape, this man Cut Nose, presented a most forbidden [sic], horrifying spectacle. With his bloody thumb he had besmeared his naked body, with his blackened face and long bushy hair like a Zulu's, and a half nose (one of his nostrils was missing) he was by far the ugliest looking and most repulsive specimen of humanity I had ever seen.

He was hung at Mankato along with thirty-seven others Dec. 26, 1862, and my father was the signal officer on that occasion—tapped the drum that cut the rope that held the trap that sent Cut Nose to the happy hunting grounds.

Our Indian captors then took us to their camp on the Rice creek, about seven miles above the lower or Redwood agency on the Minnesota river, which we reached about noon. Here we learned that on the day before all the soldiers sent out from Fort Ridgley had been massacred at the lower agency ferry. An Indian had a mule team which he said he had captured there. He had them hitched to a wagon, but was afraid he could not manage them, so Angus and I drove them about awhile.

We remained at this camp but one hour or two, when it broke up and all moved toward the main or Little Crow's camp, seven miles below. We stopped at the house of John Moore, a mixed blood Sioux, while the train moved on and camped on the hill across the Redwood river. At Moore's we were put up stairs in a dark room and told to remain quiet, for bad Indians were around, and if we were seen we might be killed. Several captive women were there besides ourselves, but owing to the darkness we did not recognize them. In a few minutes three savage looking Indians came up and ordered us away, saying that we could go to the camp on the hill. They ordered the other captives to remain, while we groped our way in the darkness down stairs and out of the house, got into the wagon and drove off, following the Indians. When we got about half way to the camp and as we were crossing the Redwood creek, we suddenly missed our Indian guides. We supposed they crawled into the bushes on the bank of the creek and hid from us, so we wandered on toward the camp.

At [the] foot of the hill a few hundred yards further we passed a white woman with six children, the eldest not more than ten years of age, two in her arms, two on her back and two traveling on behind. She was accompanied by a half-naked Indian with a gun on his shoulder and a tomahawk in his hand. We stopped and asked the woman to get in, but the Indian would not let her. He said the woman was his and would do as he pleased with her and ordered us to hurry on. He looked so fierce and ugly that we were afraid he might make quick work of us, so we passed on and went up the hill. About a half a mile further on we arrived at the camp, but were sternly told to "go on" — onto Little Crow's camp, a few miles further on. Mother begged to remain until morning, but the Indians were obdurate. She was told to "go on, go on, no Dutchman wanted." This was a heavy blow to mother, and she for the first time that day broke down and commenced to cry. She gave up all hopes and told Lonsman to drive down the road. There was no escape and we must all die. It was quite dark and Indians were returning from their bloody work. We felt that death was staring us in the face as we drove along.

But we had not gone more than a mile when an Indian woman, standing on the road side in front of her house as we were passing along, recognized mother and hailed her and we stopped. She asked us in. We drove up to the door and all quietly alighted. Indians passing along — going to and coming from Little Crow's camp below and the camp above — would stop and ask all sorts of questions — who we were, what we wanted, etc. The Indian woman would not allow Lonsman to enter the house, saying that his presence would endanger the lives of the rest of us. She advised him to run through the corn field and into the woods back of the house and follow the river down to Fort Ridgely — about sixteen miles. He laughed at the idea, saying that he was not afraid of the Indians, and started off in the direction of the camp we had just left.

It so happened that he reached the camp in safety and entered the first lodge he came to, and went in and found an old Indian woman there. She was delighted to see the white man. She had no one to live with and wanted some one to cut wood, bring water, etc., and set at once to work and prepared supper. Lonsman had not tasted a mouthful all day and was hungry and he ate heartily, and then went to bed, laying down on a buffalo robe and went to sleep. After a hearty breakfast the next morning the old woman gave him the ax and told him to chop some wood in the timber just back of the lodge, which was at one end of the camp. While at work there was quite a stir at the other end of the camp — great excitement and everybody running until not a soul was left in his immediate neighborhood. Lonsman dropped the axe and ran into the woods and made good his escape.

The excitement was caused by a white boy being stoned, clubbed and beaten to death, and shot with arrows by Indian boys. Lonsman says he went back to the old home that we had left so suddenly the day before and killed a pig, threw it on his back and walked to Henderson, a distance of some sixty miles.

Continued on page 130.

Narrative 2
NANCY McCLURE FARIBAULT HUGGAN'S ACCOUNT

NANCY McCLURE was born at Mendota in 1836. Her father was Lieutenant James McClure, an officer at Fort Snelling; her mother was Winona, a Dakota. From the age of four to fourteen, she lived with her mother and Antoine Renville, her stepfather, at Lac qui Parle, located at the junction of Lac qui Parle Lake and the Minnesota River. There she learned Dakota skills and attended a mission school operated by Dr. Thomas S. Williamson. When her mother died in 1850, she went to live with her grandmother at Traverse des Sioux. In 1851 she married trader David Faribault, Sr., and a few years later they were farming on the north bank of the Minnesota River two miles below the Redwood Agency.

When the war broke out, Nancy, her husband, and their daughter were captured and their farm destroyed. After being freed at Camp Release, Nancy settled at Faribault while her husband served with the Dakota scouts. Shortly thereafter, she and David were operating a mail service near Fort Ransom, Dakota Territory. In the 1870s, her marriage to Faribault ended, and she married Charles Huggan, a farmer near Flandreau, Dakota Territory. Her daughter, her only child, married the Reverend John Eastman, a mixed-blood who helped Nancy as an interpreter with Big Eagle's narrative.

In 1894 she wrote a series of letters to Return I. Holcombe, a St. Paul journalist, who edited them for publication in the St. Paul Pioneer Press *and the* Minnesota Historical Society Collections. *Nancy Huggan died in August 1927 at Flandreau, South Dakota.*[8]

Narrative Source: Nancy McClure Huggan, "The Story of Nancy McClure," *Minnesota Collections* 6 (1894): 438–60; *St. Paul Pioneer Press*, June 3, 1894.

AT THE TIME of the outbreak we were living two miles from the Redwood agency, on the road to Fort Ridgely. We had a log house, but it was large and roomy and very well furnished. When we first came my husband intended engaging in farming and stock raising, but he soon got back to his former business, trading with the Indians, and when they rose against the whites he had trusted them for very nearly everything he had, for they were very hard up, and the other stores would not trust them for anything. Besides the goods he sold

NANCY McCLURE, sketch by Frank B. Mayer, 1851

them on credit, he let them have fourteen head of cattle for food. The winter and spring before had been very enjoyable to me. There were a good many settlers in the country, some few French families among them, and the most of them were young married people of pleasant dispositions. We used frequently to meet at one another's houses in social gatherings, dancing parties and the like, and the time passed very pleasantly. I was twenty-five years of age then, had but one child and could go about when I wanted to, and I went frequently to these gatherings and came to know a good many people. Then came the summer, and the Indians came down to the agency to receive their annual payments under the treaty of 1851; but the paymaster with the money was delayed on the road until the time for the payment had passed. He was at Fort Ridgely with the money, all in gold, when the Indians rose. There were mutterings of trouble for some time, but at last it seemed the danger had passed away.

On the very morning of the outbreak my husband and I heard shooting in the direction of the agency, but supposed that the Indians were out shooting wild pigeons. As the shooting increased I went to the door once or twice and looked toward the agency, for there was something unusual about it. My husband was out attending to the milking. All at once a Frenchman named Martelle came galloping down the road from the agency, and, seeing me in the door, he called out: "Oh, Mrs. Faribault, the Indians are killing all the white people at the agency![9] Run away, run away quick!" He did not stop or slacken his speed, but waved his hand and called out as he passed. There was blood on his shirt, and I presume he was wounded.

My husband and I were not prepared for trouble of this kind. Our best horses and wagons were not at home. We had two horses in the stable and harness for them, but no wagon. My husband told me to get my saddle ready and we would go away on horseback, both of us being good riders. We were getting ready to do this when we saw a wagon, drawn by two yoke of oxen and loaded with people, coming down the road at a good trot. My husband said we would wait and see what these people would say. When they came up to us we saw there were five or six men, three or four women and some children, and they were all in great fright. They asked us to put our horses to their wagon — as they could travel faster than oxen — and to get in with them. This we agreed to do, and soon had the change made. When they were harnessing the horses I ran to the house to try to secure some articles of value, for as yet we had taken nothing but what we had on our backs, and I had many things I did not want to lose. Woman-like, I tried first to save my jewelry, which I kept in a strong drawer. This drawer was swelled and I could not open it, and I was running for an ax to burst it, when my husband said, "Let it go — they are ready to start." So I took my dear little daughter, who was eight years old and my only child, and we started for the wagon. Just as I was about to get in — everybody else was in — I looked up the road toward the agency and saw the Indians coming. I was afraid they would overtake the wagon; so I declined to get in, and my husband got out with me, and we took our child and ran for the woods, while the wagon started off, the men lashing the horses every jump.

Just as we started for the woods, Louis Brisbois and his wife and two [three] children, mixed-blood people, came up and went with us.[10] We all hid in the wood. In a few minutes the Indians came up, and somehow they knew we were hidden, and they called out very loudly: "Oh, Faribault, if you are here, come out; we won't hurt you." My husband was armed and had determined to sell his life for all it would bring, and I had encouraged him; but now it seemed best that we should come out and surrender, and so we did. The Indians at once disarmed my husband. They seemed a little surprised to see the Brisbois family, and declared they would kill them, as they had not agreed to spare their lives. Poor Mrs. Brisbois ran to me and asked me to save her, and she and her husband got behind me, and I began to beg the Indians not to kill them. My husband asked the Indians what all this meant — what they were doing anyhow. They replied, "We have killed all the white people at the agency; all the Indians are on the warpath; we are going to kill all the white people in Minnesota; we are not going to hurt you, for you have trusted us with goods, but we are going to kill these Brisbois." And then one ran up and struck over my shoulder and hit Mrs. Brisbois a cruel blow in the face, saying she had treated them badly at one time. Then I asked them to wait until I got away, as I did not want to see them killed. This stopped them for half a minute, when one said: "Come to the house." So we started for the house, and just then two more wagons drawn by oxen and loaded with white people came along the road. All the Indians left us and ran yelling and whooping to kill them.

We went into the house. At the back part of the house was a window, and a little beyond was a corn field. I opened the window and put the Brisbois family out of it, and they ran into the corn field and escaped. They are living somewhere in Minnesota to-day. The white people were nearly all murdered. I could not bear to see the sickening sight, and so did not look out, but while the bloody work was being done an Irish woman named Hayden came running up to the house crying out for me to save her.[11] I saw that she was being chased by a young Indian that had once worked for us, and I called to him to spare her, and he let her go. I heard that she escaped all right. Now, all this took place in less time than one can write about it.

When the killing was over the Indians came to the house and ordered us to get into one of the wagons and go with them back to the agency. This we did, my husband driving the team. The Indians drove the other team. Soon after we started an Indian gave me a colt to lead behind the wagon. About half way to the agency we saw the dead body of a man lying near the road. Just before we reached the ferry over the Minnesota river we saw a boy on the prairie to the right. There were but three Indians with us now. One of them ran to kill the boy. At this moment a German rode up to us. I have forgotten his name, but the Indians called him "Big Nose." I think he is living at Sleepy Eye, Minn., now. One of the Indians said to the other Indian, "Shoot him and take his horse." The other said, "Wait till my son comes back and then we will kill him." (His son was the one that had gone to kill the boy.) All this time I was begging them not to kill the man. I asked my husband to plead with them, but he seemed to be unable to speak a word. At last I told the German to give them his horse and run into the brush. This he did and escaped.

When we got to the ferry the boat was in the middle of the stream, and standing upon it was a young white girl of about sixteen or seventeen years of age. The Indians called to her to bring the boat ashore, but she did not obey them. They were about to shoot her, when my husband told her they would kill her if she did not do as they ordered, and she brought the boat ashore. When it touched the bank a young Indian made this girl get on a horse behind him and he rode away with her, and I never heard what became of the poor creature. When I saw her being taken away I felt as badly as if she was being murdered before my eyes, for I imagined she would suffer a most horrible fate.

When we reached the agency there was a dreadful scene. Everything was in ruins, and dead bodies lay all about. The first body we saw was that of one of La Bathe's clerks. It lay by the road some distance from the buildings. The rest were nearer the buildings, Mr. Myrick's among them. We did not stay long here, but pushed on to Little Crow's camp. We stayed that night with the Indians that brought us. Soon other prisoners, many of them half-bloods like ourselves, were brought in.

While we were in this camp we saw Capt. Marsh and his men coming from Fort Ridgely along the road towards the ferry. They could not see us, but we saw them, though at some distance. You know they were going to the agency, having heard that the Indians were rising. They stopped at our house and seemed to be getting water from the well. Poor fellows! Little did some of them think they were taking their last drink. They went on, and soon came to the ferry and fell into that bloody ambush where Capt. Marsh, Mr. Quinn and so many others were killed.

Continued on page 138.

Narrative 3
JOSEPH GODFREY'S STATEMENT

JOSEPH GODFREY'S Dakota name was Otakle or Many Kills. He was born at Mendota in 1835, the son of Joseph Godfrey, a French-Canadian voyageur, and a black woman. He grew up in the family of Alexis Bailly, a mixed-blood fur trader. He moved to the Redwood Agency in 1857 where he married the daughter of Wakpaduta of Wabasha's band.

He was present when white settlers were killed by warriors. He was the first man tried by the military commission, which sentenced him to be hanged. His testimony at the trials, however, proved useful in convicting most of the Dakotas, including his father-in-law, and mixed-bloods who were later executed at Mankato on December 26, 1862. As a reward for his testimony, Godfrey's sentence was reduced to ten years of imprisonment. Godfrey was a Dakota speaker and could speak only broken English. Isaac V. D. Heard, the recorder at the trial, edited Godfrey's statement made to the commission, added parenthetical explanations, and published it in his history of the war. Godfrey served three years of his sentence and was pardoned in 1866. He moved to the Santee Reservation in northeastern Nebraska where he died in July 1909.[12]

Narrative Source: Isaac V. D. Heard, *History of the Sioux War and Massacres of 1862 and 1863* (New York: Harper & Brothers, 1864), 191–201, 251–54.

I AM twenty-seven years old. I was born at Mendota. My father was a Canadian Frenchman, and my mother a colored woman, who hired in the family of the late Alex. Bailley. I was raised in Mr. Bailley's family. My father is, I think, living in Wisconsin; his name is Joe Godfrey. My mother is also living at Prairie du Chien. I last saw my father and mother at Prairie du Chien seven years ago. I lived with Mr. Bailley at Wabashaw, and also at Hastings and Faribault. I had lived at the Lower Agency five years. I was married, four years ago, to a woman of Wabashaw's band — daughter of Wa-kpa-doo-ta. At the time of the outbreak I lived on the Reservation on the south side of the Minnesota River, between the Lower Agency and New Ulm, about twenty miles below the agency and eight above New Ulm.

The first time I heard of the trouble I was mowing hay. About noon an Indian was making hay near me. I went to help him, to change work; he was to lend me his oxen. I helped him load some hay, and as we took it to his place we heard hallooing, and saw a man on horseback, with a gun across his legs before him. When he saw me he drew his gun up and cocked it. The Indian with me asked him, "What's the matter?" He looked strange. He wore a new hat—a soft gray hat—and had a new white leather ox or mule whip. He said all the white people had been killed at the agency. The Indian with me asked who did it, and he replied the Indians, and that they would soon be down that way to kill the settlers toward New Ulm. He asked me which side I would take. He said I would have to go home and take off my clothes, and put on a breech-clout. I was afraid, because he held his gun as if he would kill me. I went to my house and told my wife to get ready, and we would try to get away. I told my wife about what the Indian told me. I told her we would try to get down the river. She said we would be killed with the white people. We got something ready to take with us to eat, and started—we got about two hundred yards into the woods. (The old man, my wife's father, said

GODFREY,
sketch by Robert O.
Sweeny, 1862

he would fasten the house and follow after.) We heard some one halloo. It was the old man. He called to us to come back. I told my wife
to go on, but her mother told her to stop. I told them to go ahead; but
the old man called so much that they stopped and turned back. I followed them.

I found my squaw's uncle at the house. He scolded my wife and
her mother for trying to get away; he said all the Indians had gone
to the agency, and that they must go there. He said we would be killed
if we went toward the white folks; that we would only be safe to go
and join the Indians. I still had my pants on. I was afraid; and they
told me I must take my pants off and put on the breech-clout. I did
so. The uncle said we must take a rope and catch a horse.

I started with him toward New Ulm, and we met a lot of Indians
at the creek, about a mile from my house. They were all painted, and
said I must be painted. They then painted me. I was afraid to refuse.

They asked me why I didn't have a gun, or knife, or some weapon.
I told them I had no gun — the old man had taken it away. One Indian
had a spear, a gun, and a little hatchet. He told me to take the hatchet, and that I must fight with the Indians, and do the same they did,
or I would be killed. We started down the road. We saw two wagons
with people in them coming toward us. The Indians consulted what
to do, and decided for half of them to go up to a house off the road,
on the right-hand side. They started, but I stopped, and they called
me and told me I must come on. There was an old man, a boy, and
two young women at the house — Dutch people. The family's name
was something like "Masseybush."[13] The boy and two girls stood outside, near the kitchen door. Half of the Indians went to the house, half
remained in the road. The Indians told me to tell the whites that there
were Chippeways about, and that they (the Indians) were after them.
I did not say any thing. The Indians asked for some water. The girls
went into the house, and the Indians followed and talked in Sioux.
One said to me, "Here is a gun for you." Dinner was on the table, and
the Indians said, "After we kill, then we will have dinner." They told
me to watch the road, and when the teams came up to tell them. I
turned to look, and just then I heard the Indians shoot; I looked, and
two girls fell just outside the door. I did not go in the house; I started
to go round the house. We were on the back side of it, when I heard
the Indians on the road hallooing and shouting. They called me, and
I went to the road and saw them killing white men. My brother-in-
law told me I must take care of a team that he was holding; that it

was his. I saw two men killed that were with this wagon. I did not see who were killed in the other wagon. I saw one Indian stick his knife in the side of a man that was not yet dead; he cut his side open, and then cut him all to pieces. His name was Wakantonka (great spirit). Two of the Indians that killed the people at the house have been convicted. Their names are Waki-ya-ni and Mah-hwa.[14] There were about ten Indians at the house, and about the same number in the road. I got into the wagon, and the Indians all got in. We turned and went toward New Ulm. When we got near to a house the Indians all got out and ran ahead of the wagons, and two or three went to each house, and in that way they killed all the people along the road. I staid in the wagon, and did not see the people killed. They killed the people of six or eight houses — all until we got to the "Travelers' Home."[15] There were other Indians killing people all through the settlement. We could see them and hear them all around. I was standing in the wagon, and could see three, or four, or five Indians at every house.

When we got near the "Travelers' Home" they told me to stop. I saw an old woman with two children — one in each hand — run away across the yard. One Indian, Maza-bom-doo, who was convicted, shot the old woman, and jumped over and kicked the children down with his feet.[16] The old woman fell down as if dead. I turned away my head, and did not see whether the children were killed. After that I heard a shot behind the barn, but did not see who was shot. I supposed some one was killed. After that the Indians got in the wagon, and told me to start down the road. We started on, and got to a house where a man lived named Schling — a German — an old man.[17] The Indians found a jug in the wagon, and were now almost drunk. They told me to jump out. I jumped out and started ahead, and the Indians called me to come back. They threw out a hatchet, and said I must go to the house and kill the people. Maza-bom-doo was ahead. He told me there were three guns there that he had left for some flour, and we must get them. I was afraid.

I went into the house. There was the old man, his wife and son, and a boy and another man. They were at dinner. The door stood open, and the Indians were right behind me, and pushed me in. I struck the old man on the shoulder with the flat of the hatchet, and then the Indians rushed in and commenced to shoot them. The old man, woman, and boy ran into the kitchen. The other man ran out some way, I did not see how; but when we went back to the road, about twenty steps, I saw him in the road dead. He was the man I struck in the house. I heard the Indians shoot back of the house, but did not see what at. After we started to go to Red-Wood, one little Indian, who had pox-marks on his face, and who was killed at Wood Lake, said he struck the boy with a knife, but didn't say if he killed him. He told this to the other Indians.

We saw coming up the road two wagons, one with a flag in it. The Indians were afraid, and we started back, and went past the "Travelers' Home." We got to a bridge, and the Indians got out and laid down in the grass about the bridge. I went on up the road. The wagons, with white men, came on up and stopped in the road, where there was a dead man, I think; then they sounded the bugle and started to cross the bridge, running their horses. The foremost wagon had one horse, of a gray color; three men were in it, and had the flag. Just as they came across the bridge, the Indians raised up and shot. The three men fell out, and the team went on. The Indians ran and caught it. The other wagon had not got across the bridge. I heard them shoot at the men in it, but I did not see them. After the Indians brought the second wagon across the bridge, three Indians got in the wagon. After that all of them talked together, and said that it was late (the sun was nearly down), and that they must look after their wives and children that had started to go to Red-Wood. Many of these Indians lived on the lower end of the reservation. The two-horse team that they had just taken was very much frightened, and they could not hold them. They told me I must take and hold them, and drive them. I took the team, and then they all got in. We then had four teams. We started from there, and went on up. When we got to where the first people were killed, the Indians told me to drive up to the house. The two girls were lying dead. I saw one girl with her head cut off; the head was gone. One Indian, an old man, asked who cut the head off; he said it was too bad. The other Indians said they did not know. The girls' clothes were turned up. The old man put them down. He is now in prison; his name is Wazakoota; he is a good old man. While we stood there one wagon went to another house, and I heard a gun go off.[18]

We started up the road, and stopped at a creek about a mile farther on. We waited for some of the Indians that were behind. While we were there we saw a house on fire. When the Indians came up they said that Wak-pa-doo-ta, my father-in-law, shot a woman, who was on a bed sick, through the window; and that an old man ran up stairs, and the Indians were afraid to go in the house; they thought he had a gun, and they set fire to the house and left it.[19] We then started on from that creek, and went about seven miles to near a little lake (about a hundred yards from the road). We saw, far away, a wagon coming toward us. When it was only two miles from us we saw it was a two-horse wagon, but the Indians didn't know if it was white people. When it came nearer they told me to go fast. The Indians whipped the horses and hurried them on. Two Indians were ahead of us on horseback. Pretty soon we came near, and the team that was coming toward us stopped and turned round, and the Indians said it was white men, and they were trying to run away. The two on horseback then shot, and I saw a white man—Patville—fall back over his seat; and after that I saw three women and one man jump out of the wagon and run.[20] Then those in the wagon with me jumped out and ran after the women. We got up to the wagon. Patville was not dead. The Indians threw him out, and a young Indian, sentenced to be hung, stuck a knife between his ribs, under the arm, and another one, who is with Little Crow, took his gun and beat his head all to pieces. The other Indians killed the other white man near the little lake, and brought back the three women—Mattie Williams, Mary Anderson, and Mary Swan [Schwandt].[21]

Patville's wagon was full of trunks. The Indians broke them open and took the things out; there were some goods in them (Patville was a sort of trader on the reservation). They put one woman in the wagon. I drove. The other two were put separately in the other wagons. The one in my wagon (Mary Swan) was caught by Maza-bom-doo. Ta-zoo had Mattie Williams.[22] We then went on, and stopped at a creek about a mile ahead to water the horses. Then they called me to ask the woman [Mary Anderson] that was wounded if she was badly hurt. She said "Yes." They told me to ask her to show the wound, and that they would do something for it. She showed the wound. It was in the back. The ball did not come out. She asked where we were going. I said I didn't know, but supposed to Red-Wood. I asked what had been done at the agency. She said they didn't know; that they came around on the prairie past Red-Wood. I told her I heard that all the whites at the agency were killed and the stores robbed. She said she wished they would drive fast, so she could have a doctor do something for her wound; she was afraid she would die. I said I was a prisoner too. She asked what would be done with them. I said I didn't know; perhaps we would all be killed. I said maybe the doctor was killed, if all the white people were. After that we started on, and got to the Red-Wood Agency about nine o'clock. It was dark. Then the

Indians looked round, and did not see any people. We went on to Wacouta's house. He came out, and told me to tell the girl in my wagon to go into his house — that the other two girls were in his house. I told the girl; but she was afraid, and said she thought the other women were somewhere else. I told her that Wacouta said they were in his house, and she had better go. Wacouta told her to go with him, and she got out and went with him.[23] I then went on to Little Crow's village, where most all of the Indians had gone. I found my wife there. We staid some time there, and then started for the fort. They asked me to go to drive a team. After we got there they commenced to fight. They broke in the stable, and told me to go and take all the horses I could. I got a black mare, but an Indian took it away from me. They fought all day, and slept at night in the old stable under the hill. The next morning they fought only a little; it was raining. We then went back to Red-Wood. In about six days after all the Indians started, and said they would go to Mankato. They came down toward the fort on that side of the river, and crossed near the "Travelers' Home." When they got opposite the fort they stopped, and talked of trying to get in again, but did not. About noon they went on to New Ulm. I saw no white people on the road. I got to New Ulm about two hours after noon. They burned houses, and shot, and fought. They slept at New Ulm that night, and the next day went back to Little Crow's village. (This was the last fight at New Ulm; Godfrey says he was not there at the first fight. He was then at Little Crow's village.) After a few days we went to Rice Creek; staid there a few days, and started again to come to Mankato. After crossing the Red-Wood we went up the hill, and saw wagons on the prairie on the other side of the river. After the Indians had all crossed the Red-Wood, half staid there all night, and half went over the Minnesota to where they saw the wagons. Those that staid back went over early the next morning. I went with them. We got there at sunrise. We heard shooting just before we got there. They were shooting all day. They killed all the horses. (This was the battle of Birch Coolie.) At night the Indians killed some cattle, and cooked and ate some meat. Some talked of trying to get into the camp, and some tried it all night. Others talked of watching till they should drive them out for want of water. Three Indians were killed that day — so the Indians said. I saw some wounded — I should think five. In the morning some more talk was had about trying to get in. In the mean time we saw soldiers coming up, and half of the Indians started to try and stop them, and the other half staid to watch the camp at Birch Coolie. They went down to try and stop the soldiers, and afterward came back and said 'twas no use — that they couldn't stop them. Some wanted to try and get the whites into Birch Coolie, but others thought they had better go back. They fired some shots, and then started back. The Sissetons got to us while we were there the second day, about two or three hours before the Indians all left. The Indians left a little before sundown. They crossed the river at the old crossing, and went up to the site of Reynolds's house, the other side of the Red-Wood, and camped.[24] They started about midnight to go to Rice Creek. Got there about sunrise. Staid there several days.

While we were at Birch Coolie Little Crow was at the Big Woods. He got back to Rice Creek two days after we did. We went from Rice Creek to Yellow Medicine; staid there about two weeks. While there ten or twenty started every day to see if soldiers were coming. When they reported that soldiers were on the way, we moved our camp to where Mr. Riggs lived; then up to Red Iron's village; then to a little way from where the *friendly* camp was. After the scouts reported that soldiers had crossed the Red-Wood, Little Crow made a speech, and said that all must fight; that it would be the last fight, and they all must do the best they could. Scouts reported about midnight that soldiers were camped at Rice Creek. In the morning we all started down to Yellow Medicine; got there a little before sundown. Some were there earlier. We staid at Yellow Medicine all night. Some wanted to begin the attack in the night, but others thought 'twas best to wait till morning. In the morning the fight began. After the fight, went back to the old camp at Camp Release. Little Crow tried to get all to go with him, but they would not. Little Crow started away in the night. I didn't see him go. I never was out at any of the war parties except once at New Ulm (the last fight), once at the fort, at Birch Coolie, and Wood Lake. They thought that the Winnebagoes would commence at Mankato and attack the lower settlements.

Narrative 4
BIG EAGLE'S ACCOUNT

For biographical information on Big Eagle, see Chapter I, Narrative 1.

THAT AFTERNOON [August 18] word came to my village that soldiers were coming to the agency from Fort Snelling. (These were Capt. Marsh and his men.) At once I mounted the best horse I had, and, with some of my men, rode as fast as I could to meet them at the ferry. But when I got there the fight was over, and I well remember that a cloud of powder smoke was rising slowly from the low, wet ground where the firing had been. I heard a few scattering shots down the river, where the Indians were still pursuing the soldiers, but I took no part. I crossed the river and saw the bodies of the soldiers that had been killed. I think Mr. [Peter] Quinn, the interpreter, was shot several times after he had been killed. The Indians told me that the most of them who fired on Capt. Marsh and his men were on the same side of the river; that only a few shots came from the opposite or south side. They said that White Dog did not tell Mr. Quinn to come over, but told him to go back. Of course I do not know what the truth is about this. White Dog was the Indian head farmer who had been replaced by Taopi and who was hanged at Mankato.[25]

Continued on page 147.

Narrative 5
GEORGE QUINN'S ACCOUNT

GEORGE QUINN was often called George Ortley and Wakandayamani or The Spirit that Rattles as It Walks. He was born near Minnehaha Creek (present-day Hennepin County) in 1843. He may have been the son of Peter Quinn, a long-time government interpreter; his mother was Ineyahewin, a member of the Lake Calhoun band of Mdewakanton Dakotas. He learned to read and write the Dakota language from Samuel and Gideon Pond, Protestant missionaries. He lived as an Indian at Bloomington and was visiting the Redwood Agency in August 1862.

Quinn participated in the ambush at Redwood Ferry, the second battle of Fort Ridgely, and the fight at Wood Lake. He claimed to have aided in freeing twenty-five white captives but was tried by the military commission, convicted, and sentenced to be hanged. Like the majority of Indians and mixed-bloods so sentenced, Quinn received a reprieve and was sent to prison at Davenport, Iowa, where he remained until pardoned in 1866. Upon release, he moved to the Santee Reservation in Nebraska Territory and later toured the Upper Midwest selling herbal medicines. In 1898 St. Paul newspaperman Return I. Holcombe interviewed Quinn; the interpreter was William L. Quinn, the son of Peter Quinn and possibly George's half brother. The resulting narrative was finally published in 1962. Quinn died at Morton on January 23, 1915.[26]

Narrative Source: George Quinn, "Account of George Quinn," ed. Kenneth Carley, *Minnesota History* 38 (September 1962): 147–49.

I ARRIVED at Redwood Agency August 13 and four days later the outbreak began in the Big Woods (or at Acton). The next morning the work began at the Lower or Redwood Agency. I am half white man and half Indian, and I learned to read and write the Sioux language at Lake Calhoun under the instruction of the Pond brothers.[27] But I never learned to speak English and I was raised among the Indians as one of them. So when the outbreak came I went with my people against the whites. I was nineteen years old and anxious to distinguish myself in the war, but I had no wish to murder anyone in cold blood, nor did I; nobody ever accused me of such a thing. I fought the white soldiers, but not the unarmed white settlers.

I was in the attack on Captain (John S.) Marsh's company at Redwood Ferry, the first day of the outbreak at the agency, and helped to destroy that command. After the fight I and four other young men were sent down mounted to Fort Ridgely to watch the fort and see what the soldiers were doing, and to ride back and report anything important. Other parties of four or five were sent down for the same purpose. The squad I was with got to the fort very late at night. We hitched our horses and crawled up in the darkness as close as we dared to the west side of the fort and lay down and I fell asleep. When I awoke it was daybreak, and old Jack Frazer, a well-known half-breed who had made his escape from Wacouta's village the day before, leaving his family behind, was standing picket in plain view of us.[28] He called out to us to get right away from there or he would shoot us, and he said that if he did not know our fathers and mothers so well he would shoot us anyhow. We slipped down the bluff bank and did not let him see us any more. Later in the day we returned to the Redwood Agency. One party sent down to watch the fort rode some miles north of it and finally saw Lieutenant (Timothy) Sheehan's company returning to the fort in the night. A messenger was sent back to give the alarm.[29] This messenger gave the news to another scout and he rode to Little Crow's village and reported that the soldiers were coming in great numbers. There was great excitement and orders were given to break up camp and retreat to Yellow Medicine. But in a little time another scout came and said there were only about fifty men coming to re-enforce the Fort, and so the orders to break up camp were countermanded.

Continued on page 157.

NOTES

1. Anonymous, "Samuel J. Brown," typescript in possession of Alan R. Woolworth, Minnesota Historical Society; "Samuel Brown Dies," *Minneapolis Journal*, August 29, 1925, p. 1.

2. Little Dog or Sunkacistinna was Little Crow's half brother and White Spider's full brother; Anderson, *Little Crow*, 45, 193.

3. George H. Gleason, government storekeeper at the Redwood Agency, and Sarah F. Wakefield with her four-year-old son Charles and two-year-old daughter Nellie were stopped on the road to the Redwood Agency. Gleason was killed and the others captured; Wakefield, *Six Weeks in the Sioux Tepees: A Narrative of Indian Captivity* (Shakopee: Argus Book and Job Printing Office, 1864).

4. Vermont-native John Fadden was a fifty-year-old farmer, who lived near the Yellow Medicine Agency in August 1862; he was Angus Brown's father-in-law. The Fadden family fled with the refugees guided by John Otherday. Nothing more is known of the family following their flight; U.S. Census, 1860, Henderson, Sibley County, roll 574, p. 756; Arthur P. Rose, *An Illustrated History of Yellow Medicine County, Minnesota* (Marshall, Minn.: Northern History Publishing Co., 1914), 57.

5. Amanda Ingalls and her sister Jennie were fourteen and twelve years old respectively in August 1862. They were the daughters of Jedidiah H. Ingalls, who died at Hawk Creek, Renville County, on August 19. Captured with the Joseph R. Brown family, they were freed at Camp Release; Satterlee, *Detailed Account*, 35, 93.

Charles Holmes was a twenty-seven-year-old native of Sweden who lived near the Brown family. He escaped to Fort Ridgely where he joined the Cullen Guards led by Captain Joseph Anderson. He was at the battle of Birch Coulee and enlisted in the First Regiment of Mounted Rangers and later in the Second Minnesota Cavalry; Board of Commissioners, *Minnesota in the Civil and Indian Wars*, 1:534, 564, 778; Adjutant General of Minnesota, *Annual Report, 1866*, 738.

Leopold Wohler and his wife Frances were at the lime kiln, three miles below the

Yellow Medicine Agency. After Leopold's escape, his wife was kept a prisoner until freed at Camp Release; Satterlee, *Detailed Account*, 93; Bryant and Murch, *Great Massacre by the Sioux Indians*, 130–31.

6. Wanata was the leader of a mixed band of Sisseton and Yanktonai Dakotas who lived near the middle of the west side of Lake Traverse. Sweet Corn was the leader of a band of Sissetons in a village near that of Wanata. Scarlet Plume or Red Feather or Wamdiupiduta was the leader of a band of Sissetons who lived on the west side of Big Stone Lake. During the war he supported the peace party. He surrendered with his small band at Fort Wadsworth, Dakota Territory, on October 30, 1864. He was a scout for the next two years and then moved to the Sisseton Reservation where he was given land in 1875. He signed the Treaties of 1858, 1867, 1872, and 1873. The date of his death is not known; Herman Chilson, "Dakota Indian Scout Roster," unpublished manuscript in private possession; "Official Correspondence Pertaining to the War of the Outbreak, 1862–1865," *South Dakota Historical Collections* 8 (1916): 495–98; Folwell, *History of Minnesota*, 2:226; Solomon Two Stars, "Evidence for the Claimants," *Sisseton and Wahpeton Bands . . . v. the United States*, U.S. Court of Claims no. 22524, part 1, p. 84–85, 94, 198; Kappler, comp. and ed., *Indian Treaties*, 2:788, 959, 1059, 1062. For information on Standing Buffalo, see his narrative in Chapter X, p. 291, below. For information on Akipa, see Charles Crawford's narrative in Chapter V, p. 112, below.

7. Cut Nose, a Mdewakanton, was tried, convicted, and hanged at Mankato on December 26, 1862; Satterlee, *Court Proceedings*, 32–33; Transcripts of Trials of Sioux Indians, case no. 96, Senate Records 37A-F2. Dowannie or Always Singing, a Mdewakanton, participated in several murders and was hanged at Mankato on December 26, 1862; Satterlee, *Court Proceedings*, 21; Transcripts of Trials of Sioux Indians, case no. 22, Senate Records 37A-F2.

8. Thomas Hughes, *Old Traverse des Sioux* (St. Peter: Herald Publishing Co., 1929), 125–30; *History of the Red River Valley, Past and Present* (Chicago: C. F. Cooper, 1909), 2:732–33.

9. Born in Quebec in 1818, Oliver Martell moved to Minnesota in 1856 and by 1859 was operating the ferry at the Redwood Agency. When the war began, he fled to Fort Ridgely, spreading the news as he rode. He moved to Big Stone City, Dakota Territory, in 1871 and lived there until his death in December 1904; *Big Stone* (So.Dak.) *Headlight*, December 29, 1904.

10. Louis Brisbois, a native of Wisconsin Territory, worked for the traders at the Redwood Agency. He and his family escaped to Fort Ridgely, where he aided in the defense of the fort; U.S. Census, 1860, Redwood Township, Brown County, roll 567, p. 249; June D. Holmquist, Sue E. Holbert, and Dorothy D. Perry, *History along the Highways: An Official Guide to Minnesota State Markers and Monuments* (St. Paul: Minnesota Historical Society, 1967), 39.

11. Margaret Hayden, age nineteen, and her daughter Catherine, age one, escaped to Fort Ridgely. Her husband Patrick was killed at the Beaver Creek settlement; Satterlee, *Detailed Account*, 25, 99.

12. Transcripts of Trials of Sioux Indians, case no. 1, Senate Records 37A-F2; *St. Paul Dispatch*, July 24, 1909, p. 10.

13. Wilson Massipost, a widower, and his daughters Mary and Julia were killed in Milford Township, Brown County, and his son, age eight, escaped; Satterlee, *Detailed Account*, 39.

14. Wakantanka or Great Spirit, Mahoowayma or Makuwama or Comes for Me, and Wakinyanna or Little Thunder were tried, convicted on Godfrey's testimony, and executed at Mankato on December 26, 1862; Satterlee, *Court Proceedings*, 54, 74–75; Transcripts of Trials of Sioux Indians, cases no. 210, 382, and 383, Senate Records 37A-F2.

15. The Travelers' Home was an inn kept by Anton Henle along the river road in Milford Township, Brown County; Satterlee, *Detailed Account*, 40.

16. Mazabomdu or Blows on Iron, a Mdewakanton, was tried, convicted, and executed at Mankato on December 26, 1862; Satterlee, *Court Proceedings*, 14–15; Transcripts of Trials of Sioux Indians, case no. 10, Senate Records 37A-F2. The victims may have been Mrs. Messmer, Anton Henle's mother-in-law, and Anton, age eight, and Mary, age four, Henle's children; Satterlee, *Detailed Account*, 40.

17. Fifty-nine-year-old Adolph Schilling, a German settler from Mecklenburg, and his daughter Louise were killed in Milford Township, Brown County, but his wife and son Joseph escaped; U.S. Census, 1860, Milford Township, Brown County, roll 567, p. 264; Satterlee, *Detailed Account*, 40.

18. The editors have found no further information on Wazakoota.

19. Caroline Stocker was shot while sick in bed. Her husband Joseph and a neighbor, Cecelia Ochs, hid, and the house was set on fire; Satterlee, *Detailed Account*, 41.

20. Forty-seven-year-old François Patoile, a native of Canada, was married and employed as a trader at the Redwood Agency. He was killed while fleeing to Fort Ridgely; U.S. Census, 1860, Redwood Township, Brown County, roll 567, p. 246; Satterlee, *Detailed Account*, 42–43. The other white man killed was LeGrand Davies; Satterlee, *Detailed Account*, 42–43.

21. Mattie Williams of Painesville, Ohio, was visiting Valencia J. and Joseph B. Reynolds, her aunt and uncle. Mary Anderson, a Swedish immigrant whose father had been a government blacksmith, worked as a hired girl for Joseph Reynolds. Shot while being captured, she died a few days later. Mary Schwandt was born in Germany in 1848, emigrated to America in 1858, and moved to Minnesota in 1862. She wrote an account of her experiences. She died in 1939. Both Mattie Williams and Mary Schwandt testified at the trials of the Dakota Indians. See Mary Schwandt-Schmidt, "The Story of Mary Schwandt," *Minnesota Collections* 6 (1894): 461–74; Mary Schwandt Schmidt Papers, Division of Libraries and Archives, Minnesota Historical Society; Satterlee, *Court Proceedings*, 11. See also Snana's narrative in Chapter VI, p. 141, below.

22. Tazoo or Tazu or Old Buffalo, also called Red Otter, was tried, convicted, and hanged at Mankato on December 26, 1862, for the rape of Mattie Williams and participation in other crimes; Satterlee, *Court Proceedings*, 11; Transcripts of Trials of Sioux Indians, case no. 4, Senate Records 37A-F2.

23. Wakute was the successor to an earlier Dakota leader of the same name who died in about 1858. He did not participate in the war, and he was moved to the Crow Creek Reservation in the spring of 1863. He testified before an Indian Peace Commission in June 1868; [James McLaughlin, ed.], *Papers Relating to Talks and Councils Held with the Indians in Dakota and Montana Territories in the Years 1866–1869* (Washington, D.C.: Government Printing Office, 1910), 94.

24. Joseph B. and Valencia J. Reynolds, natives of New York and Ohio respectively, were instructors in a school at Shakopee's village. They fled in a buggy and reached Fort Ridgely; Bryant and Murch, *Great Massacre by the Sioux Indians*, 404–10; *Register of Officers and Agents . . . in the Service of the United States* (Washington, D.C.: Government Printing Office, 1862), 84.

25. For more on White Dog, see Satterlee, *Court Proceedings*, 25–27; Transcripts of Trials of Sioux Indians, case no. 35, Senate Records 37A-F2.

26. "Aged Medicine Man Dies, 'Dr. Quinn' Answers Call," *St. Paul Pioneer Press*, January 28, 1915, p. 12; Transcripts of Trials of Sioux Indians, case no. 200, Senate Records 37A-F2.

27. Samuel W. Pond (1808–91) and Gideon H. Pond (1810–78) arrived at Fort Snelling in 1834 to become missionaries to the Dakota Indians. Settling near an Indian village at Lake Calhoun (present-day Minneapolis), they learned the Dakota language

and served as missionaries until the early 1850s. The Ponds continued as ministers in churches founded by white settlers; Upham and Dunlap, *Minnesota Biographies,* 607–8.

28. Jack Frazer, the son of a British fur trader and a Dakota woman, was born in about 1806. After living as an Indian for thirty-five years, he adopted the ways of the whites and learned the English language. Then he worked as a fur trader until settling on a farm in 1855. During the war, he served as a scout. He died near Faribault in February 1869; Henry Hastings Sibley, *Iron Face: The Adventures of Jack Frazer, Frontier Warrior, Scout, and Hunter,* eds. Theodore Blegen and Sarah A. Davidson (Chicago: Caxton Club, 1950).

29. Lieutenant Sheehan and about forty soldiers had been ordered to Fort Ripley in central Minnesota. A messenger delivered Captain Marsh's order for them to return at once to Fort Ridgely. Upon his arrival, Sheehan assumed command of the fort; Carley, *Sioux Uprising,* 26–27; Timothy J. Sheehan Papers and Diary, Division of Libraries and Archives, Minnesota Historical Society.

CHAPTER V

Attack on the
Yellow Medicine Agency

BY MONDAY afternoon on August 18, rumors of the troubles at the Redwood Agency reached the Yellow Medicine Agency. The Indians were the first to hear the news, many disbelieving the seriousness of the reports. The ensuing debates at Yellow Medicine about the war created a division within the native community. Many mixed-bloods and some full-bloods, especially individuals who had turned to farming or who attended church, refused to take part in the war and instead saved the lives of whites. Others, working under the belief that the whites would blame all Indians for the troubles, began pillaging the traders' stores and warehouses. Late Monday night, the whites who had sought refuge in a government building decided to flee. They left in the middle of the night and were guided to safety by a few full- and mixed-bloods. A second party consisting of those whites connected to the Riggs and Williamson missions fled on Tuesday to Henderson, which they reached five days later.

The extension of the fighting to the Yellow Medicine Agency and the attitudes that the Sissetons and Wahpetons took toward the war are detailed in three narratives that are by Renville family members—Gabriel Renville, his son Victor Renville, and his half-brother Charles Renville Crawford. A fourth narrative is by Joseph La Framboise, Jr., who testified in 1901 about the conflict at Yellow Medicine. Although they were mixed-bloods, all four of these men maintained a Dakota life style. The only full-blood who left a narrative of the attack was John Otherday, one of the men who guided whites to safety. Otherday was a farmer, had a white wife, and had converted to Christianity.

Narrative 1
GABRIEL RENVILLE'S MEMOIR

GABRIEL RENVILLE or Tiwakan, meaning Sacred Lodge, was born in April 1825 at Sweet Corn's Sisseton village on the west side of Big Stone Lake. His parents were Victor Renville and Winona Crawford, both of whom were mixed-bloods. His father died in 1833, and he was reared as a Dakota by his stepfather, Joseph Akipa Renville, a full-blood. Subsequently he went to work for his brother-in-law, Joseph R. Brown, in the fur trade. Renville married three sisters in 1847, 1858, and 1860, respectively, and in 1859 settled on a farm on the north side of the Minnesota River.

When the war came, Renville helped to organize the soldiers' lodge that opposed the warriors. He remained at Camp Release after Sibley's army arrived and spent the following winter at Fort Snelling. Sibley recruited Renville to serve as a scout in spring 1863, and for three years Renville acted as the leader of the Dakota scouts, working out of Fort Wadsworth in Dakota Territory. When peace finally came to the eastern portions of Dakota Territory, Renville turned his attention to organizing the new Sisseton Reservation, leading the delegation to Washington, D.C., to negotiate and sign the Treaty of 1867. He served as chief of the Sissetons and Wahpetons at the reservation throughout the 1880s and 1890s and died at Samuel Brown's house at Browns Valley, Minnesota, on August 26, 1892. He adhered to Dakota customs throughout his life, and he never spoke English. The narrative written by him in Dakota was translated by Samuel Brown and Thomas A. Robertson.[1]

Narrative Sources: Gabriel Renville, "A Sioux Narrative of the Outbreak of 1862, and of Sibley's Expedition of 1863," *Minnesota Collections* 10 (1905): 595–613; Gabriel Renville, "Narrative," undated, Joseph R. and Samuel J. Brown Papers, Division of Libraries and Archives, Minnesota Historical Society.

MY HOME was six miles north of the Yellow Medicine Agency, on the opposite side of the Minnesota River. One evening [August 18] at seven o'clock I was told by an Indian that all the people at the Redwood Agency were killed. I wanted to know whether this report was true or false, so we crossed the river to hunt up the truth. We found nothing and came back that evening. Then the next morning before sunrise another runner came and told about the troubles at Redwood Agency. This man reported that all the people at the agency were killed, and many of them (the Indians) had come up to the Yellow Medicine Agency to attack the traders' stores there, and there was a big scare. He said this and then went on . . . [half a line is here missing from the manuscript] I went along but did not see anybody. My horses were standing in sight and I ran for one, caught it, and went back to my house. At that time another man appeared. He and the women folks stood outside in the open awaiting my return. So I didn't

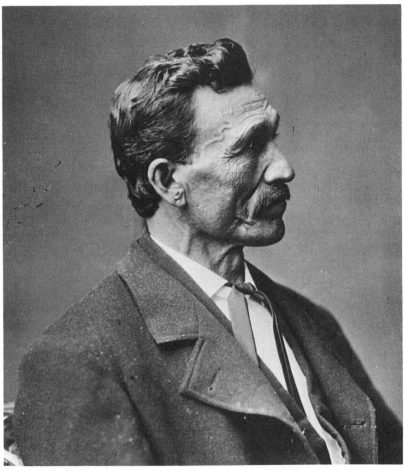

GABRIEL RENVILLE in 1880-81 in Washington, D.C.

know what to do. Then I saddled my horse and went towards the agency — that was my intention. I had some relatives at the agency that I wanted to see. I wanted to know whether they were killed or not, and I told the folks at home that if I didn't return in one hour it would be because I was killed. Now we made up our minds to take the women folks and flee to the Sissetons where our friends were. We had many relatives there. I mounted my horse and crossed the river — went about a mile and a half through the woods. Then I came to a prairie. It was the prairie lying north of the agency. Then I saw it was covered with Indians, and much smoke was issuing from the traders' stores below the agency. I then whipped up my horse and went as fast as I could. I was going through the crowd when I was stopped by some Indians who were on horseback. I said, "My friends, what is the trouble?" They said the Indians were killing all the people at the Lower Agency and were murdering the white farmers across the river there.

It was some of these who came that night [early morning hours of August 19] and drove away the storekeepers and plundered. They also reported that all the whites at the Agency had made a stand in the Agency buildings. They who reported this were of those who were not enemies to the whites.

I then went on as fast as I could towards the Agency, and stopped suddenly in front of the west door of the warehouse building. I did not see a single person, but heard very much of thumping noises. I then went around to the east door, and there saw that they had gone in that way and were plundering inside.

There was a house about four hundred yards south of the Agency buildings, from which I saw a woman come crying. I went towards her, and when I reached her I found it was my mother. She was very much frightened. When she saw that it was I, she was overcome and fell to the ground, and though she tried to get up she would fall to the ground again. I got down and took hold of her, assisting her to rise, and said, "Don't cry, but stand up. A great calamity has come to us, and we may all die. Stop crying, and try to control yourself."

I asked her what had become of the white people who belonged at the Agency. She said that that night, near daylight, John Other Day had started with them all towards the east, and that among them was one white man who had been shot but was still alive and was taken along. (This was Stewart B. Garvie.) Then she said, "Your brother has gone to your sister's. It has now been a long time since he went, but he has not come back. I expect they are all dead." She meant my sister [Susan Frenier Brown, wife of Joseph R. Brown] who lived with her children about eight miles south of the Agency. Then I said to her, "Mother, go back into the house and stay quiet there, and I will go home and come here again." I then mounted my horse, and rode as fast as I could towards my home.

About three miles north of the Agency there lived a white man who was a minister (Rev. Thomas S. Williamson). He was the first man who came among the Wahpetons to teach them, and was called the Doctor. He came out and met me, and asked what was being done and what the news was. I told him, "My friend, a great commotion has come. All the people at the Redwood Agency, and all the farmers across the river from that Agency, are reported to have been killed. But the people of the Yellow Medicine Agency, and the traders at that place, have all fled under the guidance of John Other Day last night. Everything in the stores has been taken, and those buildings have been burned. The Agency buildings have been plundered and everything taken, but they are not burned. These things are true. Therefore, my friend, flee." He replied, "I have been a long time with the Dakotas, and I don't think they will kill me. My children have all gone, and I am alone with my wife." Then I said to him, "It is reported that even the mixed-bloods who are Dakotas have been killed, and the only thing for you to do is to flee." I then went into the house and shook hands with the woman, and again urged them to escape. Their fright was very great, as could be told by their paleness of countenance; and the wild look in the eyes of all whom I met, being the same in the faces and eyes of these people, moved by [my] heart.

I came out of the house, rode swiftly away, and, fording the river, reached my home. I found the horses already hitched to the wagon, and we started in a hurry, going toward a ford which was a good crossing for wagons. I saw at that time the Doctor's children and others with them, who were crossing the river and fleeing towards the east under the guidance of an Indian who was friendly to the whites.

We crossed the river and went towards the Agency, and when we had gone about four miles some of the people I met were drunk. Two men took my horses by the bits, and accused me of fleeing towards the whites, and said that whoever did that was now an enemy. I told them I was not going there, but they did not believe me, and they used me roughly. I saw they were drunk, because one of them had a bottle tied to his arm. I then jumped to the ground, tore their hands loose from me, and took the bottle away from the man who had it. Pulling out the cork, I took a mouthful and swallowed some of it, but it burned my mouth and throat, so that I did not swallow all of it. I poured it out, and threw the bottle away and then went on. The reason why it burned my mouth was that it was white liquor and had not been mixed with water.

In a cellar under one of the buildings at the Agency was a forty gallon barrel of alcohol for the use of the Agency physician, which had been found by them and created very much of a commotion among the people who were then about the Agency. Every person had his gun, and those who were drunk were preparing to shoot at one another; but those that were not drunk held them, and that was how it came that no one was killed.

I saw this and went on to my mother's house, and found that my brother [Charles Crawford, his half brother] who had gone to where my sister and her children were living had come back. He reported that they had fled, but that some of the hostile Indians came, and that he thought they must have all been killed. These hostiles had their minds made up to kill him, but there was one who took his part and saved his life. Runners were continually arriving from the hostile Indians.

It was next reported that a detachment of soldiers that had been sent out from Fort Ridgely had been all killed [Marsh's command]. About five o'clock in the evening it was reported that Major Brown's wife, children, and son-in-law, had all been taken prisoners. Major Brown's wife was our sister.

Thirteen of us decided to go into the Agency buildings and make a stand there, because they were strong, brick buildings. In the Agent's house were Mazo-ma-ne (Walking in Irons) [Akipa's brother], Hin-tah-chan (Basswood), Shu-pay-he-yu (Intestines came out), and Pay-tah-koyag-enah-pay (Appeared clothed in Fire). In the doctor's house were Ah-kee-pah (Coming together), Charles Crawford, Thomas Crawford, and Han-yo-ke-yah (Flies in the Night). In the school building were myself (Gabriel Renville), Two Stars, and E-nee-hah (Excited). In the farmer's building were Koda (Friend), and Ru-pah-hu (Wing). It was the next morning that we did this. Then Charles Crawford and Ah-kee-pah went to get Major Brown's wife and children, and got them and brought them back.

News was coming in every day, that Fort Ridgely was being attacked, that white settlers to the east and south were being massacred, and that New Ulm was attacked. It was also reported that a party of hostile Indians, many young men, had gone north on a war party, there being white people there and also a fort [Fort Abercrombie] toward which they went.

Continued on page 186.

Narrative 2
VICTOR RENVILLE'S ACCOUNT

VICTOR RENVILLE was born at Lac qui Parle on November 13, 1849. His parents were Gabriel Renville, a mixed-blood Dakota, and Mary, a full-blood Dakota. During the 1850s, the family lived at various locations in the Minnesota River valley but finally settled at Yellow Medicine in 1859, where Gabriel worked while building a farm across the river. Victor was attending school at Williamson's mission when the war broke out. During the fighting the family moved into abandoned buildings at the agency. While the Renvilles like other mixed-bloods were made captives, they were freed at Camp Release. Victor joined his father in 1866 as a Dakota scout.

The Renville family moved from Fort Wadsworth to the Sisseton Reservation in 1867. Victor married Mary Roy on July 5, 1870, and five years later took up land on the reserve. He joined the Episcopal church in the 1880s and was ordained a priest by Bishop William H. Hare on June 26, 1895. After serving several churches on and near the Sisseton Reservation, Victor finally retired in 1925. He wrote his narrative of the war in English in about 1920, and it was edited and published in 1923. He died near Peever, South Dakota, in January 1927.[2]

Narrative Source: Victor Renville, "A Sketch of the Minnesota Massacre," *Collections of the State Historical Society of North Dakota* 5 (1923): 251–72.

ON AN AUGUST evening in 1862, Victor was returning on horseback from the agency which was four or five [six] miles from his home, when he was stopped by two Indians who were armed with guns and bows and arrows. One of the strangers motioned to him to stop and exchange saddle blankets. Victor did this, although his blanket was a newer one than that of the stranger. Then the Indian said, "Now put on your saddle and go on. I want both of them." Again Victor did

VICTOR RENVILLE
in about 1920

as he was told, wondering what these strangers could be doing in this part of the country. He thought he would stop at [Solomon] Two Stars' house on the way home and tell him of the incident and perhaps find out the mission of the strangers.[3]

When Victor arrived at the house, Two Stars came outside and said: "Tell your father that there are some spies here from the Lower Red Wood Agency who are telling that all the whites, traders and half-breeds are to be killed. This is a rumor, but your father had better look out."

Victor rode home and told his father what Two Stars had said. About eight o'clock that evening Two Stars and his wife came to Gabriel's home. They talked over the outbreak that was then just getting under way and discussed the best action for them to take in escaping the massacre. When they came to a decision it was very late, so Two Stars and his wife stayed all night at Gabriel's.

Just before daybreak Gabriel heard a knock at the door. Not knowing who it might be, he started to dress and prepare to defend himself in case of attack. Before he got to the door a man outside called to him, "I come with very bad news. At Lower Sioux Bird [*sic*] Agency traders and half-breeds were killed yesterday. I am going on to tell Dr. Riggs over the river." Gabriel never knew who the messenger was.

Gabriel awakened the rest of the household and told them that he intended to ride over to the Agency and warn the people there. If he did not return by ten o'clock they would know he had been killed and Two Stars could hitch up and take the family to Brown's Valley where they would be safe. When ten o'clock arrived, Gabriel did not appear. Two Stars hitched up the horses to the wagon and started off with the family as Gabriel had told them to do. They had not gone more than eighty rods when they saw a rider come up to the house, waving his hat for them to come back. They turned back and discovered the rider to be Tom Crawford [Gabriel Renville's half brother]. He told them that Gabriel had sent for them to come and take refuge in the brick building of the agency. Victor's mother then began to pack more of their belongings into the wagon and while she was doing this Tom Crawford rode off and Victor tried in vain to keep up with him. About half way to the agency, Victor met his father riding hard. As he had fallen far behind Crawford, Victor turned and rode back with his father past where Dr. Williamson lived.

As they approached Dr. Williamson's place they saw him standing in the road waiting to meet them. He asked Gabriel about the rumors he had heard and Gabriel told him what was going on at the agency and what had happened at the Red Wood Agency, and warned him to go east for safety. But Dr. Williamson replied that he was an old man and was not afraid, and would rather die than run away. Gabriel replied that it was the young men who were crazy and making the trouble at the reservation. Dr. Williamson's sister Anna [Jane] then went over to the house of Chief I-yank-ma-ni [Inyangmani].[4] Victor and his father went on to warn the people at the saw mill who were exceedingly frightened upon hearing of the danger they were in. As they left the mill, Victor and his father met two Indians, E-ce-tu-ki-ye and Wa-su-ho-was-te, who said that they had taken Dr. Riggs' family to the east side of the Minnesota River and were on their way to get Dr. Williamson's family and the mill employees.[5] Gabriel told them that it was a good thing they were doing.

A little further on in the woods, Gabriel and Victor met Two Stars and the rest of the family in the wagon. They joined the wagon and all rode together toward the agency. When they passed the mill and Dr. Williamson's place, they saw all the people packing up to go off. When the party arrived at the agency buildings, they found that the white people had all left and only the Indians remained, among whom, they learned, there were many Lower Agency Indians. They went to Crawford's house and outside they found Gabriel's mother crying. She said that Charles Crawford had ridden down to see if Susan Brown (Gabriel's sister) and her family were all right, but he had not yet returned and she believed he had been killed. Gabriel told her to go into the house and wait for Crawford to return. Shortly after noon of that day he returned with the news that Susan's family had left and since there were hostile Indians in the country it was very likely they had been killed. Toward evening some hostile Dakotas came into the agency and said that Brown's family was being held captive at Little Crow's house.

Continued on page 192.

Narrative 3
JOSEPH LA FRAMBOISE, JR.'S, TESTIMONY

JOSEPH LA FRAMBOISE, JR., was the son of Joseph La Framboise, Sr., a mixed-blood trader, and Oasixheaoui, a Dakota. Young Joseph was born in 1831 near the West Des Moines River (present-day Murray County), but he spent most of his youth at his father's trading house at Little Rock, a few miles below Fort Ridgely on the Minnesota River. After Joseph's father died in 1856, the family moved and was living near the Yellow Medicine Agency when the war broke out.

Once the seriousness of the conflict was understood at the Yellow Medicine Agency, La Framboise roused the Indian traders at their stores during the late hours of August 18 and convinced them to flee. He also played a major role in forming the Sisseton and Wahpeton soldiers' lodge. After the fighting had ended, La Framboise spent the winter with his family at Fort Snelling. In February he was chosen by Gabriel Renville as a Dakota scout and continued in this service for the next few years. In 1867 La Framboise moved to the Sisseton Reservation and lived there the remainder of his life. He married twice and was the father of seventeen children. On August 17, 1901, at the Sisseton Agency he testified for the claimants in the Sisseton-Wahpeton lawsuit against the federal government to have their an-

nuities restored. Thomas A. Robertson was the interpreter. La Framboise died on August 19, 1910, at Veblen, South Dakota.[6]

Narrative Source: Joseph La Framboise, Jr., "Evidence for the Claimants," *The Sisseton and Wahpeton Bands of Dakota or Sioux Indians v. the United States,* 1901–07, U.S. Court of Claims no. 22524, part 1, p. 144–57.

I WAS right near the stores at lower [upper] agency [when the news of the fighting reached Yellow Medicine] and first went to Mr. Garvey's store and saw him sitting in the door, reading either a book or a newspaper, with his feet up against the door.[7] He asked me what news there was, and I told him that there was bad news. He asked me "What is it?" I told him that it was reported that the people at the lower agency had all been killed and the stores and buildings all burnt. Then I went to Mr. Roberts's [*sic*] store and told there also what I had heard. Then I went to Mr. Forbes's store and told the people there the same thing. Then I went to Mr. Patoile's store and told them the same thing.[8] Then I came back to the store where I was employed and from there went up to the agency and told them there what I had heard, and there the agency doctor [Dr. John L. Wakefield] told me I was foolish to believe anything of that kind.[9] Then Mr. Synks, who was in charge of the agency at that time, he took me by the coat and pulled me into another room and said to me, "I believe there is something in this, because we have not received any mail for two days," and asked me what I thought was best to do.[10] I suggested to him that he get his employees and those at the agency together in a brick building that was there, in which there was a well, or near which was a well (they had guns also at the agency), get the guns and prepare to defend themselves in that building. He then said to me, "I am much obliged to you for the suggestion, and will be glad if you will be one with us." I told him I would, if possible. I then came back to the store, took my wife, and she took one of the children on her back and I carried the other one, and I took my gun (that is all we took with us), and we went away from there and went to her mother's house. We had no bedding nor clothing with us (myself and wife), except what we had on. I then went back to the store where my tent was outside the store to get, if I could, some bedding and clothing from there, and my brother-in-law went with me. We had blankets on when we went back. There is one thing I forgot there. When I went back to the store from the agency I told Captain Kennedy and Boardman to get away from there.[11] I had supposed that they did as I told them to, but I found that they had gone to the agency and then returned to the store again. When we got back in the vicinity of the store we heard whispering and whistling by people (it was dark then) near or about there. We saw a gathering of people sitting around in a circle and talking to one another, and went up to them to listen with our blankets over our heads. We saw there a gathering of the people, and in the

JOSEPH LA FRAMBOISE, JR., **at the Sisseton Agency, 1896**

center of the gathering, if I remember right, three men who had come from the lower agency, and their talk was to get these people to do as they had done, or join them in what they had done. These three men were Medawankantons. The answer to what these men had said was this, "That this is your affair, not ours." That is the answer that the people made to these three men. These three men told all that had been done at the lower agency in regard to mixed bloods also, and wanted to know what the feeling of these people was in regard to the mixed bloods. One man got up and said that he had no relatives among the mixed bloods, but that they were all his friends, and that he had no desire to injure the mixed bloods or the white men. "We had heard of your arrival and had gathered together here to consult in regard to what we should do, and you come here to where we are gathered together to try to influence us in regard to what we are going to do. What do you come here and do that for?" Then another one got up and said, "I am a mixed blood, but was raised among the Indians, dressed in breech clout, and my name is Ma-rpi-oi-car-mani (meaning he who was raised walking in the clouds). When you go against your enemies, the Chippewas, and I am with you, I am the fellow that you follow after. If anybody tries to injure the mixed bloods, I will stand by them as long as I stand alive."[12] When we first heard them consulting about the mixed bloods myself and brother-in-law had intended to shoot these men who had come from the Medawankantons, but after these two men spoke we knew we had friends there, therefore did not do anything. Then we started to where my wife was, but on the way saw a light in the store. I told my brother-in-law that I would look into the store and see if those were Indians or who they were. I peeked in through the window and saw in there Captain Kennedy and this Boardman again, putting goods up onto the shelf. I immediately entered the store and blew the light out. I took a couple of blankets and covered them over with them, trying to get them to wear them the same as an Indian wears a blanket, and took them out of the back door and started them away from there, following them myself, when the Indians rushed toward me and asked me if the white men were still in the store, in a whisper. I told them they were. I then took them farther on, put them on a road, and told them to get away the best way they could, and shook hands with them and parted with them. Then myself and my brother-in-law, Narcisse Frenier, started on a run toward where my family was, and immediately heard several shots. We immediately stopped in our run and looked back and saw a man with a white shirt on running in the road that we were going in. Thinking that somebody was running after us we stepped aside into the bushes and saw this man run by with two others close behind him, running after him. We kept still there, and shortly afterwards two men came back on the road. One of them said, "What have you done? Did you have a bullet in the gun or just a blank cartridge?" And the other one said, "No; there is no mistake about that; I was close to him. I shot him in the back and think I hit his heart." And then the other man said, "If you have done that he could not have gone any farther. He must be lying in the bushes there somewhere," and then we went on to where my family was and stayed there all night. It was dark and I could not identify these two men or tell whether they were upper or lower Indians.

Continued on page 140.

Narrative 4
CHARLES R. CRAWFORD'S TESTIMONY

CHARLES RENVILLE CRAWFORD or Wakanhinape, meaning Appearing Sacred, was born at a Dakota village located between Big Stone Lake and Lake Traverse in 1837. His parents were Akipa (Joseph Akipa Renville), a full-blood, and Winona Crawford, a mixed-blood who had been married to Victor Renville (see Chapter V, Narrative 1, above). By 1862 Crawford and his family were living at the Yellow Medicine Agency where he worked as a clerk.

Crawford witnessed several battles during the war and was brought before the military commission twice and tried for participation in the war. Each time he was acquitted. After spending the winter in the Dakota camp at Fort Snelling, he joined Sibley's 1863 expedition as a scout, serving until 1866. Crawford settled on the Sisseton Reservation thereafter, served as interpreter for the delegation to Washington, D.C., to negotiate the Treaty of 1867, and in 1875 settled on a small farm on the reservation. He joined the Good Will Presbyterian Church in 1877 and two years later received a license to preach. On August 20, 1901, at the Sisseton Agency he gave extensive testimony about the Dakota War from which the following narrative is taken. Although he had been fluent in English as a young man, he had ceased to use it and therefore needed an interpreter, who was Thomas A. Robertson. Charles Crawford died in 1920.[13]

Narrative Source: Charles R. Crawford, "Evidence for the Claimants," *The Sisseton and Wahpeton Bands of Dakota or Sioux Indians v. the United States*, 1901–07, U.S. Court of Claims no. 22524, part 1, p. 159–79.

WHEN WE got this news [of the attack at the Redwood Agency] I told Noah Synks [Sinks], and we didn't believe it in the first place, and soon after another one came. He told then what Pa-ha-tka told and said all the traders were killed. At that time George Gleason he said he would hitch up and going to start down home [to Redwood] with Miss [Mrs.] Wakefield; and this George he was a clerk at the lower agency for Galbraith. He had come from the lower agency for some reason the day before. And all that afternoon we did not hear it, much of it, until just a little before sundown there was some more news came there again, and there was an old man named Hopanduta [sic], meaning the Scarlet Second-Born Son; he said that there was some more news received from the lower agency.[14] After this trader was killed they were across the Minnesota side of the river and they killed a farmer. This Haponduta he went over to our house, and Haponduta and father and Ma-zo-mani they came back, those three of them, to the office again, and they said to Synks they had better start away, escape away from the agency, and Synks he asked them back they better stay at the warehouse until furthermore what was going on.[15] That was just about getting sundown, and there was another man named Su-pe-hi-ye, meaning His Guts Came Out.[16] Those four they say we stay and guard this warehouse; so we took a barrel pork and sugar. There is a door here outside there, and there is another door down here a hundred feet below, and there was a stairway go up, and we filled that with the barrel of sugar and pork and I took the key. I got the key yet at home. While we were doing that, it was just beginning to get dark, and John Other Day and his wife came there and he says, "I could not stay where I was. I have to get away and take my wife away." There was other people at my house, between Ta-mni-sapa's place in that flat. Then I said to Synks, "I had better go over there and find out what they were doing." He says, "Yes." So I got a horse out at a barn and went out there where this party gathered. They was all set around together bunch. I said, "What you got together here for?" A man named Pa-da-ni-apa-pi, meaning was Struck by a Pawnee, he says, "We gathered here for coming down to where the traders was.

*CHARLES R.
CRAWFORD in 1858
in Washington, D.C.*

If there was any Medewankantons come up here we want to protect these traders," and I said, "You must not do anything; that is a different band entirely," and someone says, "Hobo," meaning they were of one tribe, in a deep tone of voice.[17]

(The interpreter here explains, that about the time of the outbreak, the young men formed a kind of a secret society, and they were called hobos, and they would go through the camp nights and make kind of a deep noise, and it could not be understood whether they were saying anything or not. They were saying something in kind of a deep voice so they could understand one another, but other people could not understand them.) . . . [18]

We, that night [August 18], fastened the doors and made open above, and the white people, who were there still, had in their minds that they would remain there. I do not remember of any Indians coming there up to that time, excepting the four names I have already given. Between 12 o'clock that night and the morning of the next day, we heard noises, or sounds, and I could not tell whether they were gunshots or not. Soon after that, we saw one of the buildings down below on fire. We supposed that the Indians had attacked these other people. There was a wareroom there and other rooms, and an opening made between the two. In going from one room into another room I saw there Garvey laid out. A man, by the name of John Fadden, spoke up and said, "Garvey has been wounded." He was wounded with a gunshot, and while I did not hear any gun fired, I saw that he was wounded, and that it was a gun wound. Then these four men, whose names I have given, got very much worked up about it, and said that the best thing to be done was to have these people in the agency go away before daylight; that if we were not down, that it was probable that after they got through with their work down there to the stores, that they would come up to the agency, and that if all the people about there should join with them, meaning the Lower Sioux — (The witness here corrected the interpreter, who admitted that he had made a mistake and corrected the answer as follows:) That after the Lower Sioux got through down there and got up there, and if any of those at Yellow Medicine should join with them and attack the agency, that they probably would all be killed before soldiers could get there. They decided then to go and have Other Day go with them as their guide and also myself. They then started, which was just about daylight, and my mother was living close by the agency, and I went to see her before I started with the party. My mother asked me to go and see what had become of my sister [Susan Frenier Brown] before I went with that party. . . .

The party was standing waiting for me, and I told my mother I would go and ask Synks about it. I did so, and told Mr. Synks that I would go down to where my sister lived; they would probably be somewhere in that vicinity by the time I got there; I would see who they were and then go up to where they were. Mr. Synks said that was all right and I came back to my home and the party went on. Before

I left the party John Fadden, who was with the party, said "When we get opposite to their place, Other Day and I will go down there." This John Fadden was Angus Brown's father-in-law. . . .

The party went on and I got ready to go, but was afraid to go alone. There was a young Indian about 16 years old living at my mother's, and my mother told him to go with me. He consented to go, but we had but one horse. Just at that time a man by the name of Bo-ga-ga, meaning branching or rays of light, came there from the lower agency.[19] My mother asked this man, calling him son, "Do you know whether my daughter is killed or not?" He said, "No; the people up as far as Sacred Heart have all been killed, but I don't know of them." Then she said, "My son here is going down there, and I don't like to have him go alone; would you go with him?" He said he would. My mother borrowed a horse, and this man rode that horse. When we got to the shore opposite to where my sister lived, we found that the ferryboat was on the opposite side of the river from where we were. It was a ferryboat that took teams over, and there was a rope stretched across the river. I shouted and hollered for Angus, calling his name. It was shortly after sunrise and time for people to be up, but I could see nobody stirring about. I told the man that was with me that I would swim over, and he said, "All right; go ahead, and I will stay here and hold the horses." I took my clothes off and tied my shirt around my head and jumped in the river and swam across. I tied my shirt, after I got across, using it as a breech clout, and went up to the house. When I got to the first room, there was a table sitting there with candles on it and dishes on the table, appearing as though somebody had been eating, having a meal. I again hollered, calling Angus by name, and saying, "Are you awake?" I did that several times, but no one answered. Then I went into the upper rooms, but found no one there. There was a ravine or creek running up on each side of where the buildings were. I first went up the creek on the north side of the buildings as far as from here to the church up there (probably less than half a mile), then crossed over to the other ravine and came down that, calling for Angus and hollering for him as I went, knowing that if I followed him I would find the rest of the party, but there was no one there. I concluded then that they had gone away from there, and then it bothered me to know whether they had been killed or not. I went back up the creek again further than I had been first time, up near the head of the creek, and there met John Other Day and John Fadden. They both of them asked me where the family were, and I told them I did not know; they were not there; no one there. I have been up and down both creeks, hollering for them, but have not found anyone. There were three horses standing close by where we were. I proposed that we catch the horses; that I take one of them and they take the other two to where the party was waiting for us. They said that they did not want to spend that much time there; so I went and got one of the horses, intending to hitch it to a buggy, and told them I should do so and go and see what had become of the family, and then they went toward where the party was, and that was the last I ever saw of them. All that time I was naked, except this shirt that I had wrapped around me. I took the horse down to the house. I had seen a buggy and harness there, so I took the horse down and hitched it to the buggy, and went up into the upstairs, having in my mind that I would try and take with me some of my sister's dresses, if I could find them. I went first into one room, but there was nothing in that room. I then opened another door and went into another room, and that must have been my sister's room, for her dresses were hanging on the wall. I took down some of those and then opened a box that was used for a trunk, and in that found quite a number of boxes of cigars and Major Brown's uniform. There must have been other things in that box, but all I took out was the coat. I put those things into the box, and it was about all the box could hold, but the coat I put on. Just before I got to the landing, the river landing, the man whom I had left on the opposite shore made motions to me; seemed to be quite excited, hurrying me up by motion of his hand. I got onto the ferryboat, and by that time he motioned and said, "Hurry up! Hurry up! Come quick!" I got on the boat and commenced pulling across by the rope which was across the river, but I was very anxious to know what he was hurrying me so for and kept looking about while pulling across, and finally saw on a little knoll between these two creeks that I had been up and down two men appear and come down the hill. After I had got across those two men came to the shore and said, "Who is that; who is that?" meaning me. The man who was with me answered and said, "He is an Indian; and what are you so anxious to know for?" Then this man who was with me asked these other two men, "Where is Major Brown's wife and family?" Their answer was, "We don't know." They then said, "The white people up about here were all killed, and while we don't know what became of that family, or have not seen or heard of them, when we were leaving we saw an ox team near Beaver Creek, and about that time there was a war party starting over that way, and we heard guns fired off. If that was so, perhaps they were killed." Then the man who was with me asked them what they were doing there, meaning these two men. Their answer was, "We were going to this house to get powder and shot, if there was any there." I was out of sight. I had gone up above and had got under cover, and was standing out of sight of these men while this conversation was going on. Then this man who was with me came toward me. I was standing, holding the horse that I had in the buggy. He told me to hurry up and go home as quick as possible. I asked him if he recognized either one of those two men that he had been talking with. He said, "Yes; one of them is Wa-xi-cun-maza," meaning Iron Frenchman, and that "he is a son of Ma-rpi-ya-sa-pa," meaning Black Cloud. . . .[20]

I started for home, and in a very short time, not far from there, met two men — La-Rock and Pe-han-ke-na, meaning Snipe.[21] They were in a buggy, or single rig, and this man, whose name I gave in Indian, was driving. They were both white men. They asked me on which side of the river the ferryboat was. I told them: "It is on this side, but there are two men there from Redwood. If you go there now, they will probably kill you. I would advise you to leave your horse here and get in among the rocks and hide, and you will probably save your lives." Then they talked between themselves in French, which I could not understand, but finally said: "We will do so." They turned their horse and went into the bushes, and I came on home. A little ways further on I again met another wagon. That was an old woman by the name of Wi-no-na-gi-na, meaning the yellow firstborn girl [Elizabeth Jeffries]. She had with her her daughter, William Quinn's wife, and some children, and for a driver they had Oya-te-yan-ka, meaning sitting as a nation.[22] I told them that I had been down to my sister's; that they had gone away from their home, but that I did not know whether they had escaped or been killed. After I had crossed the river a man came there whom I was told was Black Eagle's [Cloud's] son. If you go there now, I fear you will be killed. The old woman, this yellow firstborn, said: "We had better turn back from here." I immediately started on again, and when I looked back I saw they had turned their team and were following me. Up to this time this man who went down with me had been following behind me, but just there among the rocks the road was crooked, and I drove fast and he must have gone away from me without my noticing him. After I came out onto the prairie where I could see this other team about a quarter of a mile behind me, but saw nothing of this man who had gone down there with me. I then drove on fast, and just as I was crossing the Yellow Medicine River I saw on a hill ahead of me three horsemen appear and come down the hill toward me on a gallop. When I met them I found one was my brother Tom, a young man by the name of Han-yo-kin-yan, meaning he who flies at night, and the other was Hin-ta-can, meaning basswood.[23] They said: "It was surmised that you was killed, and we were going to look for you." My brother said that my mother had been terribly frightened, thinking that myself and my sister and her family all had been killed, which caused her to go into convulsions, and she was lying on top of the hill, so Tom told me. . . .

After I got back home Daniel Renville came there and said that Mr. Riggs and the missionaries at that place had been sent away, but that Dr. Williamson was still there at home, but that there were Indians there guarding Dr. Williamson.[24] Then my half-brother, Gabriel Renville, came from across the river where he was living and said: "I will come and camp here," meaning at the agency; that it had been arranged that Dr. Williamson should be escorted away from there that night. Then my brother said: "We will now find out whether our sister has been killed or not, and then we will consult what is best for us to do to save our own lives." Then a camp was formed by Ma-zo-mani (Walking in Iron), Supe-he-yu (His Guts Came Out), Inihan (Excited), Wi-can-rpi-non-pa ([Solomon] Two Stars), brother Gabriel Renville, and my father, Akipa (Meeting), gathered together inside the building.[25]

Continued on page 201.

Narrative 5
JOHN OTHERDAY'S INTERVIEW

JOHN OTHERDAY or Ampatutokacha was called Good Sounding Voice as a young man. He was born in about 1819 near Swan Lake (in present-day Nicollet County). As the son of Zitkaduta or Red Bird and nephew of Big Curly Head, leader of a Wahpeton band at Lac qui Parle, he was well connected. While still a young man, he was a successful warrior, but in 1856 he joined the Hazelwood Republic, an association of farmer Indians who adopted some white customs. In 1857 he aided in the rescue of Abbie Gardner, who had been taken captive at Spirit Lake, Iowa, and the following year he joined the treaty delegation that visited Washington, D.C. On his return he was accompanied by a white woman whom he later married.

When the war broke out, Otherday was the leader of a small band of Wahpeton farmers who lived near the Yellow Medicine Agency. He helped to organize a party of sixty-two whites and led them to safety. The refugees' arrival in St. Paul caused a great stir that was covered by the newspapers. Using missionary Gideon Pond as an interpreter, Otherday recounted his story of the flight for publication in a St. Paul newspaper. He then joined Sibley's army as a scout. For his services, Otherday received twenty-five hundred dollars from the United States Congress, which he used to purchase a farm near Henderson. But he failed to make a living at farming and soon sold the property. By 1869, Otherday had moved to the Sisseton Reservation where he contracted tuberculosis. He died at the Fort Wadsworth military hospital on October 19, 1869.[26]

Narrative Source: John Otherday, "Highly Interesting Narrative of the Outbreak of Indian Hostilities," *Saint Paul Press*, August 28, 1862, p. 2.

ON MONDAY, the 18th, about 8 o'clock A.M., word came to the Upper Agency at Yellow Medicine, that all the white people at the Lower, or Red Wood Agency, had been murdered by the M'dewakanton Sioux. Then the Indians, at the call of their chiefs, assembled in council to the number of about 100 — Sissetons and Wakpetons, and about 30 young Yanktons who were present, but being without a chief had no voice in the council. At 12 M., while they were debating what course to take, word came that a party of soldiers had arrived at the Red Wood Agency, and were all killed. This news still further agitated the council, which was greatly divided in sentiment. The Sissetons urged the killing of all the whites, and the taking of their goods and property. They said that the M'dewakantons had already gone so far that the worst the whites could inflict would be sure to come upon them all — that the whites would regard them all alike as enemies; and since matters could in no event be worse, the best plan was to kill them all and take their goods.

The Wakpetons agreed with them that, as they were now in for mischief, they ought to take the goods of the whites, but opposed killing them. They said they had nothing against the whites, and insisted upon sending them off with their horses and wagons across the prairies.

JOHN OTHERDAY in St. Paul in 1862

Other-Day himself addressed them. He told them that they might easily enough kill a few whites—five, ten, or a hundred. But the consequence would be that their whole country would be filled with soldiers of the United States, and all of them killed or driven away. "Some of you," he said, "say you have horses and may escape to the plains; but what will become of those who have no horses." They replied to this that all this would happen anyway.

After a long debate, towards evening the Yanktons, Sissitons, and a few of the Wakpetons, rising from the council, without coming to any conclusion, moved towards the houses of the whites, for the purpose of killing them.

In the meantime he (Other-Day) took his wife by the arm, took his gun and went to the houses of the whites, informed them of their danger (for they had previously known nothing of the council) and hurried them all to the Agency house, a brick building about a mile from the place where the council was held. They assembled here armed, to the number of over fifty, resolved to defend themselves and families to the last extremity. Then he got four of his relatives to assist him in guarding the building from assault during Monday night. While there watching, the other Indians came, in groups of from five to ten, and formed a circle around the buildin[g]; thinks they intended to kill himself and his four relatives, and then attack the whites. He and his friends watched there till about daybreak, when they heard a gun near the warehouses, and about a mile further down; then another, and another, and then a general yell from the Indians, as they broke into the stores. Upon this the Indians who were sitting around watching him and his companions ran off to the warehouses, to participate in the booty, and his four friends followed them. Then he called to the whites inside to harness their horses and put off. They soon had five wagons ready, in which they put about fifty men, women, and children, and they started to cross the river a little before daybreak. After they had crossed the river and ascended the bluff on the opposite side, there was a general rush for the Agency. They were five days and four nights on the journey from Yellow Medicine to Shakopee.

Just before they started for the Agency in their wagons, Muzza-moni [Mazamani], a chief of the Wakpeton bands, came to them. He (Other-Day) asked Muzza-moni if all the civilized, or farmer Indians, were engaged in the fracas. Muzza-moni replied that only a part of them were in it. Most of those composing the Hazlewood Republic had gone to guard Mr. Riggs, their old Missionary, and were now in and around his house for that purpose. They had made up their minds to guard Mr. Riggs at all hazards. A few days before they had been furnished with powder and lead, and he thought they would defend him. He then asked Muzza-moni what had become of Dr. Williamson. Muzza-moni said that a party of Indians, probably Yanktons, were encamped near the Doctor's house; that at dark of Monday evening they rushed to his house, plundered it, and took his horses. The

Doctor and his family ran into the bushes. As the bushes and woods extended to Mr. Riggs' house, Other-Day thinks that perhaps Dr. Williamson and family have got safely to Mr. Riggs' house. There was a young woman residing in Williamson's family — a half-breed daughter of Andrew Bobinson [Robertson] — whom the Indians found in the bushes and took away, as they said she was a relative of theirs. Then he asked Muzza-moni if they had killed the half-breeds. Muzza-moni said no; they had made prisoners of them; did not know what they intended to do with them. After hearing this he came off.

In answer to miscellaneous questions by the Governor, Other-Day said that Muzza[-]moni urged him to do all he could to save the whites; that he could do nothing whatever with the Indians.

He brought away from the Agency all the whites but a few whom he could not reach — two sawyers and a woman, three clerks in Louis Robert's warehouse, and one in each of the other warehouses. There were two other warehouses, the clerks of which had locked the doors and run off in the night. Don't know what become of them.

Just as they had harnessed the horses one of the traders came to them wounded with a charge of shot in his abdomen. They brought him along with them until they came to a female nurse to whose care they left him. (This was, probably, Gavin [Garvie], who died at Cedar Creek.) He said that Jo. Brown's family, afraid of being seen if they went away in wagons, made their escape in small canoes, and floated down the river in the night, stopping at Red Wood on the way. He saw a brother of Jo. Brown who told him they had arrived safely at the Fort.[27]

In reference to the Indians engaged in the outbreak, he says that there is a stream half way between Yellow Medicine and Lacqui Parle. The Indians above that stream knew nothing of the fracas, and were not in any manner connected with it.

The chiefs who participated in the council at Yellow Medicine were as follows: The chief of Old Sleepy-Eye's band, the Lean Bear, White Lodge, the son of Lim[p]ing Devil, and Blue Face.[28] The above are Sissetons, and urged the killing of the whites.

The following are the Wappetons who opposed this advice: Muzza[-]moni; the Gun, or Walking-runner [Inyangmani], father-in-law of Little Crow; Akipa; Root-of-the-Horn; Eneehan [Inihan]; Makpi-o-Chasta; and [Simon] Anah-ungomin [Anawangmani], one of the members of the Hazlewood Republic, who has been one of its Presidents.[29]

The only reason given by the Sissetons for killing the whites, was that already stated — that the outrages at the Lower Agency would make them implacable enemies, that all the Indians would suffer for it, and that it would be no worse if they killed the whites.

Before the fracas occurred, a war party of Sioux went out from the country above Yellow Medicine against the Chippewas. They knew nothing of this affair before they went, and had not come back when it occurred.

A few days ago a panic occurred in McLeod county, from its being reported that Indian tracks were seen near Hutchinson. Other-Day says in explanation of this, that a party of ten Indian hunters went from the Lower Agency in that direction before the outbreak, and had just returned. He thinks they had no hostile intentions.

Other-Day thinks there was no preconcert in the outbreak. He had been generally present in their councils, but never heard such a thing hinted. There was no preparation at the Upper Agency at the time of the outbreak — none of the usual preparations for going to war.

The following part of Other-Day's narrative is of the utmost importance.

He says that the whole mischief began with four young men of Little Six's band, who went out from the Lower Agency, and on Sunday murdered six white people — (doubtless the six persons killed at Acton, Meeker county.)

He says that Susinaki, a young man of the Wakpeton band, of Yellow Medicine, had been down to the Lower Agency and was there when the outbreak occurred, and when he came back related to Other-Day what follows:[30]

When the four young men of Little Six's band had committed the murders above mentioned, they came back to Red Wood and made known what they had done.

In a short time the greatest excitement prevailed, and the Indians present, consisting of Little Six's, Little Crow's, Grey Iron's, and Good Road's bands, and a part of part of [sic] the Lake Calhoun band, gathered around and crowded into the warehouses. At this juncture Wabashaw, who lives about a mile from Redwood, came in, and surprised at the excitement asked, "What is all this about?" They replied that they heard the Chippeways were on the other side of the river, and were making preparations to meet them. At this instant a gun was fired, and a general rush was made for the warehouses.

Susinaki told him that Wabashaw's, Wacouta's, Red Leg's [sic], and a part of the Lake Calhoun band were absent at the the [sic] time of the outbreak, and did not participate in it, though he thinks it propable [sic] they came in afterward to share the spoils.

The above narrative, which is given in nearly the words of the interpreter, Rev. G[ideon] H. Pond, is a plain and evidently truthful recital of what came within the narrator's observation and hearing, and throws great light on the origin and extent of the disturbance.

He said that the white men collected at the Agency with their families during the night of Monday, behaved very coolly and bravely. They said that these were their wives and children, and they would die in their defense.

On the journey down some of the party seemed to be suspicious of him. Sinks only seemed to have entire confidence in him. He felt very sad at this. He would say something occasionally to reassure them. His wife would interpret it, and that seemed to make them more cheerful.

He also said that a party of 200 whites on horseback would be sufficient to go by the way of Kandiyohi Lakes — get on the other side of the Indians at Fort Ripley and in conjunction with a force operating on this side cut them off. He, himself, would undertake to guide them, and thought that it was perfectly feasible for such a force to go to Yellow Medicine and rescue the missionaries, if alive. He said the Plain[s] Indians had mostly gone west, with their wives and families, and that they knew nothing of the outbreak, and that it would take some time to gather them in.

NOTES

1. Samuel J. Brown, "Biographical Sketch of Chief Gabriel Renville," *Minnesota Collections* 10 (1905): 614–18.

2. G. Stowe Fish, ed., *Stowe's Clerical Directory of the American Church, 1926–27* (Minneapolis: The Editor, 1927), 270; U.S. Congress, *Sisseton and Wahpeton Sioux Indians*, 44th Cong., 1st sess., 1875, H. Doc. 42 (Serial 1687), 4; *The Living Church Annual: The Churchman's Year Book and American Church Almanac, 1929* (Milwaukee: Morehouse Publishing Co., 1929), 599.

3. For more on Solomon Two Stars, see his narrative in Chapter IX, p. 241, below.

4. Inyangmani or Running Walker was a Wahpeton leader at Lac qui Parle, 1830–54, when he moved with his band to a site a short distance above the mouth of

the Yellow Medicine River. Four of his daughters were wives of Little Crow; Anderson, *Little Crow*, 40–41, 42, 79, 86, 91, 186, 187.

5. For more on Ecetukiya, see his narrative in Chapter VIII, p. 199, below. Wasuhowaste or Enos Good Voiced Hail endorsed efforts to free captives and opposed the warriors. He was one of the first Dakota scouts and was with the Sibley expedition of 1863 when he was killed in mid-October near Fort Ridgely. His family was awarded $250 for his efforts in rescuing whites during the war. See *St. Paul Daily Press*, October 28, 1863, p. 2; U.S. Office of Indian Affairs, *Report, 1866*, 238.

6. [Return I. Holcombe], *Sketches Historical and Descriptive of the Monuments and Tablets Erected by the Minnesota Valley Historical Society* (Morton, Minn.: Minnesota Valley Historical Society, 1902), 68–71; *St. Peter Tribune*, August 31, 1910.

7. Scottish-born Stewart B. Garvie was thirty-one years old in 1862 when he was the agent for traders Nathan and Andrew J. Myrick at the Redwood and Yellow Medicine agencies. He was shot in the stomach on the evening of August 19 at his store near the Yellow Medicine Agency. Escaping, he sought refuge with friendly Dakotas and then accompanied the party of refugees led by John Otherday. He died of his wounds at Cedar Lake, about a dozen miles west of Hutchinson on August 22; Rose, *History of Yellow Medicine County*, 55, 59; Rebecca Almond, Diary, August 22, 23, 1862, Division of Libraries and Archives, Minnesota Historical Society; U.S. Census, 1860, Yellow Medicine Township, Brown County, roll 567, p. 246.

8. Peter Patoile, clerk and nephew of trader François Patoile at the Yellow Medicine Agency, was wounded but escaped. He later served on Sibley's expedition of 1863. See Bryant and Murch, *Great Massacre by the Sioux Indians*, 117–20.

9. Dr. John L. Wakefield, physician at the Yellow Medicine Agency, 1861–62, returned to Shakopee after the war. He died there in February 1874; Upham and Dunlap, *Minnesota Biographies*, 816.

10. Noah Sinks, a native of Ohio, arrived in Minnesota in 1857 and engaged in steamboating until 1861 when he was hired to supervise the government warehouses at both agencies. Sinks worked on the claims arising from the war until 1864 when he returned to the steamboat business. He died in St. Paul in November 1901; *St. Paul Pioneer Press*, November 24, 1901.

11. Duncan R. Kennedy and J. D. Boardman worked in a trader's store at the Yellow Medicine Agency. Kennedy moved from his native Canada to Minnesota in 1849 at the age of twenty-six and entered the fur trade at Traverse des Sioux. During the war he fled to St. Peter, met Sibley's army, and served as a courier. In about 1876 he joined the Black Hills gold rush and was still there in 1906. See Harpole and Nagle, eds., *Minnesota Territorial Census, 1850*, 10; Hughes, *Old Traverse des Sioux*, 155–57; Duncan R. Kennedy, "Narrative," in Bryant and Murch, *Great Massacre by the Sioux Indians*, 376–79; *St. Peter Herald*, March 30, 1906. Boardman fled the Yellow Medicine Agency in the group led by John Otherday. The editors have found no further information on him; Rose, *History of Yellow Medicine County*, 57.

12. The editors have found no further information on Marpioicarmani.

13. Satterlee, *Court Proceedings*, 13–14, 44–46; Transcripts of Trials of Sioux Indians, cases no. 8 and 136, Senate Records 37A-F2; E. A. Bromley, "He Was Gen. Sibley's Chief of Scouts," *Minneapolis Times*, May 8, 1901; Kappler, comp. and ed., *Indian Treaties*, 2:959; Anderson, *Little Crow*, 98, 190, 192, 227; U.S. Congress, *Sisseton and Wahpeton Sioux Indians*, 44th Cong., 1st sess., 1875, H. Doc. 42, p. 4; Moses N. Adams, John P. Williamson, and John B. Renville, *The First Fifty Years, Dakota Presbytery to 1890* (Good Will, So.Dak.: The Presbytery, 1892; reprinted, Freeman, So.Dak.: The Presbytery, 1984), Appendix, xiv; Chilson, "Dakota Indian Scout Roster."

14. Haponduta or Hepanduta or Scarlet Second-Born Son was tried, convicted, and sentenced to be hanged for participation in the war after admitting being at the

battles at Birch Coulee and Wood Lake. He received a reprieve and was at the Davenport, Iowa, prison camp, 1863–66, when he was pardoned, released, and taken to the Santee Reservation. He was then sixty-three years old and appears to have lived the rest of his life on this reservation; Transcripts of Trials of Sioux Indians, case no. 94, Senate Records 37A-F2; Satterlee, *Detailed Account*, 127; Satterlee, *Court Proceedings*, Appendix, 4.

15. Mazamani or Iron Walker was born in about 1820; he was Akipa's younger brother. He led a small band of Wahpetons from the mid-1850s and signed the Treaty of 1858. He was prominent in the peace party and opposed the war. Accidentally wounded at the battle at Wood Lake, he died in late September 1862; Anderson, *Little Crow*, 98, 190; Kappler, comp. and ed., *Indian Treaties*, 2:788; *West Central Tribune* (Willmar), September 25, 1984, p. 1.

16. Supehiye aided in the defense of the Yellow Medicine Agency. After spending the winter of 1862–63 in the Dakota camp at Fort Snelling, he was an Indian scout in 1864–66. He settled on the Sisseton Reservation in 1867 and signed the Treaties of 1867 and 1872; Chilson, "Dakota Indian Scout Roster"; U.S. Office of Indian Affairs, *Report, 1863*, 434; Kappler, comp. and ed., *Indian Treaties*, 2:959, 1059.

17. The editors have found no further information on Padanipapa.

18. Thomas A. Robertson was the interpreter for the remainder of the narrative.

19. Bogaga was a member of Shakopee's Mdewakanton band. He was charged with participation in the battles of Fort Ridgely, New Ulm, and Wood Lake. He admitted being at Fort Ridgely and Birch Coulee and was tried, convicted, and sentenced to be hanged. Receiving a reprieve, he went to the prison camp at Davenport in the spring of 1863 and may have died there or have been pardoned prior to 1866; Transcripts of Trials of Sioux Indians, case no. 106, Senate Records 37A-F2.

20. Waxicanmaza signed the Treaty of Traverse des Sioux in 1851 and the Treaties of 1867 and 1872. He served as an Indian scout in 1865 and received land on the Sisseton Reservation, where he died in 1883; Kappler, comp. and ed., *Indian Treaties*, 2:590, 959, 1059; Chilson, "Dakota Indian Scout Roster"; U.S. Congress, *Sisseton and Wahpeton Sioux Indians*, 44th Cong., 1st sess., 1875, H. Doc. 42, p. 13.

21. In subsequent testimony Crawford identified La Rock as Henry La Roche and Pehankena as a Frenchman named Fornier; Crawford, "Evidence for the Claimants," 173. The editors have found no further information on either man.

22. Evidently Elizabeth Jeffries, Angelique Quinn, and her children, Ellen, William, and Thomas, were captured. It is known that while the warriors were at the battle of Wood Lake, the two women and three children as well as the widow of Philander Prescott and her daughter Julia escaped from the Indian camp and made their way to Fort Ridgely. See [Holcombe], *Sketches Historical and Descriptive*, 58; Satterlee, *Detailed Account*, 96.

23. Thomas Crawford was born in about 1844 at Lac qui Parle and educated in mission schools there and at Hazelwood. He aided in the defense of the Yellow Medicine Agency and opposed the war. Later he served as a scout in the Sibley expedition of 1863. He settled on the Sisseton Reservation by 1867, received land in 1875, and spent the remainder of his life there; Anderson, *Little Crow*, 190, 192; U.S. Congress, *Sisseton and Wahpeton Sioux Indians*, 44th Cong., 1st sess., 1875, H. Doc. 42, p. 4. Hanyokinyan appears to have been a Wahpeton. He aided in the defense of the Yellow Medicine Agency and opposed the war. In 1863 he was chosen as an Indian scout, continuing until 1866. Then he settled on the Sisseton Reservation. See Chilson, "Dakota Indian Scout Roster." The editors have found no further information on Hintacan.

24. Daniel Renville, born in about 1840, was the son of Joseph Renville, Jr., first cousin of Gabriel Renville. He was educated at mission schools, ordained a Presbyterian minister in 1870, and served churches in the Dakota Presbytery; Adams, Williamson, and Renville, *First Fifty Years*, Appendix, xiv.

25. Inihan or Excited was a Sisseton, but he led a small band of farmer Wahpetons, who lived about two miles north of the Yellow Medicine Agency. He aided the peace party, served as a scout, 1863–65, and then settled on the Sisseton Reservation where he lived out the rest of his life. He signed the Treaties of 1872 and 1873; Solomon Two Stars, "Evidence for the Claimants," *Sisseton and Wahpeton Bands . . . v. the United States*, U.S. Court of Claims no. 22524, part 1, p. 86; U.S. Congress, *Sisseton and Wahpeton Sioux Indians*, 44th Cong., 1st sess., 1875, H. Doc. 42, p. 11; Kappler, comp. and ed., *Indian Treaties*, 2:1059, 1062.

26. Henry H. Sibley, "Narrative of John Otherday," *Minnesota Collections* 3 (1880): 99–102; "Death of John Otherday," *St. Paul Daily Pioneer*, November 7, 1869, p. 4.

27. The report of the Brown family's escape to Fort Ridgely is a good example of the erroneous and conflicting statements that circulated during the confusing early days of the war.

28. White Lodge led a portion of Sleepy Eye's band from 1859 onward. In 1857 after the Spirit Lake massacre he pursued Inkpaduta for the government. He led his band in attacks on settlers at Lake Shetek in August 1862 and took white captives westward to the Missouri River. When the army appeared he fled to Canada and died near Swift Current, Saskatchewan, in about 1870; Doane Robinson, "White Lodge," in *Handbook of American Indians North of Mexico*, ed. Frederick W. Hodge, Smithsonian Institution, Bureau of American Ethnology Bulletin no. 30 (Washington, D.C.: Government Printing Office, 1912), part 2, p. 945. Lean Bear was killed at Lake Shetak in August 1862; Solomon Two Stars, "Evidence for the Claimants," *Sisseton and Wahpeton Bands . . . v. the United States*, U.S. Court of Claims no. 22524, part 1, p. 91. The editors have found no further information on Blue Face.

29. Simon Anawangmani or He Who Goes Galloping Along, a Wahpeton, was born in about 1808. He signed the Treaty of Traverse des Sioux in 1851. A student at Williamson's Lac qui Parle mission school, he was the first Dakota man to become a Christian convert. He was an elder in the Hazelwood Church, 1854–63, and prominent in the Hazelwood Republic. He and others protected the missionaries in August. He took a captive woman, Mrs. Neuman, and her three children to Fort Ridgely and then joined Colonel Sibley's army as a scout, serving until 1865. The Dakota Presbytery licensed him to preach in July 1866. He signed the Treaty of 1873 and received land on the Sisseton Reservation in 1875. He died at the Sisseton Agency in the summer of 1891; Adams, Williamson, and Renville, *First Fifty Years*, 15; John P. Williamson, "Simon Anawangmani," *Iapi Oaye (The Word Carrier)* 20 (December 1891): 1; Satterlee, *Detailed Account*, 96; [Holcombe], *Sketches Historical and Descriptive*, 59–61; Kappler, comp. and ed., *Indian Treaties*, 2:589, 1062; U.S. Congress, *Sisseton and Wahpeton Sioux Indians*, 44th Cong., 1st sess., 1875, H. Doc. 42, p. 22.

30. The editors have found no further information on Susinaki.

CHAPTER VI

The Gathering at
Little Crow's Village

DURING the first few days of the war, the sense of organization that seemed apparent in the attack on the Redwood Agency broke down. Small war parties, commanded by members of the soldiers' lodge, went in every direction, carrying death and destruction into the countryside. While Dakota warriors raided along both sides of the Minnesota River, a village formed around Little Crow's house. It soon contained several thousand people, including more than three hundred mixed-blood and white captives. The village quickly became the command center of the war, the Dakotas staying at that location until August 25.

White captives, all women and children, left more than a dozen vivid accounts of the threats, uncertainty, disorientation, and occasional mistreatment they experienced in Little Crow's camp. Mixed-bloods, and even some full-bloods, often faced the same problems that white captives did. Many left accounts of life in the camp that provide rich source material for understanding the racial dynamics of the war.

Of the five narratives that follow, four were recorded by mixed-bloods. Almost all of them reveal the fear that entire families would be killed, and most give evidence of the major roles full-bloods played in saving the lives of their mixed-blood relatives. The one narrative from a full-blood, a woman, shows that some Indians felt great compassion for the white captives brought into Little Crow's camp. Indeed, Snana, the author, saved a German girl by adopting her.

Narrative 1
SAMUEL J. BROWN'S RECOLLECTIONS

For biographical information on Samuel J. Brown, see Chapter IV, Narrative 1.

AS SOON as we got into the house the good Indian woman hurried us up stairs out of the way, and got something to eat for us. We had not eaten a mouthful all day, and the children particularly were over-joyed when supper was announced, after which and as soon as we had donned the Indian dress — the leggins and blankets — which had been given to Angus and I, two of Little Crow's head warriors who happened in advised mother to send her sons to the Chief's camp. Fearing treachery she at first demurred, but finally consented and Angus and I and the two Indians started for Little Crow's camp, three or four miles down the river. Our mission was to call upon the chief and deliver to him a message from mother. The mission was a delicate one, for we did not know what would be our fate, Little Crow being regarded as a very dangerous man. We arrived at the camp sometime after dark. It was all excitement — singing, dancing, shouting, yelling and the beating of the tomtom. We walked through the crowd and into the chief's house unnoticed by the rabble. Little Crow was in his own house and the great camp was pitched around it — number[ing] some 250 or 300 lodges.

We found the chief at home, with his three [four] Indian wives and five white women that he was keeping.[1] He greeted us very cordially and at once asked about mother, and gave us a blanket apiece and told us to go after her immediately, for he wanted to see that she was properly cared for — made comfortable. He ordered one of his head warriors to return with us.

Of course we were delighted over the success of our mission. Mother was afraid we might be killed, but now we had good news for her. We hurried back and hitched up the oxen and all got into the wagon and started for [Little] Crow's camp. It was now very dark, but we had no difficulty in keeping the road. We were constantly meeting Indians who were returning from the attacks on New Ulm and Fort Ridgely. They would stop and peer at us through the darkness and act threateningly, but after an explanation by the warrior who was our guide we would be permitted to pass on. But on one occasion our lives were in imminent danger. We met a party of drunken Indians who wanted to kill us, and our friend, the warrior-guide, interceded and saved our lives. Upon telling them who we were and that Little Crow had sent for mother and that he would defend his charge with his life, if necessary, they sobered up and let us go.

We finally reached the camp, which was in a perfect uproar as before, and all got out of the wagon and proceeded in Indian file through the camp to the chief's house, which we reached at about 10 o'clock at night.

When mother entered[,] the chief arose from his couch and stepped up and greeted her very cordially, and then handed her a cup of cold water and told to [sic] her [to] drink, saying that she was his prisoner now. We were all hurried up stairs and told to remain quiet. The chief gave us robes and blankets and told us to lie down and go to sleep. He would sneak up stairs and ask mother (in a whisper) if she was comfortable, how the children were, etc. He was anxious to get into conversation with her, and finally said to her that he wanted her to know all about the troubles that have so suddenly come upon his people, and he wanted to tell her about it. He said in substance that his young men had started to massacre; that he at first opposed the movement with all his might, but when he saw he could not stop it he joined them in their madness against his better judgment, but now did not regret it and was never more in earnest in his life; that the plan was for the Winnebago Indians to sweep down the Minnesota river from Mankato to St. Paul[,] the Chippewa Indians down the Mississippi from Crow Wing to St. Paul, and the lower Sioux down between the two rivers from lower agency through the big woods at St. Paul; that all would meet in the neighborhood of the confluence of the two rivers and make a grand charge on Fort Snelling; that this was a stone fort and might take a day or two to batter the walls down.

The chief was very kind to us, and assured us that we would not be harmed, that he would take as good care of up [us] as he would if we were members of his own family.

The wily old fellow! He was working for the aid and support of the Upper Sioux. He knew of mother's influence over Standing Buffalo, Waanatan, Scarlet Plume, Sweet Corn[,] Red Iron, A-kee-pah, and other influential Sisseton and Wahpeton chiefs. He was afraid, he said once, that he could not keep Blair alive until morning, that the young men outside were bloodthirsty and desperate, and should they learn that a white man was in camp there was no telling what might happen.

The chief got some vermillion and daubed Blair's face with the red paint, and gave him a new red Mackanac blanket and a pair of red leggins, and pulled off his own moccasins and put them on Blair's feet, and then cautioned us to remain quiet, as bad Indians were near by, and then went back down stairs.

About midnight someone came to see Little Crow. He told the chief that it was rumored about camp that a white man and some strangers were in the house, — that the warriors were very angry about it, and he wanted to know if there was any foundation to the rumor. When told that there was, and that we were Sisseton mixed bloods and his friends, the man got very angry and insisted that we should all be killed at once. He said that no prisoners ought to be taken — that the Sissetons were a different people and had no claim whatever on the Lower Sioux and the mixed bloods of that tribe are no better than white people, and should be treated the same as the whites.

He wanted Little Crow to call a council at once. But the chief told the man that we were his friends, that Standing Buffalo, Scarlet Plume, Ah-kee-pah, and Sweet Corn were his friends, and he would protect us, that it was too late for a council that night, and then compelled the man to leave.

As soon as the man had gone away, Little Crow came quietly upstairs and told mother that he had just had a stormy interview with his (Crow's) private secretary, that the secretary had just left the house in a very angry mood. We had heard through a stove pipe hole all that had been said, so that we were prepared. Mother and Little Crow talked over the matter, and they both agreed that not only was Blair's life in danger, but the lives of all of us, including that of Little Crow himself. The only hope was to get Blair away — send him off in the dark. My mother and Mrs. [Lydia Brown] Blair resolved to do this. They at once went to work to get him ready. They gave him what crackers they had, and Little Crow gave him a shawl to wrap around his head, and then summoned his head warrior and instructed him to lead Blair down stairs and out through the camp, and down through the woods to the river bank — a few hundred yards back of the house — and leave him there to make his escape as best he could. Little Crow said to Mrs. Blair: "I have known your mother for many years. She is a good woman, and in sending your husband away I am risking my life for her and for you all to-night. Be brave, your husband shall live."

After a sad farewell, Blair was taken away. He was dressed in full Indian costume.

Fort Ridgely was but about fifteen miles away, and yet the poor fellow was seven days getting to it. He was a consumptive and could not stand any hardships. He forded the Minnesota river a few minutes after the Indian had left him and crawled into a thicket where he remained until the next night. He then traveled until exhausted from hunger and fatigue. He lay in the tall grass on the flats opposite the Lower Agency, near the road. Indians on the warpath were constantly passing and he could not go on. Finally becoming crazed with hunger and from sheer desperation, and after five days and six nights of hiding, he got up at daybreak one morning and staggered out to the road and started out for the fort, about ten miles distant, which he reached after the lapse of seven days and eight nights from the time he left Little Crow's house.

The exposure was too much for his naturally weak frame and he kept sinking until February following, when at Henderson with his wife and children around him, death claimed [him] as a victim.

It has been said that upon Blair's arrival at the fort he was terribly emaciated, weak, and hardly able to walk or to speak; that he could only mutter a few words and that with difficulty and incoherently; that upon learning that he was a son-in-law of Major Brown, and because he was dressed in full Indian costume and had his face painted — a la Sioux brave — he was looked upon with suspicion and placed under arrest, as a spy; that he was kept in durance vile until the arrival of Gen. [Colonel] Sibley, who ordered his release instanter, and severely reprimanded the commanding officer. In justice to Col. [Lieutenant] Tom [Timothy] Sheehan, who was then, I believe, the officer in command at the fort, I will say that he denies this story in toto.

We passed a miserable night, did not sleep a wink. We were afraid that we might be attacked and massacred, that we might at any moment be fired upon by the half crazed Indians outside. The night passed, however, without any attempt to take our lives.

The next morning (Wednesday, the 20th) old Aunt Judy (Hazatonwin) a good old Indian woman whom we had known for many years, and who was now the mother-in-law of Little Crow's head warrior, came to the house and took us away. She took us to her daughter's teepee or lodge, near by, and gave us something to eat. She kept us there and took as good care of us as she could. I shall never forget the crackers and molasses she used to feed us on. We had all we wanted. She would never let us go hungry. She was always asking about our comfort — was afraid mischievous Indians might attempt to scare us or drunken Indians might shoot us. She got her son-in-law to guard us at night.

One evening as my sister (Mrs. Blair) had just been frying hard bread or crackers, and had just put away the frying pan half filled with hot grease near the doorway or entrance to the lodge, when a drunken Indian came in and squatted there. He made insulting remarks and then turned to go out, and as he did so accidentally placed his hand in the hot pan of grease. With a yell of pain he rushed out and disappeared in the darkness. He never came back.

On Saturday, the 23rd, Ah-kee-pah arrived from Yellow Medicine. He had heard that Little Crow held us captives, and had come back to take us away — to take us back to Yellow Medicine, where our relatives and friends were living. Soon after his arrival one of Little Crow's warriors taunted the Wahpeton chief with cowardice, saying, among other things, that [he] (Ah-kee-pah) had not so much as killed one white man — not even a babe. He stepped in the midst of the crowd that had gathered around him and made a speech that opened their eyes. He declared that there was no bravery in killing helpless men and women and little children, but that it was simply cowardice, and cowards would only boast of it — that if he had found that any of his relatives had been harmed he would have gone about tomahawking the whole camp, "slaughtering the braves (?) like slaughtering a lot of beaver on dry land." He said, "when the sun arose that was to witness the horrors of an indiscriminate massacre of the whites in the valley of the Minnesota, regardless of age or sex, by the lower Sioux, the upper bands were peacefully attending to their crops on their own reservation, or hunting the buffalo on the distant prairies, the report of that day's work reached our ears in a more astounding tone than that of the voice of the Great Spirit issuing from the 'dark clouds of the west.' "

The next morning, on Sunday, the 24th, we left Little Crow's camp and started for Yellow Medicine, Ah-kee-pah putting us all into one wagon and driving, his head soldier armed to the teeth and on horseback accompanying us. We were now in the hands of our relatives and friends and felt safe.

Near the Redwood river we saw the dead body of poor George Gleason (whom we had seen but a few days before,) lying in the road with a stone imbedded in his skull. We saw no other dead bodies near or in fact between that and the upper agency.

It appears that when Mr. Gleason and Mrs. Wakefield came along they met some Indians who shot the man and took the woman prisoner.

We reached Yellow Medicine that afternoon and at once moved into one of the vacated agency buildings, the residence of Dr. Wakefield, and remained there until Thursday, the 28th, when Little Crow's whole camp moved up from the Lower Agency. They passed by and ordered us to follow them, which we did. We moved up and located our camp near a creek west of the Hazlewood mission station, lately vacated by Rev. S. R. Riggs. The Upper Indians made this their camping ground, while the Lower Indians pitched their camp on the opposite side of the creek, the two camps being about a mile apart.

Continued on page 169.

Narrative 2
CECELIA CAMPBELL STAY'S ACCOUNT

For biographical information on Cecelia Campbell Stay, see Chapter III, Narrative 1.

Narrative Source: Cecelia Campbell Stay, Interview, in Alexander Seifert, "Notes of Committee Selecting Historical Data from New Ulm, Minn.," August 5–6, 1924, typescript, Sioux Uprising Collection, Division of Libraries and Archives, Minnesota Historical Society.

THE NEXT MORNING [August 19] orders came that Little Crow wanted everyone to move into his Village—they had to be in one camp. So we went up there, and this was then, Tuesday morning, and we seen the Indians trotting around, always going to the west it seemed. They had small pails about so high (indicating) and square, about 8 x 12 inches, in which they had all kinds of ropes; they was all wrapped around it, with a handle so that you could carry it. And mother had told us, "You finish up here and you will get some Pole Dashes[?].["] Mrs. Finley's brother, why, he says, ["]you are going to have some Tadoo [potato?] Soup,".[2] "Yes," they said, but they don't seem to be very proud of it; and I am not sure, but it looked as though they were having scalps there. I didn't know for sure, but that is the way it lokked [sic] to me. It was Tuesday we moved in there [Little Crow's village] and mother was not satisfied to stay where she was; she was not well enough off. She told father, she didn't want to go to Littlee [sic] Crow's village, and didn't like to stay in a teepee; she would rather live in a house, she says. He said, "you are better off here with Passing Hail to stay here, he says, he is the best friend we have got, he and his band. You know where you are well off, you can go and see that it won't be safe anywheres for you.["] So we went up there and one of them came and put on an Indian dress, and he took off her white clothes. When they took my sister, Emily, and they changed her and she cried like a whild [child] while they were dressing her, and mother says, "that is all right; that is just as right to live in a teepee, you won't get your clothes soiled." And so pretty soon they came, all ragged. Then one of Little Crow's wives ran in the hut and we heard Little Chief [?] say: "All the beasts that there are here, stay right here." "Somebody talking mean." (Little Crow was not there just then). So mother turned around to see if we were all gone, and she missed my oldest child (sister) Emily. "Why," she says, ["]where is Emily?" I Says, "didn't you see Little Crow's wife keep her back, She was going to stand outside. I seen her standing outside in the yard with her,["] and she said, "I will save Emily anyway". [Little Crow's wife probably believed that all Campbell family members were to be killed.] Emily has the name Wee-noon-nah [Winona]. And mother says, "did she [Little Crow's wife] say that?" She says, "Yes." "Don't look good to me," Mother says, ["]we will all be butchered.["] . . .

Just then Little Crow's soldier came around the house, and he said, "what is all this about?"[3] And he had a hatchet on his arm, like this (indicating), and he kept it pointing that way (indicating), that we recognized where he came from. So then he waited a while, and then he swung the hatchet this way (indicating) and said: "If any of our men," he says, "come one here, I see if you hurt any of my relatives, or not." And he says, "You will lie on the ground if you hurt a one." And so it was all quiet. And mother told them, ["]you go to him, he is the one who saved us", and he put his arm around her and she cried. She is the only one that felt like crying. Mother says, "Let us go back to your father". Father says, "Old Woman, you are going to stay over there in the house", and she didn't say anything. "No," I said, "we don't want to stay in no house, rather than go over there."

"How did they receive you?" she says. So we youngsters told them all about it. So he says, "yesterday morning he was caught right in his bed." He was to die at daylight, or leave. And so they made him the black sheep. He said, "he would rather have us alive in his bed, than to die at daylight." And we never offered to go back to Little Crow's anymore. But at the same time Little Crow did some good things, for he saved Charley Blaire, Major Brown's son-in-law. He gave him a blanket — and I had a letter here this spring from Allenson [George G. Allanson], and he said he had been down with his mother, that is Lois [Ellen] Brown, and she showed him the ravine where Little Crow had taken this Charles Blaire to go down to save his life.[4] And he happened to be the first one, I guess, to die at Ft. Ridgely. The first cannon that was shot, was intended for him, and he died. . . .

Then we stayed there a few days [at Little Crow's village], through the battles, you see, at New Ulm, two battles, at Ridgely. After those battles some of the men that left the Fort and came back to us. These were the happy Indians, and they came back and they were the ones that told us that the Fort was not taken. And we saw that column of smoke which went just straight and just as high as from those big pipes you see in the cities — right straight up in the air. Grandmother says, "Our friends are all gone in the Fort. The Fort must be burning up." And then these fellows come in by Sundown and said, "No, it was not taken; but that they were burning some buildings there."

We settled there and then we moved up, and we moved up and settled down here [the Yellow Medicine Agency] and made them all camp into one big circle, on this [north] side of the Yellow Medicine River. Close by the Yellow Medicine River, there is a flat prairie there, and there was a big field of potatoes. Here they camped . . . on the side of the Yellow Medicine River, and we helped ourselves to the potatoes. The patch was just as you go up the bluff this way (indicating) there was one building right on that side of that field, and that is the field where the big potatoes patch was, and we lived on them potatoes during the time that we were there. We were at this place until after the Birch Coulee siege, which was Sept. 2nd, I think — the Birch Coulee Siege, and in not a great while after that, we moved up and we came up to here, what they call Hazel Run, or Hazelwood. We camped there. While there Standing Buffalo came down, I suppose, to look into matters, I don't know what. He was against their outbreak. He was from the Upper Agencu [Agency] and he wanted that we should quit them all and go with them up to the Upper Agency [Indians].

Continued on page 249.

Narrative 3
NANCY McCLURE FARIBAULT HUGGAN'S ACCOUNT

For biographical information on Nancy McClure Faribault Huggan, see Chapter IV, Narrative 2.

THE NEXT DAY [August 20] the Indians under Little Crow went to attack Fort Ridgely. When they came back [to Little Crow's village] they reported that there were many half-breeds in the fort that fought against them, and shouted to them: "We will fix you, you devils; you will eat your children before winter." This made them very bitter against us, for they said we were worse than the whites, and that they were going to kill all of us. Most of them had whisky, and it was a dreadful time. Towards evening a heavy storm came up, and a thunderbolt struck and killed an Indian. Some one raised a cry, "They are killing the half-breeds now!" I caught up my child and ran. I saw my husband [David Faribault], with Alex Graham, running into Little Crow's corn field, and I saw him no more that night. An Indian woman went with me, and we did not stop until we got to Shakopee's camp, seven miles away. It was Indians, any way, the best I could do, and I had some distant relatives in that camp, and I would rather trust myself there than with Little Crow's drunken and infuriated warriors. My friends treated me very kindly—gave me a dry blanket and some dry clothes for my little girl, who was quite sick by this time. It was an awful night. Towards midnight the Indians brought in a lot of captive white women and children, who cried and prayed the rest of the night. How I felt for them, but of course I could not help them.

The next morning I left my child with my Indian friends and I and the woman who had come with me went back to Little Crow's camp to see what had become of my husband and how things were. No one had been killed except the Indian who was struck by lightning. To our surprise we found my husband in the camp, and my companion's husband sitting over him very drunk, and with a butcher knife in his hand! The woman took the knife from her husband, and all was quiet for a time. My husband said he came back soon after we left, and that the Indian had been following him and threatening to kill him all night.

The team of horses we let the white people have at our house took them safely to Fort Ridgely. Just outside the fort one of the horses dropped dead. The other was left on the prairie, and the Indians that attacked the fort caught it. I think it was the fourth day of the outbreak that I was strolling through Little Crow's camp, when I saw my horse "Jerry." I untied him and was leading him away when an Indian ran up and said: "Here, I captured that horse at the fort, and he is mine." I told him I did not care how he got him; he was mine, and I was going to take him. At last he allowed me to have him. I had that horse at Camp Release, and took him with me to Faribault, Minn. The funny part of this story is that this same Indian is living here, near Flandrau, now. About two years ago he wanted to borrow some money from one of the banks here and wanted me to go with him and recommend him to the bank. He said he thought I ought to go, as he let me take that horse!

Another day the cry was raised that the half-breeds were all to be killed. Little Crow held a council and would allow no Indians to attend it that had half-breed relatives. We thought this looked bad for us, and there were all sorts of alarming reports. Three young Indians came and sat by our camp and talked, and were heard to say that when the half-blood men were killed one of them should have me for his wife; I presume they meant the one that should murder my husband. A few minutes afterward my uncle, with three of his cousins, rode into the camp. My uncle's name was Rday-a-mannee (the Rattling Walker).[5] He was a very brave, good man, and had taken no part in the outbreak. To my great joy, he said he had come to take us away. When Little Crow heard this he came out and told my uncle that he would not allow any one to take away half-bloods from the camp, and if any one tried to he would order his warriors to kill him. How proud I was of my brave uncle when he made this reply: "Little Crow, I only want the people who belong to me, and I will take them. You think you are brave because you have killed so many white people. You have surprised them; they were not prepared for you, and you know it. When we used to fight the Chippewas you were all women; you would not fight. If I leave these people here you will worry them to death. Now, I am going to take my people, and I would like to see the man that will try to stop me!" With this we started, and some of the Indians raised the war-whoop. But we kept on, my uncle and his cousins riding in the rear, their guns in their hands, and Little Crow and his warriors looking sullenly but silently at us.

Continued on page 244.

Narrative 4
JOSEPH LA FRAMBOISE, JR.'S, TESTIMONY

For biographical information on Joseph La Framboise, Jr., see Chapter V, Narrative 3.

BEFORE this camp [located north of the Yellow Medicine River and set up on August 28] was formed and before the lower Indians had moved up there, it was reported that a brother of mine, Alexis La Framboise, who was down there near the lower agency, was in a house surrounded by the hostiles, and they were going to kill him.[6] Three of us went there and got him and started for the upper agency. Some of the Lower Sioux came up and tried to step [stop] us. They stood across the road ahead of us (my brother was in a buggy with his wife) and fired guns over our heads. When we got within hearing, they told us that all of them were going to move up that way, and that we should not go until they were ready to go. There were three of us and my brother, making four. He was a single-handed man — had only one hand. I turned around toward my brother and told him to whip the horses up and rush ahead, and, if possible, to knock that fellow down that was trying to stop us. There were about 10 of the party that were trying to stop us from coming up this way. He did as I told him to, whipped up the horses, and rushed up toward these men, and when they saw he was coming so fast they went aside and let him pass through. Then myself and these other two men, August Frenier and John Frenier, dropped behind the buggy, facing these other men, and backed away from them until we got beyond shooting distance, and then went on.[7] We met with no others on the way, and arrived at Yellow Medicine.

Continued on page 198.

Narrative 5
SNANA'S STORY

SNANA *or Tinkling or Maggie Brass was born at Mendota at the mouth of the Minnesota River in 1839. She and her mother, Barleycorn, belonged to the Kaposia band of Mdewakantons. She was educated at Dr. Williamson's mission school at Kaposia, 1849–52, and moved with her mother to the reservation in late 1853. The next year at the age of fifteen, she married Wakinyanwaste or Good Thunder. They had several children, but all died young. Both Snana and her husband joined the Episcopal mission church in 1861, being the first Dakotas to do so. They favored peace rather than war, and during the first few days of fighting, Snana purchased and protected a fourteen-year-old German girl, Mary Schwandt. Mary remained with Snana until being turned over to Colonel Sibley at Camp Release.*

After the war, Snana and her husband lived in the Dakota camp below Fort Snelling, where two of their children died. Good Thunder joined the Sibley expedition as a scout in the spring of 1863, and Snana went to live at Faribault. In about 1865 Snana separated from Good Thunder, and a few years later she moved to the Santee Reservation in Nebraska. There she married Charles Brass, a Dakota man, and lived with him until his death in 1894; they had one son and two adopted daughters. In that year, Return I. Holcombe edited and published Mary Schwandt Schmidt's narrative, which led to a reunion of the two women. Snana visited Mary in St. Paul, and the two friends kept in contact with each other. In 1901 Snana wrote her story in English for Holcombe, who edited and annotated it. She also testified for the defendants in the Sisseton and Wahpeton trials in 1901. Snana died on April 24, 1908.[8]

Narrative Source: Snana, "Narration of a Friendly Sioux," *Minnesota Collections* 9 (1901): 426–30.

AN INDIAN MAN whose name was Good Thunder then offered some special things to my mother for me to be his wife, which was, as we may say, legal marriage among the Indians. But I insisted that, if I were to marry, I would marry legally in church; so we did, and were married in the Protestant Episcopal church.

Some years after we got married, we were the first ones to enter the Christian life, which was in 1861. We were confirmed in the same church. On account of our becoming Christians we were ridiculed by the Indians who were not yet taught the gospel of Jesus and who could not yet understand what Christianity meant.

I want everybody to understand that what little education I have was taught me by the kind family of Dr. Williamson. It has been of very great use to me all through my life; and it led me from the darkness of superstition to the light of Christianity in those dark days among my people.

Then came the dreadful outbreak of 1862. About eight days before the massacre, my oldest daughter had died, and hence my heart was

SNANA *in about 1860*

still aching when the outbreak occurred. Two of my uncles went out to see the outbreak, and I told them that if they should happen to see any girl I wished them not to hurt her but bring her to me that I might keep her for a length of time. One evening one of my uncles came to me and said that he had not found any girl, but that there was a young man who brought a nice looking girl. I asked my mother to go and bring this girl to me; and my uncle, having heard of our conversation, advised my mother that she ought to take something along with her in order to buy this girl. Hence I told her to take my pony with her, which she did.

When she brought this girl, whose name was Mary Schwandt, she was much larger than the one I had lost, who was only seven years old; but my heart was so sad that I was willing to take any girl at that time. The reason why I wished to keep this girl was to have her in place of the one I lost. So I loved her and pitied her, and she was dear to me just the same as my own daughter.

During the outbreak, when some of the Indians got killed, they began to kill some of the captives. At such times I always hid my dear captive white girl. At one time the Indians reported that one of the captives was shot down, and also that another one, at Shakopee's camp, had her throat cut; and I thought to myself that if they would kill my girl they must kill me first. Though I had two of my own chil-dren at that time with me, I thought of this girl just as much as of the others.

I made her dress in Indian style, thinking that the Indians would not touch her when dressed in Indian costume. I always went with her wherever she went, both in daytime and night. Good Thunder never helped me in any way to take care of this girl, but he always went with the men wherever they went. Only my mother helped me to take care of her; especially whenever she would wash, she always provided the soap and towel.

Continued on page 257.

NOTES

1. Three of these women were Urania S. Frazer White, Helen Mar Paddock Car-rothers, and Amanda M. Macomber Earle. The other two "women" were probably Julia White, then fourteen years old, and Julia Earle, then thirteen years old; Bryant

and Murch, *Great Massacre by the Sioux Indians*, 275–92; Helen M. [Carrothers] Tarble, *The Story of My Capture and Escape during the Indian Massacre of 1862* (St. Paul: Abbott Printing Co., 1904), 31–32; Mrs. N. D. [Urania S.] White, "Captivity among the Sioux, August 18 to September 26, 1862," *Minnesota Collections* 9 (1901): 403–4; "List of Captives," *St. Paul Pioneer*, October 3, 1862, p. 1; "The White Prisoners," *St. Peter Tribune*, October 10, 1862, p. 1.

2. Angelique Findley was the mixed-blood daughter of Louis Ogien and a Sisseton Dakota. Then thirty-four years old, she was the widow of Antoine F. Findley, a trader. During the war, she cared for twelve-year-old William A. Findley, her stepson; Harpole and Nagle, eds., *Minnesota Territorial Census, 1850*, 46; Statement of Samuel I. Findley, Roll of Mixed-Blood Claimants, 1856, Records of the Bureau of Indian Affairs, NARG 75.

3. This soldier may be Gray Bird or Zitkahtahhota, who was a member of Little Crow's band. By 1859 he had joined the Mdewakanton farmers band. When Little Crow assumed leadership of the war, he appointed Gray Bird as his head soldier or war leader; he was also the speaker for the soldiers' lodge. He was a leader at the battles at New Ulm and Birch Coulee. It is probable that he fled with Little Crow after the battle of Wood Lake as his name does not appear in the trial records; Anderson, *Little Crow*, 143; Mdewakanton and Wahpekute Annuity Rolls, 1849–1860, Records of the Bureau of Indian Affairs, NARG 75; Antoine J. Campbell, "Evidence for the Claimants," *Sisseton and Wahpeton Bands . . . v. the United States*, U.S. Court of Claims no. 22524, part 2, p. 257; Carley, *Sioux Uprising*, 43.

4. See George G. Allanson, *Stirring Adventures of the Jos. R. Brown Family* (Sacred Heart, Minn.: Sacred Heart News, [1930?]).

5. Rattling Walker or Rdayamani was the son of Mazakutemani or The Walking Shooting Iron (not Paul Mazakutemani). He was Nancy McClure's maternal uncle, and Nancy and her grandmother (her mother's mother) lived with him at Traverse des Sioux in 1851 as members of Red Iron's band of Sissetons. Rattling Walker and his mother fled to Manitoba and lived out their lives there; Nancy McClure Huggan, "Story of Nancy McClure," *Minnesota Collections* 6 (1894): 439–40, 453–54; Frank Blackwell Mayer, *With Pen and Pencil on the Frontier*, ed. Bertha L. Heilbron (St. Paul: Minnesota Historical Society, 1932; Minnesota Historical Society Press, Borealis Books, 1986), 167–68.

6. Alexis La Framboise was born in 1840 and grew up at his father's Little Rock trading post on the Minnesota River in present-day Nicollet County. Before the war he lived at the Redwood Agency. He later testified before the military commission and was a Dakota scout, 1863–66. He signed the Treaty of 1873 and moved to the Sisseton Reservation where he received land in 1875. He died in March 1876; Satterlee, *Court Proceedings*, 28; *The Dakotan* 5 (August 1902): 130; *Iapi Oaye (The Word Carrier)* 5 (May 1876): 20; U.S. Congress, *Sisseton and Wahpeton Sioux Indians*, 44th Cong., 1st sess., 1875, H. Doc. 42, p. 20; Kappler, comp. and ed., *Indian Treaties*, 2:1062.

7. Augustin Frenier or Mazakoyaginape or Appears Clothed in Iron was born in 1840, the mixed-blood son of Xavier Frenier, who lived at the Yellow Medicine Agency in 1856. Augustin enlisted in the Renville Rangers and fought to defend Fort Ridgely, but he left and was charged with desertion. He was tried, convicted, and sentenced to be hanged. Receiving a reprieve, he spent three years in the prison camp at Davenport. Pardoned in 1866, he went to the Santee Reservation. John Frenier was the twenty-eight-year-old son of Jacob Frenier and a Sisseton Dakota. At his trial he admitted being at the battle of Birch Coulee but denied participation in it. Instead, he claimed to have been on a war party to the Big Woods during much of the war. He was convicted and sentenced to five years in the prison camp at Davenport; the editors have found no further information on him. See Roll of Mixed-Blood Claimants, 1856,

Records of the Bureau of Indian Affairs, NARG 75; Satterlee, *Court Proceedings*, 48, Appendix, 6; Transcripts of Trials of Sioux Indians, cases no. 143 and 149, Senate Records 37A-F2.

8. Schwandt-Schmidt, "Story of Mary Schwandt," *Minnesota Collections*, 6:461–74; Maggie Brass, "Evidence for the Defendants," *Sisseton and Wahpeton Bands . . . v. the United States*, U.S. Court of Claims no. 22524, part 2, p. 379–85.

CHAPTER **VII**

The Battles

AS THE INDIANS gathered at Little Crow's village, several, including Little Crow, planned strategy for the war. The most significant obstacle to Dakota control of the upper Minnesota River valley was Fort Ridgely, standing not more than a dozen miles away on the north side of the river. After the defeat of Captain Marsh, the fort had a troop strength of only forty men, most of whom were untried volunteers. Fifteen miles southeast of the fort stood New Ulm, a town settled primarily by Germans. While of no military value, New Ulm held a considerable amount of food and other goods. The Dakotas knew that they would have to capture both the fort and New Ulm in order to sustain the war effort, drive the whites from the Minnesota River valley, and gain control of the southwest portion of the state.

Although a few Indians approached the perimeter of New Ulm on August 19, firing into the town, the battle for the valley began in earnest the next day when about four hundred Indians attacked Fort Ridgely. Fortunately for the defenders, another fifty soldiers plus the hastily recalled Renville Rangers had arrived during the previous night along with many refugees. These additions brought the strength of the command to about 180 men. In typical frontier style, the fort lacked a stockade, but the largest building was made of stone, and the garrison had artillery. Fighting against superior odds, the defenders managed to hold the fort. The Indians returned on August 22 but again were unable to overrun Fort Ridgely.

Becoming discouraged, a large Indian force turned instead to New Ulm, where the fiercest battle of the war occurred on August 23. The townspeople, pushed into a four-block-square area, withstood a powerful Dakota assault. Two days later, the Dakotas abandoned Little Crow's village, fleeing north to the upper reaches of the Minnesota River.

One other engagement, involving fewer combatants, occurred September 1–2 at Birch Coulee. The coulee, located across the river from the Redwood Agency, was selected as a campsite by an army burial detail, consisting of two companies, sent out from the fort after the Dakotas had apparently evacuated the region. The Indians, however, surprised and nearly annihilated the eighty-odd men in a vicious two-day fight. The relief of the burial detail by Colonel Sibley ended the war in the south; thereafter, the action shifted to the region north of the Yellow Medicine Agency.

Several fascinating narratives of the battles were left by Dakota full- and mixed-bloods. The two most interesting are by full-bloods Big Eagle and Hachinwakanda, or Lightning Blanket, both of whom participated on the Indian side. Two other accounts by mixed-bloods come from George Quinn and Joseph Coursolle. Quinn took part in the second attack on the fort but was on a horse-stealing expedition during the battle at Birch Coulee. Coursolle joined the volunteers at Fort Ridgely and was made a corporal.

·

Narrative 1
BIG EAGLE'S ACCOUNT

For biographical information on Big Eagle, see Chapter I, Narrative 1.

I WAS NOT in the first fight at New Ulm [on August 19] nor the first attack on Fort Ridgely [on August 20]. Here let me say that the Indian names of these and other places in Minnesota are different from the English names. St. Paul is the "White Rock;" Minneapolis is "the Place Where the Water Falls;" New Ulm is "the Place Where There Is a Cottonwood Grove on the River;" Fort Ridgely was "the Soldiers' House;" Birch Coulie was called "Birch Creek," etc. I was in the second fight at New Ulm and in the second attack on Fort Ridgely. At New Ulm I had but a few of my band with me. We lost none of them. We had but few, if any, of the Indians killed; at least I did not hear of but a few. A half-breed named George Le Blanc, who was with us, was killed.[1] There was no one in chief command of the Indians at New Ulm. A few sub-chiefs, like myself, and the head soldiers led them, and the leaders agreed among themselves what was to be done. I do not think there was a chief present at the first fight. I think that attack was made by marauding Indians from several bands, every man for himself, but when we heard they were fighting we went down to help them. I think it probable that the first attack on Fort Ridgely was

BIG EAGLE
in 1858 in
Washington,
D.C.

made in the same way; at any rate, I do not remember that there was a chief there.

The second fight at Fort Ridgely [August 22] was made a grand affair. Little Crow was with us. Mr. Good Thunder, now at Birch Coulie agency, was with us. He counted the Indians as they filed past him on the march to the attack, and reported that there were 800 of us. He acted very bravely in the fight, and distinguished himself by running close up to the fort and bringing away a horse. He is now married to the former widow of White Dog, and both he and his wife are good Christian citizens. We went down determined to take the fort, for we knew it was of the greatest importance to us to have it. If we could take it we would soon have the whole Minnesota valley. But we failed, and of course it was best that we did fail.

Though Little Crow was present, he did not take a very active part in the fight. As I remember, the chief leaders in the fight were "The Thief," who was the head soldier of Mankato's band, and

Mankato ("Blue Earth") himself. This Mankato was not the old chief for whom the town was named, but a sub-chief, the son of old Good Road.[2] He was a very brave man and a good leader. He was killed at the battle of Wood lake by a cannon ball. We went down to the attack on both sides of the river. I went down on the south side with my men, and we crossed the river in front of the fort and went up through the timber and fought on that side next the river. The fight commenced about noon on Friday after the outbreak. We had a few Sissetons and Wakpatons [sic] with us, and some Winnebagoes, under the "Little Priest," were in this fight and at New Ulm.[3] I saw them myself. But for the cannon I think we would have taken the fort. The soldiers fought us so bravely we thought there were more of them than there were. The cannons disturbed us greatly, but did not hurt many. We did not have many Indians killed. I think the whites put the number too large, and I think they overestimated the number killed in every battle.[4] We seldom carried off our dead. We usually buried them in a secluded place on the battle-field when we could. We always tried to carry away the wounded. When we retreated from Ridgely I recrossed the river opposite the fort and went up on the south side. All our army but the scouts fall back up the river to our villages near Redwood agency, and then on up to the Yellow Medicine and the mouth of the Chippewa.

Our scouts brought word that our old friend Wapetonhonska ("The Long Trader"), as we called Gen. [Colonel] Sibley, was coming up against us, and in a few days we learned that he had come to Fort Ridgely with a large number of soldiers. Little Crow, with a strong party, went over into the Big Woods, towards Forest City and Hutchinson. After he had gone, I and the other sub-chiefs concluded to go down and attack New Ulm again and take the town and cross the river to the east, or in the rear of Fort Ridgely, where Sibley was, and then our movements were to be governed by circumstances. We had left our village near the Redwood in some haste and alarm, expecting to be followed after the defeat at Ridgely, and had not taken all our property away. So we took many of our women with us to gather up the property and some other things, and we brought along some wagons to haul them off.

We came down the main road on the south side of the river, and were several hundred strong. We left our camps in the morning and got to our old villages in the afternoon. When the men in advance reached Little Crow's village—which was on the high bluff on the south side of the Minnesota, below the mouth of the Redwood — they looked to the north across the valley, and up on the high bluff on the north side, and out on the prairie some miles away, they saw a column of mounted men and some wagons coming out of the Beaver creek timber on the prairie and going eastward. We also saw signs in Little Crow's village that white men had been there only a few hours before, and judging from the trail they had made when they left, these were the men we now saw to the northward. There was, of course, a little excitement, and the column halted. Four or five of our best scouts were sent across the valley to follow the movements of the soldiers, creeping across the prairie like so many ants. It was near sundown, and we knew they would soon go into camp, and we thought the camping ground would be somewhere on the Birch Coulie, where there was wood and water. The women went to work to load the wagons. The scouts followed the soldiers carefully, and a little after sundown returned with the information that they had gone into camp near the head of Birch Coulie. At this time we did not know there were two companies there. We thought the company of mounted men (Capt. Anderson's) was all, and that there were not more than seventy-five men.[5]

It was concluded to surround the camp that night and attack it at daylight. We felt sure we could capture it, and that 200 men would be enough for the undertaking. So about that number was selected. There were four bands — my own, Hu-sha-sha's ("Red Legs"), Gray Bird's and Mankato's.[6] I had about thirty men. Nearly all the Indians had double-barreled shotguns, and we loaded them with buckshot and large bullets called "traders' balls." After dark we started, crossed the river and valley, went up the bluffs and on the prairie, and soon we saw the white tents and the wagons of the camp. We had no difficulty in surrounding the camp. The pickets were only a little way from it. I led my men up from the west through the grass and took up a position 200 yards from the camp, behind a small knoll or elevation. Red Legs took his men into the coulie east of the camp. Mankato ("Blue Earth") had some of his men in the coulie and some on the prairie. Gray Bird and his men were mostly on the prairie.

Just at dawn the fight began. It continued all day and the following night until late the next morning. Both sides fought well. Owing to the white men's way of fighting they lost many men. Owing to the Indians' way of fighting they lost but few. The white men stood up and exposed themselves at first, but at last they learned to keep quiet.

The Indians always took care of themselves. We had an easy time of it. We could crawl through the grass and into the coulie and get water when we wanted it, and after a few hours our women crossed the river and came up near the bluff and cooked for us, and we could go back and eat and then return to the fight. We did not lose many men. Indeed, I only saw two dead Indians, and I never heard that any more were killed. The two I saw were in the coulie and belonged to Red Legs' band. One was a Wakpaton named Ho-ton-na ("Animal's Voice") and the other was a Sisseton. Their bodies were taken down the coulie and buried during the fight. I did not see a man killed on the prairie. We had several men wounded, but none very badly. I did not see the incident which is related of an Indian, a brother of Little Crow, who, it is said, rode up on a white horse near the camp with a white flag and held a parley and had his horse killed as he rode away. That must have happened while I was absent from the field eating my dinner.[7] Little Crow had no brother there. The White Spider was not there. I think Little Crow's brothers were with him in the Big Woods at this time. The only Indian horse I saw killed that I remember was a bay. Buffalo Ghost succeeded in capturing a horse from the camp.[8] Late in the day some of the men who had been left in the villages came over on their horses to see what the trouble was that the camp had not been taken, and they rode about the prairie for a time, but I don't think many of them got into the fight. I do not remember that we got many re-enforcements that day. If we got any, they must have come up the coulie and I did not see them. Perhaps some horsemen came up on the east side of the coulie, but I knew nothing about it. I am sure no re-enforcements came to me. I did not need any. Our circle about the camp was rather small and we could only use a certain number of men.

About the middle of the afternoon our men became much dissatisfied at the slowness of the fight, and the stubbornness of the whites, and the word was passed around the lines to get ready to charge the camp. The brave Mankato wanted to charge after the first hour. There were some half-breeds with the whites who could speak Sioux well, and they heard us arranging to assault them. Jack Frazer told me afterward that he heard us talking about it very plainly. Alex Faribault was there and heard the talk and called out to us: "You do very wrong to fire on us. We did not come out to fight; we only came out to bury the bodies of the white people you killed." I have heard that Faribault, Frazer and another half-breed dug a rifle pit for themselves with bayonets, and that Faribault worked so hard with his bayonet in digging that he wore the flesh from the inside of his hand. One half-breed named Louis Bourier attempted to desert to us, but as he was running towards us some of our men shot and killed him.[9] We could have taken the camp, I think. During the fight the whites had thrown up breastworks, but they were not very high and we could easily have jumped over them. We did not know that Maj. Joe Brown was there; if we had, I think some of our men would have charged anyhow, for they wanted him out of the way. Some years ago I saw Capt. Grant in St. Paul and he told me he was in command of the camp at Birch Coulie.[10]

Just as we were about to charge word came that a large number of mounted soldiers were coming up from the east toward Fort Ridgely. This stopped the charge and created some excitement. Mankato at once took some men from the coulie and went out to meet them. He told me he did not take more than fifty, but he scattered them out and they all yelled and made such a noise that the whites must have thought there were a great many more, and they stopped on the prairie and began fighting. They had a cannon and used it, but it did no harm. If the Indians had any men killed in the fight I never heard of it. Mankato flourished his men around so, and all the Indians in the coulie kept up a noise, and at last the whites began to fall back, and they retreated about two miles and began to dig breastworks. Mankato followed them and left about thirty men to watch them, and returned to the fight at the coulie with the rest. The Indians were laughing when they came back at the way they had deceived the white men, and we were all glad that the whites had not pushed forward and driven us away. If any more Indians went against this force than the fifty or possibly seventy-five that I have told you of I never heard of it. I was not with them and cannot say positively, but I do not think there were. I went out to near the fortified camp during the night, and there was no large force of Indians over there, and I know there were not more than thirty of our men watching the camp. When the men of this force began to fall back, the whites in the camp hallooed and made a great commotion, as if they were begging them to return and relieve them, and seemed much distressed that they did not.

The next morning Gen. Sibley came with a very large force and drove us away from the field. We took our time about getting away. Some of our men said they remained till Sibley got up and that they fired at some of his men as they were shaking hands with some of the men of the camp. Those of us who were on the prairie went back to the westward and on down the valley. Those in the coulie went down back southward to where their horses were, and then mounted and rode westward across the prairie about a mile south of the battle-field. There was no pursuit. The whites fired their cannons at us as we were leaving the field, but they might as well have beaten a big drum for all the harm they did. They only made a noise. We went back across the river to our camps in the old villages, and then on up the river to the Yellow Medicine and the mouth of the Chippewa, where Little Crow joined us.

Continued on page 234.

Narrative 2
LIGHTNING BLANKET'S ACCOUNT

LIGHTNING BLANKET or Hachinwakanda was also known as Red Star or Wichunkpeduta and later as David Wells. He was born in 1832 in a Mdewakanton village on the lower Minnesota River and moved with his band to the reservation in late 1853. He participated in the first and second battles of Fort Ridgely but surrendered at Camp Release in late September.

After being tried and convicted by the military commission, Lightning Blanket was sentenced to be hanged. He received a reprieve and spent three years in the prison camp at Davenport, Iowa. While in prison, he became literate in Dakota, converted to Christianity, and in 1864 married Manikiyahewin, the youngest widow of Little Crow. Upon his receiving a pardon in 1866, they moved to the Santee Reservation and in the 1880s settled in Minnesota near Morton. His wife died at Morton on March 3, 1900. In 1908 he narrated an account in Dakota of the first and second battles of Fort Ridgely to Joseph Coursolle, who translated it into English. It was published in the Morton newspaper in 1908 and many times afterward. He died at Morton in about 1914.[11]

Narrative Source: Lightning Blanket or Hachinwakanda (David Wells), "Story of the Battles of Fort Ridgely, August 20 and 22, 1862," *Morton Enterprise*, August 28, 1908, p. 1.

THE EVENING of the second day of the Sioux war (August 19), the Indians came into Kagaw Chestin's (Little Crow's) village west of the Lower Sioux Agency, opposite where the village of Morton now stands, and reported all whites who had not been killed had gone to Esa Tonka (Ft. Ridgely) and Wakzupata (Village-on-the-Cottonwood — New Ulm). Little Crow with several of the chiefs, Pazuta Zha (Medicine Bottle), Shakopada (Little Six) and Wamada Tonka (Big Eagle) favored the attack on these two places, but the other two chiefs, Wapasha (Wabasha) and Wapecouta (Leaf Shooter), would not agree, because Wabasha was jealous of Little Crow. They sat up all night with their blankets around them until the sun was just coming up in the morning when they announced to us young men that Wapasha and Wapecouta would not go, but we were to get ready immediately to fight the white men at the Fort and New Ulm. The young men were all anxious to go, we dressed as warriors, in war paint, breech clout and leggings with a large sash around our body to keep our food and ammunition in. We started at sunrise and crossed the river at the agency on the ferry, following the road to the top of the hill below Faribault's creek, where we stopped for a short rest. There the plans for attacking the Fort was [were] given out by Little Crow. It was agreed to follow the road and ridge along the bluff to the creek west of the Fort, (Makaiyutapi-yomni-wakpada) Three Mile creek. Then those on foot were to go directly east to the creek which runs around the Fort, then follow the creek down to the north and east side of the Fort. These men were under Big Eagle and Medicine Bottle. The men on horseback with Little Crow and Little Six were to go down the creek to the river bottom then follow the old crossing road up to the bluff south and west of the Fort.

After reaching the Fort, the signal, three big shots (volleys), to be given by Medicine Bottle's men to draw the attention and fire of the soldiers, so the men on the east, Big Eagle's, and those on the west and south, Little Crow's and Little Six's could rush in and take the Fort.

We reached the Three Mile creek before noon and cooked something to eat. After eating we separated, I going with the footmen to the north, and after leaving Little Crow we paid no attention to the chiefs; everyone did as he pleased. Both parties reached the Fort about the same time, as we could see them passing to the west, Little Crow on a black pony. The signal, three big shots (volleys), was given by our side, Medicine Bottle's men, after the signal the men on the east, south and west were slow in coming up. While shooting we run

LIGHTNING BLANKET in about 1857

up to the buildings near the big stone one. As we were running in we saw the man with the big guns, whom we all knew and as we were the only ones in sight he shot into us, as he had got ready after hearing the shooting in our direction. Had Little Crow's men fired after we fired the signal[,] the soldiers who shot at us would have been killed. Two of our men were killed and three hurt, two dying afterward. We ran back into the creek and didn't know whether the other men would come up close or not, but they did and the big guns drove them back from that direction. If we had known they would come up close we could have shot at the same time and killed all, as the soldiers were out in a big opening between the buildings. We did not fight like white men, with one officer; we all shot as we pleased. The plan of rushing into the buildings was given up, and we shot at the windows, mostly at the big stone building, as we thought many of the whites were in there. We could not see them, so were not sure we were killing any. During the shooting we tried to set fire to the buildings with fire arrows, but the buildings would not burn, so we had to get more powder and bullets. The sun was about two hours high when we went around to the west of the Fort and decided to go back to Little Crow's village and come back and keep up the fighting next day. After leaving the Fort we buried the two who were killed in a little creek, or draw, west of the Fort, from behind which the men had been fighting. We buried them on the creek, one above and the other below the road, about forty rods apart, taking dirt from the road to cover them. I do not know how many were killed on the east, west, and south sides, but don't think there were any. We always thought no whites were killed, or not many, as it was hard to see them. There were about 400 Indians in this attack, no women were along. They all stayed at Little Crow's village. The cooking was done by boys ten to fifteen years of age, too young to fight.

We left the camp early in the morning, arriving at Little Crow's village about the middle of the day, from that time until night we made bullets and everyone who had powder brought it in, getting the most of it from the agency buildings. That night about 400 Sisseton and Wahpeton warriors from Big Stone Lake, who had started on hearing of the war, joined us, and early the next day (August 22), we started with about 800 warriors, but the grass was very wet with dew, more than the day of the first attack, so the sun was quite high before we traveled very far and it was just before the middle of the day when we reached the Fort. We followed the same road, crossing at the agency as we did before and divided forces at the Three Mile creek, footmen going north and horsemen south, with [the] same chiefs as in [the] first attack. I was again with the men on the northeast and north side. There were no women along, but the boys were taken for the same purpose as before, driving cattle and making campfires. We did not stop to eat this time, but each carried something to eat in his legging sash and we ate in the middle of the day while fighting. The plan of attack was the same as on [the] first battle, three big shots from the north, followed by a rush of the men on the east, south and west all at the same time. Little Crow had given strict orders on account of the first failure. Just before all was in readiness three young men belonging to Medicine Bottle's party on the northeast side of the creek saw a mail carrier coming into the Fort on the Wakzupata (New Ulm) road, shot at him but didn't kill him, then shot twice more and killed him. This the men on the south and west heard and took for the signal, ran up to the top of the hill, and began shooting. By the time the others had commenced, the big guns were fired at them, (the one on the south and west), who then ran back under the hill, by this time all were shooting, most all of us being hid. We saw many more soldiers than were there [in] the first attack but kept up shooting until dark. During the day many small buildings were burned, and we tried to burn the big ones with fire arrows. Some were burning, when a rain put out the fire. The sun was now getting low and after we saw the men on the south and west driven back by the big guns, and could see Little Crow and his men going to the northwest, we decided to go around the creek to the northwest and join them to see what to do, as our fire arrows had failed to burn the buildings and drive the whites out into the open. After joining them it was supposed we were going back to Little Crow's village to get more warriors. When we got to the Three Mile creek it was dark and we cooked beef and Little Crow told us there was no more warriors and a discussion followed, some wanted to renew the attack on the Fort the next morning and then go to New Ulm, others wanted to attack New Ulm early the next morning and come back and take the Fort. We were afraid soldiers would get to New Ulm first. Little Crow wanted to go to New Ulm to reach there first, before sunrise. He was angry and said he would take the ones who wanted to go and capture New Ulm. He left the camp that night and started for New Ulm with part of the men, should think about half of them, 400. The rest remained in camp that night and went back to Little Crow's village next morning.

Narrative 3
GEORGE QUINN'S ACCOUNT

For biographical information on George Quinn, see Chapter IV, Narrative 5.

I WAS in the second attack on Fort Ridgely. In this fight I came up on the south side to the stables and tried to get a horse. As I was leading it out a shell burst in the stable near me and the horse sprang over me and got away, knocking me down. When I got up I saw a mule running and I was so mad that I shot it. Good Thunder was in this fight and got a horse. I saw him and another Indian shooting at the windows of a house on the west side of the Fort. Some white men were firing from these windows at the Indians. Little Crow, Wabasha, Shakopee, Big Eagle, and Mankato were all at the first Ridgely fight.

I saw Little Priest and three other Winnebago there. Big Eagle and The Thief tried to prevent the second attack on Fort Ridgely, by saying it was no use to attack it, for it could not be taken without too great a loss. The Thief was not at the first fight; I know he was not.

I was over in the Big Woods trying to steal horses when the fight at Birch Coulee began. I got to the battle ground just as Sibley came and ended the fight. Red Legs' brother, Wahkeeyah Hotonna, or Thunder Voice, was killed at Birch Coulee.[12] His body was wrapped in a blanket and taken to the old site of Shakopee's village near the mouth of the Redwood and buried. Several Indians were wounded, and among them was William Columbus, now living at Morton; he had his powderhorn shot off too.[13]

Continued on page 258.

Narrative 4
JOSEPH COURSOLLE'S STORY

For biographical information on Joseph Coursolle, see Chapter III, Narrative 5.

LEAVING Marie I hurried to the office of Captain Joe Anderson who was recruiting for his Mounted Company.[14] Here I signed up and was appointed a corporal on the spot.

The Fort [on August 18] was buzzing with preparations for defense against an attack from Little Crow, expected any moment. I grabbed a shovel and began digging dirt for barricades with the others. Day and night the work never stopped but every time I could get away, even for a minute, I ran to the refugee barracks to see Marie and my tiny boy. Every time I went he seemed weaker than before.

No Sioux came the next day [August 19] but the following morning [August 20] they rode up, circling the Fort out of range of our muskets. Then we saw dismounted warriors, naked except for headbands and breech clouts crawling toward the Fort from the ravines and the woods. At a shouted signal from the chiefs they attacked from every side, rushing at us with screaming yells. Arrows and bullets whizzed above our heads as we returned their fire.

A flaming arrow stuck in the shingles of the officers quarters and a blaze started to spread.

"Corporal Coursolle," shouted Captain Anderson, "climb up on that roof and chop out the fire!"

"Every Indian bow and gun will be shooting just at me," I thought. My legs felt wobbly but up the ladder I went, two rungs at a time. Bullets and arrows whistled past my head. Never did an axe swing faster than mine as I whacked out the fire. The ladder was too slow; I rolled off the roof and landed with a grunt on the soft top of an earthwork wall. I thought there would be more holes in me than a sieve. But I didn't have a scratch. They were bum shots.

Most of the time we stopped their charges with musket fire but when they bunched up thick we let 'em have it with a cannon and they ran as though the devil was chasing them.

After a few charges that day they gave up and crawled away, dragging their dead warriors back to the horses.

No Indians appeared the next day and we worked feverishly at the defenses piling up stones, logs, bags of feed, hunks of sod — anything we could get our hands on that would stop lead and arrows.

We were mustered in early on the morning of August 22 and right after the ceremony I hurried to the refugee barracks. When I saw Marie fear almost stopped my heart from beating. She led me to her corner of the room and turned back a blanket covering a tiny body. Our baby Joe had closed his eyes forever.

There was no time for mourning. I ran to the carpenter shop where I picked up a small box with a cover. I hurried with the box to the post cemetery, dug a little grave and fitted the tiny coffin in the opening. Then I wrapped my son in a blanket and carried him in my arms to the grave. Marie and the Chaplain walked with me. Gently I lay my baby boy to sleep while the Chaplain said a prayer. Marie and I wept as I held her in my arms.

Then we heard war cries of the Sioux and the rattle of rifle fire. Hastily I kissed my heart-broken wife and raced to the barricades to take my place in the battle.

There were many more warriors in this attack than there were in the first battle. There seemed to be thousands. They were ten to our one and we knew we must stop them or every person in the Fort would be killed — except the women. And we knew they would rather die than face the fate of prisoners.

Suddenly they [the Sioux] rushed toward us, painted and screaming.

One big brave came straight at me. "Maybe you are the one who took my girls," I thought. I took careful aim and muttered, "Take that!" as I pulled the trigger. But I am not sure I hit him.

The first wave of charging Sioux couldn't face our fire. They broke and ran pell-mell back to the forest. Again and again we heard the chiefs urging them back to the battle but each time they rushed they lost their nerve. On one charge they were only twenty feet away and we braced for bayonet fighting. But Lt. Sheehan and his squad pulled a cannon to our position and fired a howitzer right into their faces. Again they panicked and ran howling out of range.

That stopped the attacks for a long spell but in the late afternoon we could see them bunching up in an open area southwest of the Fort. This coming charge, I knew, would be "for keeps." My scalp tightened and the palms of my hands were wet with sweat.

In addition to the twelve pound howitzers we had one twenty-four pounder held in reserve for an emergency. The Indians didn't know we had this secret weapon.

In previous attacks the Sioux had rushed the Fort from all sides. This time they were consolidating for one grand, overwhelming charge.

The gunners placed two twelve-pounders and the twenty-four pounder to meet the assault. The big gun they loaded with a double charge of canister.

The rallying point of the Sioux was in range of the artillery but Little Crow didn't know how far our guns would carry. At the instant the Indians joined forces, all three cannons roared. The shells tore great holes in the ranks of the warriors and the crashing boom of the twenty-four pounder rumbled and echoed up and down the river bluffs. The Indians skedaddled and the fighting was over.

During one of the earlier charges a soldier who was running across an open space between the Fort buildings was struck by an Indian bullet. A young fellow, fighting next to me, ran out from shelter, picked him up and brought him back to the firing line. The rescuer was a member of Company A, Sixth Minnesota, cool-headed and a crack shot. His name was Denais Felix and I took a real shine to him.[15]

All the time, day and night, Marie and I were driven nearly frantic by our concern for Minnie and Elizabeth. Were they hungry? Were they cold? Were they mistreated? Were they alive? Were they DEAD?

"At last the Fort is safe," I thought. "Now I must find them."

"What can you do alone?" asked Captain Joe when I asked permission to go. "Get killed, that's all. And what good would that do? We need every man. Soon Sibley will come with many more soldiers. Then we will catch Little Crow and find your daughters."

It was six days before Sibley came and every hour a torture for Minnie [Marie] and me. Four days more dragged by after he arrived with hundreds of troops. But at last Sibley ordered the Rangers and Company A of the Sixth to scout the country, bury dead settlers, the ambushed members of Company B of the Fifth at the Agency ferry, and search for survivors. I was glad Company A of the Sixth was going along; Denais Felix would be a good man to have by my side.

Marie came to see us off. "Don't worry," I told her as confidently as I could, "I will bring them back."

The things we saw that day were too terrible to describe. Scattered along the road and at burned cabins we found the bodies of settlers, mostly men and boys. Fifty we buried before reaching the ferry. There the most gruesome sight of all awaited us. On the road lay the bodies of thirty-three young men [of Marsh's command], most of them in two files where they fell when the Sioux fired from almost point-blank range — killed in their tracks without returning a shot. All had been scalped and the uniforms had been stripped from their bodies. We dug at a furious pace in our haste to conceal the fearful sight.

We moved back from the ferry to make our camp. It seemed an endless night, thinking of our dead comrades so near at hand and the way our own bodies would look if the Sioux returned. I was gripped in an agony of fear as I pictured my black-eyed little girls in the hands of these blood-crazed warriors. But I was helped by one ray of hope. We had seen no bodies of little girls. Had Elizabeth and Minnie been spared?

As we moved out in the morning we crossed Birch Cooley creek. Here I saw small piles of k[i]nnikinick branches from which the bark had been freshly shaved. I also saw fresh footprints in the sand. I knew the Indians used kinnikinick to wad their guns. I often used it myself. It worked better than paper. I was sure the Indians were not far away.

We followed the valley a few miles west, then climbed the bluff to the prairie road that led to the settlement of Beaver Falls. It was another day of horror; burying putrid bodies exposed for ten days in the August sun.

That night we camped on the west bluff of Birch Cooley creek, on an open prairie not far back from the steep, wooded ravine.

I guess we were all scared of the Indians. I know I was. So I told my sergeant about the k[i]nnikinick and the fresh tracks I had noticed that morning on the banks of the creek a mile or so downstream. I asked him to give this information to Captain Grant who was in command. But instead of reporting to Grant he reported to "Major" Brown. Brown wasn't an officer. He had come with us to look for missing relatives and friends. He had been an agent in charge of a government supply post and all such agents were called "Major."

"Don't worry about Indians," said Brown, "there are none within a hundred miles. You're just as safe as if you were home in your own beds!"

I had seen nobody all that day who could give me news of Elizabeth and Minnie and I was tormented with worry when I crawled under a wagon to sleep. We were dog tired, but in spite of "Major" Brown's assurance, many of us, mostly those with Sioux blood, dug shallow holes to lie in. These little holes saved the lives of many!

The history books say the first shot of the battle was fired the next morning by a sentry who thought he saw a wolf slipping through the prairie grass.

That is not the way it started. My friend Desjeuner, who was part Indian like myself, was on duty and he told me what happened.[16] "I saw something move. I looked close and saw an Indian kneeling with an arrow fixed to his bow. I thought 'I never have killed a man. I hate to kill a man now but if I don't kill him he will kill me.' So I shot him in the head."

Other heads stuck up out of the grass and another sentry fired. Then hundreds of half-naked Sioux leaped to their feet and rushed toward the wagons surrounding the camp, yelling and shooting.

Most of us were asleep when the firing started and for a time we didn't know what was happening. Some men stood up to form a firing line but soon flopped down on their bellies like the rest. All of us had turned in for the night with muskets loaded so we returned the fire before the warriors reached the wagons. We saw Indians fall. Soon all of them dropped to their knees and scampered away on hands and knees through the waving grass. Hurrah! We had turned back their surprise attack! They had planned to kill us all while we slept.

There were nearly a hundred horses on the picket ropes and many of them were hit by the first volley the Indians fired. Some dropped dead and others broke loose and galloped terror-stricken in the wagon

enclosure. The warriors had poured in such a murderous fire that all
horses but one soon were killed. We used their bodies as barricades.
The unscathed horse seemed to have a charmed life and we clung to
a faint hope that somebody might mount him and dash through the
besieging braves to summon relief from Fort Ridgely. But the Indians
concentrated their fire and finally the poor beast crumpled and fell.

The Indians had no courage for close range fighting and they
didn't charge again. They didn't have to risk death in a running attack
because of a low-lying hill to the north on which they could lie concealed and shoot down into our camp. Big trees on the rim of Birch
Cooley ravine on the east gave them sniping shelter. From one of these
trees an Indian rifle cracked and usually some poor fellow in camp
stopped a bullet. I watched until I saw the barrel of a rifle stick out
through the leaves. Then I fired. A painted body came tumbling
down like a dead squirrel. "One less," I murmured to Denais Felix.

The shooting of the sniper started a big commotion and we could
hear much jabbering and yelling under the shelter of the bluff. Then
I heard a loud voice calling in Sioux, "Hear me, Hinhankaga. We saw
you shoot. You killed the son of Chief Traveling Hail. Now we kill
your little girls!"

"They are alive!" I almost shouted in relief. Then my heart was
chilled with dread. Would they now be killed?

Denais lay beside me behind a dead horse and the wheel of a wagon. A bullet struck a spoke of the wheel directly in front of his eyes
and splinters flew in his face. But he wasn't hurt a bit. "Ha, Hinhankaga, I was lucky that time!" A comrade a few feet away turned
his head to see what had happened. A bullet crashed into his brain
killing him instantly.

Our ammunition was running low but the reserve supply was in
one of the wagons and any man who stood up to break it out would
be the target for hundreds of bullets and arrows.

I was one of the men ordered to get it. We hunched along on our
backs behind the shelter of the dead horses until we were directly under the wagon. Then we quickly raised our feet and tipped the wagon
over. One of the men got a bullet through his leg but we got the ammunition! We slid the boxes along the ground, each man helping himself and pushing the boxes on to the man next in line.

Then we discovered a terrible mistake — all the bullets were for
larger bore rifles! With our knives we whittled lead from the minie
balls. It took forever to pare one down to fit. If the Sioux had charged

then our goose would have been cooked. You bet we made every bullet count after that!

While we were whittling bullets one of the Sioux ran toward us waving a white flag. "Sergeant Auge, find out what he's after," ordered Captain Grant. The messenger spoke in a loud voice in his native tongue.[17]

"What did he say?" asked Grant.

"We are as many as the leaves on trees," translated Auge. "Soon we come and kill every soldier. We do not want to kill our brothers. All in camp who have Dakotah blood come out. We will not harm you."

"You are free to go," said Grant. "Auge, ask each man to make his choice."

"Hinhankaga, what do you say?" asked Sergeant Auge.

"If I go," I thought, "Traveling Hail's band will chop me up like pemmican meat. I stay!"

Every man with Dakotah blood said, "I stay."

We did not trust the Sioux.

When the roll was complete Auge shouted in Sioux: "Fah! Cowards! You do not dare. Every man in camp has five guns ready to shoot. You fight like Chippewas! Go back and stay with the squaws!" Then he spat derisively at the messenger.

The boastful charge never came. I guess they decided to starve and choke us out. That would have been an easy thing to do. We had no food; we had no water. There was no help we could give to our many wounded comrades who groaned on their blankets. That was the longest night of my life.

Our only hope was help from Fort Ridgely. Had our firing been heard twelve miles away? Was Col. Sibley disturbed over our failure to return?

We had no way of knowing that a relief force was on its way! The firing had been heard and Col. Sibley had sent Col. McPhail and two hundred men to investigate![18]

McPhail marched to the opposite side of the ravine. He was afraid he wasn't strong enough to attack. He sent a messenger to Sibley for reinforcements and went into camp.

We knew he was there and cursed because he stopped. Perhaps he didn't know what torture that night meant to us; the nauseating stench of death, the desperate thirst for water, the gnawing pangs of hunger, the death rattle in the throats of dying men.

In the morning, after another night of suffering and terror, other companies of the Sixth marched in without firing a shot, as again the Indians skedaddled.

In our camp the rescue party found eighty-seven dead horses, twenty-two dead soldiers and sixty half delerious, wounded comrades.

We marched back to the Fort where I cried when I told Marie I had not found the children. My heart ached because I had to hurt her with such a cruel disappointment.

Continued on page 239.

NOTES

1. George Le Blanc or Provençalle was the mixed-blood son of Louis Provençalle, a fur trader, and Muzanakawin, a Mdewakanton. He was born in about 1825. He was listed in the 1850 census as being a hunter and farmer and appears to have been at Traverse des Sioux. He was present at the signing of the Treaty of Traverse des Sioux in 1851. By 1860 he had married and moved to Redwood Township, where he was a farmer. As a Mdewakanton, he became involved in the war and was killed at the second battle of New Ulm on August 23; Roll of Mixed-Blood Claimants, 1856, Records of the Bureau of Indian Affairs, NARG 75; Harpole and Nagle, eds., *Minnesota Territorial Census, 1850*, 71; U.S. Census, 1860, Redwood Township, Brown County, roll 567, p. 252; Satterlee, *Detailed Account*, 47.

2. The Thief or Wamanonsa went to Washington, D.C., as part of the Mdewakanton delegation and signed the Treaty of 1858. It is probable that he fled with Little Crow after the battle of Wood Lake as his name does not appear in the trial records; Kappler, comp. and ed., *Indian Treaties*, 2:784.

Mankato or Blue Earth succeeded his father as war leader of a Mdewakanton band in the late 1850s. As leader, he signed the Treaty of 1858. He was one of the leaders at the battle of Birch Coulee; Kappler, comp. and ed., *Indian Treaties*, 2:784; Carley, *Sioux Uprising*, 43.

3. Little Priest or Hoonkhoonokaw was a Winnebago leader. He and a dozen Winnebagos were at the ambush at Redwood Ferry and at the first battle of New Ulm. On his return to the reservation, he is said to have tried to incite a war, but he did not succeed. On October 4, 1862, he and ten others were arrested and tried at Sibley's camp in Mankato for participating in the war. Antoine J. Campbell was the chief witness against them, but all were acquitted. In May 1863 they were removed to the Crow Creek Reservation. Soon they went to the Omaha Reservation in Thurston County, Nebraska Territory. Little Priest led a company of Omaha Indian scouts against the Teton Sioux. Severely wounded near the Powder River, Montana, in March 1866, he was taken to his home where he died on September 12, 1866; Hughes, *Indian Chiefs of Southern Minnesota*, 99–106.

4. Lieutenant Thomas P. Gere estimated the Dakota losses at the second battle of Fort Ridgely at one hundred men, but this seems excessive. The Dakotas themselves could recall the names of only two men killed; Carley, *Sioux Uprising*, 30.

5. The burial party was composed of Company A of the Sixth Minnesota, com-

manded by Captain Hiram P. Grant, and some fifty mounted men of the Cullen Guards, commanded by Captain Joseph Anderson, as well as seventeen teamsters and an unknown number of civilians — about 170 men in all; Carley, *Sioux Uprising*, 41.

6. Hushasha or Reg Legs was born in about 1804 and began a long career as a Wahpekute leader in 1849. He signed the Treaty of Mendota in 1851 and the Treaty of 1858. He was at the second battle of New Ulm and the battle of Birch Coulee. His name does not appear in the trial records. He and his band were moved to the Crow Creek Reservation in May 1863; in 1866 they moved to the Santee Reservation. He died there in about 1898; Kappler, comp. and ed., *Indian Treaties*, 2:593, 784; Hubbard and Holcombe, *Minnesota as a State*, 326; Santee Sioux Annuity Rolls, 1900–1907, Records of the Bureau of Indian Affairs, NARG 75.

7. Captain Hiram P. Grant, commander of Company A of the Sixth Minnesota, stated in his official report that a Dakota warrior on a white horse approached their camp on the morning of September 3, conversed with an interpreter, and claimed that they were ready to charge the camp and would grant no quarter. Any mixed-bloods could leave and would be protected. Grant's men fired, killing the horse, but the rider escaped. Robert K. Boyd, a participant in the conflict, confirms Grant's statement; Board of Commissioners, *Minnesota in the Civil and Indian Wars*, 2:218; Robert K. Boyd, *The Battle of Birch Coulee: A Wounded Man's Description of the Battle with the Indians* (Eau Claire, Wis.: Herges Printing, 1925), 14.

8. Little is known about Buffalo Ghost or Tatankawanagi aside from the fact that he was a son of White Lodge, a Sisseton leader; Hubbard and Holcombe, *Minnesota as a State*, 349.

9. Alexander Faribault was the mixed-blood son of Jean B. Faribault and the brother-in-law of Nancy McClure Faribault Huggan. He was born at Prairie du Chien in June 1806. He was a fur trader and land speculator, the founder of the town of Faribault, and a delegate to the Minnesota Territorial legislature in 1851. During the war he raised a unit of volunteers. He used some of his land to resettle those Dakotas who remained in Minnesota after the war. He died at Faribault on December 28, 1882; *Minneapolis Tribune*, December 30, 1882; Charles E. Flandrau, *Encyclopedia of Biography of Minnesota* (Chicago: Century Publishing and Engraving Co., 1900), 454–55; Carley, *Sioux Uprising*, 42, 81; Upham and Dunlap, *Minnesota Biographies*, 216.

Louis Bourier is probably Peter Boyer, a twenty-one-year-old mixed-blood who enlisted in the Renville Rangers at the Redwood Agency on August 14, 1862. He served through the battle of Fort Ridgely and accompanied Captain Joseph Anderson's Cullen Guards to Birch Coulee. He was killed at the beginning of the battle while on guard duty one hundred yards west of the camp. No evidence exists to show that he attempted to desert; Hubbard and Holcombe, *Minnesota as a State*, 351; Board of Commissioners, *Minnesota in the Civil and Indian Wars*, 1:485, 2:213, 214.

10. Hiram P. Grant, a native of Vermont born in 1828, moved to St. Paul in 1855. He was captain of Company A of the Sixth Minnesota Regiment at the battle of Birch Coulee and rose to the rank of lieutenant colonel. In the 1880s and 1890s he created controversy by claiming that he, instead of Major Joseph R. Brown, had been in command at this battle. He died at St. Paul in October 1897; Upham and Dunlap, *Minnesota Biographies*, 272; Board of Commissioners, *Minnesota in the Civil and Indian Wars*, 2:212–13, 215–19.

11. *St. Paul Pioneer Press*, October 17, 1897, p. 12.

12. The editors have found no further information on Thunder Voice.

13. William Columbus or Tunkannamani or Walks under a Stone was born at Kaposia (present-day South St. Paul) in 1811 and was a relative of Little Crow's. He was appointed the band's war leader in 1846. Years after the war, he claimed to have been one of the first Mdewakantons to have dressed in white man's clothing and to have

farmed. He also claimed that his participation in the war was with reluctance. Tried, convicted, and sentenced to be hanged, he was reprieved and sent to the Davenport prison camp in 1863. Pardoned in 1866, he went to the Santee Reservation. He returned to Minnesota in the late 1880s and died at Morton in 1900; Satterlee, *Court Proceedings*, 23–24; Transcripts of Trials of Sioux Indians, case no. 31, Senate Records 37A-F2; *St. Paul Pioneer Press*, October 17, 1897, p. 12; Hubbard and Holcombe, *Minnesota as a State*, 182.

14. Joseph Anderson was born in Ohio in 1826, moved to Minnesota Territory in 1855, and was a cattle dealer. During the war he commanded the Cullen Guards and was mustered out in November 1863. He moved to Texas in 1877 and then to Oklahoma. He died at Oklahoma City on June 23, 1897; Upham and Dunlap, *Minnesota Biographies*, 15; *St. Paul Globe*, June 26, 1897.

15. Dennis Felix, son of Pierre Felix and a mixed-blood Mdewakanton, was born at Mendota in about 1842. In mid-August 1862 he enlisted in Company A of the Sixth Minnesota and was discharged at the close of the Civil War in August 1865. He married Elizabeth Coursolle, Joseph Coursolle's daughter, and probably settled near Prior Lake; Roll of Mixed-Blood Claimants, 1856, Records of the Bureau of Indian Affairs, NARG 75; Board of Commissioners, *Minnesota in the Civil and Indian Wars*, 1:330; "The Ordeal of Hinhankaga," as told by Clem Felix to F. J. Patten, typescript, ca. 1962, Division of Libraries and Archives, Minnesota Historical Society.

16. Desjeuner is probably George Degnais, a mixed-blood who enlisted in the Renville Rangers. He served in the defense of Fort Ridgely. The editors have found no further information on him; Joseph Fortier Papers, Division of Libraries and Archives, Minnesota Historical Society; Board of Commissioners, *Minnesota in the Civil and Indian Wars*, 1:780.

17. Sergeant Auge was twenty-two-year-old James Auge, a native of Canada who enlisted in Company A of the Sixth Minnesota at Mendota on July 25, 1862. He was a corporal and an interpreter at the battle of Birch Coulee and was later promoted to sergeant. After serving in the Civil War he was discharged in August 1865. The editors have found no further information on him; Board of Commissioners, *Minnesota in the Civil and Indian Wars*, 1:330, 2:218; U.S. Census, 1860, Eagan Township, Dakota County, roll 568, p. 50.

18. Colonel Samuel McPhail was born in Kentucky in 1828 and served in the Mexican War. He moved to Minnesota Territory in 1850 and founded the towns of Caledonia and Brownsville in Houston County. During much of the Civil War, he was colonel of the First Regiment of Minnesota Cavalry. In 1864 he founded the town of Redwood Falls on the upper Minnesota River and lived there for many years and practiced law. He died near Taunton on March 6, 1902; Upham and Dunlap, *Minnesota Biographies*, 480; Franklyn Curtiss-Wedge, *The History of Redwood County, Minnesota* (Chicago: H. C. Cooper and Co., 1916), 1:442–45.

CHAPTER VIII

The Flight North and the Emergence of the Peace Party

FOLLOWING the unsuccessful attempts to storm Fort Ridgely and New Ulm, the leaders of the war ordered the evacuation of Little Crow's village. Their decision was based on the presence of the army under Colonel Sibley farther down the Minnesota River and its obvious intentions to march north. The five-mile-long train of Indians left on August 26, reaching Yellow Medicine Agency two days later. They were now in the territory of the Sissetons and Wahpetons. Within hours of their arrival, a heated debate broke out concerning the continuation of hostilities and the fate of the captives. As a result a peace party, started by Sissetons and Wahpetons, emerged and rapidly attracted the support of many disgruntled Mdewakantons, most of whom had been farmers. The peace party soon made it difficult for the Dakota warriors to sustain the war effort.

The initial debate over the war began on August 28 near Yellow Medicine and lasted until August 31, when the warriors left the agency to mount a series of further raids against the white settlements. One of these raiding parties under Little Crow entered the Big Woods and looted and burned the towns of Forest City and Hutchinson. A second moved down the right bank of the Minnesota River, eventually crossing the stream and attacking the army burial detail at Birch Coulee. After the Indians returned on September 6–7, further discussions ensued that brought several Dakota leaders, including Standing Buffalo and Wanata, in from the plains. In these debates, Sisseton and Wahpeton spokesmen emphatically disagreed with the course taken by the Mdewakantons and even threatened to prevent Little Crow and his people from camping on their lands. Red Iron, a Sisseton leader, was adamant about preventing the occupation of his lands by Mdewakantons. After yet another retreat northward occurred on September 9, Red Iron met the warring Indians a few miles south of Lac qui Parle and ordered them to stop. By this time there were two distinct camps. One was hostile to whites and interested in continuing the war; the other desirous of peace negotiations with Colonel Sibley and determined to gain control of all the captives.

Many important narratives have survived from this crucial period in the war. Most come from mixed-bloods who were involved in forming the peace party, especially the accounts of Samuel J. Brown, Thomas A. Robertson, Gabriel Renville, and Victor Renville. Paul Mazakutemani, a full-blood, was chief spokesman for the peace party. Shorter, yet significant, statements regarding the debates can also be found in the Sisseton-Wahpeton claims testimony. Among the more important pieces of testimony are the narratives of Joseph La Framboise, Jr., Ecetukiya (He Who Brings About What He Wants), Charles Crawford, Wicanrpi (Star), and Lotitojanjan (Light Face). Lorenzo Lawrence, a full-blood and one-time ally of Little Crow's, wrote an account of his rescue of several captives. All of these narratives show the wrenching devisiveness that developed among the Dakotas over the issues of war, captives, and plunder.

Narrative 1
SAMUEL J. BROWN'S RECOLLECTIONS

For biographical information on Samuel J. Brown, see Chapter IV, Narrative 1.

WE REACHED Yellow Medicine that afternoon and at once moved into one of the vacated agency buildings, the residence of Dr. Wakefield, and remained there until Thursday, the 28th, when Little Crow's whole camp moved up from the Lower Agency. They passed by and ordered us to follow them, which we did. We moved up and located our camp near a creek west of the Hazlewood mission station, lately vacated by Rev. S. R. Riggs. The Upper Indians made this their camping ground, while the Lower Indians pitched their camp on the opposite side of the creek, the two camps being about a mile apart.

On that day the government buildings at Yellow Medicine, and all the stores and other buildings there were burned and totally destroyed by the Indians. Our house followed suit.

In the evening several hundred of Little Crow's warriors came over to our camp on horseback, whooping, yelling, and firing off their guns. They surrounded our camp and ordered the Upper Sioux to move at once to the camp of the Lower Sioux on the opposite side of the creek, saying that this was the will of the Soldiers' Lodge and must be obeyed; that unless we complied *instanter* our lodges would be cut up and destroyed, and we would be punished severely. The Upper Sioux protested against this most vigorously. They said plainly that they would not only not comply with the insolent demands of the Lower Sioux, who inaugurated the outbreak and must assume all responsibilities connected with it, and who moved into the country of the Upper Sioux without invitation, but would take up arms against them and die on the spot rather than move into the camp of the insane followers of Little Crow. Bitter wrangling followed, and the visitors finally left with threats of returning in the morning with a larger force and compelling obedience.

The Upper Sioux, immediately upon the departure of the Lower Sioux warriors, sent out runners to the several camps and houses of the farmer Indians near by, and called in the people. In an incredibly short time several hundred half-naked and painted Indians came running into camp, armed to the teeth with guns, bows and arrows, knives, and pitchforks, ready for a fight. They at once set to work and pitched a large teepee or lodge, in the center of the camp, and formed a "soldiers' lodge" — a sort of committee of ways and means, composed of warriors of the tribe, from whose decision there is no appeal — and immediately decided upon taking some offensive action — to let Little Crow and his warriors understand once [and] for all that they would not be permitted to ride rough shod over the whole Sioux nation, and that they were tresspassers upon the lands of the Upper Sioux and had better behave themselves, or they would be ordered and driven off.

This was the *nucleus* of the friendly camp that was afterwards so instrumental in saving the lives of the captives.

On the next morning, the 29th, the lower Indians, some 300 or 400 half naked and painted warriors, came again, all on horseback, whooping and yelling as before, and surrounded our camp, but on noticing the soldiers' lodge in the center the visitors hastened away. They had evidently come for mischief — to carry out their threats of the day before — but the business appearance of the big lodge in the center opened their eyes and scared them away.

Immediately after they left, the "friendlies" (hereafter I shall call them that instead of Upper Sioux) got their chiefs and warriors together, painted their faces and bodies, took their guns, bows and arrows and knives, mounted their horses, and proceeded to the camp of the

Lower Sioux. They were going to demand all the property in the hands of Little Crow and his people belonging to the Sisseton and Wahpeton mixed bloods. The Lower Sioux had cattle, horses[,] wagons, carriages and other property belonging to my mother, and I was taken along to identify them. There were 75 or 100 in the party and all went singing, shouting, yelling, and firing guns. We entered the camp amid great excitement, and proceeded direct to the Soldiers' Lodge, pitched on a mound in the center of the camp. We rode up to within about fifty feet of the lodge, and surrounded it and then dismounted, and held our horses by the bridle bits, while Little Paul [Mazakutemani], the spokesman for the friendlies, stepped to the front and delivered a speech in which he demanded the property.[1] There were upwards of 100 of the chiefs and warriors of the hostiles (hereafter I shall call them that instead of the lower Sioux) lounging about in and around the big lodge. They were savage looking fellows, but that fact did not deter Little Paul from expressing himself without any fear whatever. Objections to the demand were at once interposed and bitter wrangling, followed, and, for a time the interview seriously threatened a bloody termination. The demands were, however, finally acceded to, after finding that the friendlies were determined to have their own way. The hostiles suggested that we should go through the camp and hunt up our property. We did so and discovered a horse belonging to my mother standing near a lodge, tied to a wagon. I pointed it out and the party went up to take it when the Indian rushed out of the lodge and ordered us not to touch the animal. The friendlies said they must have it and one of them went toward the horse when the hostile drew a bow from its quiver and quickly fixed an arrow in it and vowed he would pierce it through and kill it on the spot rather than let it go. The friendlies told him that we were warriors and belonged to the soldiers' lodge and must not be fooled with, and one of them dismounted and ran up to the horse, cut the rope or halter with which it was tied and led it away, the hostile not daring to make good his threat. It looked serious for a few moments. If the hostile had shot the horse the friendlies would surely have shot him to pieces, and there is no telling where the troubles would have ended.

(Explanatory — In the introductory chapter of "Reminiscences" in defining the relations of the Upper and Lower Sioux tribes it was stated that seventeen of the former and 286 of the latter were condemned to death. This was the finding of the court, as we understand it, afterwards modified by President Lincoln's review and decree, but Mr.

Brown wishes the words "or imprisonment" added, which would correctly read "condemned to death or imprisonment." Of the Indians hung at Mankato two belonged to the upper bands and thirty-six of the lower bands. In addition Little Six and Medicine Bottle were hanged at Fort Snelling in 1863 or 1864 [November 11, 1865], and John Campbell at Mankato in 1865, making in all thirty-nine of the lower bands hung during the Indian war, which commenced Aug. 18, 1862, and ended June 1, 1866, according to official records.[2] Inquiry has also been made as to the fate of Standing Buffalo. He was killed in a fight with the Crow Indians, Mr. Brown thinks, in 1866.[3] "He was always a friend of the whites—loyal to the last—a truly good Indian.")

The fate of the captives hung on a very slender thread. When the hostile was told we were warriors and belonged to the soldier's [sic] lodge and mnst [must] not be fooled with he pointed to me and sneeringly remarked: "Is he not a captive? You must be hard up for warriors."

We next went where our carriage stood and took that away, and then to another place and secured another one of mother's horses. We then went singing and whooping and firing off guns back to our camp. Here we remained for some days, the friendlies and hostiles camping apart. But for the dangers braved by these friendlies, but for the firm stand taken by them, not a captive would have been saved — all would have been killed, including mixed-bloods and "farmer" Indians. As it was we barely escaped massacre at the hands of the hostiles on any occasion.

The Indians are found [fond] of telling of their adventures, their exploits on the warpath. It is sickening to hear them boast of their devilish deeds. They say it is like play to fight the whites. Little Crow, who comes whenever he can to chat with mother, remarked one day that since the second attack on Fort Ridgley he had been suffering with a headache.

"What gave you the headache, were you scared so much as that?" she asked.

"Why," says he, laughing. "I was lying on the brow of a hill near the fort taking a nap when we were teasing the whites, shooting them through the windows of the fort and hearing them scream and cry like babies. I lay with my head on a huge rock for a pillow, and hearing the boom of a big gun I woke suddenly and peered over the rock to see what the matter was, and saw a cannon ball coming. I quickly dodged and struck my head on the rock and have had a pain ever since.["]⁴ "But seriously," he went on, "I am worried—ammunition is giving out. We could of course use clubs, sticks and stones, and drive the whites out of the country, but they were numerous like the grass on the prairies—that it would take a long time." (These boasts were made to keep up the courage of the young men.)

On Saturday, the 6th of September, Scarlet Plume, a leading Sisseton chief, arrived from above, from his camp at the head of Lake Traverse. He assured mother that she would not be detained as captive much longer, that as soon as the Sissetons returned to their planting grounds on Lake Traverse from their buffalo hunt on the plains northwest of there, where they now are, they would come down in a body and take us away by force, if necessary, and deliver us over to the whites.

I witnessed a singular spectacle today. One of Little Crow's warriors swallowed a bird whole, feathers and all. The warrior's son, a boy about ten years old, had shot and killed with his bow and arrow a little bird that had been hopping about on the prairie, and brought it home in triumph, when the father, in honor of the feat, and as an encouragement for the little warrior to preserve [persevere] in that line and perform greater deeds, called the crowd together and taking the bird and dipping it in grease swallowed it and then smacked his lips with gusto and relish.

On Monday, the 8th, the camp criers of both camps went around telling the people to break camp the next morning and proceed up the river. We had camped here since the 28th of August. Very early Tuesday morning, the 9th, both camps broke up and started, making a train five or six miles long, and arrived at Red Iron's village that afternoon.⁵

When we approached the village, which was afterwards known as Camp Release, Chief Red Iron and his warriors came out to meet us and there came very near being a serious row between the Red Iron faction of the Upper Sioux and Little Crow's people. The former came up whooping and yelling and firing off guns and ordering the latter to halt. They were told to proceed no further into the Sisseton country, saying, "you commenced the outbreak, and and [sic] must do the fighting in your country. We do not want you here to excite our young men and get us into trouble," and so the whole train stopped and went into camp.

The Robertson boys [Thomas A. Robertson and Thomas Robinson], whom the friendlies had dispatched to the Fort on a mission of peace a few days ago returned today and we were informed [that] the father [Joseph R. Brown] was sick there, suffering from a gun shot wound received in the battle of Birch Coolie.

The afternoon was lively. No sooner were the camps pitched than dancing and feasting was commenced. Some rode about on horseback, singing war songs. Charley Crawford, with father's uniform on and a prancing steed, made a fine appearance. George Washington on charger was "nowhere." The dancers had the long red whiskers of a white man dangling from a pole in the center of the ring around which the half-crazed warriors and their women and girls danced. One after another the half-naked and painted warriors would spring into the ring and make a speech. Each would boast of the exploits, relate his daring deeds. Then all would join in a the [sic] demoniac dance, with yells, whoops and songs and the beating of the tom-tom.

One hideous looking fellow jumped into the ring and gave the drum a tap with the flat side of his tomahawk, which act was a signal for the drummers to cease beating, and proceeded to narrate his adventures that day. He said he had despatched three—a man, a woman, and a child—and then proceed[ed] to act out the sufferings of his victims. He declared that he had destroyed a whole family for which he deserved much honor. That he went into a stable and shot a white man in the back and then beat his brains out with the but[t] of his gun, then rushed into the house where he found the wife kneading bread and a babe in a cradle near by. He grabbed the shrieking woman by the hair of the head and threw her violently against the wall, then took the babe, put it into the bread pan, and shoved it into the hot oven, then turned and shot the woman as she was trying to get up, then set fire to the house and hurried away and joined his comrades.[6]

On Wednesday the 10th, six of the friendlies with some captive women and children started from [for] the fort, but were discovered by some of Little Crow's warriors and brought back. This has intensified the feeling of bitterness existing between the opposing factions, and [they] "do not speak as they pass."

Little Crow is fast losing his hold upon the young men and this fact worries him greatly and the old warrior is getting heartily discouraged. He told mother today that he intended to spend the coming winter in the Green Lake region of the big woods and kill as many whites as he could, but if he should get killed himself it would be all right. He did not want to be caught and hung.

Frank Robertson — one of the captives — and I took a long walk on the prairie today. We wished, and wished and wished that this "cruel war was over," and that we were back with the boys at "old Seabury" again.[7]

On Sunday the 14th, the friendlies and the hostiles got into a rumpus again. There came near being bloodshed. Ah-kee-pah's life was threatened. He has refused all along to join in the dances or take part in any demonstration against the whites. His band today struck their lodges and moved out and away from the main camp and established one of their own, and declared that they would fight and die like men rather than submit to the insults and indignities heaped upon them by Little Crow's warriors.

On Monday the 15th, Waanatan, the Charger, an influential chief of the Upper Sioux, arrived from the north. He told mother that most of his people were out on the buffalo ranges and had brought but few of his warriors with him and did not expect to accomplish much. His mission was, he said, principally to consult with Little Crow about the captives and to suggest that they be released and sent to the fort (Ridgeley) — at least such of them as were taken on or in the vicinity of the upper reservation — also to demand the restoration of such goods, provisions and other articles that the hostiles took from the government supply house and traders at Yellow Medicine.

On Thursday the 18th, the friendlies met in council for the purpose of taking some action towards rescuing the captors [captives] and delivering them over to Col. Sibley. Some favored taking our family alone to the fort on the ground that it would not be practicable to include all the captives — that to include them all would excite bitter opposition on the part of the hostiles — who out-numbered the friendlies five to one — and might result in a general massacre and the death of every captive in camp. Little Paul [Mazakutemani] and others, however, opposed this plan, saying that no distinction should be made between the captives — that to take one family only would endanger the lives of those left behind — that all should be taken from the hostiles and delivered over to the whites at once, that with proper management and pluck and earnestness on the part of the friendlies, the hostiles would quail and every captive could be taken away and delivered over to their friends. But the idea was dropped for the time being — the ceuncil [council] concluding that the time was not yet ripe enough for any open action in behalf of the captives. They all came and danced around our lodge that night. This was done as a mark of respect for mother.

Waanatan told mother today that he was going to start back north tomorrow and would return in fifteen days with all his warriors and take us away, by force if necessary, and deliver us to Col. Sibley.

On Friday the 19th, the hostiles and the friendlies quarreled and came near fighting. The quarrel was ostensibly over the division of the plunder, but really over the captives. The latter wanted to take all the captives away and deliver them to the whites at the fort, while the hostiles wanted to massacre the whole outfit. The quarrel got very hot — threats made and guns fired. Tomahawks were shook at us and our situation was critical indeed. Poor mother! She has been crying all day, and has not tasted food since yesterday morning. She tries to hide her feelings, and the danger that confronts us, but we know it all and feel anxious for her. The day was a most sad and gloomy one for us. Night came but we could not sleep.

Lame Jim's son came to our lodge with his gun and tenderly cared for us during the night. He vowed he would shoot the first man that undertook to harm us in anyway. Saturday the 20th, was another bad day for the captives. My brother and I and all who were kept advised of the situation of things sat up with others of our friends to watch for prowling Indians. Faithful Taxunkemaza (Lame Jim's son) with gun in hand walked around our lodge all night long ready to kill "two at a blow." Lame Jim was a brother of "Old Bets" and was well known in early days in and about St. Paul.[8]

Little Crow was very angry to find that the captives were apprised of his plans to massacre them during the night, and that they were prepared to defend themselves. In the morning he threatened our lives — said that the captives must all be killed. He ordered his warriors to massacre us, but no one dared to execute his order — no not one.

Continued on page 222.

Narrative 2
THOMAS A. ROBERTSON'S
REMINISCENCES

THOMAS A. ROBERTSON was born at Gray Cloud Island (present-day Washington County) on October 24, 1839. His father was Andrew Robertson, a Scotsman who was an interpreter and superintendent of schools on the reservation, and his mother was Jane Anderson, a mixed-blood Dakota. He was educated at the mission schools and accompanied his father to the treaty negotiations in Washington, D.C., in 1858 as an interpreter.

He was made a prisoner in the war and was forced to be present at the second battles of New Ulm and Fort Ridgely, but by September 1862 he was a courier between Little Crow and Colonel Sibley. During the battle of Wood Lake, he stayed with the peace party to protect the captives, among whom were his mother, brothers Frank and Angus, and sister Marion Hunter. He was tried by the military commission for participation in the war but won an acquittal. He spent the winter of 1862–63 in the Dakota camp at Fort Snelling and then moved to the Crow Creek Reservation in Dakota Territory.

He was made chief of a Dakota scout camp at the head of the Redwood River until October 1866. The following year he moved to the Sisseton Reservation where he spent the rest of his life. He served as a jurist for the reservation and was an interpreter at the Sisseton-Wahpeton claims hearings in 1901. In about 1917 he wrote a lengthy reminiscence of his life for his children. He died at Veblen, South Dakota, on January 30, 1924.[9]

Narrative Source: Thomas A. Robertson, "Reminiscence of Thomas A. Robertson," *South Dakota Historical Collections* 20 (1940): 568–601.

ON OUR RETURN from the two battles mentioned above [second battles of Fort Ridgely and New Ulm], the camp was ordered to move to Yellow Medicine. On this move to Yellow Medicine John Moores, who was a step-brother to Mother, took charge of her and the rest of the family and as he had many friends and relatives among the Indians I felt that they were comparatively safe for the time being; so when some young men of old Red Iron's band wanted me to go with them, I consented and went with them to their village about twelve or fifteen miles up the Minnesota from Yellow Medicine.[10] While at

Red Iron['s] my brother Frank and another young man were sent as messengers to have me appear before Little Crow at the camp at Yellow Medicine. I at once went with them and on arriving at the camp found that a council was being held discussing a note that had been brought in that was found posted on the battle ground of Birch Couley. This note was from General [Colonel] Sibley and has been read and interpreted by James [Antoine Joseph] Campbell, David Faribault, and other mixed bloods that could read English. When I got to the council grounds Little Crow beckoned me to sit beside him, which I did; then he handed me the note, which was only a few lines, and said, "I have had this letter read and interpreted by several, but I want to be sure what is in the letter, so I sent for you. Now read it and tell me what it says", so I read the note and interpreted it to him, after which he said, "Now I know because I know I can depend upon you to tell the truth. You can go now where you please". After hunting about for a while I finally found Mother and the rest of the family who were still with Uncle John Moores, and I stayed with them up to the time of the release of the prisoners at Camp Release. I will state here that in this note General Sibley said, "Send two mixed bloods under a white flag and they will be protected from harm and return to you."
. . . The Council that was being held finally decided to send an an-

THOMAS A. ROBERTSON in 1858 in Washington, D.C.

swer to this note of General Sibley's and chose two mixed bloods, one of whom was Thomas Robinson who was willing and ready to make the trip; but no other mixed blood was willing to take the chances and go with him.[11] He, Tom, came to me and told me this. I then said, "I will go with you if you can get Little Crow's consent". He said, "I will go to him and see what he says". Sometime after this he came back and said, "Little Crow does not want you to go on this trip but told me to go and find somebody else. I have looked about but can find nobody. They are all afraid". I had known Little Crow since I could remember and knew he was friendly towards me and our family so after thinking the matter over a few minutes I concluded that perhaps he, Little Crow, did not want me to take the chances, so I said to Tom, "Let's you and I go together and see him again". So we went and found him alone in his tent. When we went in and he saw me he said, "Tunskuyolu" and told me to sit down beside him. Then Tom told him that he had been to everyone of the mixed bloods, but none of them would consent to go except me; that this note of Sibley's should be answered but that he did not like to try to make the trip alone. Then Little Crow, laughing, said, "Are you not afraid?" I said no that I was not afraid to go anywhere he told me to. Then he (Little Crow) said, "You two can go then", and handed Tom the answer to General Sibley's note. Tom then said, "It is a long walk; we will get back as soon as we can". Then he (Little Crow) said, "You won't have to walk. I will get you a rig". We went back to our tent. Soon after a small mule and single buggy was brought to us and told that that was our rig, and by the way, this little mule, before we got back, proved to be much more than she looked. She was the best mule of her size I ever saw in my life. She was not much on the trot but she would lope from sunrise to sundown and then some.

We started and on our way, just before we got to the Yellow Medicine River we came to an Indian grave over which was stuck a pole with a yard square of sheeting fastened onto it, and painted blue in the center. As we did not have even a white handkerchief we took this along with us hoping to make this work as a flag of truce; but somewhat in doubt as to how the blue center would work for that purpose. Just before we came to the Redwood River we came to a house that had been occupied by the government farmer for Little Six's band who were located on or about the Redwood. We stopped to give the mule a breath and went into the house. Everything had been taken or destroyed, but on going into the cellar we found a part of a keg of soft soap. Having still our blue center flag in mind we took this along and stopping at the river we spent one half hour washing this out, which, when we got done would, at a distance, do fairly well, but in close quarters was still somewhat bluish; however, it was the best we had.

Continuing on, about four or five P. M., we came to the creek about one and one half miles from Fort Ridgely. Up to this time we had not yet come in sight of the fort. Here, hiding our arms, we again started on our way and getting on top of the bank of the creek, we came in plain sight of the fort, where we could see there was quite a commotion, and that a man from the fort had started out on the road to meet us.

About half way between the creek above mentioned and the fort was the picket line inside of which cattle were being butchered. Just before we got to this picket line I got out and met this man that was coming outside of the picket line. After saluting he asked me where we were from. I told him from Little Crow's camp. He then asked me what we were there for. I told him we had a message for General (at that time Colonel) Sibley, to be delivered to him and no one else. He said, "That's right, you stick to that 'till you get to Sibley", and by the way, this man was Colonel McPhail, the officer of the day, who I became well acquainted with after these trouble[d] times were over, and with whom I have played many a game of billiards. He died several years ago somewhere near Redwood Falls.

To continue, he then told Tom, who was still sitting in the rig, to come on but as Tom did not seem to understand what was wanted, I went back and led the mule up to where the colonel stood. He told me to get in and he himself getting in and sitting on our lap, he himself drove the mule into camp. A detachment of soldiers had been sent out and surrounding us they guarded us into the lines to Colonel Sibley's tent; and up to this time it looked a little squeamish for us, as anyone from the hostile camp, red, white, or black, was considered by many a hostile and a murderer.

After giving us our supper we were separated. I was taken to another tent and questioned as to the conditions in the hostile camp, the condition of the prisoners, etc. This was done by some officer appointed for that purpose. Tom was questioned by Colonel Sibley himself. Anticipating that something of this kind would be done, we on our way had talked these matters up and had agreed on what answers we would give to the main questions that we were liable to be asked. This turned out to be a happy forethought as though separated, our answers agreed on all the main points asked us.

No one can realize the situation in which we were placed, for while we were ostensibly messengers from Little Crow and the hostiles, I was, in secret, a messenger in the interests of the friendly element and the release of over 150 prisoners in the hostile camp.

We stayed at Fort Ridgely that night and the next morning, early, an escort took us outside the lines and, taking up our arms where we had left them, we wended our way back to the hostile camp which we reached without further adventure which would be of interest to you children.

On reaching camp we found the friendlies had not been idle, and had formed a separate camp composed mostly of the mission Indians and their friends with Little Paul, as he was called, as their leader (Indian name — Mazakutemani) and a few Whites and some mixed bloods that had been taken under their protection during the first days of the outbreak.

A great ado has been made over the acts of John Otherday, old man Simons [Simon Anawangmani], and Lorenzo Lawrence.[12] I happen to know the early history of at least two of these men — John Otherday and Lorenzo Lawrence. John Otherday was a desperate character among his own people and was both feared and hated. On the trip to Washington in 1858 he brought back with him a white woman that he took out of a house of ill-fame whom he married after he got back on the reservation. Aside of whatever friendly feeling he might have had towards the Whites, he was interested in getting his wife back to her own people, as well as getting himself away from his own people, some of whom were liable to shoot him at any time under cover of these troublous times, for this Otherday received from the government $1000 which was all right enough — perhaps he ought to have got more. Lawrence also was, among his own people, a tough character. He and another man at one time shot and killed two of Little Crow's brothers, and Lawrence afterwards married one of the widows and lived with her up to the time of her death, so he also had other things in view when he put himself under the protection of the Whites. As to Simons, I have nothing except I think he was all right; but Little Paul was really the man of the hour. He bearded the lion in his den, as it were. He told Little Crow and his people in open council, "You think you are brave because you have in the last few days killed a lot of defenseless women and children. You are cowards. You think to get me and my people to help you in this work? No, never. These prisoners will have to be given back to their people and the sooner you do it the better it will be for you. You are figuring now to leave this country and get under the protection of the English, but you must remember the chief of the English is a woman and she can never be friendly to a people who will kill and butcher and otherwise abuse such as she is, as well as killing innocent little children. No, you will never get my help". This council broke up with this so called friendly party taking a firm stand to work for the release of all prisoners. I tell this to show that Little Paul really did more than those that guided small parties out of the hostile country. Little Paul was a member of the Presbyterian church, a Christian, as well as a good and brave man.

One more incident I will relate of this Little Paul. The summer after the Inkpaduta outbreak at Spirit Lake it was reported that three prisoners were in his hands — Mrs. Noble, Mrs. Marble, and a Miss Gardner, a young girl about 15 years old.[13] It was learned afterwards that Mrs. Noble was shot in the water while crossing the Sioux River. Jacob Greyfoot (Sihorota) and his brother went out somewhere between the Jim [James] River and the Missouri and brought in Mrs. Marble and reported they could not get Miss Gardner as she was in the hands of the notorious White Lodge, and he would not give her up.[14] Little Paul, hearing this, said, "I will go and get her", so he in company with some other Indians, I forget now who went out and found White Lodge somewhere on the James River, and after some dickering and wrangling he finally got Miss Gardner and started home with her. A runner came in to Yellow Medicine and reported that Little Paul's pony had played out and that he wanted help. Father sent me out with a rig and I met Little Paul and Miss Gardner at Lacquiparle and brought them into the Yellow Medicine Agency, where we were then living. After Miss Gardner, under Mother's care, got rested up, Father, myself, Little Paul and, if I remember right, one or two others, took her to St. Paul and delivered her to the authorities there. I met this same Miss Gardner only a few years ago at Browns Valley. If she is still living she is at Okoboji, near Spirit Lake, where the rest of her family of six were killed.

After the council mentioned above in which Little Paul defied Little Crow and his cohorts, Little Crow decided to send again a message to Colonel Sibley in answer to the one we brought back on our first trip, and Tom Robinson and I were again chosen to take this message.

In the meantime the friendly or peace party had not been idle. We were to start on this second trip the next morning. That night Goodthunder came to me and told me some of the friendlies wanted to send a letter to Colonel Sibley, and wanted me to write it for them. I had in my pocket a short piece of pencil and an old memorandum book, but we had no light so Goodthunder went out and found somewhere a short piece of candle. He split a stick and sticking the candle in the split end and covering this and myself with a blanket he lit the candle and I, in as few words as possible, wrote what he told me they wanted to say. I then asked him who was sending the letter, and he said, "Put Wabashaw and Taopi's names to it", and this I delivered to Colonel Sibley on our second trip. The reason for my hiding the light when I wrote this was that some of the hostiles were becoming suspicious of us two messengers, especially myself, and I had to be very careful about what I did. The original of this note I am told is somewhere among the historical records in St. Paul.

On this second trip we had part way with us my brother Angus and Uncle John Moores. They went with us to get a wagon that we had seen near the road on our first trip. They got the wagon and returned to Beaver Creek to wait for our return. This was sometime after the Battle of Birch Couley.

On this second trip we did not stay overnight at Fort Ridgely, but started on our return the same day, quite late in the afternoon. When within about two miles of the battle ground of Birch Couley, on a little rise ahead of us and near the road, we saw something pop up and drop out of sight again. We, of course, at once took it to be an Indian or someone else that was way-laying us. In a second our guns were ready, and we turned out of the road a little to circle around this mound or rise in the ground from which when we got opposite, a hawk rose and flew away. This was just after sundown. Perhaps some of you recall having seen other hawks do this same thing. We, of course, had a laugh over our scare but it goes to show that we had to be, and were, on the alert all the time. It got dark before we got to the battle ground of Birch Couley—a moonless, still, and soggy night—and circling around and past the battle ground (the stench was terrible; I thought we would never get away from it) we finally came to the top of the bluff back of our old house. Somewhere in this vicinity we expected to meet my brother and Uncle John Moores, but no particular place had been agreed upon and for a few minutes we were in a quandary what to do. Tom Robinson who, as you know, was with me said, "We can't halloo as that would arouse any Indians that might be lurking about here." After thinking a few minutes it came to my mind that in our boyhood days when my brother and myself, while in the woods in the evening hunting the cows, in order to keep in touch with one aonther [sic] would one of us imitate the note of the bob-o-link and the other would answer in the same note. Putting my fingers in my mouth I did this and we waited a minute — but no answer. I repeated it and immediately came an answer from away down in the woods below our old house. I knew at once that it must be them. We went on down the hill and met them about half way to where they had made camp in the woods. Arriving in camp we found that they had dug up potatoes in some settler's garden, and finding also some chickens somewhere, they had a large pot on boiling; so, taking care of our mule that we had unhitched at the foot of the hill, we filled up on chicken, potatoes, and soup, and as we had got some tobacco at the fort, we had our smoke, and lying down on our blankets we were soon in our righteous slumber. My brother told me afterwards that they had heard my first call but wanted to be sure, but when the second call came he knew it must be I as the same thought came into his mind that had into mine — suggesting this call out of our dilemma.

The next morning we were up early and by daylight were on our way again. After crossing the Minnesota, a short distance from where we had made our camp, we met a small bunch of sheep of which we killed three, loading them into Moores' new wagon, took them along. About half way between Redwood and Yellow Medicine we met a small party of our friends of the so-called peace party, and soon after that a party of the hostiles headed by Little Crow's brother (Onktomiska) White Spider who, a few years ago, died at Flandreau [Morton].[15] This looked suspicious to us but, as about an equal number of our friends had joined us, we were not much alarmed. Soon after both parties left us — White Spider and his party claiming they were hunting cattle. Three of our own friendly party soon followed them, I think to keep in touch with them and to see that they did us no harm. We saw nothing more of either party during the rest of our trip. During the day a steady rain came up and lasted all day and the following night so by the time we reached (Iyangmani) Runningwalker's abandoned village about sundown we were thoroughly soaked to the skin. We found the old chief Runningwalker's house still standing. This was built of logs with a mud chimney for a fireplace, and a rough pine board table for furniture. Glad to get under any shelter we soon un-hitched our team and mule and securing them, we secured a liberal supply of wood and soon had a roaring fire going in the old mud fire-place. By this time it was getting dark so, taking in our belongings and stripping off our clothes and hanging them about the fireplace to dry, we were as we thought prepared for a night of comparative comfort, but found to our sorrow that we had counted without our host — our hosts — as when the place began to get warmed up it was literally swarming with fleas, fleas, fleas, and then more fleas. After taking off my clothes I had taken possession of the one pine board table. On this I layed and sat — mostly sat — the whole blessed night and was surely glad when morning came and we were once more on our way.

We found on getting back that the camps, both hostile and friend-ly, had been moved to within a short distance from Red Iron['s] vil-lage, now Camp Release. As we neared camp we saw Little Crow on a knoll singing and dancing and as we got nearer we heard him say-ing, "The British are coming to help me and they are bringing Little Dakota". This Little Dakota was a small cannon or howitzer at some time left by some exploring party near where Jimtown [Jamestown, North Dakota] is now, and so named by the Indians. It was after-wards, by the Indians, thrown into the Jim River and I presume lays there yet.

Our message from Colonel Sibley to the friendlies or peace party was, if possible, to get possession of all the prisoners and form a sepa-rate camp and hold the prisoners; that he was now thoroughly pre-pared and would be on the move against the hostiles the next day; that all those that had committed murders and other outrages against the Whites would be punished and all those that had been friendly and acted as such would be duly considered and protected as such.

Continued on page 229.

Narrative 3
GABRIEL RENVILLE'S MEMOIR

For biographical information on Gabriel Renville, see Chapter V, Narrative 1.

AFTER these many things had come to pass, the hostile Indians, with their families, moved up towards the Yellow Medicine Agency, and had now arrived. Then Tah-o-yah-tay-doo-tah, or Little Crow, the chosen chief of the hostile Indians, came to where we were, and told us to get out of the houses that we were in. He said, "These houses are large and strong, and must be burned. If they are not burned, the soldiers will come and get into them, Therefore get out, and if you do not you will be burned with the buildings." So we got our horses and hitched them to our wagons, into which we put our belongings, and started north.

When we had gone about a mile and a half, we came to where the hostile Indians had formed a camp. As we were passing through the camp, I saw many white prisoners, old women, young women, boys and girls, bareheaded and barefooted, and it made my heart hot, and so I said to Ah-kee-pah, Two Stars, and E-nee-hah, "If these prisoners were only men, instead of women and children, it would be all right, but it is hard that this terrible suffering should be brought upon women and children, and they have killed many of even such as these."[16] I therefore had in mind to call a council, invite the hostile Indians, and appoint Mazo-ma-ne and Marpiya-wicasta (Cloud Man) to say to the hostiles that it was our wish that the prisoners should be sent home. Ah-kee-pah, Two Stars, and E-nee-hah, agreed with me in my idea, and they told me to go on and do so.

We had by this time got about five miles from the Agency, at the home of Mr. Riggs. These houses were not yet burned and were occupied by some of the friendly Indians. John B. Renville was with them, and we made our camp near them.[17]

I told Mazo-ma-ne and Cloud Man what I wanted of them, and they said they would do as I wished. I then went to the people that were in the Hazelwood Mission house, and told them what I was planning to do, and they also told me to go ahead and do it, and J. B. Renville gave me a calf to kill to feed the people that were to be called to that council. This was in the evening. The next morning early I killed a cow which I had tied up, and picked out two men, Tah-ta-wah-kan-hdi and Hin-ta-chan, to do the cooking.[18]

When all was ready, but before the invitation was sent to the hostile camp, a large body of horsemen came towards us from that camp, two hundred or more. They all had their guns, their faces were painted, and they were gaily dressed. They came and stopped at our camp. Then I said to them, "We were about to send for you to come here to a council. But as you are here, whatever your purpose may be in coming, for the present get off your horses and have something to eat." They then got down, and after they had eaten they mounted again, and, forming around our camp, said, "We have come for you, and if you do not come, the next time we will come to attack you;" and firing their guns into the air they departed.

By this time Cloud Man, Mazo-ma-ne, and all those of our people who were about there came, and were much angered and said, "The Medawakantons have many white prisoners. Can it be possible that it is their object to make the Wahpetons and Sissetons their captives too? Call together those who are Wahpetons and Sissetons, and we will prepare to defend ourselves."

I at once sent out the two young men whom I had helping [me], and they on horseback went about and gathered our people together. When about three hundred had arrived, we painted our faces and got our guns, and, mounting our horses and singing, went towards their camp. When we arrived near the hostile camp, we kept firing our guns into the air until we got within the circle of their encampment, and then rode around inside and came out again where we went in.

It was decided at that time that we would get all our people together and in the future act on the defense. With this understanding, all started to bring in their families for the purpose of forming one general camp of those friendly to the whites and apart from those who were hostile. We formed our camp in a circle west of Mr. Riggs' Hazelwood Mission buildings, and a large tent was put up in the center of the camp.

A soldiers' lodge was organized, and four men, myself, Joseph La Framboise, Marpiya-hdi-na-pe, and Wakpa-ee-yu-way-ga, were chosen as the chief officers or directors of this soldiers' lodge, to act for the best interests of the Sisseton and Wahpeton peace party.[19]

After these four had been duly installed and authority given them, the first question discussed was the release of the prisoners, both whites and mixed-bloods; and it was decided that the effort should be made to have these prisoners returned to the whites, excepting that the men who were able to fight might be retained. The reason for this decision of the directors of the soldiers' lodge was that the hostile Indians would claim that if the men were released they would turn right around and fight them. Little Paul (Maza-ku-ta-ma-ne) was chosen as spokesman to present this to the hostile Indians.

Then the Medawakantons, the very enemies of the white people, called a big council, and invited us to it. So we prepared ourselves by arming ourselves and painting our faces, and went over to their camp. It was decided, before we started, that now was the time for Little Paul to present the case for the release of the prisoners. When we arrived at the council, the Medawakantons made many speeches, in which they urged strongly the prosecution of the war against the whites to the fullest extent. Then Little Paul arose and made a speech, in which he said all he was instructed to say in regard to the release of the prisoners.

The spokesman of the Medawakantons was Wa-ki-yan-to-eche-ye (Thunder that paints itself blue), who arose and said that the captives should not be released, that the hostile Indians had brought trouble and suffering upon themselves, and that the captives would have to stay with them and participate in their troubles and deprivations.[20] Many others spoke on their side. It was a big meeting, nearly a thousand people being present, and there was much excitement up to the time of the breaking up of the council.

It was now reported that many soldiers had got together at Fort Ridgely, and Little Crow with about four hundred men started for the Redwood Agency. About this time a detachment of soldiers had been to the Redwood Agency, and on their return camped at Birch Coulie. They were attacked that night by this party and were fighting until daylight. During that fight a mixed-blood [Peter Boyer] ran out of the soldiers' camp, but was killed as soon as he got among the Indians. After that a large party of soldiers came from Fort Ridgely, which stopped the fighting, as we were told.

Some who had been at that battle said that they thought they recognized Major Brown's voice, and it caused me to think much, for we had his wife and children with us. I then went to our soldiers' lodge, and, taking my place there, said that as it had been reported that many had been killed at the battle of Birch Coulie, we ought to send a party to investigate and find out, if possible, about how many were killed. My reason for this was that I wanted to come to some conclusion as to whether Major Brown was dead or alive. We then discussed the question, and it was decided that some one ought to be sent down there, and I suggested Charles Crawford.[21] Others said that there ought to be two, so Wa-su-ho-was-tay [Enos Good Voiced Hail] was named, and these two were selected and sent to investigate the battle ground of Birch Coulie. When the Medawakantons heard of this, they also sent two of their men.

Our men came back the next day. They reported that they had been to the battle ground, and there were more than ten graves, but that they could tell nothing about how many were buried in each grave.

Charles Crawford said that he had found a paper on the battle ground, but that those who were with him did not know that he had found it, and then he gave me the paper. This paper, he said, had been put into a cigar box and tied to a small pole or stake and stuck up on the battle ground. General Sibley's name was signed to this paper, so I knew that he had written it. I took it to our council lodge, and had it carefully read.

In this paper General Sibley wanted to know why it was that the Indians had become hostile to the whites, and that if any of them wished to see him they could do so, but must go in the road in plain sight, and that they would not be harmed and could return again. On getting this news, the minds of our people were still more drawn towards the whites.

Then we had a consultation in regard to the mixed-bloods, who, though they were white, were children of the Indians. It was thought to be wrong that their property should be taken from them, and that therefore their horses and wagons should be returned to them. After we had discussed the matter, it was decided to demand the property, and Little Paul was chosen as spokesman to present the matter to the hostile Indians.

We again painted our faces, took our guns, and went to the Medawakanton camp; and when we arrived at their soldiers' lodge, Little Paul said what he was told to say. Then the public crier of the Medawakantons arose and said, "The mixed-bloods ought not to be alive, they should have been killed. But now you say their property should be returned to them. We will never do so."

Little Crow spoke next, and said that he was the leader of those who had made war on the whites; that as long as he was alive no white man should touch him; that if he ever should be taken alive, he would be made a show of before the whites; and that, if he was ever touched by a white man, it would be after he was dead.

So the hostile Indians would not consent to have the property of the mixed-bloods returned; but Joseph Campbell's wagon, Mrs. J. R. Brown's wagon and horse, and Mrs. Andrew Robertson's wagon, were taken by us and returned to them. As we could see by this time that if any more of this property was taken by us and returned to the owners it would cause a fight between us and the hostile Indians, we stopped and went back to our camp.

After these things had happened, about three hundred horsemen came from the Medawakanton camp with their guns, singing and shouting their war cry. They came around on the outside of our circular camp, and, stopping in front of our entrance way, shot at the tops of our tepees, and shouting their war cry departed.

In the face of all this opposition of the hostile Indians, we were still determined to keep on the course we had laid out for ourselves, and again getting together decided that some person or persons should be sent to General Sibley's headquarters at Fort Ridgely. When the Medawakantons heard of this, they made the threat that anyone who was sent to Fort Ridgely would be killed. There was much discussion over the matter, but finally, when Little Crow said he was in favor of some one being sent, the two Toms (Thomas Robinson and Thomas A. Robertson) were designated as the ones to go, and they went.

We then got together again in our council lodge and decided to move our camp, having in mind to do everything in our power to discourage the hostile Indians. We hoped that finally they would see that we were so determined in our purpose that it would be wise for them to consent to our proposition in regard to the prisoners, and we therefore moved our camp.

About this time the two who had gone to Fort Ridgely for news returned. They had seen General Sibley, who had told them that he was not the enemy of those who were friendly to the whites, but was most assuredly the enemy of those who were the enemies of the whites; that he must have the captives returned first; and then he would meet the hostile Indians as men.

We then moved our camp, and the hostiles also moved theirs. They went north till they came to Red Iron's village, where they were halted, and, a great commotion occurring, a scattered camp was made. Some shots were fired, but no one was killed. The result of this move at Red Iron's was that the hostile Indians went no farther at that time.

When all had moved away from Yellow Medicine, Simon Anawag-ma-ne took a captive woman and her child who could talk English, and, hiding with them, fled towards the whites. Lorenzo Lawrence also about that time took his own family and a white woman and hid in the river bottom. Finding a canoe, he put them into it and started down the river in the night. On his way he came across a mixed-blood woman, who, with her children, was hiding, and taking them along he arrived safely with them at Fort Ridgely.

The making of the scattered camp, caused by the halting and commotion at Red Iron's village, had the effect of breaking up the hostile soldiers' lodge, and to some extent the influence that it had exercised over their own people. Therefore when it was proposed that messengers should again be sent to General Sibley, a few of the Medawakantons felt inclined towards the whites, and, secretly getting Thomas A. Robertson to write a letter for them, sent it by him to General Sibley. This letter was signed by Taopi, Good Thunder, and Wabashaw. There were other letters written to General Sibley, but all unknown to the hostile Indians.

The friendly Indians were by this time becoming much stronger, and getting together formed a camp west of the mouth of the Chippewa river. Then Taopi, Good Thunder, Wah-ke-yan-tah-wah, and a few others, came into the friendly camp.[22]

At this time the messengers that had been sent to Fort Ridgely the second time returned and reported that General Sibley was preparing to advance, and that the troops were crossing over to the west side of the Minnesota river.

At this camp it was reported to us that the so-called Medawakanton soldiers were coming to attack us, and we determined to defend ourselves. We soon saw them coming and got our guns, and then getting behind our tents selected about twenty of our men, among them Mazo-ma-ne, [Solomon] Two Stars, Basswood, Wa-su-ho-was-tay [Enos Good Voiced Hail], Wa-ki-ya-hde, and A-chay-tu-ke-yah, with Mazo-ma-ne as spokesman, to go and meet them and tell them that they must come no farther, but go back, and that, if they persisted in coming on, we would fire on them.[23]

So these men went to meet the Medawakantons, and forming in line waited for them to come. When they got near, Mazo-ma-ne commanded them to halt, and said to them, "If you come any nearer we will shoot. Why are you treating us in this way? You have brought about the destruction of everything we had to live on. Do you also want to make captives of us? No, you can never make us your captives. Go back." So they went back, without coming any farther.

The horses had eaten all the grass down to the ground, so we moved our camp about a half mile to the east. There again the Medawakanton soldiers came, and having taken us unawares pushed over some of our tents, but on being ordered to stop they quit and went back to their camp.

Continued on page 230.

Narrative 4
VICTOR RENVILLE'S ACCOUNT

For biographical information on Victor Renville, see Chapter V, Narrative 2.

FOR ABOUT two weeks, the friendly Dakotas and the half-breeds stayed together at the agency brick building. Soon the hostile Indians began coming up into the Yellow Medicine country. Some warriors sent word up to the agency and demanded that the buildings be vacated. The hostiles said that the soldiers were on the way there and unless the buildings were destroyed they would furnish a fort for the troops. So rather than have the buildings burned over their heads the whole band set out for Dr. Riggs' place.

On the way they learned that the hostiles were camped about a mile and a half from the agency and that they were holding a number of women and children prisoners. They also learned that the agency building had been burned. Gabriel [Renville] did not like to see these women and children prisoners suffering. He said that it was fair to take men prisoners, but not the women and children. When they arrived at Dr. Riggs' place, where the buildings were not yet burned by the hostiles, the party made camp. There were already a number of Indians encamped there and among them was John B. Renville, a son of the Joseph Renville [Victor's great uncle] mentioned above. Gabriel went to them and told them of the women and children captives. They agreed with him upon a plan to liberate them. Gabriel called to him two head chiefs of the Upper Agency Indians, [Paul]

Ma-za-ku-te-ma-ni (Cloud Man),[24] and Ma-zo-ma-ni, and told them to go to the hostiles and try to persuade them to give up their prisoners because they were not fighting women and children.

So they called a council of all those camped here and Gabriel supplied a beef. They decided also to call in the head chiefs of the hostiles who were camped a few miles away. The friendly Indians and the half-breeds had gathered in council ready for the feast, but before they could send their messengers to the other camp they saw a band of armed hostiles riding toward them with their chiefs in front. When they came up to within two or three rods of the council, Ma-zo-ma-ni rose up and said to them: "We were about to send for you. Get down and eat with us and tell us why you come."

The women and children stood in a dense mass back of the council circle, afraid of what might happen. Finally after some discussion among themselves, the warriors got down and ate with the others in the council. When they were about through, Ma-zo-ma-ni stood up and made a speech. He said that the hostiles were fighting the whites, a very strong nation, and that the white women and children had been taken captive.

"We think," he told them, "that you are fighting only the men, so you can let the women and children go back to their people. This is what we ask."

One of the soldier band among the hostiles stood up and answered that they knew the white people were too strong for them, but their object was to make the white women and children stay with them and suffer with them when the whites drove them out of the country. Following this speech, the hostile warriors mounted and before riding away they said that all the half-breeds and friendly Indians must come to their camp and unite forces with them the next day, otherwise they would return and force them to join.

After the hostiles left, an old man, Nach-pi-ya-wi-ca-xta [Cloud Man], got up and said that these hostiles, after breaking all treaties and causing the friendly Indians to lose their annuities, were now planning to make them all captives. He also said that they must send out messengers to call all the camps together and prepare to attack the hostiles. Accordingly, two messengers went out and in about two hours all the friendly Indians came together, in all about fifty or sixty tents. About a hundred well armed fighting men, led by two chiefs, set out for the hostile camp. They rode in among the tents of the hostiles, shouting and firing their guns, and the next day the hostiles did not attack the friendly camp.

In two or three days the friendly camp increased to one hundred tents and again the warriors rode over to the hostile camp planning on capturing the white prisoners. The friendly warriors could accomplish nothing and barely avoided a fight with the other camp.

When word was received of the approach of more hostiles, the friendly Indians struck camp and went up the river, pitching camp on the west side. The hostiles followed and camped a mile away. The friendly Indians then held a council and sent General Sibley a letter written by Thomas Robertson, who had escaped from the hostile camp. He, with a comrade, carried the letter to Fort Ridgely. Robertson was allowed to enter the fort blindfolded and was able to explain to Sibley what the friendly Indians were trying to do. He also carried Sibley's letter back to the friendly camp with the message that the general was not fighting his friends among the Indians and half-breeds.

Continued on page 238.

Narrative 5
PAUL MAZAKUTEMANI'S STATEMENT

PAUL MAZAKUTEMANI or He Who Shoots as He Walks was also called Little Paul. A son of Old Eve, a Wahpeton, and a Mdewakanton man, he had many relatives in the Wahpeton village at Lac qui Parle, including his nephews Solomon Two Stars and Ecetukiya. He was one of the first pupils in Williamson's mission school in 1835, becoming literate in the Dakota language. He was an early convert to Christianity, became a farmer, and helped to organize the Hazelwood Republic. In spring 1857, Mazakutemani was one of three Dakotas who rescued Abbie Gardner, a white captive, after the Spirit Lake massacre.

During the war, Mazakutemani acted as spokesman for the opponents of the war and advocated freedom for the captive women and children, speaking out boldly in the many councils that occurred during late August and early September. After the captives were turned over to the whites at Camp Release, he became a scout for Sibley, serving throughout the plains campaigns. In 1867 he was awarded five hundred dollars for his services on behalf of the captives and the army. In about 1880 Mazakutemani wrote his reminiscences of the war in Dakota and sent the manuscript to the Reverend Stephen Riggs, who translated the narrative for publication by the Minnesota Historical Society. Prominent in civil and religious affairs throughout his life, Mazakutemani died at the Sisseton Reservation on January 6, 1885.[25]

Narrative Source: Paul Mazakutemani, "Narrative of Paul Mazakootemane," *Minnesota Historical Collections* 3 (1880): 82–90.

AS I WENT from tent to tent in the Dakota camp I saw a great many white women and children captives. On that account my heart was very sad, and I became almost sick. I considered what I could do to save these captives. And He who is merciful and strong helped me, and in answer to my prayers gave me strength. So I went into the as-

PAUL MAZAKUTEMANI in about 1862

sembly of all the Dakota braves, and I said to them, "If you will give me leave in your council, I will speak to you of a certain matter." They gave me leave to speak. Then I stood up and said, "When this people in times past have assembled in council I have been their speaker; but that time is past. I want to speak now to you of what is in my own heart. Give me all these white captives. I will deliver them up to their friends. You Dakotas are numerous — you can afford to give these captives to me, and I will go with them to the white people. Then, if you want to fight, when you see the white soldiers coming to fight, fight with them, but don't fight with women and children. Or stop fighting. The Americans are a great people. They have much lead, powder, guns, and provisions. Stop fighting, and now gather up all the captives and give them to me. No one who fights with the white people ever becomes rich, or remains two days in one place, but is always fleeing and starving. You have said that whoever talks in this way shall not live — that you will kill him. Stop talking in that way, and if any one says what is good, listen to it."

Then White Lodge's son, who is called "Strike the Pawnees," arose and said, "If we are to die, these captives shall die with us" — and to this they all said "Yes."

I then returned home and made a great feast myself, to which I invited more than two hundred men. When they came together I again demanded the captives, and made a long speech. They had said they would fight the Americans and make friends with the British. To this I answered, "When you say you will fight the Americans and attach yourselves firmly to the British, you say what is not true. Forsake then your evil doings, for the British will dislike every one who is wicked and disobedient, even though he be a white man. This is my thought: listen to it, and deliver up to me the captives."

Then Rattling Runner, one of the chief braves said to me, "The braves say they will not give you the captives. The Mdawakontonwans are men, and therefore as long as one of them lives they will not stop pointing their guns at the Americans."[26]

Next to him a man who is called The Thunder that makes itself blue said to me, "Although we shall die bravely, and though the captives die in the way, I don't care. Don't mention the captives any more."

When they had said these things, they arose and departed, and as they went home they sang a soldier's song: —

"Over the earth I come;
Over the earth I come;
A soldier I come;
Over the earth I am a ghost."

This is the song they sang. I disliked it very much; and although my young men were few, I said to them, "Take your guns; this people have wrought a great wickedness which I will cut in two." So they took up their guns. I then gathered all the horses and wagons that had been taken from the half breeds and restored them to them. Then I called especially upon my friends among the Sissetons. After this I invited the Sissetons and the Mdawankontons all — and on the one side were Sissetons, and on the other side the Mdawakontons. I took my stand in the midst. They said they would kill me; but as I wished to die in the midst of a great multitude, I spoke thus: "Sissetons, the Mdawakontons have made war upon the white people, and have now fled up here. I have asked them why they did this, but I do not yet understand it. I have asked them to do me a favor, but they have refused. Now I will ask them again in your hearing. Mdawakontons, why have you made war on the white people? The Americans have given us money, food, clothing, ploughs, powder, tobacco, guns, knives, and all things by which we might live well; and they have nourished us even like a father his children. Why then have you made war upon them? You did not tell me you were going to fight with the white people; and how then should I approve it? No, I will go over to the white people. If they wish it they may kill me. If they don't wish to kill me, I shall live. So, all of you who do not want to fight with the white people, come over to me. I have now one hundred men. We are going over to the white people. Deliver up to me the captives. And as many of you as don't wish to fight with the whites, gather yourselves together to-day and come to me — all of you who are willing."

Having said these things to them, I removed my tent out to one side, the same day. Then His Thunder, who had Mr. Spencer, one of the captives, came and pitched his tent by mine.[27] And all who valued the friendship of the Americans came also — such as Simon [Anawang-mani] and Lorenzo [Lawrence] of the Wahpetons. Also two Sissetons, viz., Wamdisuntanka (Great-tailed Eagle) and Hayokisna (Hayoka alone.)[28] These were both good men, and each had a captive boy; but they took care of them as their own children. The captive that Great-tailed Eagle had was without clothes. He sold a horse and bought clothes and dressed up the captive boy very well. And I thought he did a good deed.

Continued on page 256.

Narrative 6
JOSEPH LA FRAMBOISE, JR.'S, TESTIMONY

For biographical information on Joseph La Framboise, Jr., see Chapter V, Narrative 3.

LITTLE CROW'S Soldiers' Lodge came around in our camp [on August 28 or August 29] and said that we must form a camp together with them, and made threats that if we did not do that [then] they would injure us. We did not do as they told us to, and they came around the second time, and that time commenced pushing down our tents. . . .

Then the Sissetons and Wahpetons, in order to defend themselves, also formed what we called a Soldiers' Lodge, choosing four men as the councilors of that lodge, and also leading men among the people, who would belong to that lodge. . . .

I was one of those four; one of them was Gabriel Renville; another was a full-blooded Indian by the name of Wa-kpa-i-yu-we-ga, meaning River Crosser, and the fourth man was Pa-da-ni-ku-wa-pi, meaning He who was chased by the Pawnees. Then us four who were chosen as councilors for this lodge got together, and at that time the mixed bloods who were with the Lower Sioux wanted to get away from them, but could not. They would not let them go, so we talked together of what would be best to do in regard to them, and at the same time chose Paul Muzakutamani as spokesman of that lodge. Then Paul Muzakutamani went over toward Little Crow's and stood near Little Crow's lodge and said, "You have been threatening us and trying to get us to join you in what you have done. We have consulted amongst ourselves in regard to this matter and have decided not to do so, and for that reason have formed a Soldiers' Lodge of our own, and we are now ready to defend ourselves. Our Soldiers Lodge will very shortly now come to test themselves, and they will demand of you the horses, wagons, and other property that you have taken from these mixed bloods, and also the mixed bloods themselves." He then came back, and the Soldiers' Lodge got together, got their weapons (myself among the rest) and went to Little Crow's camp. When we got to Little Crow's camp, we asked these mixed bloods where the property was — horses and other things that had been taken away from us. We took them through the camp and they pointed out the property that belonged to us, and we took this property away from Little Crow and returned it to those to whom it belonged. When going our rounds in the camp one man ran out of his tent with his gun in his hand and took hold of the horse that we were taking away, and said that we should not take that horse, and ran up and took hold of the rope that the horse was tied with, when this man, by the name of River Crosser, ran up to him and cut the rope off with his knife above where the man was holding. Then River Crosser, who had a club given him the same as I had, went up to this man and said, "I am a soldier; do you think that I do not mean that I am one?" and struck him with his club and knocked him down. In the meantime the man that came out had his gun in his hand ready to shoot. I jumped down off my horse and took the gun and broke it. Then they stopped all resistance against what we were doing, and we picked up all the property in the camp and went back with it to where we were.

Narrative 7
ECETUKIYA'S TESTIMONY

ECETUKIYA or He Who Brings What He Wants was also called Big Amos. He was born in 1834, probably at Lac qui Parle. He and his brother, Solomon Two Stars, were the sons of Cloud Man, a Wahpeton leader; his father's brother was Paul Mazakutemani. Ecetukiya attended the mission school at Lac qui Parle and joined the Hazelwood Republic in the late 1850s.

Ecetukiya united with the peace party during the war and helped the missionaries escape from the Yellow Medicine Agency. He spoke in council against the hostile forces and was one of a small group that rescued Sophia J. Huggins, widow of missionary Amos Huggins, and her two children. After spending the winter of 1862–63 in the Dakota camp at Fort Snelling, he became one of Gabriel Renville's scouts in the spring and served for several years. In 1867 he was a delegate at the negotiations in Washington, D.C., for the creation of the Sisseton Reservation where he received land in 1875. On August 15, 1901, at the Sisseton Agency, South Dakota, he testified before the U.S. Court of Claims Commission about events in the war; Thomas A. Robertson was the interpreter. Ecetukiya lived the rest of his life on the Sisseton Reservation. The exact date of his death is not known.[29]

Narrative Source: Ecetukiya, "Evidence for the Claimants," *The Sisseton and Wahpeton Bands of Dakota or Sioux Indians v. the United States*, 1901–07, U.S. Court of Claims no. 22524, part 1, p. 120–29.

THE PURPOSE of the council [on August 28 or 29] was to consult in regard to this outbreak, but before anything was said, the Lower Sioux came to this council in a body and said to them that they [Sissetons and Wahpetons] must all move and camp where they, the Lower Sioux, were camped, and that they must move that day, but the answer to that was, "We have something here for you to eat and were going to have you come and eat with us," the Sissetons and Wahpetons said to the Mdewakantons or Lower Sioux. . . .

The Mdewakantons said no more at that time, but Paul Maza-ku-te-mani again got up and said this was no small matter; that it was a great matter, meaning the outbreak, and that he wished that they would deliver over to them, the Sissetons and Wahpetons, the prisoners they had with them, and that they would return them to the whites, and then consider what it was best for them, the Sissetons and Wahpetons, to do for their own good. . . .

I was present at the council [held on September 6]. I said nothing myself, but I heard what was said. The Sissetons had then come down, that is, those whose names have just been mentioned [Standing Buffalo, Mazakutemani, Red Iron, Scarlet Plume, Wanata], and the first one that got up and spoke was Wa-a-na-tan, who said, "I live by the white man," meaning the whites assisted in his living, "and by the buffalo. I fear that you are going to annihilate all these for me, therefore you shall not advance north of here." Then Standing Buffalo got up and spoke and said, "While I am but a boy, I am the chief of our people. My father had dealings with the white people and I am afraid that you are going to destroy them all, and I dread the idea even that the connection that my father had with the white people, meaning the treaties that had been made between my father and the white people, should be destroyed. We live by the white people and by them alone.

It would be well if you would end this thing now," meaning to stop fighting.

Narrative 8
CHARLES R. CRAWFORD'S TESTIMONY

For biographical information on Charles R. Crawford, see Chapter V, Narrative 4.

ABOUT THAT TIME [August 28 or 29] the Medawakantons were moving up toward where we were, and Little Crow came to the agency where we were and said to Ma-zo-mani [Crawford's uncle] and my father [Akipa]: "We are going to form a camp out yonder on the plains, and you must move out there." By that time my father had got my sister [Susan Brown, his half sister] and brought her up there, and their answer to Little Crow was: "We will not do that. What we want to do is to try and save the lives of these," meaning my sister and her family. That is all that was said there, and Little Crow went away. Immediately after Little Crow went away my brother Gabriel [Renville] came in and said: "Hurry up. Before Little Crow forms his camp we will go up to Hazelwood where others are forming a camp." Angus [Brown] and myself immediately hitched up the oxen (we had no horses) to the wagons, and we moved up to within about a quarter of a mile of the missionary buildings, west of the buildings, and we (I mean those of us who were there together at the agency — there were no others there where we camped, but there were others, right at the mission buildings were other Indians). When we came there, about the time we came there, Little Crow and his people were forming a camp between I-yan-mani and Ta-wa-mni-sa-pa, meaning Black Pleiades, houses.[30] Shortly after that four of Little Crow's men came over to where we were camped and ordered us to move over to their camp. My brother Gabriel's answer to them was: "We will not do so." Then Ma-zo-mani said: "We will not go over. We are not going to mix up with you in your camp or your affairs." Then my father, Akipa, said to them: "What are you doing here? Why don't you stay down there where you have committed these acts? We are not going over to you." Then their answer to him was: "Well, that being the case, we will go back and more of us come, and then we will take you over." Then my father said: "Hurry up and go back and come over here quick, you cock suckers." . . . [Counsel for the claimants objected unsuccessfully to this language.]

What Akipa meant to have them understand was that he had no fear of them; that he despised them. The Indians had no curse words, or oaths, and they used this expression to express their contempt. When they got mad they used this expression. Little Crow's men then went back to their camp, and just then Mar-pi-ya-cax-ta (Cloud Man) came to where we were and asked us what those men were saying. He was told they wanted us to move into Little Crow's camp, and he said "No, no; you must not do that. There are enough of you to make a stand, and you must not do as they told you to. It would not be well for you to do as they want you to." Then they got together and went toward Little Crow's camp singing what we call a brave song, which they do when they do not care whether they die or not — a battle, or soldiers' song. Then Akipa, Ma-zo-mani, Mar-pi-ya-cax-ta, Maza-ku-te-mani, and my brother Gabriel got together and consulted what was best to be done. They concluded to make a stand by themselves away from the hostiles, and hold John B. Renville and his wife, and the Brown family, and others, and try to get back to the whites; and if they could not do it sooner, to have them return to the whites when they got to the British line at Pembina. Soon after that Little Crow moved his camp about 2 miles from where they were camped before to within about a half a mile of where we were camped, but we remained where we had camped first. Between the time that Little Crow formed his first camp to the time that I have just mentioned of his having moved further on — in between those times, these five men whose names I have given consulted together in secret and concluded to ask Little Crow for at least a portion of the prisoners in his hands, and, if they could get them, to then take those and the others that they had with them; that is, Renville and the Brown family, and take them together and try and have them sent back to the whites; and if they could not do that, then they would take them on with them to Pembina and send them to their friends from the British side, and they chose Cloud Man and Ma-zo-mani as the ones to ask Little Crow for these prisoners. Those five men then went out in the camp and told the others what they had concluded to do, and we all met together and went over to Little Crow's camp (I was among the rest that went over there). Little Crow's camp was in a circle. We went into that circle; came into the center of the camp. Paul Maza-ku-te-mani then went around as a crier, and said that he was calling a council and wanted them all to come together there where we stood in the center of that camp. After the people got together, Paul Maza-ku-te-mani got up and said: "We have come here to talk. Why do you not get up and say what you have got to say" (speaking to these two men that had been chosen as spokesmen by their own people—that is, Ma-zo-mani and Cloud Man), and went on and said, "Your killing of the whites is a big thing, or great thing, that you have done" (addressing the hostiles) "and I feel as if the world was coming to an end. We have come to ask of you the prisoners in your hands. If you will deliver them over to us, we will see that their lives are saved." A young man on Little Crow's side then got up and said, "We will not deliver the prisoners over to you." Then Paul said in answer, "If you will not give us the prisoners, you shall not cross our line onto our lands."

Continued on page 259.

Narrative 9
STAR'S TESTIMONY

STAR or Wacanrpi was also called Adam Magaiyahe or Lightning Goose. He was born in 1832 and was a member of Red Iron's Sisseton band. Reared as a Dakota, he neither understood nor spoke English. He claimed to know little about the war, but he had attended the council on September 6 at the mouth of the Chippewa River where Standing Buffalo and other Sisseton leaders expressed their desire for peace. He was present at the battle of Wood Lake but only to protect his cousin, Simon Anawangmani. Star was given land on the Sisseton Reservation in 1875. In 1882 he was listed as one of the reservation's more prosperous farmers. On August 14, 1901, at the Sisseton Agency, South Dakota, he testified before the U.S. Court of Claims Commission concerning the war; Thomas A. Robertson was the interpreter. No information is available on his date of death.[31]

Narrative Source: Star, "Evidence for the Claimants," *The Sisseton and Wahpeton Bands of Dakota or Sioux Indians v. the United States,* 1901–07, U.S. Court of Claims no. 22524, part 1, p. 101–5.

WHEN Little Crow and his people came near to where we were living myself and others took our guns and went out and met him and his people and ordered them not to go upon our lands. . . .

There were present Standing Buffalo, Wa-a-na-tan, Scarlet Plume, and Red Iron was already there—that was his home. Wa-a-na-tan in that council got up and said: "I live by the white man and the buffalo. These people who have done this act have destroyed everything I have—the treaties with the whites and everything else—and for that reason I shall object to their going across my land." Standing Buffalo also spoke and said that everything of his had been destroyed by the acts of these people, therefore he should object to their going onto or across his lands. Then Red Iron spoke and said: "My friends"—meaning the Sissetons that were there—"I can not bear the thought of everything of mine being destroyed, therefore I shall stay here where I belong until General Sibley comes here, and I will shake hands with him, and then he may do what he pleases with me." After that council was ended, Wa-a-na-tan and Standing Buffalo and the others started back to their homes—that is, they and their people that were there with them. That is what I know about it.

Narrative 10
LIGHT FACE'S TESTIMONY

LIGHT FACE or Lotitojanjan was born in 1834 and was a member of Cloud Man's band of Sissetons. He was on a hunting expedition north of the Yellow Medicine Agency when the war broke out. But he and other members of the band witnessed the battle of Wood Lake and acted as bodyguards for their relatives—Simon Anawangmani, Lorenzo Lawrence, and John Otherday—who had gone inside Sibley's lines. Light Face settled on the Sisseton Reservation after the war and became a farmer. On August 13, 1901, at the Sisseton Agency, South Dakota, he testified before the U.S. Court of Claims Commission concerning the latter phases of the fighting; Thomas A. Robertson was the interpreter. No information has surfaced on his date of death.[32]

Narrative Source: Light Face, "Evidence for the Claimants," *The Sisseton and Wahpeton Bands of Dakota or Sioux Indians v. the United States,* 1901–07, U.S. Court of Claims no. 22524, part 1, p. 94–101.

THE FIRST council that I knew of was when the Sissetons went from here [Sisseton Agency] down there [near Lac qui Parle], or from up this way down there, and a council was called. . . .

Wa-a-na-tan got up and spoke [on September 6] and said that he lived only by the white man and, for that reason, did not want to be an enemy of the white man; that he did not want the treaties that had been made to be destroyed. . . .

There is something more that Wa-a-na-tan said that I forgot to tell and that is this, that if they, the Medawakantons, did not stop fighting the whites I [Wanata] will stop them from going upon the Yankton or Yanktonais' lands. . . .

I mean these lands out here that Wa-a-na-tan's father had marked out at sometime; the lands that belonged to him and his people, and when Wa-a-na-tan was speaking at that time he meant those lands.

Narrative 11
LORENZO LAWRENCE'S STORY

LORENZO LAWRENCE or Face of the Village or Towanetaton was born near Big Stone Lake in about 1822. His parents were Left Hand and Catherine Totedutawin, both full-blood Dakotas; through his father Lorenzo was related to the Renville and Little Crow families. He studied in Williamson's mission school at Lac qui Parle, 1835–45, but attended a preparatory school at Oberlin, Ohio, for the 1842–43 school year. With his mother he helped to build the mission church at Lac qui Parle in 1841–42. From about 1838 to 1848, he frequently accompanied Little Crow who was then living at Lac qui Parle. When Little Crow returned to Kaposia to claim the chieftainship, Lorenzo assisted him and killed a rival claimant, who was Little Crow's half brother, and married the widow.

Returning to Lac qui Parle, he farmed and worked around the mission and began dressing as a Euro-American. He moved with the Stephen R. Riggs family to Pajutazee in 1854 where he was a founder of the Hazelwood Republic. In 1861 he became the first Dakota Indian to receive citizenship.

He opposed the war and rescued Jannette De Camp and her three children and Mrs. Magloire Robideau and her five children by taking them as well as his own wife and five children to Fort Ridgely. He was a scout at the battle of Wood Lake and aided Sibley's army afterward. An award of five hundred dollars was given to him in 1867 for his services. He homesteaded on the Lac qui Parle mission site in 1868 and moved to the Sisseton Reservation in 1877. He wrote a long account of his life in English in 1894 and died near Peever, South Dakota, on April 25, 1897.[33]

Narrative Source: Lorenzo Lawrence, "Story of Lorenzo Lawrence," 1894, Lorenzo Lawrence Papers, Division of Libraries and Archives, Minnesota Historical Society.

IT WAS more than thirty years ago, in the year 1862, that the Mdewakanton Sioux made war upon the Big Knives. And now because it was a long time ago when the Mdewakanton Indians tell stories of those times, a good many of them will tell about rescuing so many captives at that time. Especially there is the man called Taopi, who is said to have saved 255 captives; and Bishop H[enry] B. Whipple tells the story. But now for myself I will try to tell the exact truth about how I took ten captives to the soldiers at Fort Ridgley. There was a great company of men saw me bring them in. But my chief witnesses are General [Colonel] H. H. Sibley to whom I delivered them, and Dr. T[homas] S. Williamson, and Rev. S[tephen] R. Riggs, and Rev. S[amuel] D. Hinman, and Mr. George Spencer, and what all these men witness to cannot be untrue. But for these things I have never exalted myself, or asked a reward of the Government. Even when I was a boy I tilled the soil, so in later years I have planted potatoes and corn for a living. And I have never appealed to the State of Minnesota to keep me from starvation because I had saved her towns or rescued her citizens who were captives. And I have never asked the Government to pay me for false claims. But as I know my statements are true, when I am so old that I cannot plant corn and potatoes I may with justice call upon the Great Father or the State of Minnesota for help. But as long as there is strength in my arm to toil for a living I think it is best to do so. I want to be a good citizen.

Now I will tell something about how I escaped from the Indians with the captives. It was when the big Indian camp was at Yellow Medicine where I lived [the warriors reached the Yellow Medicine River on August 28]. One day mother came and said to me; Son, in the morning the whole nation is going to move the camp up to Red-iron's Planting. So now, my son, go to the river and get the canoes all ready, and I will come again when it is dark. So I went to the river and got three canoes all ready, and put them in the water. As soon as it was dark mother came, and said, Son this is the last night we shall be together. You will flee with these White women and children, but I must stay with the nation. So let us pray to God to show us the way we should go. So we prayed.

After it had been dark a good while, and no one was walking around my house to see what I was doing, I went down in the cellar where I had the captives hid. Mother wanted to see them; so I opened the door and brought them out. Mother rose and shook hands with Mrs. [Jannette] De Camp, and kissed her and said: My sister, the power of God is very great, the power of the Indians is not great. If it is God's will, in less than a month all these Indians will be captives. Mrs. De Camp answered, Yes they can kill the body but they can't kill the soul.

Then I said to the women: This night bake all the bread you can, there are a great many children. Then I said again to them. Have every thing in readiness, for by daylight in the morning, before the Indians gather up the nation for the march, we must hide somewhere in the woods. And when night comes again we shall flee in the canoes. Mrs. De Camp asked if there were any canoes to go in. I answered, Yes, they are all ready. Mrs. De Camp asked again, Brother Lawrence, do you think we can escape from the Indians. And I answered, Yes, that is a hard question to answer now, but if we pray to God he will show us the way to go. It [was?] nearly time for day break, so I asked the women, How many loaves of bread have you baked. They said, Four. And I said, Mrs. De Camp, my sister, You take care of the loaves of bread and keep them for the children. If one cries for hunger give it five or six bites, and save what you can from the large ones. Remember we do not know how long it will be before we get out of this wilderness. So save the bread all you can, so we can have it for the one who is going to starve to death. And now we heard the Indians beginning to stir in the Camp. And now the noise became fearful. There were calls and cries and singing. And we fled to the thick woods in the bottom near where Dr. Williamson had lived [on the Minnesota River]. And there was a big cane swamp there, and we ran into that till the water was up to our knees, and we stood there. And then we found a large musk-rat house, and we put all the children on that and some of them went to sleep there, but we stood in the water waiting for all the Indian Camp to move away. It was now about four o'clock in the afternoon and I said, Behold women, the noise of the camp has all died away. I think the Indians have all gone. Let us go out to the dry land. And I also said, Now I think I will go and peep over the hill and see if they are all gone. But the women said, Don't go, don't go. Perhaps they will kill you, and then we will all die. But I persisted, saying, Why if I go and see whether they are all gone or not then we can tell better what course we should take; and I shall go very secretly. Then we all came to dry land, and they were all very cold because they had stood so long in the water. Then I went up the hill peeping over its brow here and there to see if any of the Indian camp was left, but it was all gone, not a human being was to be seen, nothing but the old dirty grounds they had left. Then I looked and behold the missionary's house and our nice little church had been burned and the embers were still smoking. Then I looked for my house and they had burned it too. Then I looked around for my mother and my brother [Joseph Kawanke] and my sister [Sarah], and they with their families were all gone, and everything was destroyed by fire. As I stood there looking at these things a terrible oppression came over my heart. I was weighed down with great grief. I had been e[x]pecting something of the kind because I had heard the Indians say that when they left they would burn everything behind them. So every day I had been keeping watch around the church to see what would happen. You see I thought a great deal of that church. It was with a great deal of toil that we built that house, and I could not bear the thought of it being destroyed. I was only one man and they were a great company. . . .[34]

But one thing I was glad I had done. When I heard what the Indians were doing, I thought that was what they would do, and one day I went and hired a young man that was very strong, and I went and hired him for two dollors [sic] to help me, and we went and took the bell down from the church, and put it in a hole in the ground, and buried it. Then I went to the Mission house and every body had fled, but I went in and got the boxes with Indian Bibles and Indian hym[n]-books, and took them and buried them too, so I knew they were not burned, and I was glad of that.

Then I went to look at my own house and I found everything burned. But I found the chickens had run off and hid in the bushes. So I caught four of them, and then I went back to where I had left the women, and I said to the women. Now dress these chickens as quick as you can, and I will go and hunt a kettle and we will stew the chickens and give the children a good meal here in the bushes, and to-night we will all flee in the boats.

Then as I thought how I was to take all those women and children through all the dangers and keep them safe it made my heart shake, and I thought over the best way to do with all my might. And then as it was growing dark we had prayers. We sung the hymn, "Nearer my God to thee." Then we prayed these words, O God, our Father in heaven, this night be with us in our secret wanderings, and guide us in the way we should go.

Then after prayers we went to the river where I had prepared the boats. By that time it was very dark. And we stood there ready to get into the boats, and the women said, What will you do with the dog? If you put him in the boat he will tip it over and drown some of us. And they were very afraid to let him in. So I said, Well this is my dog, I will kill him. So I called Fox, Fox, and he came up wagging his tail, and I caught and gagged him, and then broke his skull without his making any noise. I prized this dog very highly, and it hurt me very much to do it, but I thought even our own bodies are not worth much just now. Then we all got in the boats. But it was very dark so we could not see where we were going, and the women were very much afraid. So I said to them. Why are you afraid? Just think God is watching you and you won[']t be afraid. Then we went on and kept going all night. About daylight it commenced raining, and the wind blew from the north and we were all cold, and they begged me to stop and make a fire. So we stopped in the brush and I made a big fire, and the children were all glad to get near it and warm. And then the children commenced asking for something to eat, and they gave each of them a little piece of bread. Then I told my boys Moses and Thomas to climb up in the trees, perhaps they could see a hostile scout. Then they clumb [sic] up and looked across the river and saw a little girl, and the poor little thing could hardly walk, and directly they saw her mother come out of a ravine and take her back with her. So I went and waded over the river, it was over four feet deep, and went in the direction they had gone, and it was a woman named Mrs. Robideau and her six [five] little boys and girls, who had run off to hide from the Indians.[35] And it was so cold she had taken off her dress, and tied it over the brush for a shelter, and they were all huddled under that nearly froze. So I gathered them all up and took them over the river to our fire, and we were all glad to see each other. Then I said, Let us have prayers now. And we sung

"All hail the power of Jesus' name,
Let Angels prostrate fall,
Bring forth the royal diadem,
And crown him Lord of all."

Then we prayed thus: O Lord our God, watch over us this day, and turn the eyes of the Indians so they won't see us. And we prayed with all our heart.

That was a very windy day, and rainy too. We stayed hid all day, because we knew we could not travel without some one seeing us, and if they saw us they would not spare our lives. And the women too were afraid to stir out in the day time. So I thought it was best to be quiet, and the children lay by the fire where they could be warm and slept. When dark came we all went to the boats again, and got in and rowed quietly away. That was a very dark night, and cold too, and the women and children suffered very much. And we could not see, so the boats would run into trees or rocks or shoals, and I would have to get out and wade and shove the boats into the channel again. So we worked all night, and at daylight we again stopped in a thicket, and stayed there all that day. Soon after the sun rose three cows and a sheep wandered up close to where we were, and the women said, Oh, kill one of the cows so we and the children won[']t starve to death. I got my pistol out and was getting ready to shoot, when they said, Oh, don[']t shoot, there's a sheep with the cows. Perhaps you can catch it and kill it with a knife. So I pulled out my knife and started after the sheep. I chased it and it ran, and I ran and ran, but it was very swift, and I tired myself all out for nothing. I came back to where the folks were and they were all laughing to see me run after the sheep. Then the women said. We told you not to shoot because we were afraid some of the bad Indians would hear it and find us. But we would rather run the risk than starve to death. It was the second day now that we grown people had eaten nothing, and I had been working hard two nights, so I knew I must have something to eat or I would lose my strength. So I took a little rope, and I went up softly towards the cows and spoke gently to them, and afterwhile one of them let me put the rope around her horns, and I led her up to where the folks were, and I took the pistol and shot her dead. When the women saw it they thanked the Lord for the food and were very glad. I went to work as hard as I could to skin it. And when I had got a good deal skinned the children all came around. And they were so hungry that they commenced picking off the fat and chewing it, and I told them not to do it, but they were so eager they paid no attention to me, they could see nothing but the meat; and I looked at them and pitied them. So I commenced at once cutting out pieces of the meat with my knife which was nothing but a pocket knife, and gave the pieces to my wife, who had made a fire, and the women all set to work roasting them on the fire, and as soon as the meat was a little roasted they would give it to the children. There was not any other knife in the crowd, so they all had to work with their fingers and teeth like dogs. Afterwhile we had all got what we wanted to eat. Then I said, Now we are all refreshed let us sing and pray. So we sung a hymn, and then prayed towards heaven with all our heart.

Then I said, Now all you women, Today roast before the fire all the meat you can, to take along. Tonight again we shall paddle the boats as hard as we can all night. And God having mercy on us, not an Indian will see us. So all the women roasted what meat they could that day. When it was dark we again went to the boats and started off. That night was very cold. There was some frost. And there were rapids; and a great many shoal places in the river, and the boats would get stuck and I would have to keep getting out in the water to shove them off, and I had no change of clothes; so I was wet all the time, and got very cold. We stopped at daylight, and pretty soon we heard a chicken crow, and we concluded there must be some settler near there. We waited expectantly till daylight. Then we looked around and saw a house some distance off. So I went to see who was there. When I got close I saw that the door stood open. Then I saw where some one had been at work hewing a log with a broadax, and he had been shot while he was at work, for there he lay dead by the log[,] on his face, and two bullet holes in his shoulder. I looked all around quick, and I found the body of a boy with a bullet hole in his head.[36] Seeing these dead bodies moved my heart very much. I looked around and found a spade at the stable, and I took the bodies and buried them as well as I could. I then went to the door of the house and I wrote on a piece of paper: I am Lorenzo Lawrence. I am fleeing from the Indians with some White women and children, and my own wife and children. We are going down in boats, and when we came here we found the dead bodies of a man and boy, and I buried them near the house under the mound of dirt. I have ten captive women and children that I am fleeing with, and I write this so any one who comes can tell who was here. Then I tacked the paper on the door. Afterward I went in the house and took a kettle and dish and knife, and went back to where the women and children were. And we made a fire and stewed some of the meat we had, and the women and children were very glad to get some cooked meat and soup. And the women asked me, What did you see at the house where you went. But I did not want to tell them I had found the dead bodies and buried them, because I thought it would frighten them, so I did not tell them that. That was the Sabbath day, and we rested there all day. And I was sick too. I had the head ache and pains in my bowels, and so lay still all the time. And the women were troubled and said[,] Perhaps you won[']t get over it, and what will become of us all then. But I said to them: Don[']t [be] afraid. All these nights I have been jumping out in the water to shove the boats off when they got stuck, and keeping my cold wet clothes on, and that is what is the matter with me. But don[']t be troubled about it. I think I will get well. And whenever you are afraid just remember God is taking care of us. Then I will tell you where we are. This place has a big name among the Indians. Long ago when there were hardly any Whites ever came among the Indians, old Mr. [Joseph] Renville[, Sr.,] had a camp here, and was trading with the Indians. And the Indians then worshipped bear skins, and called them Sacred skins. But old Mr. Renville took a piece of a bear's skin and made himself a hat of it. So the Indians named this place Sacred Hat.

We stopped over there till the next morning, and then we started from there very early. We had not gone far, perhaps a little over two miles when we heard a cannon down towards Fort Ridgely. We heard it plain. They heard it in all the boats.[37] The women clapped their hands for joy, and said, White men fired the cannon. But some of the women answered: Perhaps the Indians have whipped the soldiers and captured the cannon and are firing it. Then I laughed and said, No the Indians could never capture the cannon from the Soldiers. Then I said, Let us now stop and give thanks to God. I think you will live now, and see your friends again. And the women sung, Nearer my God to thee. And then we sent up joyful prayers to God.

They all felt better then, and so paddled the boats faster, without so much fear. That day we kept hearing the cannon very often, which enlivened the women, and they talked away as they paddled, and revived me very much. And towards evening we drew near to the Redwood ferry. And some of the women said, There were a great many soldiers killed at the ferry. Let us not camp close by them. So we were looking for a place to camp before we got there, and going along slow.

There were three big conoes [*sic*] and one little one. And Thomas
Lawrence and Willie De Camp were in the little canoe, and they were
going along careless, like boys. The big boats were ahead and they
were in the little boat behind us, and they let their canoe run on a snag
in the water,[.] The boat turned over and threw them both into the
water. Thomas held on to the boat, but poor Willie floated off, and
when I looked back I saw him just sinking in the water. I jumped into
the water and commenced feeling around for him. My wife jumped
in the water too, and hunted for him. Afterwhile she called out;
Come, I have got hold of him. I started towards her but she had pulled
him out before I got there. I thought I saw a movement in him, and
I took my coat and wrapped him in it, and watched for his breath.
Presently I saw he breathed, and I said, Willie can you breathe, and
he said, Yes. Then I said to his mother, Your son is alive. And she felt
great joy. We were all frightened to think how near one of us came
to dying, and our memory was refreshed, and we knew well that God
was watching over us, and we were filled with gratitude to him. So
we stopped there and stayed that night. In the morning we awoke early and started. We had gone about two miles when we came to Redwood ferry. It was still quite early, and it filled us with gloomy
thoughts as we rowed past, and looked at the mounds along the bank
where the soldiers, who had so lately been killed, were buried.[38] We
had gone on some distance when I saw the body of a soldier in the water, where it had floated against the bank. I told the folks in the other
boats to go on a little way and wait for me. Then I stopped and went
to where the body was lodged, and I saw it was the body of an officer,
with a sword on this side, and epaulets on his shoulders.[39] I think it
was the Captain so many of whose soldiers were killed at the ferry.
I pulled it out on the bank, and dug a hole as well as I could and buried it. We all then went on. We wanted to get to Fort Ridgely that
night, but we had had nothing to eat that day, and were not strong
[enough] to row the boats. Afterwhile we saw a field of corn close by
the river. So we stopped and made a fire, and got some of the corn
and roasted it, and we were so hungry we eat it before it was done,
and we kept on roasting and eating a long time, and forgot we were
in a hurry to get to the fort that night. And some of them lay down
and went to sleep because they were very tired too. So it was way after
noon when we got started again. We went on that afternoon listening
to the noise of the soldiers at the fort, for there were a great many
there then. And as we came near it was getting dark, and we knew

the guards would be standing around the fort, and if we went near in the dark we were afraid they would shoot us. So we stopped across the river from the fort and stayed that night. It rained very hard that night, and a strong wind from the east was blowing, and we got soaked to the skin, and were cold and miserable, and spent the night without sleep. In the morning we got in our boats and went on about half a mile and came to where there was a big flat-boat the soldiers had got ready to cross the river in. We stopped by it, and the women and children crawled under it, and I stood on the boat looking around, and presently a soldier came whistling along the road to the boat, and when he came near he said, "Good Morning", and I said the same. He said, "You are out here early." I said. "I come from the hostile Indians, and there is a lot of women and children under the boat, who were prisoners, and fled with me." When he heard that he jumped down to where they were, and shook hands with them all, and passed a few words with them, and started back on a run. And very soon we saw a squad of soldiers coming, and they lined up in front of us. Then the officer came forward and shook hands with all of us, and talked some little while with the White women. By that time some wagons had come, and they loaded us all in and took us into the fort, and there they stopped with us at one of the nice houses, and gave us seats where we rested a little, and then they invited us off to a room to eat, and we sat down to a table where we saw different kinds of food, and it made us all hoppy [happy], and we gave thanks, and as we ate I talked to them and said, "Now I have brought you prisoners all safe to where you will live, and thank God that he has helped me to do it. And you too must be grateful to God. Remember when you were fleeing for your lives, in your hiding places you could all pray to God every morning, and he heard you, and I am glad. So now as long as you live you must remember that, and worship God." Thus while we were eating I talked away to the ten captives. When we finished and went back to the room where we were before, an officer came and talked to Mrs[.] De Camp and said, "You know this is a ter-rible time we are having, and we have had some fearful battles, and a great many have been killed, both Whites and Indians. And we had a fearful fight up at Birch Cooley, and I come to tell you Mr[.] De Camp was killed there." When the poor woman heard that she cried very hard. She had talked to me a great deal about her husband, and now I felt sorry for here [her]. And she had told me too that if I got her away from the Indians, her husband would do a great deal for me.

But that was not what I thought of when I was in so much trouble getting away with them, but it was that I pitied them and wanted them to live. Then I said to here [her], There is no one lives or dies but what God knows it. So trust in God. Then she said to me. "Brother Lawrence, thank you for talking thus to me. I thank God with all my heart that you saved me. If I had found my husband alive he would have done everything he could for you, I am sure. But he is killed, and I feel so sad." Then I said, "Yes, but you have all your children alive with you, and so while you cry remember to trust in God, and in his good mercy he will wipe the tears from your eyes." The rest of us were all very sorry too that the husband of one of the ten captives I had brought away, had been killed, but still we knew that God was merciful, and so we said, God is good.

The next morning I was asked to go outside of the fort to the large camp of soldiers who were there on their march against the hostile Indians. I went and they took me to where the Commander and head officers were. Gen. [Col.] H. H. Sibley, and Rev. S. R. Riggs and others were there. Then they said to me. Lorenzo Lawrence, we have almost raised you, and know you like a book. Now we want you to tell us the truth about what you know about the Indians, and swear to it by this Bible we have laid here. So I arose and took the Bible in my hand and said, I believe this book is the Word of God, who has brought me alive here this day, and turned the eyes of the hostile Indians away so they did not see me or hurt me. And now I will tell you wise men the whole truth about what I know.

NOTES

1. For more on Little Paul Mazakutemani, see his narrative in Chapter VIII, p. 194, below.

2. John L. Campbell, the son of mixed-bloods Scott Campbell and Margaret Menanger, was born in March 1833 at Mendota and was educated there. He was active in the fur trade on the upper Minnesota River and joined Brackett's Battalion in November 1861. He deserted the army and returned to Minnesota in March 1864. He then broke out of the Fort Snelling guardhouse and joined the Dakotas who were living near Fort Garry, Manitoba. In April 1865 he led a raiding party to the vicinity of Mankato that murdered the Jewett family. He was captured and lynched at Mankato on May 3, 1865; St. Paul Pioneer, May 7, 1865, p. 1; Williams, History of the City of Saint Paul, 135.

3. For more on Standing Buffalo, see his narrative in Chapter X, p. 291, below.

4. After the war a story circulated that Little Crow had been stunned by a cannon

ball and therefore took no part in the fighting at Fort Ridgely. Brown's account contradicts this story. See Hubbard and Holcombe, *Minnesota as a State*, 337.

5. Red Iron or Mazasa or Sounding Iron was a Sisseton leader born in about 1810 near Lake Traverse. He opposed but signed the Treaty of Traverse des Sioux of 1851 and led his band to the reservation in 1854. He was a member of the 1858 treaty delegation that sold Dakota lands north of the Minnesota River. During winter 1862–63, he and Akipa, his older brother, cared for the Dakota prisoners in the camp near Mankato. He converted to Christianity and accompanied the exiled Dakotas to Crow Creek and then served as an Indian scout, 1865–66. He received a grant of land on the Sisseton Reservation and lived there until his death in 1884; Hughes, *Indian Chiefs of Southern Minnesota*, 60–65; *Le Sueur News*, September 5, 1907; "Red Iron," J. Fletcher Williams Papers, Division of Libraries and Archives, Minnesota Historical Society; Kappler, comp. and ed., *Indian Treaties*, 2:590, 788; U.S. Congress, *Sisseton and Wahpeton Sioux Indians*, 44th Cong., 1st sess., 1875, H. Doc. 42, p. 5.

6. The victims were probably John Kochendorfer, his wife, and his daughter Sarah of Middle Creek Township, Renville County. Four other children escaped to Fort Ridgely; Satterlee, *Detailed Account*, 28, 99.

7. The Bishop Seabury Mission was established in 1858 at Faribault by the Reverend James Lloyd Breck as an Episcopal seminary; *St. Paul Pioneer Press*, November 21, 1943.

8. Taxunkemaza or His Iron Horse was tried and acquitted by the military commission; Satterlee, *Court Proceedings*, 20; Transcripts of Trials of Sioux Indians, case no. 21, Senate Records 37A-F2.

9. Transcripts of Trials of Sioux Indians, case no. 135, Senate Records 37A-F2; Satterlee, *Court Proceedings*, 42–44.

10. John Moores was the son of Hazen Mooers, a trader, and a Dakota woman. He was born in 1826 near Red Wing's village at the mouth of the Cannon River and lived there with his mother until he was about fifteen years old. He then joined his father and learned about the fur trade. They moved to the Redwood Agency in 1853, and by 1855 John was clerking for James W. Lynd. He was active in the war protecting the captives and spent the winter of 1862–63 in the Dakota camp at Fort Snelling. After scouting for the army, 1863–67, he settled on a claim in Lincoln County and married a sister of Thomas Robinson's. He died on January 1, 1899; A. E. Tasker, *Early History of Lincoln County* (Lake Benton, Minn.: Lake Benton News Print, 1936; reprinted, 1973), 294; *Tyler Journal*, January 6, 1899.

11. Thomas Robinson was the son of Dennis Robinson and a Mdewakanton woman. He was born in about 1826. In 1856 he was living at Wabasha and was married to a daughter of Wakute. He moved with Wakute's band to the reservation in the early 1850s. There he appears to have lived as a Dakota, supplementing his annuity by hunting and trapping in winter months. He and his family spent the winter of 1862–63 in the Dakota camp at Fort Snelling. He was a scout, 1863–66, and then settled near his friend, John Moores, in Hope Township, Lincoln County, where they farmed. He died on September 29, 1887; Roll of Mixed-Blood Claimants, 1856, Records of the Bureau of Indian Affairs, NARG 75; Chilson, "Dakota Indian Scout Roster"; Death certificate, Lincoln County Records, Lincoln County Courthouse, Ivanhoe.

12. For more on John Otherday, see his narrative in Chapter V, p. 119, above; for Lorenzo Lawrence, see Chapter VIII, p. 205, below.

13. For information on the Spirit Lake massacre, see Folwell, *History of Minnesota*, 2:400–415.

14. Jacob Grayfoot or Siharota and his brother, Makpiyakahoton or Loud Voiced Cloud, were sons of the Wahpeton leader Wakanmani or Spirit Walker, whose village was near the mouth of the Lac qui Parle River. They rescued Margaret Ann Marble in May 1857; Doane Robinson, "A Visit with Grayfoot," *Monthly South Dakotan* 3

THE PEACE PARTY / 217

(1901): 285–88. Makpiyakahoton was tried and acquitted by the military commission. In 1875 he received land on the Sisseton Reservation. Satterlee, *Court Proceedings*, 55; Transcripts of Trials of Sioux Indians, case no. 246, Senate Records 37A-F2; U.S. Congress, *Sisseton and Wahpeton Sioux Indians*, 44th Cong., 1st sess., 1875, H. Doc. 42, p. 19.

15. For more on White Spider, see his narrative in Chapter III, p. 60, above.

16. For more on Akipa, see Charles Crawford's narrative in Chapter V, p. 112, above; for Solomon Two Stars, see Chapter IX, p. 241, below.

17. John B. Renville, the son of Mary and Joseph Renville, Sr., was born at Lac qui Parle in October 1831. He was educated at the local mission school and at an Illinois college, taught school at the Yellow Medicine Agency, and was held captive with his white wife during the war. He was ordained as the first Dakota minister of the Presbyterian church in 1865. He died at the Sisseton Reservation in December 1903; Adams, Williamson, and Renville, *First Fifty Years*, Appendix, xiv, xv.

18. Tahtawahkanhdi or Takewakanhdi or Wind Out of Lightning appears to have been a Wahpeton who aided the peace party. He probably was the Takewakankeda who received land on the Sisseton Reservation in 1875, but nothing more has been found about him; U.S. Congress, *Sisseton and Wahpeton Sioux Indians*, 44th Cong., 1st sess., 1875, H. Doc. 42, p. 7.

19. For more on Joseph La Framboise, Jr., see his narrative in Chapter V, p. 108, above. The editors have found no further information on Marpiyahdinape or Wakpaiyuwega.

20. Wakinyantoechye or The Thunder that Paints Itself Blue was a Mdewakanton who probably belonged to Little Crow's band. In the early stages of the war he acted as the Mdewakanton spokesman and opposed the release of white captives. During his trial by the military commission he admitted being at Fort Ridgely and New Ulm but denied active participation in battles. Convicted and sentenced to be hanged, his sentence was remitted, and he was held at the Davenport prison camp. He was pardoned in 1866 and moved to the Santee Reservation; Heard, *History of the Sioux War*, 158; Satterlee, *Court Proceedings*, Appendix, 12; Transcripts of Trials of Sioux Indians, case no. 322, Senate Records 37A-F2.

21. For more information on Charles Crawford, see his narrative in Chapter V, p. 112, above.

22. Wahkeyantahwah or Wakeyantawa or His Tent was also called Waziduta or Red Pine. He was tried, convicted, and sentenced to be hanged. He received a reprieve and was sent to the prison camp at Davenport, Iowa. He was pardoned in 1866; Satterlee, *Court Proceedings*, Appendix, 3; Transcripts of Trials of Sioux Indians, case no. 75, Senate Records 37A-F2.

23. The editors have found no further information on Wakiyahde or Achaytukeyah.

24. Cloud Man or Machpiyawicaxta (Mahpiyawicasta) was a Wahpeton leader. His sons were Solomon Two Stars and Amos Ecetukiya; his brothers were Eagle Help and Paul Mazakutemani. He signed the Treaty of Traverse des Sioux in 1851. The date of his death is not known. He is often confused with the Mdewakanton Cloud Man who had lived at Lake Calhoun, 1828–39; Anderson, *Little Crow*, 41, 86, 188; Kappler, comp. and ed., *Indian Treaties*, 2:589.

25. John P. Williamson, "An Indian Hero Gone," *Northwestern Presbyterian*, February 7, 1885, p. 1.

26. Rattling Runner or Hdainyanka belonged to Little Crow's band of Mdewakantons but was Wabasha's son-in-law. As a leader he signed the Treaty of Mendota in 1851. He supported the Dakota warriors and was at the battles at New Ulm, Fort Ridgely, and Wood Lake. He served as the Mdewakanton speaker before the battle of Wood Lake and offered great rewards to men who fought well. He was tried, convict-

ed, and hanged at Mankato on December 26, 1862; Hubbard and Holcombe, *Minnesota as a State*, 402; Kappler, comp. and ed., *Indian Treaties*, 2:592; Satterlee, *Court Proceedings*, 19–20; Transcripts of Trials of Sioux Indians, case no. 19, Senate Records 37A-F2; Carley, *Sioux Uprising*, 61, 72–73.

27. His Thunder or Wakinyantawa, also called Chaska, was a member of Little Crow's band and his head soldier until the war and was noted as a warrior in fighting the Ojibway. On the morning of August 18 he saved the life of George H. Spencer, his friend, at the Redwood Agency and took care of him thereafter. He then refused to participate in the war. He was a scout for the Sibley expedition of 1863 and was poisoned on his return trip from the Missouri River. His family was awarded $250 for his saving Spencer's life; Bishop, *Dakota War Whoop*, 50–60; Wall, *Recollections of the Sioux Massacre*, 277; U.S. Office of Indian Affairs, *Report, 1866*, 238.

28. Wamdisuntanka or Great Tailed Eagle served as a Dakota scout, 1864–67. He then settled on the Sisseton Reservation. Nothing further is known of him; Chilson, "Dakota Indian Scout Roster"; Charles Crawford and Samuel J. Brown, Census of the Lake Traverse Indians, October 3, 1867, p. 12, Joseph R. and Samuel J. Brown Papers, Division of Libraries and Archives, Minnesota Historical Society. Hayokisna or Heyoka Alone was also called Sweaty Clown. He served as a scout at Lake Traverse, Bears Den, and the head of the Coteau in 1865; Chilson, "Dakota Indian Scout Roster."

29. Kappler, comp. and ed., *Indian Treaties*, 2:959; U.S. Congress, *Sisseton and Wahpeton Sioux Indians*, 44th Cong., 1st sess., 1875, H. Doc. 42, p. 7.

30. The editors have found no further information on Black Pleiades or Tawamnisapa.

31. U.S. Congress, *Sisseton and Wahpeton Sioux Indians*, 44th Cong., 1st sess., 1875, H. Doc. 42, p. 27; U.S. Office of Indian Affairs, *Report, 1882*, 40.

32. U.S. Congress, *Sisseton and Wahpeton Sioux Indians*, 44th Cong., 1st sess., 1875, H. Doc. 42, p. 25; U.S. Office of Indian Affairs, *Report, 1882*, 41.

33. Anderson, *Little Crow*, 41, 42, 44, 45, 51, 57, 79, 91, 156, 188, 189, 190; [Holcombe], *Sketches Historical and Descriptive*, 57–59; *Grant County* (Milbank, So.Dak.) *Review*, April 29, 1897, p. 4. Jannette E. De Camp left a narrative of her experiences during the war; see "Mrs. J. E. De Camp Sweet's Narrative of Her Captivity in the Sioux Outbreak of 1862," *Minnesota Collections* 6 (1894): 354–80.

34. Five and one-half pages of the narrative have not been included. Lorenzo at this point recounted the history of the church building.

35. Magloire Robideau, a native of Canada, married sixteen-year-old mixed-blood Madaline Dumarce in about 1855. In 1859 they took a land claim on Hawk Creek in Renville County. In mid-August 1862 he enlisted in the Renville Rangers and participated in the defense of Fort Ridgely and the battle of Wood Lake. He was discharged in late November 1862 and returned to his family, which was still at Fort Ridgely. They returned to Hawk Creek in 1867 and were living there in 1870; U.S. Census, 1860, Hawk Creek Township, Renville County, roll 373, p. 375, 1870, roll 9, p. 148; Board of Commissioners, *Minnesota in the Civil and Indian Wars*, 1:780; Curtiss-Wedge, *History of Renville County*, 1:106, 549; Roll of Mixed-Blood Claimants, 1856, Records of the Bureau of Indian Affairs, NARG 75.

36. The identities of these victims cannot be ascertained.

37. The cannon fire probably came from Sibley's relief column, which was trying to reach the troops surrounded at Birch Coulee.

38. The burial detail had been at the ferry on September 1, buried about twenty soldiers, and moved on to camp at Birch Coulee.

39. Captain John S. Marsh had drowned after his command was ambushed at Redwood Ferry.

CHAPTER IX

Wood Lake and
Camp Release

THE SQUABBLING over the captives came to an end on September 21 when news reached the Dakotas that an army of fourteen hundred men commanded by Colonel Sibley was marching up the Minnesota River valley. The Dakotas realized that they could not allow Sibley's army to advance any farther, and after some debate the soldiers' lodge determined to make one final, all-out assault on the whites. The Indian army of about six hundred men departed that evening for battle the following morning. Messengers had informed the leaders that Sibley's troops had camped just south of the Yellow Medicine Agency near a small body of water called Wood Lake.

During the late night hours of September 22, the soldiers' lodge and other Indians, some of whom were friendly to the whites, debated strategy. Little Crow wished to attack Sibley's position before sunrise, using the cover of darkness to create confusion. The plan was a good one, since Sibley's men were inexperienced and would panic easily. Several Indians, who were opposed to the war in general but were seemingly on the side of the warriors, dreaded the outcome. They promptly accused Little Crow and his followers of cowardice and persuaded the warriors to adopt different tactics. The battle was set for dawn. The fighting erupted when a few white men went out to collect potatoes for breakfast. Indians, lying in ambush near the potato patch, fired on them. While the element of surprise was effective initially, the Indians could not withstand the fire power of the regrouped army and failed to rout the whites. This defeat ended the dream of expelling the settlers from the upper Minnesota River valley.

During the battle, the friendly Indians who had remained in camp dug rifle pits in the centers of their lodges and took possession of many of the captives still held in the warriors' camp. Thus when the defeated Indians returned, most of their hostages had been taken from them, and their choices had been reduced to two — stay and surrender or flee to the Dakota plains. Many Mdewakantons retreated

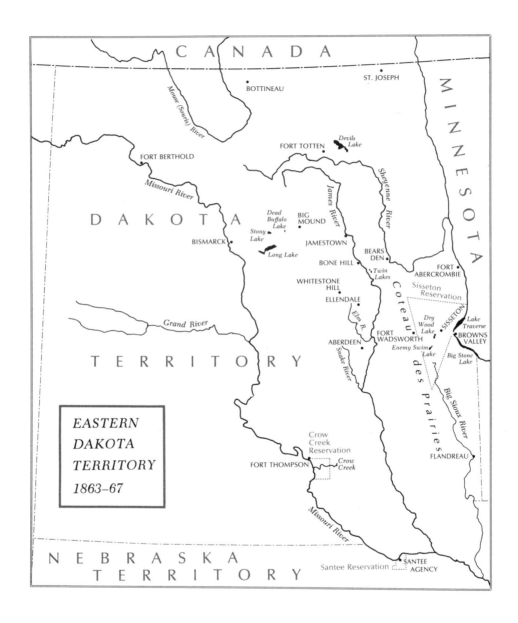

CANADA

BOTTINEAU

ST. JOSEPH

MINNESOTA

Mouse (Souris) River

FORT TOTTEN

Devils Lake

FORT BERTHOLD

Missouri River

Sheyenne River

James River

D A K O T A

Dead Buffalo Lake

BIG MOUND

Stony Lake

BISMARCK

Long Lake

JAMESTOWN

BEARS DEN

FORT ABERCROMBIE

BONE HILL

Twin Lakes

Sisseton Reservation

WHITESTONE HILL

ELLENDALE

Grand River

Elm R.

Dry Wood Lake

SISSETON

Lake Traverse

FORT WADSWORTH

BROWNS VALLEY

T E R R I T O R Y

ABERDEEN

Enemy Swim Lake

Big Stone Lake

Snake River

Coteau des prairies

Big Sioux River

EASTERN
DAKOTA
TERRITORY
1863–67

Crow Creek Reservation

FLANDREAU

FORT THOMPSON

Crow Creek

Missouri River

N E B R A S K A
T E R R I T O R Y

Santee Reservation

SANTEE AGENCY

with Little Crow, but others decided to test the promise made by Sibley through the mixed-blood messengers that only those Indian men who had killed noncombatants would be punished. Camp Release, the village holding the peace party and the majority of the captives, soon sheltered a growing number of Indians—some previously hostile and all now professing friendship with the whites.

Sibley's army marched into Camp Release on September 26 and freed those who had been held captive. Two days later Sibley organized a military tribunal of five officers of volunteer regiments to examine evidence regarding Indian participation in the war. By November 5 the tribunal had tried 392 men, handling as many as forty cases in one day, and sentenced 307 to be hanged. Although many of these men had joined the war reluctantly, the tribunal usually determined their guilt by using their own incriminating testimony and condemned anyone who admitted being at a battle and firing a weapon. The defendants in the trials had no lawyers to represent them, were not allowed to bring in witnesses in their own defense, and were given no time to prepare. Despite the fact that few of the men on trial knew the English language and interpreters had to be used, the interpreters were not sworn in. At no point in the trials did anyone intervene on the behalf of the defendants.

As the prisoners, chained together, and their dependents, numbering more than sixteen hundred people, were moved down river to Mankato, Henderson, and St. Paul, the townspeople of the frontier communities made a number of assaults on the caravans, throwing stones and bricks. Governmental authorities finally appeased the anger of the white settlers on December 26 when thirty-eight men were hanged for crimes against civilians. This number was determined by President Abraham Lincoln, whose legal advisers concluded that evidence against the remainder of the Dakota warriors in custody was insufficient to warrant capital punishment. In the spring the remaining prisoners were sent to a prison camp in Davenport, Iowa, and their families to the Crow Creek Reservation in south central Dakota Territory.

The final days of the war have been chronicled by many full- and mixed-bloods. The narratives demonstrate that many mixed-bloods and full-bloods played a crucial role in preventing the slaughter of captives and in bringing about a resolution to the war. All who had opposed the war and all who had been captives rejoiced in seeing Sibley's troops march into Camp Release. Several full-bloods who surrendered later showed the bitterness that developed when they realized that they would be imprisoned for participating in the war.

Narrative 1
SAMUEL J. BROWN'S RECOLLECTIONS

For biographical information on Samuel J. Brown, see Chapter IV, Narrative 1.

NEWS came that the troops were sighted at the Redwood and that they would reach the Yellow Medicine bottom about Sunday, the 21st [of September].

The Soldiers' Lodge (from whose decision there was no appeal) had solemnly decreed to attack the troops there and to slaughter them — wipe the white marauders from the face of the earth. Little Crow wants [wanted] the Sissetons to go along — take teams and help haul away the plunder. But they refused, saying they did not care to be mixed up in the quarrel.

On Monday morning, the 22nd, Little Crow's camp crier went around saying that the Soldiers' Lodge had decreed that every man in camp must go at once to Yellow Medicine and meet the troops, that anyone bringing in the scalp of Sibley, [Joseph R.] Brown, [William H.] Forbes, [Louis] Roberts [Robert], or [Nathan] Myrick, or the American flag, would receive as a present from the tribe all the waupum [*sic*] beads in camp and be showered with all the honors within the gift of the people, and be thereafter looked up to as the hero and chief warrior of the tribe.

In the afternoon of that day there was nobody left in camp but old men and boys and old women and girls, and most of the captives. As we were told by the friendlies to be prepared to defend ourselves against the hostiles upon their return from Yellow Medicine, we immediately set to work digging holes in the center of the lodges big enough for the women and children to get into, and ditches outside and around for the men.

On Tuesday the 23d, the Indians returned from Wood Lake. They had met the troops there instead of at Yellow Medicine and been most beautifully threshed [*sic*] that day.

Little Crow was despondent. He was almost heart broken. He

stepped outside his lodge and spoke to the people. He told them that he was ashamed to call himself a Sioux. "Seven hundred picked warriors whipped by the cowardly whites," he said. "Better run away and scatter out over the plains like buffalo and wolves," he continued. "To be sure," he went on, "the whites had big guns and better arms than the Indians and outnumbered us four or five to one, but that is no reason we should not have whipped them, for we are brave men while they are cowardly women. I cannot account for the disgraceful defeat. It must be the work of traitors in our midst"—meaning the friendlies.

There were 738 Indians on the battle ground at Wood Lake, and the actual number was ascertained in this way: At the crossing of a creek near Dr. Williamson's mission house, two trusty warriors were stationed on the road leading to the battle ground. As each brave passed he handed to the warriors a stick. When all had reached Yellow Medicine bottoms, a few miles from where the battle took place, these sticks were counted and found to number 738. Little Crow told mother this in my presence.

On Wednesday, the 24th, Little Crow called all his warriors together and told them to pack up and leave for the plains and save the women and children, the troops would soon be upon them and no time should be lost. "But," he said, "the captives must all be killed before we leave. They seek to defy us," he went on, "and dug trenches while we were away. They must die."[1]

The camp of the friendlies, where trenches were dug and earth works thrown up, and where the captives had been secreted, was pitched a little way from the main or hostile camp, and was rapidly increasing in numbers so that the captives felt comparatively safe. Indeed, when the friendlies had threatened to take Little Crow and his whole camp and turn them over to the troops and several hundred of the hostiles had come over into our camp with their captives and vowed they would stand by us, we simply laughed at Little Crow's bombastic talk.

Upon realizing the condition of things Little Crow and some two or three hundred of his followers hurriedly fled, "folded their tents and stole quiet[l]y away."

On Friday morning, the 26th, Gabriel Renville, Joseph Lu Tramboise [La Framboise, Jr.] and two or three other friendlies took, at the risk of their lives two white captives, a girl and a boy, that were being carried off by a party of nine of the hostiles. This party had been to the Big Woods in the vicinity of Hutchinson and were on their way back and passing the camp with these captives when intercepted.

About noon the entire camp was all excitement. The troops were approaching. Every man and woman in the camp, and every child old enough to toddle about, turned out with a flag of truce — every Indian became suddenly good. All were were [*sic*] friendly to the whites and anxious to shake hands with Sibley, Brown, Forbes, Robert and Myrick, the five for whose scalps reward has been offered. White rags were fastened to the tips of the tepee poles, to wagon wheels, cart wheels, to sticks and poles stuck in the ground, and every conceivable object and in some grotesque manner and ludicrous way.

One Indian who was boiling over with loyalty ahd [*sic*] love for the white man threw a white blanket on his black horse and tied a bit of white cloth to its tail, and then that no possible doubt might be raised in his case he wrapped the American flag around his body and mounted the horse and sat upon him in full view of the troops as they passed by, looking more like a circus clown than a "friendly" Indian.

When the troops suddenly appeared on an eminence a mile away and there was no doubt that they were coming to our rescue the captives could hardly restrain themselves — some cried for joy, some went into fits or hysterics, and some fainted away. It was a joyful [scene], yet most sad and gloomy.

No grander sight ever met the eyes of anybody than when the troops marched up with bayonets glistening in the bright noon day sun and colors flying, drums beating and fifes playing. I shall never forget it while I live. We could hardly realize that our deliverance had come. The troops passed by and pitched their tents a quarter of a mile from us and at once spiked their guns which commanded our camp.

Very soon Col. Sibley with his staff and a body of guard[s] came over into our camp and after calling the Indians together made formal demand for the captives which were readily given up.

Then my father and Major [William J.] Cullen, Doctor [Asa W.] Daniels and one or two other personal friends came.[2] We went with them to the soldiers' camp and remained there until sent to Henderson a few days subsequently — my father and I only of the family remaining with the expedition.

There were about 150 lodges in the Indian camp at the time of the arrival of the troops. But a few days subsequently the camp had increased to 243 lodges. Some had been captured and brought in, while others came in of their own accord, and including the captives (and exclusive of the soldiers[)] there were at Camp Release 2188 souls, as follows:

Indians	1,918
Captive white men	4
Captive white women and children	104
Captive mixed bloods	162

The names of the four white men who made [were] kept captives by Little Crow were as follows:

1 — George Spencer.
2 — Peter Romsseau [Rousseau].
3 — Louis La Belle.
4 — Peter Rouillard.[3]

I mention this to correct the impression that there was but one white man (Spencer) made prisioner by the Indians.

Upon my release from captivity I was at once put upon the U.S. scout roll and detailed for duty with Major Thomas J. Galbraith, United States Indian Agent. I acted as interpreter.

On the 4th of October I was ordered to inform the Indians that such of them as were not required as witnesses in the trial then going on must at once break camp and proceed to Yellow Medicine, — that this was rendered necessary on account of the stock of provisions running out, and that I was to go along as inte[r]preter. We left the camp, (Camp Release) the same day under the escort of some soldiers under Capt. J. Whitney of the Sixth regiment, Minnesota Volunteers, and proceeded to our destination.[4] The large number of cattle, horses, wagons, carriages, and buggies, and about 1250 Indians, (286 were men, the residue women and children) and about 150 soldiers, with their provisions and baggage wagons, made the train a long one.

At Yellow Medicine, which we reached the same day, the Indians were all put to work digging potatoes and gathering corn. In a week we had filled several root houses and cellars — had housed about 6,000 bushels of potatoes and 1,500 bushels of corn.

While thus engaged, and by exercising a justifiable piece of strategy, I assisted in causing the arrest and in safely detaining in custody all the Indian men (except forty-six who were above suspicion, and three or four who had "smelled a mice" and ran away during the night) and disarmed them and chained them in pairs together — that is, the right leg at the ankle of one was chained to the left leg at the ankle of another.

This successful and justifiable piece of strategy took place at the government warehouse, built by my father when he was agent a few years before, a large two story building fifty feet long, which the hostiles had burned and destroyed when they passed up on the 28th of August, but the walls of which were still standing, and was accomplished in the following manner: About a hundred yards from this building the soldiers had pitched their tents, while the Indians camped under the hill along the Yellow Medicine creek, a half or three quarters of a mile distant. I was ordered one day to proceed to the camp and inform the Indians that the annuity roll was to be prepared the next morning, and that they must all come at an early hour and present themselves to the agent at the warehouse and be "counted." They were delighted to learn that they were at last to get their money. The annuity payment for that year had not yet been made, and this *ruse* worked like a charm.

About 8 o'clock the next morning the Indians flocked to the warehouse anxious to be "counted." Major Galbraith, Captain Whitney and two or three "clerks" were found seated at a table behind one end of the building with pens, ink, paper, etc., hard at work on the "rolls" while one of the officers and myself were stationed in a doorway at the opposite and further end. As each family would step up to the table one of the "clerks" would rise and count or number them with his finger, one, two, three, etc., and after announcing the result with a flourish and motioning for them to pass on, a soldier would step up and escort the Indians to the other end of the building where I was stationed. As they reached the farther end and turned the corner and came in front of the doorway, I would tell the men to step inside and allow the women and children to pass on to the camp, telling them, as I was instructed to do, that the men as heads of families must be counted separately, as it was thought the government would pay them extra. I would then take their guns, tomahawks, scalping knives, etc., and throw them into barrels, telling them they would be returned shortly. In this way we succeeded in arresting and safely detaining in custody 234 of Little Crow's fiercest warrior[s]. And since the Indian men outnumbered the soldiers two to one and were fully as well armed, I think that in this case "the end justified the means."

In the evening of that day and before the Indians were put in irons, one of them broke from the guard and escaped to the camp where he was captured by the friendlies and brought back.

We remained at Yellow Medicine until the 12th, when we left for the lower agency, arriving there on the 15th—the entire expedition from Camp Release arriving at the same time.

Here we remained for upwards of three weeks, the time being consumed in the trial of the indicted Indians.

On the 9th of November, the uncondemned Indians and their wives and families, and the wives and families of the condemned and absent Indians, numbering in all 1,658 souls, were started off for Fort Snelling, Lieut. Col. [William R.] Marshall of the Seventh regiment, Minnesota Volunteers, with an escort of three companies of soldiers, being in command.[5]

At the same time 392 condemned Indian men and seventeen Indian women as cooks, laundresses, etc., four papooses, and four of the friendlies, as assistants in the care of the prisoners, were started off for Mankato, making 417 in all, Col. Sibley and the main portion of the expedition and Major Brown, superintendent in charge of the Indian prisoners, accompanying these.

I went along with Col. Marshall's detatchment—the train measuring about four miles in length. At Henderson, which we reached on the 11th, we found the streets crowded with an angry and excited populace, cursing, shouting and crying. Men, women and children armed with guns, knives, clubs and stones, rushed upon the Indians, as the train was passing by, and before the soldiers could interfere and stop them, succeeded in pulling many of the old men and women and even children from the wagons by the hair of the head, and beating them, and otherwise inflicting injury upon the helpless and miserable creatures.

I saw an enraged white woman rush up to one of the wagons and snatch a nursing babe from its mother's breast and dash it violently upon the ground. The soldiers' [sic] instantly seized her and led or rather dragged the woman away, and restored the papoose to its mother—limp and almost dead. Although the child was not killed outright, it died a few hours after. The body was quietly laid away in the crotch of a tree a few miles below Henderson and not far from Faxon.

I witnessed the ceremony, which was, perhaps, the last of the kind within the limits of Minnesota; that is, the last Sioux Indian "buried" according to one of the oldest and most cherished customs of the tribe.

And here my thoughts reverted to the case of the Indian brave at the dance who boasted in "ghoulish glee" that he had roasted a babe in the oven, and I contrasted it with the case before me. An uncivilized heathen in the one case, and a *civilized christian* white woman in the other!

There was another incident that took place at Henderson which is worth mentioning. I refer to a brave and noble act by one of the bravest and noblest of men — Lieut. Col. Marshall, afterwards governor of Minnesota.

While the train was passing through the town one of the citizens with blood in his eyes and half crazed with drink rushed up with a gun levelled at Charles Crawford [Samuel Brown's uncle],[6] one of the friendlies, and was about to fire, when "the bold charger of the plains," Lieut. Col. Marshall, who happened along on horseback, rushed between them and struck down the gun with his sabre and got Crawford out of the way, thus saving a life at the risk of his own.

Prior to the outbreak my father was a major general of the state militia and had a uniform of that rank in his house at the time it was ransacked and plundered by the Indians. Crawford secured this and wore it in camp, at dances, feasts, etc. He was a tall, broad shouldered man, a good rider and fine figure on horseback, and having pants with stripes down the legs, a coat with epaulettes, a cocked hat, sash, sword, spurs, and a prancing steed, he was a noticeable figure at all gatherings. The captives noticing this, and not knowing it was done for their benefit, naturally supposed he was a hostile of the worst kind, and hence the feeling against him.

As the records of the millitary commission that tried the Indians — of which Gov. Marshall was a member — shows that Crawford was brought before it twice, and underwent a most searching examination each time, and was adjudged "not guilty" on every charge, there ought to be no doubt of the man's innocence.

Crawford rendered valuable service in the war following the outbreak, and is now pastor of the Presbyterian church at Good Will, South Dakota.

On the 14th we reached Fort Snelling and placed the Indians in camp.

Here most of them remained — in charge of the military — until the following spring, when they were turned over to the interior department, put into steamboats and taken down the Mississippi river to the Missouri, and up the latter stream to a point called Fort Usher or Usher's Landing, but afterwards as Fort Thompson or Crow Creek Agency, D. T., about 200 miles above Yankton. In 1866 these Indians were removed down the Missouri to a point now known as Santee Agency, Nebraska.

Of the condemned Indians sent to Mankato thirty-eight were hung there on the 26th of December, and the residue — except those that died from sickness — remained there until the following spring when they too were dumped into a steamboat and taken down the river to a military prison near Davenport, Iowa, where the most of them remained in *durance vile* until 1866, when they were released and returned to their friends and relatives on the Missouri.

Continued on page 271.

Narrative 2
THOMAS A. ROBERTSON'S REMINISCENCES

For biographical information on Thomas A. Robertson, see Chapter VIII, Narrative 2.

SOON after this [delivering Colonel Sibley's message], runners came reporting that Sibley was on his way, in fact, runners were coming in every few hours. The hostiles at once made preparations to meet him, and as runners again came in with word that Sibley was making his camp at Wood Lake or Lone Tree Lake — as the Indians called it — they decided to attack the camp that night or early in the morning, and everybody was ordered to go that night.[7] As usually supposed, these orders were not from Little Crow but by the Soldiers' Lodge, of whom the notorious Cutnose, who was one of the 38 hung at Mankato, was the head, and who was virtually in command at all the battles. This battle ground of Wood Lake is about 12 or 15 miles from where we were then camped. As soon as it got dark nearly all the men, both hostile and friendly, started, but on the way and in the dark, most of the friendlies dropped out and came back to camp and after the battle, when the hostiles came back defeated and discouraged, they found that in their absence the friendlies had formed a separate camp; had secured all of the prisoners; had dug pits inside the tents for protection of prisoners; and were prepared to meet them on any grounds they wished to take, but being beaten and on the run, by the next morning no hostile camp was in sight, and so practically ended for that year the Indian outbreak of 1862. I was one of those who stayed behind and helped form the separate camp, and dug pits for the security of the prisoners.

To some who may read this I may seem too egotistical, but my only desire is to state the facts as I now remember them — and some of which I was not present — as they were related to me by those who were and whom I could rely on for truthfulness.

By the next morning, after the battle of Wood Lake, there was no hostile camps [*sic*] in sight, as during the night they had left and scattered out through the country farther west. As the details of the Battle of Wood Lake are a matter of official record and as I was not present, I will leave them to be looked up elsewhere.

The next day Colonel Sibley and his command came in sight, so a few of us went out and met him and reporting to him the situation as it then was, conducted him to what has ever since been called Camp Release. Some detachments of cavalry were at once sent out after the hostiles, and in a few days brought in a few families that had been overtaken somewhere on the Jim [James] River. During the next few days quite a number of the hostiles whose families had remained with us, came into our camp, but were at once reported and put under guard with the others. I suppose you will at once think what others, which I will explain by stating all were disarmed and excepting in a very few cases the whole camp put under guard. No one could leave this without a special permit from Colonel Sibley. Any Indian could come into this camp, but none ever got out. We were near the timber on the Minnesota River so in a few days log pens were put up, and as fast as they were apprehended the men were put into these log pens and strongly guarded.

Narrative 3
GABRIEL RENVILLE'S MEMOIR

For biographical information on Gabriel Renville, see Chapter V, Narrative 1.

THEY [the warriors] later moved their camp about a half mile to the westward. It was at that time [September 22] that the hostile Indians decided that they were ready to go and meet General [Colonel]

Sibley's command, ordering everybody to go, and making the threat that those who did not go would be punished by their soldiers' lodges, and that now was the time to wipe out General Sibley's command, which they said they intended to do. This was the reason that some of the friendly Indians were told to go down there to see if the soldiers would all be killed, and the others to stay and take care of the camp.

The start was now made to meet the troops. Sibley had gone into camp about one and a half miles south of the Yellow Medicine river, and the Indians were camped on that river. A consultation was then had as to how it was best to attack Sibley's command, the council being held in the evening. Little Crow's plan was to quietly advance under cover of the darkness until the guards fired, and then rush in, and, as soon as the troops rose up, to halt, fire one volley, charge forward, and massacre them.

Then I spoke and said, "It is not true, what you have said about there being only a few of the soldiers. There are many more than you have said. They also have spy-glasses, and have seen the Indians coming here. They have their big guns in readiness, and are prepared for a surprise. Therefore what you say is not right."

Then [Solomon] Two Stars spoke and said, "I do not think your plan is a good one, because if the attack is made at night only a part of us will go, and many will not go. Your plan therefore would fail. I have been told that over here in the west they would lie in ambush for the troops, and when they came up to them the Indians would rush in, cutting the command in two, and then would kill them all. I think that would be a better plan for you."

The reason for Two Stars saying this was, that, if the attack was made in daylight, the friendly Indians would have an opportunity to let the troops know what was planned. Thus the plan of attack was argued until daylight.

When the morning came, some of the soldiers who were going for potatoes were fired upon by the Indians and chased back into their camp, and two companies of soldiers came out and drove the Indians back. Then all the hostile Indians rushed in, and drove back the two companies of soldiers, and killed three of them before they reached their camp. Afterward the Indians surrounded the camp, and fired on the troops from all sides. As soon as the soldiers were ready, however, they came out of the camp and pursued the Indians, killing many of them. The Indians then withdrew and went back to their camp, and the next morning fled to the northward.

During this time the friendly Indians in their camp had been digging pits outside of their tents, and being armed went about taking and bringing into their camp the white captives, putting them into the pits, and thus rescuing them from their great sufferings.

About this time a war party, with some prisoners in their possession, were reported passing to the westward of the friendly camp. Therefore I and Too-kan-shaw-e-che-ya, with others, pursued them, and after some resistance they were compelled to give up the prisoners, and we brought them into the friendly camp.[8] Strict guard was kept all that night.

The next day General Sibley arrived with his command, who made their camp to the eastward of the friendly camp, near the Minnesota river. With joyous handshaking we met, and the white prisoners were taken into the soldiers' camp.

During this time some of the hostile Indians with their families had been returning under cover of the night, and pitched their tents among the friendly Indians. This was reported to General Sibley, who issued an order demanding that all arms and amunition that had been taken out of the stores and government warehouses should be given up, and this was done.

Then word came that the Indians would be sifted as you would sift wheat, the good grain to be put into the bin, but the chaff and the bad seeds to be burned. This was done, and all those who by good evidence were proven to have done anything against the whites were put into irons. Indian scouts were appointed and followed after the hostile Indians, many of whom were overtaken in their flight and brought back.

Soon after that the friendly Indians, with those of the hostiles who had sneaked in, were all ordered to move with their families to the Yellow Medicine Agency. A camp was formed on and about the Agency grounds, with a detachment of soldiers to guard them.

At this time a few of the Indians from this camp crossed the Minnesota river and fled, and another party went off in the night and fled north. These things happening, the commander at this place ordered every man, woman, and child, to come, and a list was made of all those who were under his charge. All able-bodied men were shut up and put under guard, but shortly afterwards those who were friendly were released.

Again, another one of those who were under guard got away, and the commanding officer ordered that, if he was not found and delivered over to the soldiers, the head men should be locked up in his place. Search was immediately made, he was found and captured, and was delivered over to the soldiers.

As myself and Ah-kee-pah [Gabriel's stepfather], and our families, had not been implicated in any of the outrages against the whites, we were given the privilege of being outside of the Indian camp, coming and going as we pleased. This being the case, I went back to my old home across the Minnesota river.

Soon after this, General Sibley with his command, bringing the Indians that were there with him, moved down to the Yellow Medicine Agency, and thence, taking all that were there, moved down to the Redwood Agency.

Everything that I owned at my old home had been taken or destroyed by the hostile Indians. Having nothing to live on, and the outlook being very dreary, I moved my camp to Redwood Agency, and pitched my tent with the friendly Indians who were then camped on the north side of Sibley's command. The families of those who had been suspected of doing anything against the whites were camped on the south side of the troops.

From this encampment, after the proceedings of the military court had been closed, and when all parties had come in from hunting the hostile Indians, those who were friendly, with their families and the families of those who had been convicted, were taken to Fort Snelling, and the convicted men were taken to Mankato.

On the way, when they were passing through the town of New Ulm, the whites were very much excited. Both men and women, coming with stones, bricks, and pitchforks, and anything they could lay their hands on, and rushing through the ranks of the soldiers who were guarding them, attacked the chained prisoners in the wagons, and knocked many of them senseless. The guards, striking these whites with their sabers, drove them back. Finally, with much difficulty, they were brought through the town. Arriving at Mankato, the convicted men were there imprisoned.

Ah-kee-pah and [his brother] Red Iron, though not prisoners, were with those who were at Mankato, and were quartered with the soldiers outside of the Indian prison.

Thirty-eight of those who were convicted and sentenced to be hung paid the penalty. When they were waiting for the drop, these men sang and recounted their war deeds and sent farewells to their absent relatives, and while all this was going on the time came, the rope was cut, and thirty-eight hostile Indians hung in the air, each with a rope around his neck.

The friendly Indians and their families, and the families of the prisoners, on their way to Fort Snelling, passed through Henderson, at which place the whites were very much angered and threw stones at the Indians, hitting some of them, and pulled the shawls and blankets off the women, and abused them much. But they finally got through the town without any one being killed, and formed a camp beyond the town, in an open prairie.

They were then taken down on the east side of the Minnesota river, and went into camp at some distance from Fort Snelling. Shortly after this the camp was moved again, being located close to the Minnesota river. These camps were always well guarded, but in spite of that many of the horses and oxen belonging to the Indians were stolen, including three horses that belonged to myself and Charles Crawford [Gabriel's half brother].

Then a fence was built on the south side of the fort and close to it. We all moved into this inclosure, but we were so crowded and confined that an epidemic broke out among us and children were dying day and night, among them being [Solomon] Two Stars' oldest child, a little girl.

The news then came of the hanging at Mankato. Amid all this sickness and these great tribulations, it seemed doubtful at night whether a person would be alive in the morning. We had no land, no homes, no means of support, and the outlook was most dreary and discouraging. How can we get lands and have homes again, were the questions which troubled many thinking minds, and were hard questions to answer.

Continued on page 273.

Narrative 4
BIG EAGLE'S ACCOUNT

For biographical information on Big Eagle, see Chapter I, Narrative 1.

FOR SOME time after the fight at Birch Coulie the greater part of the Indians remained in the camps about the Yellow Medicine and the mouth of the Chippewa. At last the word came that Sibley with his

army was again on the move against us. Our scouts were very active
and vigilant, and we heard from him [an unidentified Indian scout]
nearly every hour. He [Sibley] had left a letter for Little Crow in a
split stick on the battle-field of Birch Coulie, and some of our men
found it and brought it in, and correspondence had been going on between us ever since. Tom Robinson [Robertson] and Joe [Antoine
Joseph] Campbell, half-breed prisoners, wrote the letters for Little
Crow. It seems that some letters were written to Gen. [Colonel]
Sibley by the half-breeds which Little Crow never saw. I and others
understood from the half-breeds that Gen. Sibley would treat with all
of us who had only been soldiers and would surrender as prisoners of
war, and that only those who had murdered people in cold blood, the
settlers and others, would be punished in any way. There was great
dissatisfaction among us at our condition. Many wanted to surrender;
others left us for the West. But Sibley came on and on, and at last
came the battle of Wood lake.

When we learned that Sibley had gone into camp at the Wood
lake, a council of the sub-chiefs and others was held and it was determined to give him a battle near there. I think the lake now called Battle lake was the old-time Wood lake. As I understand it, there once
were some cottonwoods about it, and the Indians called it "M'da-
chan" — Wood lake. The larger lake, two miles west, now called
Wood lake, was always known to me by the Indian name of "Hinta
hauk-pay-an wo-ju," meaning literally, "the Planting Place of the
Man who ties his Moccasins with Basswood Bark." We soon learned
that Sibley had thrown up breastworks and it was not deemed safe to
attack him at the lake. We concluded that the fight should be about
a mile or more to the northwest of the lake, on the road along which
the troops would march. This was the road leading to the upper country, and of course Sibley would travel it. At the point determined on
we planned to hide a large number of men on the side of the road.
Near the lake, in a ravine formed by the outlet, we were to place another strong body. Behind a hill to the west were to be some more
men. We thought that when Sibley marched out along the road and
when the head of his column had reached the farther end of the line
of our first division, our men would open fire. The men in the ravine
would then be in the rear of the whites and would begin firing on that
end of the column. The men from behind the hill would rush out and
attack the flank, and then we had horsemen far out on the right and
left who would come up. We expected to throw the whole white force

into confusion by the sudden and unexpected attack and defeat them
before they could rally.

I think this was a good plan of battle. Our concealed men would
not have been discovered. The grass was tall and the place by the road
and the ravine were good hiding places. We had learned that Sibley
was not particular about sending out scouts and examining the country before he passed it. He had a number of mounted men, but they
always rode together, at the head of the column, when on a march,
and did not examine the ground at the sides of the road. The night he
lay at Wood lake his pickets were only a short distance from camp—
less than half a mile. When we were putting our men into position
that night we often saw them plainly. I worked hard that night fixing
the men. Little Crow was on the field, too. Mankato was there. Indeed, all our fighting chiefs were present and all our best fighting Indians. We felt that this would be the deciding fight of the war. The
whites were unconscious. We could hear them laughing and singing.
When all our preparations were made Little Crow and I and some
other chiefs went to the mound or hill to the west so as to watch the
fight better when it should commence. There were numbers of other
Indians there.

The morning came and an accident spoiled all our plans. For some
reason Sibley did not move early as we expected he would. Our men
were lying hidden waiting patiently. Some were very near the camp
lines in the ravine, but the whites did not see a man of all our men.
I do not think they would have discovered our ambuscade. It seemed
a considerable time after sun-up when some four or five wagons with
a number of soldiers started out from the camp in the direction of the
old Yellow Medicine agency. We learned afterwards that they were
going without orders to dig potatoes over at the agency, five miles
away. They came on over the prairie, right where part of our line
was. Some of the wagons were not in the road, and if they had kept
straight on would have driven right over our men as they lay in the
grass. At last they came so close that our men had to rise up and fire.
This brought on the fight, of course, but not according to the way we
had planned it. Little Crow saw it and felt very badly.

Of course you know how the battle was fought. The Indians that
were in the fight did well, but hundreds of our men did not get into
it and did not fire a shot. They were out too far. The men in the ravine
and the line connecting them with those on the road did the most of
the fighting. Those of us on the hill did our best, but we were soon

driven off. Mankato was killed here, and we lost a very good and brave war chief. He was killed by a cannon ball that was so nearly spent that he was not afraid of it, and it struck him in the back, as he lay on the ground, and killed him. The whites drove our men out of the ravine by a charge and that ended the battle. We retreated in some disorder, though the whites did not offer to pursue us. We crossed a wide prairie, but their horsemen did not follow us. We lost fourteen or fifteen men killed and quite a number wounded. Some of the wounded died afterwards, but I do not know how many. We carried off no dead bodies, but took away all our wounded. The whites scalped all our dead men—so I have heard.

Soon after the battle I, with many others who had taken part in the war, surrendered to Gen. Sibley. Robinson [Robertson] and the other half-breeds assured us that if we would do this we would only be held as prisoners of war a short time, but as soon as I surrendered I was thrown into prison. Afterward I was tried and served three years in the prison at Davenport and the penitentiary at Rock Island for taking part in the war. On my trial a great number of the white prisoners, women and others, were called up, but not one of them could testify that I had murdered any one or had done anything to deserve death, or else I would have been hanged. If I had known that I would be sent to the penitentiary I would not have surrendered, but when I had been in the penitentiary three years and they were about to turn me out, I told them they might keep me another year if they wished, and I meant what I said. I did not like the way I had been treated. I surrendered in good faith, knowing that many of the whites were acquainted with me and that I had not been a murderer, or present when a murder had been committed, and if I had killed or wounded a man it had been in fair, open fight. But all feeling on my part about this has long since passed away. For years I have been a Christian and I hope to die one. My white neighbors and friends know my character as a citizen and a man. I am at peace with every one, whites and Indians. I am getting to be an old man, but I am still able to work. I am poor, but I manage to get along.

Narrative 5
VICTOR RENVILLE'S ACCOUNT

For biographical information on Victor Renville, see Chapter V, Narrative 2.

GENERAL [Colonel] Sibley then [on September 21] assembled his troops and started marching upon the hostiles. When he drew near he sent a young man to ride to the friendly camp and get the assistance of the warriors there. He told them that if they did not fight with him they would [not] be punished. So the friendly Indians rode out to help the soldiers and warned them of what the hostiles planned to do.

Little Crow, chief of the hostiles, then ordered all friendly Indians to join him in the attack on Sibley's forces. He called a general council of friendlies and hostiles to meet where the trader's house had stood at the Upper Agency. Little Crow told them that he had counted the soldiers' tents and that they were fewer than his own. He stated that his plan of attack was to surround the soldiers at night, stampede their horses and mules, and take the troops by surprise.

Gabriel [Victor's father] got up and opposed this plan because he feared the hostiles would succeed in defeating the soldiers. He said that the camp could not be taken by surprise as the troops had sentinels posted on every side. He also declared that in a night attack many young warriors would be killed, so he proposed to wait until the soldiers were on the march when they could be ambushed and taken by surprise. About half of the council agreed with Gabriel and the debate continued until morning without result.

Early in the morning the half-breeds and friendly Indians rode out ahead of the attacking hostiles and by showing themselves here and there, gave plenty of warning. When the attack began the soldiers were ready and by the unexpected use of cannon the enemy was driven off. The hostiles now rode back to their own camp and began to make ready to escape. This gave the friendly Indians and half-breeds an opportunity to ride into the hostile camp and snatch the women and children captives from the Indians who were about to carry them off. They carried these prisoners to their own camp which they defended with ditches and breastworks. Over the camp of the friendly Indians floated a white flag as a sign that they were not hostile to the whites.

Sibley's forces scoured the country for hostile Indians and succeeded in taking more than four hundred. The troops then rushed in upon what remained of the hostile camp and took all the captives and supplies. They then established a court and tried their Indian prisoners. Each man was questioned and asked to give an account of himself. Those found to have committed atrocities were placed in irons and many of them were later hanged.

Continued on page 275.

Narrative 6
JOSEPH COURSOLLE'S STORY

For biographical information on Joseph Coursolle, see Chapter III, Narrative 5.

WE DRILLED and drilled and drilled while more troops came pouring in. Soon there were two thousand soldiers in the Fort and an almost endless train of wagons hauling in supplies. I thought we had enough to lick General Lee but Sibley kept drilling us for two whole weeks!

All that time I was tormented with anxiety, wondering whether Traveling Hail's warriors had killed Elizabeth and Minnie [Coursolle's daughters].

At last we left! Our company was in the lead and the column stretched back through the woods farther than I could see. I was glad we had the cannons with us. The big guns scared the daylights out of the Sioux.

We moved like snails. I could have crawled on my stomach and made faster time. Again we cursed Sibley. He was so slow! Every day we started the march in the middle of the foremoon [forenoon], halted for a noon meal, camped at four o'clock, dug rifle pits and built barricades. Why waste such precious time! We would never catch the Indians dawdling like this!

Endless rumors ran through the column. "All white captives have been killed." "All whites have been taken to Sisseton." "All whites are prisoners and are in camp near the Yellow Medicine river." How I wanted this last one to be true for that was where we were marching! There, if alive, Minnie and Elizabeth would be found!

We camped at Wood Lake and in the morning a squad of men on a foraging expedition surprised an ambush Little Crow was setting up to cut off the head of our column. The third Minnesota got into the fight first. As we were forming to advance, Company A of the Sixth went by on the double and Denais Felix yelled, "Hurry up, Hinhanhaga [Hinhankaga]! We'll lick 'em this time!"

And lick 'em we did! When the artillery started firing they skedaddled like scared rabbits.

The next day we knew the white prisoners were in camp only a short distance away. Today I would see Minnie and Elizabeth! Or - - ? ? ? the thought they could be missing drove me nearly crazy.

"Hurry! Hurry!" I shouted. Then Sibley ordered a dress parade! For two hours we manouvered and then passed in review. I would have been court-martialed if Sibley had heard what I called him under my breath! And instead of going in to the rescue we camped again that night!

Even Sibley must have caught the urge for the next morning we moved faster. Soon we could see smoke rising from the prison camp. No order was given but every man in the column broke into a run. To run faster I threw away my musket and dashed ahead calling, "Elizabeth! Minnie!" Then I saw a group of ragged women and children running to meet us.

Elizabeth saw me first. "Papa! Papa!" she cried and threw herself into my arms. Just behind came Minnie, her short legs spinning. There was room in my arms for both! For a long time I held them close with their arms hugging my neck. If only Marie had been there too!

When at last I set them down Elizabeth hugged one leg and Minnie the other. I looked them over carefully. Their bony little bodies were covered with dirt where the skin showed through torn clothing. They were unharmed! They were the loveliest little girls in the whole wide world!

"Elizabeth," I asked, "what happened after I left you and Minnie by the river?"

"You told us to hide. Some Indians came down the path. We kept still and they didn't see us. Pretty soon another Indian came and he saw us. 'You come with me,' he said. He had a long knife and we were afraid. We followed him to his house. He told me, 'Stand up straight.'

Then he put a barrel over my head. It was dark inside and I couldn't see. I heard him tell Minnie, 'You sit here.'

"Then other Indians came. One of them said, 'We take your girl.' 'No,' said the Indian who found us by the river, 'She my girl. Anybody touch her I shoot him.' Then he took the barrel off my head. 'Look, this one my girl, too.' When the Indians saw me they laughed and went away.

"Then the black man with the curley hair came running; You know, the man who cut hair at the Agency. 'What shall I do? What shall I do?' he shouted. 'Run! Run!' said the Indians. He ran toward the river. The Indians shot their guns and he fell down. He kicked a little and then he didn't move any more.[9]

"The Indians didn't hurt us. But we didn't have good things to eat like mama makes. Sometimes we got awful cold. We slept on the ground. We didn't even have a blanket. And, oh, we were so lonesome! We wanted to see you and Mama and Cistina Joe and Duta."

It was easy to say, "Mama is must [just] fine and oh, how SHE wants to see YOU! And she will see you soon!" But it wrung my heart to tell them that never again would they see their baby brother. I couldn't bear to tell them how Duta died. I told them only that he had gone to a happy land where he was playing every day with Cistina Joe.

Narrative 7
SOLOMON TWO STARS'S TESTIMONY

SOLOMON TWO STARS or Wicanrpinonpa was born in about 1827 at Lac qui Parle; Cloud Man, his father, was a leader of the Wahpetons. His brother was Ecetukiya; his uncle, Paul Mazakutemani. A member of Inyangmani's band, Two Stars received a Dakota upbringing. He was living near the Yellow Medicine Agency when the war broke out.

Two Stars joined the peace party that resisted the Dakota warriors. He ridiculed Little Crow's plan to attack Sibley's troops at night near Wood Lake and helped to convince the soldiers' lodge that the assault should be undertaken during the morning hours. He testified against several Dakotas before the military tribunal, and he became a scout for General Sibley in 1863. Two years later his force of twelve men met and killed a hostile Indian party of sixteen near present-day Webster, South Dakota.

Two Stars settled on the Sisseton Reservation in 1867 where he received an allotment in 1875. He signed the Treaties of 1867, 1872, and 1873. In 1900 he met Doane Robinson, an early historian of the Sioux, and gave him valuable information regarding the early history of his people. On August 10, 1901, at the Sisseton Agency he testified for the claimants in the Sisseton-Wahpeton lawsuit against the federal government to have their annuities restored. Thomas A. Robertson was the interpreter. Two Stars died near the Sisseton Agency on June 6, 1914.[10]

*SOLOMON
TWO STARS
in 1907*

Narrative Source: Solomon Two Stars, "Evidence for the Claimants," *The Sisseton and Wahpeton Bands of Dakota or Sioux Indians v. the United States,* 1901–07, U.S. Court of Claims no. 22524, part 1, p. 75–93.

THAT EVENING [September 22], while they made the stop at Yellow Medicine (that was very close to Wood Lake), Little Crow came up on the hill and looked over and saw the camp of General [Colonel] Sibley (there were a few tents at the rear of the camp, and those probably were the officers'), and his plan was to wait until dark and then crawl up as near as they could to the camp and to all fire at once and rush in and wipe them out. . . .

Gabriel Renville [Two Stars's second cousin] was there and got up and answered Little Crow and said no; I have been up on the hill and I have seen the camp too, and there are more there than you say there are, and if you attack the camp you will get wiped out; and if you are going to do anything you had better do it in the daytime. Then I got up and told Little Crow I thought they were mistaken in their plan of attack, and that they would undoubtedly have pickets out quite a distance from the camp, and they would know whether anybody was coming near before they could get within a reasonable distance to attack the camp, and that being the case they would be driven back before they could get near the camp. . . .

Then I also told Little Crow I understood that where the Tetons attacked the troops they did it in the daytime; got as close as they could to them without being known, and then made a sudden rush upon them, and then they could handle them very easily, and that they had better do the same thing. Of course, I was saying this to try and not to have the attack made in the night, but to have it in the daytime. . . .

Then Rda-ya-in-yan-ke, Rattling Runner, one of the leaders in the fight, got up and said he thought that was the best plan; therefore they would lie still that night until daylight, and they decided to make the attack in the daytime. . . .

When they decided to make the attack in the daytime, then I and the party that were sent there moved up a little ravine or creek, away from the rest of them to sleep during the night, and about daylight we awoke and somebody stood up and said that they ought to go out and see what they were doing, and one of them did so, and said that the Indians had left and gone off somewhere; so we got together and went around by the battle ground there, and when we got out there they were already fighting. . . .

[After the battle] General Sibley did not advance to Yellow Medicine. . . . Simon [Anawangmani], John Otherday, and Lorenzo Lawrence came up ahead of the troops. Simon came up onto one of the hills and commenced to wave a blanket or something to let them know that he was somebody, and they recognized him as Simon; and it happened that Simon's son was there on the hostile side, and he brought his father out to the hostile line and they surrounded him and was consulting whether to kill him or not, and it happened that some of his own men were there with his son and protected him, and then I and my party, when we heard that Simon was out there, went over there, but found that he had been spirited away to General Sibley's lines.

Narrative 8
NANCY McCLURE FARIBAULT HUGGAN'S ACCOUNT

For biographical information on Nancy McClure Faribault Huggan, see Chapter IV, Narrative 2.

SOME DAYS after we got to the mouth of the Chippewa, Little Crow's and Shakopee's bands and all the other Indians came up. We all stayed here until Gen. [Colonel] Sibley and his troops came into the country, and then the Indians went out to meet them. In a few days we heard the booming of the cannon in the battle of Wood lake. Commonly the roar of cannon is a dreadful sound in the ears of women, but to us captives in the Indian camp the sound of Gen. Sibley's guns was as sweet at [as] the chimes of wedding bells to the bride. Very soon stragglers came in bearing wounded, singing the death song and telling the tale of defeat. They were cursing the half-breeds, saying that Gen. Sibley had numbers of them with him in the battle, and that every shot that one of them fired had hit an Indian. It did me real good to learn that so many of my race had stood loyal and true and had done such good service. You know that only a very few half-breeds took part in the outbreak. The Indians have always bitterly hated the half-breeds for their conduct in favor of the whites in that and other wars, and they hate them still. It seems they can forgive everybody but us.

But then came the word that the defeated Indians would take vengeance on the half-breed captives and the whites, too, as soon as they got back. It was another exciting time. Some of us dug holes in the ground and hid ourselves. I dug a hole large enough to hide myself and child in a few minutes, and I had only a little fire shovel to dig with, but I made the dirt fly. When the excitement was over — for the alarm was false — I tried again to dig with that same shovel, and somehow it wouldn't dig a little bit! I kept that shovel for years, but finally lost it.

When the warriors came back they had numbers of wounded, and the death song was going all night. I began to be very brave. The soldiers were near, the half-bloods were in the saddle and I felt that I would soon be safe. An Indian woman near me began abusing us. She said: "When we talk of killing these half-breeds they drop their heads and sneak around like a bird-dog." Her taunting speech stung me to the heart, and I flew at that woman and routed her so completely that she bore the marks for some time, and I am sure she remembered the lesson a great deal longer! Perhaps it was not a very ladylike thing to do, but I was dreadfully provoked. Most of my companions were greatly pleased, and the Indians did not offer to interfere.

I heard the Indians plan their part of the battle of Wood lake. About twenty of the chiefs and head warriors sat down near our tent one evening and talked it all over in my hearing. I do not now remember who all of them were. Little Crow was there, and with him were Pa-ji-ro-ta (Gray Grass), Hu-sap-sa-pa (Black Leg) and his brother, Ta-taka-wa-nagi (Buffalo Ghost), Shakopee (Six) and others.[11] I did not understand the plan very well, but it was agreed that Gen. Sibley's forces were to be cut into two or three parts by the Indian movements. A strong party was to go into a large ravine. Another party was to show itself at another point and attract the attention of the soldiers; then the ravine party was to come up and cut the white forces in two, and so on. When I heard all this it did not alarm me the least bit. I knew that Gen. Sibley and Col. Marshall and Col. McPhail and the other officers would have something to say and do about that fight. But the Indians were confident, and, as they were leaving the camp, many of them said: "We will have plenty of pork and hardtack to-night!"

NANCY
HUGGAN in
about 1920

At last Gen. Sibley came and surrounded our camp. A great many officers came with him, and I remember that Col. Marshall was one of them. They came into the camp and took away the white captives first. Gen. Sibley knew me, and told me to take my child and go with them. I asked him if all the half-bloods were going and he said they were not. I did not understand it all then, and I said I would stay awhile. Maj. Fowler,[12] who was married to my husband's sister, then came and told me I had better go, as the soldiers were greatly enraged at some of the half-bloods, and their officers were afraid they could not "hold them." I told him I had a half-brother and a half-sister there, and I would stay to protect them. So I stayed that night there, and went over into Camp Release in the morning. I was a witness before the military commission that tried the Indians, and called several times, but I could not recognize any of the prisoners as those I saw taking part in the murders of the whites. I was sorry that the guilty wretches I had seen were not brought up. I think I was at Camp Release about two weeks.

I cannot tell all of the scenes I saw while I was a captive. Some were very painful. I knew a great many of the white prisoners I was with, but now I only remember the names of Mrs. [Helen] Crothers [Carrothers], Mrs. [Urania] White and her daughter and Miss [Mattie] Williams. Some of the women came to me at times and asked me to let them stay with me. It was hard to refuse them, but I thought it best. I saw many women, some of them French women, that I had met the winter before at the country dances and other parties I have spoken of. I saw George H. Spencer quite often; he was still suffering from his wounds.

The night before the troops came to Camp Release, twenty or thirty Indians came in with a young white girl of sixteen or seventeen. She was nearly heartbroken, and quite in despair. When the half-breed men saw her they determined to rescue her, and we women encouraged them. Joe Laframboise and nine other mixed bloods went boldly up and took the girl from her brutal captors. The Indians threatened to shoot her if she was taken from them; but Joe was very brave, and said: "We are going to have her if we have to fight for her; and if you harm her it will be the worse for you. Remember, we are not your prisoners any more." So they took her, and she was rescued at Camp Release. Two other half-breed boys acted very bravely on this occasion — the Robertson boys; each was named Thomas, but they were not related.[13] One of them is living at Sisseton; the other died five years ago, but his family lives near Flandrau.

One day Shakopee came to our camp and talked with me. He said he would not have taken part in the outbreak but for the fact that his son had gone off hunting and the whites had killed him. "And now," said he, "my arm is lame from killing white people." A few days afterward his son returned all safe. The only time I spoke to Little Crow was the day my uncle came for us. He ordered my husband to hitch up a team for him that he had taken. The horses were not well broken and were quite wild, and he could not hitch them up himself.

When we were at Camp Release a Mrs. Huggins, who had been the wife of Amos Huggins, who had been killed, lived near us.[14] He and I were children together at Lac qui Parle. One day her little girl, three years of age, a bright child, came to our tent when my husband and I were eating dinner, and we gave her a seat with us. The little thing said: "This is not like the dinner mamma made the day papa was killed. The Indians killed my papa on his very birthday. We were going to have a good dinner. Mamma made a cake and everything nice, and papa came home with a load of hay, and the Indians shot him. But my papa isn't dead for sure. He is in heaven with God. You know, Mrs. Faribault, God is everywhere." We could not eat another bite after that.

I think the only time I laughed while I was a captive was at an Irish woman, another captive.[15] She was about forty-five years of age and not very shapely of form. Just before Camp Release we made many moves of a mile or two. The Indians had taken her ox team, and had often let her ride on the marches; but on the last march they made her walk. She came to our camp and inquired of my husband for John Mooer. She had on squaw clothes, had a baby in her arms, her face was very dirty, her hair towzled, and she was sputtering away in her Irish brogue and was a comical sight. She knew my husband, and she said: "Mr. Faribault, where are we goin' anyways?" My husband said: "We are going to the whites pretty soon." Then she said: "Well, I wish they would do something; I am sick of this campin' and trampin' all the time. That's my team they have, and the blackguards do be makin' me walk, and, be gosh, I am goin' to see John Mooer about it," and off she went to find Mr. Mooer.

While the Indians were away fighting at Wood lake, I and others of the mixed-bloods could have gone away from the camp; but Little Crow said if any of us did so those who remained should be killed; and so I thought it better to stay. Some women went away all the same, and escaped, too—Mrs. [William] Quinn, Mrs. [Philander] Prescott, with their children, and others. They seemed to know that Little Crow's threat was only a bluff, but he might have carried it out had he won that battle.

At last a lot of us released captives were started off for the settlements below. There were seven wagon loads of us in the party, whites and mixed-bloods, all women. At St. Peter's a store building was cleared out, cooking stoves put up, and bedding given us. An officer, whose name I am sorry I cannot remember, was in charge of us. Joe Coursalle, a noted half-blood scout, was with us.[16] In the evening the German, whose life I saved the first day of the outbreak, came into the room. He was intoxicated, had a knife in his hand, and said he was looking for an Indian to kill. The officer had gone out, but Coursalle was in and said to the reckless fellow, pointing to me, "Here is the woman that saved your life." This seemed to quiet him, and he thanked me very kindly. Then the officer came in and said to him: "Get out, you rascal. If you want to kill an Indian so bad, go West, to the front. There are lots of them out there, and they want to fight," and he put him out.

I went to Faribault and stayed at the home of my brother-in-law, Maj. Fowler, for some time. My husband remained with the troops under Gen. Sibley. All we had left was my horse, "Jerry." Our property had all been taken or destroyed by the Indians, but our log house was not burned. Our loss, besides what the Indians owed my husband, was fully $3,000. Our home was at Faribault for two years. We then moved back to Redwood, and then to Big Stone lake. Here, through Mr. [William] L. Quinn, the scout, who has always been my staunch friend, my husband got employment as interpreter under Maj. Crossman [Crosman], who, with a party of soldiers, was on the way to build Fort Ransom, 150 miles northwest of Big Stone lake.[17] We reached the site of the new fort in June, 1867. My husband was placed in charge of the scouts at this fort.

Narrative 9
CECELIA CAMPBELL STAY'S ACCOUNT

For biographical information on Cecelia Campbell Stay, see Chapter III, Narrative 1.

Narrative Source: Cecelia Campbell Stay, "Camp Relief [Release] in 1862," [1924?], typescript, Sioux Uprising Collection, Division of Libraries and Archives, Minnesota Historical Society.

LETTERS had been sent back and forth, between the Indians and Gen. [Colonel] Sibley. Big Tom Robertson [Robinson] and Little Tom Robertson, son of Jane and Andrew Robertson, were sent with the letters to the fort.

They would not let Father go, thinking he would post the army on the Indian position. I don't know how many times they went. I am quite certain they went twice. There was a trip made to Hutchinson vicinity. Flour was wanted. Flour the camp had to have. So the camp had not so many men some days. The camp [of the warrior Indians] would be very quiet, just old men, women and children. The Little Chief and his nearer relatives, Spencer's comrads were always on their guard for there was no telling, just when our turn came to die.

We moved to Stony Run, I don't know the exact date, we must have been all of a week at Hazelwood, and another week at Stony Run. From there we moved to Camp Relief [Release], our last western stand.

The plan made and carried out, the friendly indians should camp by themselves whatever the hostiles did, even if they had to fight them. Gen. Sibley was coming toward Wood Lake, and we were camped away from the hostiles. One night father came in looking pleased. He says to mother, "Old Woman, We are going to have a council in our tent to-night." "Are you," said she, "What about?["] He said, "The friendly chiefs were going to have a council[."] Then he was going to write letters to Gen. Sibley, and he was selected to carry them too.

Mother says, "They will kill you if they catch you." He said, he expected they would try. But he would go around them. He expected every route would be guarded to prevent anyone passing the enemies lines. We youngsters laid down on our hard beds (the ground). and slept so sound we heard nothing.

Next morning father was gone to Wood Lake with Joseph La Frambois[e] and Joseph (Rooyer) Rouilliard (how strange that all three should be named Joseph). The Indians were watching to prevent his reaching the army.

They were going to give him a slow death even if they had to stick needles all over him if caught going. But they did not get him and he did get to General Sibley. Thanks to the Renville Rangers, those brave boys, And some of the 3rd Regiment (Minnesota). They rushed for him shouting, "Kill the damned Traiter". Kill Him. While history tells [us] today they had not stood the ground nor duty like he had done. Perhaps they will think more of him when they read this little volume, and feel, "What if they had been in his place, standing between two fires as it were, Indians watching to kill him, the 3rd Regiment wanting to hill [kill] him." Supposing they had killed him. Do you think they would have got the prisoners alive then? I think not. It was well understood that if the army crowded them they would kill every drop of white blood in their hands. Those three men who went with the flag of Truce to meet Gen. Sibley have all the chance of a reward in heaven. For the Beatitudes say — "Blessed are the peacemakers — for they shall be called the children of God."

Gen. Sibley gave his instructions to father. We had long before camped away from the hostiles and called the friendly camp. Before

Father left us they dug a large round hole in the middle of our tent where we were to crawl in, and another long trench outside for the Indians to s[t]and in, to fight in, to fight defending us, if it came to battle between them and the Hostiles. They promised Father whatever happened, they would fight defending his family, as long as there was a drop of hearts blood alive within him. There we waited in suspense. Cannot tell what our plight was, only those who understood the language, they alone could feel the ominous[ness] of the hour in which our lives hung suspended by a thread.

During one moonlight night before that, a woman came running across the prairie, from the Hostile Camp, thru our camp. We stood out and she told mother the hostiles were coming to kill our family, as they suspected father had gone to meet the soldiers, with letters, and he was apt to give Gen. Sibley information, that would defeat them. Father asked them soon after about their threats. To give him a slow death, but they denied having said anything, as they held him in too high regard. Father was gone more than one night. For the first night they dug the trenches and held the council, next night Iron Elk's sister Ha Pana (Second Daughter) came to mother, and whispered in her ear that they had talked of taking the two oldest off. She wanted us to go with her until father came back. So Mother ordered us to follow the woman. We did not want to go, and leave them but she said it was on account of the trench. There was no room for us to sleep, which sounded strange as we had slept there the night before.

We went without asking any questions. We came to Blue Eyes['s] Tent, her sister was there, we were told where to sleep.[18] Emily slept near Blue Eyes['s] daughter, and I slept with the one who came after us. She moved her bundles, then I lay down, and she put her bundles all up against me, so no one could see there was anyone lying there. Before daylight I heard Father's voice in our tent, which was close by. It did not take us long to go back. Father's voice always had a charm for his dauther [daughter] Celia, and so, I shall always drop a word, which shall always bloom as roses around his pathway, and he shall know that while friends have turned fickle, and enemies dangerous, his daughter has watched and prayed, that all will yet come right. Now [How] carefully that noble man's name has been kept from history. When he did so much to alleviate the wrongs of the Red Man. How he soothed wounded feelings, by kind words, and wise counsels and material aid. He could not see one come to him for naught, and risking his own life and welfare for these prisoners. How they promised of their own accord to help him by a good word, when back to civilization, without asking. Where are those good words?

They have been carefully blotted out, even Gen. Sibley had to come in for his share of sneering criticism. Gen. Sibley had done just what all level heads thought best at the time. He took time and cooly did his duty to save lives. If he had taken Gen. [George A.] Cu[s]ter's rush he would have ended the same way, and accomplished nothing. Gen. Sibley is not praised for saving lives but Gen. Custer is lauded for losing his life and army when it was not necessary. Frontier men are cautious, at the same time brave, and the knowing how and accomplishing, is a trait, not to be sneered at. Indians are not drilled like an army. They are wily foe, full of schemes and plans to waylay and ambush. So a soldier drilled for civilized warfare is not the one to send to meet the Indians. Take our Renveille [Renville] Rangers for instance, They will always take the honor. Why not drill in that manner for the Frontier. Well here we come to Camp Release and Camp Relief as the Soldiers camp and Friendly Camp were called by us while talking with some of our soldier friends.

Gen. Sibley had told father as they were short of rations he could not force any marches, but on the 3rd morning he would be in sight about ten o'cllck [o'clock], and if he did not come to meet him with a flag of truce, at that point after he saw the bayonets shining at that distance he would fire the cannons into our camp, as by not meeting him with a flag of truce at that time he would know that father was a traitor, so would serve us accordingly.

We were divided into the Friendly Camp and Hostile Camp about two weeks before Gen. Sibley's battle at Wood Lake in Yellow Medicine, County, Minnesota. The morning after the battle of Wood Lake, Little Crow sent word to father to come, he wanted to see him. Our Indians did not want him to go, as it might be to kill him. Father smiled and said, "I'll go, I don't want to show them any cowardice. I think it[']s to kill me, but I'll go.["] "Well, they said, we will not let you go alone." So eight Indians went along with him. They may have had knives but there were no arms to be seen about them. They walked up to the council tent pitched upon a knoll. The tent belonged to Beausejour, a French Canadian. He had been practicing curcys [circus] acts before the outbreak. The lower corner of the door was carried up and fastened back so the end of the tent was open. Little Crow sat inside just to the right of the open door. They spread a robe or blanket in the center for father to sit on. The warriors were all dressed and painted, standing outside next to their chief, all leaning on their guns. Father said, "What a fine lot of men they were." There was a silence, then father spoke "Cousin," he said (they had always called each other cousin) "I heard you wanted to see me so I have come." Little Crow answered and said, "Yes, cousin, I am going away, if there is a last favor you would like to ask of me I would like to grant it to you." Father answered. "Yes, cousin, we are most safe now. Gen. Sibley will be here soon, and I would like that you and your warriors would give yourselves up" Little Crow with a derisive laugh says, "Wo Pa Tun Han Ska." ["]The long merchant Sibley would like to put the rope around my neck but he won't get the chance.["] Father said, "I don't think they will hang anybody[;] they never did before." "No, cousin," he said, "anything else, but to give myself up to hang by the neck like a woman. If they would shoot me like a man I would, but otherwise they will never get my live body."

Father then said, "if you can't do that, then I would like to get the prisoners.["]

Little Crow said, "Yes, you shall have them[.]" To his warriors he said any of you that have a prisoner or anything that belongs to them, give them back, and fetch them to this man. All answered "Ho" (Yes). And all turned around and hurriedly left to comply with the request of the only man, as Little Crow said, they could love and respect. He had never turned a deaf ear to them. Had always been like brothers, until the outbreak. So this last favor showed how they called upon the only man they could favor in their last adieu.

There is something holy and impressive to see these warriers who had for a space of five weeks, and three days spurned father's warnings and advice, and at the last moment show him so much regard.

Truly the works of God are indeed mysterious. Father took the names of the prisoners as fast as they were brought to him. There were 107 he got right there (Record 109)[.]

When he started with them to the Friendly camp, they trotted after him with great bundles tied up in white sheets and table clothes [cloths] so heavy they would drop them to the ground, then to fling them back over their shoulders. I[t] would swing around and drop to the ground again.

Some carried little children. They asked father many questions about their folks. Father knew they would never see them again. Some might have been saved. He did not know. He hated to shatter their hopes by telling them the sad facts. He gradually distanced them to keep the truth from them awhile longer. He would not be the first to tell them. There might be a shadow of doubt their lives were lost. There were [was] no hope of seeing their loved ones again.

They were all safely put amongst the Friendlies until Gen. Sibley came on the third morning. I am quite sure it was the 26th of Sept. when the army came. The Renville Rangers stood in a row opposite our tent. We girls went and shook hands with those we knew, and Emily gave Dick Hoback, the picture and ten dollar bill Mary Anderson had commissioned her to give him, for her folks.[19]

While looking out for glistening bayonets, the news came in camp that there was a war party going west by prairie trail with three prisoners. Father sent right off for his horse and word to Joseph La Frambois[e] and John Moore to each take a horse and come with him so there would be one to each prisoner if they had to take them by force. He expected trouble with their captors. Mother reasoned and wept, telling father to think of all that camp and his family, if Sibley should come and command them. She came and knelt down clasping her arms around his kneed [knees], but he loosened her hold of him and said, "Old Woman, go into the tent and lie down (she had tooth ache about two weeks then) those prisoners love their lives. Their lives are just as sweet to them as ours to us. It is my duty and may be the only chance they would have to see whites again."

Mother went into the tent to console herself, weeping quietly, lying on the ground, and away went father, galloping over the prairie for dear life, followed by the other two. They spread apart along the line of marching Indians as he knew the most important is always in the lead, so he took the head one. Talked to the leader. He had a Swede girl 14 years old prisoner, refusing to give her up, it was his squaw. Father put his hand out, the girl grasped it. When asked how she had confidence in a stranger, she said she would trust a white man anytime before an Indian. She knew they were disputing about her[;] each pulled his way to get her from the other.

The Indian saw he would not get her away from father, so he aimed his gun at father's breast to shoot. When [Then] one Indian looking on, stepped up and pushed the gun away, telling the other, more than one would like [lie] by him if he was harmed, that Father's brother, Uncle Hypolite, was married to his cousin.

At the same time he gave a lift to the girl on his horse, back of father astraddle, that was as good as a signal to the rest, they gave up their prisoners too. A little boy 8 years old. They were taken at Madelia. The girl and her old mother, and the neighbor's boy who was hearding cattle. The old woman came along until she was so foot sore and tired she sat down and refused to go further. They shot her dead, and then went their way with the other two until father got them away. You may be sure it did not take them long to get back to camp. Gen. Sibley and staff stood on an eminence each looking thru a spy glass by turn. Father has seen them too. He hurried the girl off, telling those standing around to help her off she could hardly walk, so helpless and tired. He called for a white handkerchief or cloth but it was hard to find a white cloth after five or six weeks of Indian life. At last some one came out with a cloth that was yellow with wear, and off again he went. He had lost his hat, it had been shot off by the enemies, and he had been going bareheaded since his trip to Wood Lake to meet Gen. Sibley. All eyes watched eagerly toward those shining bayonets. Until Gen. Sibley came up, where father stood with the head men of the Sioux tribe in a circle, where they met the general. Then father and Gen. Sibley went thru the camp side by side. The proudest incident of my life to have seen a duty well performed and well ended so far, and to see those two men neither could have done without the other in that last dark day of trouble of death and devastation.

Narrative 10
TAOPI'S STATEMENT

For biographical information on Taopi, see Chapter III, Narrative 7.

THE INDIANS came back from their defeat at Wood Lake and immediately prepared to retreat up the river to Big Stone Lake. They threatened to kill the friendly Sioux before leaving. We intrenched our tipis, digging down four or five feet that the women and children might be safe in case of attack. We could at any time have saved a few of the prisoners and escaped. But after General Sibley's letter we wished to save all of them or as many as possible. At first most of the Indians ran away with those routed at Wood Lake. But when they knew that the general would probably spare our lives, they kept coming back into our camp every night, until after his army arrived. I was instructed to save the prisoners if possible. By God's help we succeeded, and the bad men were foiled. The prisoners numbered one hundred whites and about one hundred and fifty of mixed blood. There were two hundred and fifty-five in all. Many of the Indians of the Farmers' Band aided me in my undertaking. I wish especially to mention Wakinyanwaste (Good Thunder) the head man of my band, Wakinyantawa (who saved Mr. Spencer), and Wahacankamaza who carried the letter over the prairie.[20] The two young men, Thomas Robertson and Thomas Robinson, who carried the letter to General Sibley, ought to be rewarded. They did it at the risk of their lives. I wish also to state that I tried to send a letter to General Sibley before. I asked Mr. Spencer to write it for me, but he could not as he was wounded in the right arm.

This is all I have to say.

Narrative 11
PAUL MAZAKUTEMANI'S STATEMENT

For biographical information on Paul Mazakutemani, see Chapter VIII, Narrative 5.

AFTER this [formation of the camp for the peace party] they gathered up the captives and gave them to me. And now Gen. [Colonel] Sibley came with his army. I remained at our camp near the mouth of the Chippewa, while a great part of the Dakotas fled. When the white troops came near, I raised a white flag. Gen. Sibley came on and encamped near me, and so I shook hands with him and with all the officers. Then I said, "I have grown up like a child of yours. With what is yours, you have caused me to grow; and now I take your hand as a child takes the hand of his father. My hand is not bad. With a clean hand I take your hand. I know whence this blessing cometh. I have regarded all white people as my friends, and from this I understand this blessing has come. This is a good work we do to-day, whereof I am glad. Yes, before the great God I am glad."

Gen. Sibley said to me, "This is good. Henceforth I will take you into my service." Since that I and my children have lived well. And from that time more than ever I have regarded myself as a white man, and I have counselled my boys accordingly.

Continued on page 278.

Narrative 12
SNANA'S STORY

For biographical information on Snana, see Chapter VI, Narrative 5.

THE SOLDIERS [Sibley's army] seemed not to come near to us, but instead of that they could be heard at a distance beating the drum day after day, which I did not understand. Of course we who had captives wished the soldiers to come to us or to kill all the bad Indians.

Once, when the soldiers came near us, all the bad Indians were trying to skip from the country, mean and angry; but at this time I dug a hole inside my tent and put some poles across, and then spread my blankets over and sat on top of them, as if nothing unusual had

SNANA
in 1899

happened. But who do you suppose were inside the hole? My dear captive girl, Mary Schwandt, and my own two little children. When the soldiers camped beside us, my heart was full of joy.

General [Colonel] Sibley was in command of the army, and he advised us to camp inside of his circle, which we did. He was so kind that he provided for us some food just the same as the soldiers had; and I thought that this was something new to me in the midst of my late troubles. When I turned this dear child over to the soldiers my heart ached again; but afterward I knew that I had done something which was right.

From that day I never saw her nor knew where she was for thirty-two years, until the autumn of 1894; when I learned that she lives in St. Paul, being the wife of Mr. William Schmidt. Soon I went to visit her, and I was respected and treated well. It was just as if I went to visit my own child.

Narrative 13
GEORGE QUINN'S ACCOUNT

For biographical information on George Quinn, see Chapter IV, Narrative 5.

I WAS in the Wood Lake battle. I was one of a party of thirteen that was placed toward the rear of Sibley's force in a ravine which ran from the lake. We were nearly all of Wacouta's band and our leader was Chetanwekechetah, or the Killing Hawk.[21] His wife was Jack Frazer's niece. He was killed and eight more of the thirteen were shot by the force that attacked us. Our line was across the route the soldiers were on to dig potatoes at the Yellow Medicine Agency, and a dog with the soldiers barked at our men as they lay in the grass and so they were discovered. Little Crow stayed on the field till the fight was over. He had no arms but a large six-shooter. I do not think he fired it. Mankato's body was buried back in our camp, I think, and not in the banks of the Yellow Medicine, as Big Eagle says. Old Simon came among the Indians during the fight, with a white rag on a stick and wanted the other Indians to stop fighting, and some of them obeyed him. Old Mahzomanne (Walks on Iron [Mazamani]) went out from the Indian side with a white flag, but a cannon ball took off his leg and he died. He had taken no part against the whites.

I surrendered at Camp Release and gave my gun to Samuel J. Brown. He put me under guard, but said I would not be a prisoner very long. I was a prisoner for four years, being sent to Rock Island. Nothing was proved against me except that I was in some of the battles against the whites. I took no part in killing the settlers and was opposed to such work.

Narrative 14
CHARLES R. CRAWFORD'S TESTIMONY

For biographical information on Charles R. Crawford, see Chapter V, Narrative 4.

I WAS tried twice [by the military tribunal], and I will tell of both times. The day that General [Colonel] Sibley came to Camp Release an officer came to me and told me that I was wanted at headquarters. I went over there and went in. I found in there a number of officers, and among them one whom I knew afterwards to be Colonel Crooks, who wrote a paper about me, stating that I was accused of killing a white man. He asked me if that was so. I told him no; and then he said to me "If you lie about this, there is a man who knows about it and will tell on you." I then told them, as I have told you here, about going to hunt for my sister, and all that, up to the time that I went to the battle of New Ulm. Then the guard went and brought Lorenzo Lawrence. Lawrence was asked if he knew me, and he said yes; then he was asked if he knew of my killing a white man. He said no. "Why do you then accuse this man of killing a white man?" — this question was put to Lawrence. He said he heard that. Then Lawrence was asked how he heard of it, and Lawrence said he didn't know. Then he was asked how it came that he heard of it, and he said again "Oh, I heard of it." Then Lawrence was asked who told him this, and he said that he had heard it, but didn't know exactly where he had heard it. Then Lawrence came out and one Anton [Antoine] Frenier was brought in, who accused me of breaking open a barrel of whisky, getting the Indians drunk, and starting with them on a war party.[22] That is what Frenier accused me of, but that is not true, because I was not

CHARLES CRAWFORD
at the Sisseton
Agency, 1896

there. The second thing I was accused of was by a white man, a soldier [John Magner], that claimed that I was very close to him at the battle of Wood Lake, chasing him, and that he just barely saved his life by my not being able to catch him. At that trial we told of our being on the west side of the battlefield during the battle. When this soldier was questioned, he said that this band was on the east side of the road and on the east of the battle grounds; but we were not on that side at all. That was all of the trial.

Narrative 15
GEORGE CROOKS'S ACCOUNT

GEORGE CROOKS or Wakanajaja, meaning Holy Lightning, was the son of Tukonwechaste or Sacred Stone Man and Mahkahta or Woman Who Goes on the Earth. He was born on January 1, 1856, near the Redwood Agency. His parents, Christian members of the Mdewakanton farmer band, protected many white captives during the war. Afterwards Crooks and his mother lived at Faribault, while his father worked as a scout for General Sibley. Crooks married Alice Boyd or Blue Star in July 1880; in about 1889 they moved to Birch Coulee, where he farmed and sold musical instruments. He died at Morton, Minnesota, on April 1, 1947.

In 1988, when this book was first published, it included an account attributed to George Crooks that first appeared in the Morton Enterprise *in 1909. Its bitter message was the story of a disastrous journey to Fort Snelling in the fall of 1862, during which white settlers attacked a caravan of captives at New Ulm and killed his older brother.*

After this book's publication, another George Crooks account came to light. Published in the Redwood Gazette *almost four weeks after the Morton piece, it denied any connection to the earlier, lurid account. A reminiscence he recorded in 1937, now at the Minnesota Historical Society, also makes no reference to the New Ulm trip.*

The account as first published, apparently invented by O. W. Smith, editor of the Enterprise, *was reprinted in at least three other southern Minnesota newspapers. It provides yet another complication in the continuing historiography of the Dakota War—and also, no doubt, sold papers. Excerpts from both articles are included below.*[23]

Narrative Source: Morton Enterprise, January 29, 1909, p. 1.

THE EXCITEMENT of the Indians knew no bounds when they realized they were in the power of the soldiers and the scene was terrifying to behold, fear and despair completely carried them away and the impression gained an everlasting hold on [my] youthful mind. It was repeatedly told us we were all to be executed. . . .

After the surrender the Indians were loaded into old Red River carts and started for the Lower Agency and Mankato. The carts were small, drawn by an ox, and it was with difficulty for any more than four persons to occupy the box. In the cart I was forced to occupy were two Indian men and my sixteen-year old brother. We were bound securely and on our journey resembled a load of animals on their way to market. . . .

As we came near New Ulm . . . I crouched down beside my brother completely overcome with fear. In a short time we reached the outskirts of the town and the long looked for verdict—death, seemed at hand. Women were running about, men waving their arms and shouting at the top of their voices, convinced the driver the citizens of that village were wild for the thirst of blood, so he turned the vehicle in an effort to escape the angry mob but not until too late, they were upon us. We were pounded to a jelly, my arms, feet, and head resembled raw beef steak. How I escaped alive has always been a mystery to me. My brother was killed and when I realized he was dead I felt the only person in the world to look after me was gone and I wished at the time they had killed me. . . .

I can truthfully say the experience photographed on my youthful mind can never be defaced by time.

Narrative Source: Redwood Gazette, February 24, 1909, p. 1.

THE GAZETTE last week received a call from Geo. Crooks, the Sioux Indian whose alleged account of his recollections of the Indian uprising was copied from the Morton paper two weeks ago. Mr. Crooks mildly objects to being reported in this way, inasmuch as he never wrote or sanctioned the account as printed, and more particularly because the story as printed is to some extent absolutely false. . . . We print the following abstract of Mr. Crooks' recollections. . . .

"I had nothing to do with the story which appeared in the Morton paper and do not know who wrote it. It is true that I was about six years old at the time of the trouble, but it is all wrong about my brother and some other things said in the paper. My brother was 25 years old at that time instead of 16, as the paper said, and instead of being killed at New Ulm, died a natural death from consumption in '66, four years after the trouble, at Crow Creek agency.

"As I was only six years old, my recollections at that time are not important. I know, however, that the women and children were taken from Camp Release and went in carts to St. Peter, and not to New Ulm or Mankato at all, neither did my brother or the prisoners go through New Ulm, as I understand. My brother was among those tried and acquitted at Mankato. I never heard of any Indian prisoner being killed at New Ulm. . . ."

Narrative 16
GOOD STAR WOMAN'S RECOLLECTIONS

For biographical information on Good Star Woman, see Chapter II, Narrative 2.

THE INDIANS who fought the whites turned against the Indians who refused to join them. It was a custom of the Sioux, when in danger of attack from the Chippewa, to put the women and children in one or two wigwams, and dig a trench in the middle so they could crouch in that and be below the line of fire. The earth that was removed to make the trench was piled outside the wigwam, forming an embankment. Good Star Woman's family were "friendly Sioux" and she remembers being placed in such a shelter, with the other children and the women.

At length the friendly Sioux got someone to write a letter and take it to Fort Snelling. The man had to go a long way around, but he returned safely and said the soldiers were coming. He told the Indians what to do when they saw the soldiers and said they must make a white flag to wave, and must point their guns down toward the ground. They did as he told them, and the soldiers circled around and had them pack their goods. The soldiers brought wagons for the women and children, while the Indians who had horses took them, and put their belongings on travois. Good Star Woman's father had a horse and travois and she travelled that way, with her two younger sisters. Her father covered them with a buffalo hide with the hair on the outside, but she sometimes lifted the corner and peeked out. When they passed through towns the people brought poles, pitchforks and axes and hit some of the women and children in the wagons. Her father was struck once and almost knocked down. The soldiers rode on each side of the column of Indians and tried to protect them but could not always do so. A boy was driving an ox cart and the white people knocked him down. Some Indians died from the beatings they received.

At night they camped close together, and the soldiers camped in a circle around them. Once an Indian was struck and killed. They scraped the fire aside and buried him under it, so the whites would not find his body. They went on the next morning.

In the meantime the Sioux who had started the trouble had run away to safety.

At length the pitiful column of friendly Sioux reached Fort Snelling. A high fence was put around their camp, but the settlers came and took their horses and oxen. They were provided with food. The soldiers drove a wagon among the tents and gave crackers to the children and bread to the older people. Measles broke out, and the Indians thought the disease was caused by the strange food. This was the first time they ever had the disease. All the children had measles and one of her sisters died. Sometimes 20 to 50 died in a day and were buried in a long trench, the old, large people underneath and the children on top. A Roman Catholic priest brought a box for each body and put them in the trench until spring, then he "buried them right." He was good to the children and told them to come to church and he gave them candy and apples. The children liked the singing in the church. (Who was this priest? Doubtless his name is recorded in history but the Sioux remember only his good deeds.)[24]

Good Star Woman said that some Sioux were taken from Fort Snelling to St. Louis and put in chains.[25] The remainder were kept there all winter, and in the spring were told they would have to move. They were put on a steamboat and taken down the river, but the boat was leaking and some had to be taken off. After a while they were put in box cars and taken over to the Missouri river where they were again put on a steamboat. Their destination was Fort Thompson [Crow Creek Reservation, Dakota Territory] where they were kept in a stockade for three years. Many starved to death there. The Indians were almost naked. They wound burlap around their legs to keep warm. Many of the women had to wear burlap gotten from the soldiers, and nobody had any sleeves in their garments. If the men got drunk they had to carry bricks all day.

Such is the story of Good Star Woman, one of the Friendly Sioux who remembers the uprising of the hostile Indians.

NOTES

1. Other narratives contradict this statement regarding Little Crow's attitude toward the captives; see Cecelia Stay's narrative in Chapter IX, p. 249, below.
2. Dr. Daniels, a resident of St. Peter, set up a hospital there to treat wounded refu-

gees and served as army surgeon under Sibley's command; Carley, *Sioux Uprising*, 41, 42.

3. Rousseau, La Belle, and Rouillard were French-Canadian traders who had Dakota wives and mixed-blood children; U.S. Census, 1860, Hawk Creek Township, Renville County, roll 373, p. 375.

4. Joseph C. Whitney had lived for some years in Minneapolis where he was a Presbyterian minister. On August 16, 1862, he received a commission as captain of Company D of the Sixth Minnesota. His unit went to the relief of Fort Ridgely and participated in the battle of Wood Lake. Company D served at Camp Release where it guarded Dakota prisoners, on the Minnesota frontier in the winter of 1862–63, on the Sibley expedition to Dakota Territory in 1863, and again guarded the frontier during the winter of 1863–64. Whitney then served in the Civil War, 1864–65. He returned to Minneapolis where he was in business until his death in 1896; Upham and Dunlap, *Minnesota Biographies*, 852–53; Board of Commissioners, *Minnesota in the Civil and Indian Wars*, 1:311–18, 327, 335.

5. William Rainey Marshall (1825–96) arrived in Minnesota Territory in 1849, started a hardware business in St. Paul, and founded the *St. Paul Press*. He served in the Civil War with the Seventh Minnesota as lieutenant colonel, colonel, 1863–65, and was brevetted a brigadier general. He was governor of Minnesota, 1866–70, and railroad commissioner, 1876–82; Upham and Dunlap, *Minnesota Biographies*, 490.

6. For more on Charles Crawford, see his narrative in Chapter V, p. 112, above.

7. The battle was actually fought near Lone Tree Lake. An error, perhaps made by a guide, led to its being called Wood Lake. The original Wood Lake lay in the next township to the west. See Folwell, *History of Minnesota*, 2:177n52.

8. Tunkanshaiciye or Sacred Stone that Paints Itself Red or Solomon Tukanshaiciye was born at Lac qui Parle in 1833, educated in the mission school, and joined the Hazelwood church in 1858. He was tried, convicted, and sentenced to be hanged for participating in the battles at Fort Ridgely, New Ulm, Birch Coulee, and Wood Lake. His sentence was remitted, and he was imprisoned at Davenport, 1863–66. Licensed to preach by the Dakota Presbytery in 1867 and ordained in 1868, he served as pastor of Dakota churches on the Sisseton Reservation until 1879 when he moved to Manitoba to work among refugee Dakotas. In 1890 he returned to the Sisseton Reservation and became pastor of the Buffalo Lake church. He died in 1910; Adams, Williamson, and Renville, *First Fifty Years*, Appendix, xvii; Stephen R. Riggs, *Mary and I: Forty Years with the Sioux* (1880; Boston: Congregational Sunday-School and Publishing Society, 1887), 374–81; Satterlee, *Court Proceedings*, Appendix, 4; Transcripts of Trials of Sioux Indians, case no. 92, Senate Records 37A-F2; Obituary, in possession of Alan R. Woolworth.

9. William Taylor, a well-known barber and musician in St. Paul, often attended annuity payments at the Redwood Agency; Williams, *History of the City of Saint Paul*, 249; Heard, *History of the Sioux War*, 67.

10. Doane Robinson, "The Fight at Webster," *Monthly South Dakotan* 3 (1901): 324–27; Samuel J. Brown, "Two Stars and Little Crow," *The Dakotan* 5 (1903): 323–25; U.S. Congress, *Sisseton and Wahpeton Sioux Indians*, 44th Cong., 1st sess., 1875, H. Doc. 42, p. 10; Kappler, comp. and ed., *Indian Treaties*, 2:959, 1058, 1062; *Inter Lake Tribune* (Browns Valley), June 25, 1914, p. 3.

11. Gray Grass, a Mdewakanton, was tried by the military commission, convicted, and sentenced to be hanged. His sentence was remitted, and he spent three years in the prison camp at Davenport. At his trial he admitted firing three shots at the battle of Birch Coulee. Other witnesses stated that he was a member of the warriors' soldiers' lodge; Satterlee, *Court Proceedings*, Appendix, 3; Transcripts of Trials of Sioux Indians, case no. 62, Senate Records 37A-F2. Little is known about Black Leg other than that he was one of several sons of White Lodge, leader of a Sisseton band. He probably

accompanied his father to the Missouri and then to Canada; see Chapter V, note 28, above.

12. Stephen H. Fowler was born in Connecticut in 1820. He was commissioned a second lieutenant in the U.S. Fifth Infantry in November 1838 and served in the Mexican War, being brevetted a major. While serving at Fort Snelling he met and married Emily R. Faribault, the mixed-blood daughter of Alexander Faribault and Elizabeth Marie Graham, in 1841. On August 25, 1862, he was given the rank of lieutenant colonel by Colonel Sibley and placed in charge of a regiment of unmounted men, which was never actually organized. During the trials following the war, he gave advice on procedures. By 1870 he and his family were farming in Walcott Township in Rice County; Francis B. Heitman, *Historical Register and Dictionary of the United States Army* (Washington, D.C.: Government Printing Office, 1903), 1:433; Folwell, *History of Minnesota*, 2:150; U.S. Census, 1870, Walcott Township, Rice County, roll 9, p. 541.

13. Thomas A. Robertson and Thomas Robinson.

14. Amos W. Huggins, a missionary to the Dakotas, was killed at the Lac qui Parle school on August 19 by one of a group of three men. The actual murderer was a man named Tainna or Leather Blanket. With him was a warrior named Hosihdi or He Brought the News; he was tried, convicted, and sentenced to be hanged, but he was not executed. Both belonged to Red Iron's Sisseton band. The editors have found no further information on these two men. An onlooker was Tatekage or He Makes the Wind, the grandson of Wakanmani or Spirit Walker, leader of a Wahpeton band. Although young and perhaps mentally defective, he was tried, convicted, and hanged at Mankato on December 26, 1862; Folwell, *History of Minnesota*, 2:121; Satterlee, *Court Proceedings*, 49–50, 58–59; Transcripts of Trials of Sioux Indians, cases no. 155, 272, Senate Records 37A-F2.

15. The identity of this woman cannot be ascertained.

16. For more on Joseph Coursolle, see his narrative in Chapter III, p. 57, above.

17. William L. Quinn was born near Fort Snelling on November 4, 1828. His parents were Peter Quinn, an interpreter, and Mary Finley, a mixed-blood. He was employed as a clerk in the Indian trade for many years. In 1862 he and his family were at the Yellow Medicine Agency where he worked in William Forbes's store. He was in St. Paul when the war began but soon searched for his family who were captives but had escaped to Fort Ridgely. He was a scout, guide, and at times a messenger, 1862–65, and chief of scouts at Fort Wadsworth, 1867–70. He then lived in St. Paul until his death on March 5, 1906; *St. Paul Pioneer Press*, April 29, 1894, March 7, 1906.

Major George H. Crosman entered West Point from Pennsylvania in 1854 and received a commission in August 1861. He served through the Civil War and was brevetted a major at Gettysburg. He served at Fort Wadsworth and on June 18, 1867, went with the Tenth Infantry Regiment to Bear's Den Hillock on the Sheyenne River to build a military post. He left that post in the spring of 1868, was mustered out in January 1871, but was still living in 1895; Heitman, *Historical Register and Dictionary of the United States Army*, 1:341; Dana Wright, "Military Trails in North Dakota," *North Dakota History* 17 (1950): 242–45.

18. The editors have found no further information on Blue Eyes.

19. Dick Hoback had been engaged to marry Mary Anderson; Schwandt-Schmidt, "The Story of Mary Schwandt," *Minnesota Collections*, 6:469.

20. Wahacankamaza or Iron Shield was a Mdewakanton. He and his family spent the winter of 1862–63 in the Dakota camp at Fort Snelling. He was a scout at Lake Traverse in 1865 and in 1866 was awarded $150 for carrying the letter signed by Taopi and for caring for white captives. After living at Santee, Nebraska, for some years, he returned to Minnesota in about 1887 and was living near Morton when he died in De-

cember 1907 at the age of 75; U.S. Office of Indian Affairs, *Report, 1863,* 433, *1866,* 238; Chilson, "Dakota Indian Scout Roster"; Obituary, in possession of Alan R. Woolworth.

21. The editors have found no further information on Chetanwekechetah.

22. Antoine Frenier was a mixed-blood with Sisseton and Yanktonai ancestors. He was born in 1827 and educated in Canada. By 1854 he was at Lac qui Parle in charge of Martin McLeod's trading post. By 1858 he had moved to the Yellow Medicine Agency and was an interpreter for the Indian agent. During the war he played an active role as a scout for the army and was an interpreter at the trials. He went to Fort Snelling during the winter of 1862–63 and became controversial by charging both full- and mixed-bloods with involvement in the war. In summer 1863 he joined the James L. Fisk expedition to the Montana gold fields as an interpreter and guide. On his return alone down the Missouri River, he was killed, probably by Santee Dakotas, in early June 1864; U.S. Office of Indian Affairs, *Report, 1858,* 53, 67, *1863,* 269; Heard, *History of the Sioux War,* 85–86, 96–97; Helen M. White, *Ho! For The Gold Fields: Northern Overland Wagon Trains of the 1860s* (St. Paul: Minnesota Historical Society, 1966), 78–79, 83, 113–14; *St. Paul Pioneer Press,* June 30, 1864, p. 1.

23. *Minneapolis Times,* August 15, 1897. The false Crooks account was originally reprinted in *Redwood Gazette,* February 3, 1909, p. 1; *Hector Mirror,* February 12, 1909, p. 1; *New Ulm Review,* February 10, 1909, p. 1; and perhaps in other papers. George's mother, who was also known as Mary Crooks, sought out and protected two white captives, Urania White and her baby. Mary's name is on the monument erected at Morton by the Minnesota Valley Historical Society to "commemorate the brave, faithful, and humane conduct of the loyal Indians." See White, "Captivity among the Sioux," *Minnesota Collections,* 9:395–426; [Holcombe], *Sketches Historical and Descriptive,* 46–50, 61–63.

24. Father Augustin Ravoux (1815–1906) arrived in St. Paul in 1841 and spent several years as a missionary to the Dakotas. He counseled the condemned warriors in Mankato in December 1862; Upham and Dunlap, *Minnesota Biographies,* 628; Williams, *History of the City of Saint Paul,* 113–15.

25. The Dakota men who had been tried and convicted by the military commission and received prison sentences were held at Mankato until spring when they were moved to a prison camp at Davenport, Iowa.

CHAPTER **X**

The Final Days

AS THE newly promoted General Sibley and his officers examined the evidence against the many Dakota Indians who surrendered in late 1862, the final chapter of the war took shape on the plains northwest of Camp Release. Perhaps as many as 250 Mdewakanton men had fled Sibley's army in late September, joining the bands of Sioux who lived on the plains. Among the latter were Sissetons and Wahpetons, most of whom had not participated in the fighting in the Minnesota River valley, and large numbers of Yanktons, Yanktonais, and Tetons. While the Tetons made their home in the Missouri River valley and to the west, the Yanktons and Yanktonais frequently resided at Devils Lake, an oasis of sorts in the middle of the vast northern plains. By early November, Sissetons, Wahpetons, and a few Mdewakantons turned to the lake for refuge, making it the focal point of Dakota activity in the west.

Little Crow, as spokesman for the Mdewakantons, sought to mold the Sioux bands into an alliance that would resist the whites. The plan came to naught because the Yanktons quickly rejected such a coalition, and the leaders of the Sissetons and Wahpetons held the Mdewakantons responsible for starting a war that they wished had never happened. By springtime as it became evident that General Sibley would launch a campaign against the Sioux, all remaining thoughts of an alliance among the western tribes faded. Little Crow reacted to this failure by deciding to return to Minnesota in June with his son, Wowinape, and a few others. He was fatally shot by a white farmer on July 3, 1863, near Hutchinson.[1] His son survived the attack and left a narrative of the chief's last weeks. By the time of Little Crow's death, the Mdewakantons who had followed him to the plains had scattered.

As the Sioux on the plains debated the war issue, Sibley made plans to invade the stronghold around Devils Lake. Being aware of the need for accurate information regarding the whereabouts of the Indians and fearing that the warring faction would mount raids during the winter, he decided to form a scout camp and recruited Dakota mixed-bloods and full-bloods. The scouts, dominated by the Renvilles and the mission Indians, played important roles in protecting the whites living on the frontier, the summer campaign into Dakota Territory, and the eventual surrender of most of the Indian participants in the war. The scouts also carried messages between the plains Sioux and Sibley's camp. Nevertheless, they were not successful in preventing a clash between Sibley's army and the Indians at Big Mound, about forty miles east of present-day Bismarck, on July 24, 1863. The skirmish, known as the battle of Big Mound, began when a Sisseton warrior shot Dr. Josiah S. Weiser, an army surgeon, during an impromptu negotiation. The army pursued the Sioux westward to the Missouri, fighting at Dead Buffalo Lake on July 26 and Stony Lake on July 28. More than a hundred Indians were killed and a quantity of food, utensils, and other goods destroyed. By fall, the Dakota War came to a close.

The narratives that have survived from this period recount the organization of the scout camps, the negotiations that occurred on the plains, and Sibley's expedition into Sioux lands during the summer of 1863. They show once again the divisiveness that existed among the various Dakota groups over the issues of war, negotiations with the whites, and peace.

Narrative 1
FRANK JETTY'S REMINISCENCES

FRANK JETTY was born in the vicinity of the Yellow Medicine Agency in about 1858. His father was Francis Shetais or Stay (or Jetty), a French-Canadian hunter and trapper, and his mother, a Dakota Indian. When the war began, his father fled to Fort Ridgely, and his mother took his sister and him to her Dakota relatives, accompanying them into northern Dakota Territory. In the spring of 1864 he was given into the safekeeping of a métis couple, Moses Azure and Leocadie Martelle. He grew up at St. Joseph, Dakota Territory, married Juilienne Dubois, and raised eleven children. He spent the rest of his life in the vicinity of St. Michael, North Dakota. The date of his death is unknown.

When he was about thirty-seven years old, he sought out his parents, both of whom had remarried. His mother and her husband, a

Dakota full-blood, lived on the Sisseton Reservation in eastern South Dakota. His father had married Cecelia Campbell and lived near Lac qui Parle.

Narrative Source: Frank Jetty, "Frank Jetty's Life — Related by Himself to the Grey Nuns at St. Michael's Mission, St. Michael, North Dakota," typescript, ca. 1952, Cecelia Campbell Stay Papers, Provincial Archives of Manitoba, Winnipeg, Manitoba.

WHEN the Indian warriors saw the soldiers arrive [near Camp Release in September 1862], they fled in this direction (Devils Lake). My mother too, fled here with my sister Josephone and myself, we were the halfbreeds of the band. For fear of being killed, the peaceful Indians fled along with the rest. This happened in 1862. That year my mother spent the winter on the Lake shore (Devils Lake). My mother showed me the place where she stayed. It is right here behind your heating building. (St Michael, N. Dak.) There was a thick woods along the shore, where my mother went fishing with her cousin, White-Dog. . . .

The next spring we left for the prairies between here (St. Michael, N. Dak.) and Bismarck. In June the Government sent Scouts to find out where the Indians were. When the Indians saw the regiment coming, they thought the soldiers were coming to fight. But this was not the reason. They wanted to bring back the Sioux to Yellow Medicine, Minn. from whence they had come.

The Indians fled again, and the soldiers followed with the intention of overtaking them at the Missouri River. When the Indians arrived between Mandan and Bismarck, N. Dak., below the hills of the river shore, they camped. Sibbly [sic] and his soldiers watched them four miles from the encampment to encircle them the next morning. When the Indians preceived [sic] that they were discovered, they started to improvise boats with small trees on which they tied buffalo hides. All during the night the Indian swimmers guided these boats across the river with ropes held between their teeth. Thus, all who could not swim and the women, children and belongings were carried across. Only a poor old squaw who had died during the night remained behind. The Indians had prepared her well. The next morning, the soldiers found her sitting, waiting for them. When the soldiers waw [saw] they were tricked, they returned.

In the Fall, the Indians recrossed the Missouri River and went to Turtle Mountains, Bottineau, N. Dak. near the present site of Peace

Gardens. There they spent the winter for this was good hunting-ground. Here, too, was the Fort of the Hudson['s] Bay Co., where the Indians could exchange pelts for munitions, guns, food and clothing.

The next Spring [1864], they left Turtle Mountains and came to Pleasant Lake to hunt Buffalo and here they met the half-breeds who came from Walhalla and Pembina to hunt. The Bois Brulis (Burnt Woods) [métis] and the Sioux met. The good Indians who had children with white blood feared that they would be killed by the wicked Indians. In the group were ten boys and four girls with white blood. Their parents asked the half-breeds if they would take these children and care for them so that the bad Indians would not kill them. They always had fear of the Sioux or of the soldiers. Thus, the Sioux gave these children to the Half-breeds to have them brought up.

Myself, age 6 was adopted by Moses Azure and his wife, Leocadie Martelle. She had been educated by Rev. Father [George A.] Belcourt for the Sisterhood . . . but did not persevere. Moses Asure's brother, Antoine, adopted Josephone, my sister, age 9, but the following year she ran away to her mother. My sister left during the night to follow her mother to the camp after her mother visited her. My mother continued to follow the Sioux with my sister. Later my sister married M. Augustin LaFreniere. I was raised and married in Walhalla.

Narrative 2
SAMUEL J. BROWN'S RECOLLECTIONS

For biographical information on Samuel J. Brown, see Chapter IV, Narrative 1.

Narrative Source: "Little Crow's Famous Trip to the Missouri River," told by Samuel J. Brown to Marion P. Satterlee, undated typescript, Marion P. Satterlee Papers, Division of Libraries and Archives, Minnesota Historical Society.

THE NEXT DAY after the battle of Wood Lake, Where the Lower Indians intended to wipe out Sobley's [sic] army, but were defeated and routed instead, Little Crow returned to his camp crestfallen, saddened and disheartened. This camp was opposite the mouth of the Chippewa River, and was afterward known as Camp Release. Standing outside of his teepee, and calling his warriors together, he told them to pack up and leave, and save their wives and children: that the troops would soon be upon them and no time should be lost. In the evening of that day, Little Crow with his family and about 200 warriors with their families, under cover of the darkness, struck thier [sic] tents and hurriedly fled toward Devil's Lake, about two hundred miles away, arriving there a month or so later. It was from this place (Devil's Lake, where he intended to remain for the winter), that Little Crow made his famous trip to the Missouri. Soon after his arrival there, the wily chief planned to go to Fort Berthold on a mission of peace with the Gros Ventres, Mandans, and Ree tribes, the object being to endeavor to induce them to join in raids on the whites in Minnesota the following spring. With his two hundred trusty warriors he set out on his journey, arriving at his destination in due time. Approaching the Mandan village in the usual style of peace-making among the Indians — dancing, whooping and firing of guns, and making as much bluster and noise as possible, while holding aloft and extending the peace pipe, they were met by the Berthold Indians, who at once fired upon the visitors. The Ree Indians having crossed over from the west side commenced the attack. The recent killing of many of their warriors (by other tribes of Sioux), Including the killing and scalping of one of their leading chiefs, made them (the Rees), unforgiving. The Gros Ventres and Mandans had also suffered much from the Sioux, and were glad to help their Ree friends: so, Little Crow's men were overwhelmingly outnumbered and in consequence were beaten and most unmercifully slaughtered. They were compelled to flee for their lives. Many were overtaken and killed and their scalps taken. Among the number so killed was Little Dog, (Xunka-Cistinna, pronounced Shunka-Cis-Tinna, the Indian who warned the family of Maj. Joseph R. Brown, of the massacre at the Lower Agency in 1862.) This was Little Crow's undoing: the failure of his cherished plans — the failure to win the friendship and assistance of these Indians, as well as the feeling against him on account of the loss of many of his men — and the memory of the Wood Lake disaster — so disheartened him that upon his return he at once broke camp and started for the British Possessions, accompanied by about 100 of his men with their families. The rest of the people who survived the slaughter scattered out in different directions, some going south to their friends on the Missouri, in the nieghborhood [sic] of the Grand River, and some northwest hunting buffalo along the Mouse River, (presumably, on to the Assineboin River). Little Crow and his party went to Turtle Mountain, (neighborhood of St. Joseph, D. T.) and camped there for the winter, going on to Fort Garry [Manitoba] in the spring of 1863, where he and his band arrived about April. Soon after his arrival there, or about the middle of June, he with sixteen others went on a marauding expedition to the settlements in Minnesota and he was killed while picking berries near Hutchinson, by Nathan Lamson and his son Chauncey, on July 3d, 1863.

Narrative 3
GABRIEL RENVILLE'S MEMOIR

For biographical information on Gabriel Renville, see Chapter V, Narrative 1.

THEN I went to General Sibley [in late December 1862] and had a talk with him, and suggested to him that some mixed-bloods be picked out as scouts and sent to Redwood Agency. But this was a difficult matter to consider, so General Sibley called into consultation the officers under him, and a letter was written to the great father in regard to it. An answer came, and I was asked who I thought should be sent out there. I gave in the names of myself, Michael Renville, Daniel Renville, Isaac Renville, John Moore[s], Thomas Robinson, and four full-blood Indians.[2]

I was laughed at, and was asked whether I thought it was a light matter to so soon send out these full-blood Indians. My answer was, "You told me to pick out reliable men. I have done so. There are full-blood Indians who are more steadfast and more to be depended upon than many of the mixed-bloods. This is why I have chosen them." The question was referred to the authorities at Washington, and in about a month the answer came that this might be done. [Solomon] Two Stars, E-chay-tu-ke-ya [Big Amos], E-nee-hah, and Wah-su-ho-was-tay [Enos Good Voiced Hail], were chosen.

In the month of February, 1863, having got permission from General Sibley and rations, we came out of the inclosure at Fort Snelling and started on our journey. In passing the different towns on the way the people saw we were armed, and, surmising our occupation, they respected us and did not molest us in any way. We arrived at Fort

Ridgely, and passing up the Minnesota river made our headquarters on Rice creek. The white men who had brought us thus far in sleighs then returned. Other scouts were added to these until ten of us had made our camp at Rice creek. Alexis and Joseph La Framboise came to where we were, and were included as scouts by General Sibley, and we staid there together.

After a short time we took provisions and blankets and started on a scouting expedition up the Minnesota river. We came to Yellow Medicine, and then went on up the Minnesota to the Chippewa river. There we found signs of the hostile Indians, and commenced searching for their camp. They had sent their families away, and had waited for us to come, as we learned afterward; but we were so long getting there that they finally followed their families, and we lost track of them. Then we came back and reported. Later we went on another scouting expedition to the westward. We kept working in this way till spring. . . .

Three other scouts came up in a steamboat from Mankato, namely, Ah-wee-pah, Thomas Crawford, and Han-yo-ke-yan.[3]

When General Sibley had completed his plans for the expedition against the Sioux in 1863, he notified the troops that were in camp near the Redwood river what day he would be there. Great preparations were made, and amid the playing of bands and waving of flags he was received with much distinction and honor.

It was decided there as to which scouts were to go on the expedition, and which were not to go. The following are the names of those who were not to go, but to remain and scout with their headquarters at Fort Ridgely:

Two Stars,	Ah-we-tan-e-nah,
Joseph Le Blanc,	Mah-pe-yah-wah-koon-zay,
Antoine Renville,	Wah-hah-chan-kah,
Han-yo-ke-yan,	

The following are the names of those who were to go as scouts with General Sibley's expedition:

Gabriel Renville,	Little Paul,
Michael Renville,	David Faribault, Sr.,
J. B. Renville,	William L. Quinn,
Daniel Renville,	Alexis La Framboise,
Isaac Renville,	Joseph La Framboise,
Joseph Renville,	We-yon-ske,
E-ne-han,	Chay-tah-shoon,

A-chay-tu-ke-yah,	Taopi,
John Moore,	Wah-ke-yah-tah-wah,
Thomas Robinson,	Ah-kee-pah,
Charles Crawford,	Kah-wan-kay,
Thomas Crawford,	Joseph Campbell,
Kah-tah-tay,	Narcisse Frenier,
Anawag-ma-ne,	Joseph Coursall,
Wah-kon-bo-e-day,	Good Thunder
Henry Ortley,	Wa-su-ho-was-tay.

The expedition then started, going by the way of Yellow Medicine, Lac qui Parle, Yellow Bank, and the foot of Big Stone lake, to the planting grounds of the Sissetons at the head of lake Traverse. Thence they went by the way of the big bend of the Sheyenne river, Bear's Den, and the Bald hills, to Eagle hill, and from there it was not far to the Missouri river.

There were Indians camped at this place, and some of General Sibley's scouts came suddenly upon some of the Indians. Little Paul was the first one to see them and reported it, and I was the first one who shook hands with the Indians who were coming. Some of them wanted to shoot me, but through the bravery of O-win-e-ku, who was a relative of mine and took my part, I finally met and shook hands with them.[4]

Narrative 4
VICTOR RENVILLE'S ACCOUNT

For biographical information on Victor Renville, see Chapter V, Narrative 2.

GENERAL SIBLEY gave the Renvilles permission to go back to their homes but Gabriel did not care to do this because all his buildings had been burned and there were still hostile Indians wandering about the country. Instead of returning home, Gabriel suggested that Sibley let him pick a band of warriors to scout the surrounding country for hostiles and tell the friendly Indians that it was safe to return. Sibley had to get permission from General Pope before he could grant this.[5] When he received the permission Gabriel picked the following warriors: Antoine, Michalle [Michael], Isaac and Daniel Renville, John

Moore[s], Big Tom Robertson (not the one living near Lidgerwood), [Solomon] Two Stars, E-ce-tu-ki-ye [Big Amos], Wa-su-ho-wa-shte [Enos Good Voiced Hail], E-ni-han, Joseph La Framboise and Alexius [Alexis] La Framboise. General Sibley sent these scouts out from Fort Snelling in wagons with white drivers. Camp was made up the Minnesota River half way between the two agencies and about thirty-five miles from Fort Ridgely.

From March to June, 1863, this band of scouts was at work. Half the party would go out at one time, leaving the other half to guard the camp. Supplies were hauled from Fort Ridgely with two teams that the two La Framboise[s] had taken with them.

Following is a list of camps at which scouts were stationed from 1863 to 1865:

1. Sheyenne River post; Indian name, To-an-kan-xa-ci-ye; located at the south side of a big bend of the Sheyenne. Charles Crawford acted as outlook here and killed several Indians on hostile raids.

2. Twin Lakes; Little Paul in charge.

3. Skunk Lake; Indian name, Ma-ka-le-de; the half-breed, Scott, in charge.

4. Bone Hill; Indian name, Hu-hu-pa-ha; located south of Jamestown on the James River; Charles Crawford in charge previously at Station No. 15. Sam Brown reports that he saw a ring of buffalo bones on this hill. This ring was about three feet in diameter and composed entirely of the small bones taken from the front leg of the buffalo back of the shin. There were very many of these bones placed so close together that they touched each other. The west bank of the James River at Jamestown was called the place where they cut bows. Rock Elm trees supplied the wood for these bows. At an early time the Upper Yanktons lived here. The Dakota name for Jamestown is E-ta-zo-pe-o-kak-se.

5. Elm River; Indian name, Pe-wak-pa; located fifty or sixty miles west of Fort Wadsworth; in charge of Joe Roulliard; Elm River flows into the James.

6. Snake River; Stands-Firmly (E-kan-a-gin-ka) in charge of post.[6]

7. Drifted Guts; Indian name, Shu-pe-cho-ge; Inihau [Inihan] (Excited) in charge; located southwest of Fort Wadsworth near Enemy Swim Lake; named from some guts found drifted in upon shore of Enemy Swim Lake.

8. Hawk's Nest; Indian name, He-cha-o-te; located south of Camp No. 7; Two Stars in charge.

9. Dry Wood Lake; Indian name, Tshau-she-sha; located near Sisseton on east side of the lake.

10. Lake Traverse; Indian name, Ptan-sin-ta; located just above the iron post on the hill; Sets-Fire-to-Hail (Wa-su-e-de-ya) in charge. This scout was killed May 1, 1869, by Flat Mouth and his band[.][7]

11. Cottonwood Grove; Indian name, Na-go-zhu-na; Gabriel Renville, superintendent of scouts, in charge. This was the main camp and was located five miles east of Aberdeen on the James River.

12. Oak Grove; Indian name, U-to-ho-zhu; located on the east bend of the James River, thirty miles south of Aberdeen. E-sha-na-ji-ka [E-kan-a-gin-ka] in charge.

13. Surrendered Camp; located on Fish Lake, six miles northeast of Fort Wadsworth on the road to Fort Abercrombie. Scarlet Plume (Red Feather) came into Sibley's camp just before the battle of Big Mound and before Dr. Weiser was killed to see Gabriel Renville and tell him that his band and that of Standing Buffalo were ready to surrender. This camp was a headquarters for all surrendered Indians willing to stop fighting and return to the reservation with their families. In 1863 about fifty of the scouts were sent from this camp to meet fifteen lodges of Indians who were coming down from Canada to surrender. They met the party five miles north of Fort Wadsworth. Gabriel found among them two Indians known to have committed atrocities during the massacre and gave orders for them to be shot. One of the scouts, Star, shot one of the hostiles while he was seated smoking with his companion. Star's rifle missed fire the second time and the other Indian ran. The Indians in camp scattered and all the scouts opened fire on the fleeing Indian. Joe Demarrais, Jr., brought him down just as he leaped over a mound.[8] During the chase one Indian woman was wounded by a spent ball. The hostile shot by Star was found to be the grandson of Inkapadute. The father of the other hostile warrior wailed for an hour and then stopped and said, "I told my son not to go into the fighting against the whites."

14. Fort Wadsworth; Indian name, Kettle Found (Cgar-i-ye-ya-pi); Sam Brown in charge.

15. Head of Coteau Station. Twelve or fifteen miles about north of Fort Wadsworth. Commander chief of scouts, Charles Crawford. Given by Samuel J. Brown and [of] Brown's Valley.

In June, 1863, Sibley came to headquarters camp on his expedition against the Sioux and took with him all the scouts at the head-quarters, in all about twenty. He furnished them with horses and rifles. Up to that time they had received blankets from Fort Ridgely, and such guns as had been taken from the hostiles.

The force was reorganized in 1864 and by 1865 numbered two hundred. In July, 1864, Fort Wadsworth was established. The soldiers lived in tents and dugouts during the following winter. The next year, 1865, buildings were erected.

Narrative 5
PAUL MAZAKUTEMANI'S STATEMENT

For biographical information on Paul Mazakutemani, see Chapter VIII, Narrative 5.

THERE was then [1864] a fort [Wadsworth] built at the head of the Coteau des Prairies; and the officer in command made known the will of the Great Father. He said that all the Dakotas who wished for good might come to the head of the Coteau and live. "Come, come," he said to the Dakotas, "the Great Father is merciful, and will have mercy on any one who is needy." This he said giving them the invitation. Then all the men who wished for the friendship of the white people came in, and with their people desired good. These are the chief men — Wasukiye, Wamnahize, Wasuiciyapa, Wamdisuntanka, Isakiye, and Hupacokamaza.[9] These first shook hands with the white people and desired that they and their children might live.

I talked with these men, and said to them, "Why did you flee? You were not implicated in the war of the Lower Sioux with the white people. What did you fear, that you fled and did not come back for a long time?"

They said, "Indeed we knew that the Americans were furious, and therefore we fled. But now our Great Father says we may live, and therefore we have come back."

I went with them to see the commanding officer of the fort, with whom they had a talk. He said to them, "The Great Father has commanded me to invite all the Indians to come back who do not want to fight. The Great Father wishes to have no more fighting; therefore he has commanded me to call in all the Indians, and he says you shall do no more fighting." To this they said "Yes."

Then Great-tailed Eagle, one of the Dakota chiefs, stood up and said, "The guns, and the tobacco, and the lead, and the knives which we have are all made by the Americans. If we fight the Americans we must use these things that we have of them, to fight with. Therefore we dislike the fighting. By the help of the Americans we live; and we do not wish to fight the Americans with the things they have made. I desire only that which is good, and therefore I have come to shake hands with you that I may live."

To this the commanding officer replied, "You have spoken well. Before the snow comes, I will send your name to the Great Father."

The Hail that strikes itself, another Dakota chief, said, "Shall one who is a chief seek what is bad? I am a chief, and therefore I seek only the good."

To this the officer replied, "Yes, you speak well. Your Great Father seeks only that which is good."

After these words, when winter was coming on, another Dakota chief came in—this was Scarlet Eagle Tail and his people. Seven chiefs and their people were now here.

About this time the commanding officer employed them as scouts, and every Dakota that they saw, who came to the region of Fort Wadsworth on the war path, they killed. In all they killed thirteen. So the rebellion was stopped, and all the people desired to return to what was good.

Narrative 6
WOWINAPE'S STATEMENT

WOWINAPE or The Appearing One or Thomas Wakeman was born in August 1846 at the Mdewakanton village of Kaposia. His parents, Little Crow and Mazaiyagewin or Iron Cluster Woman, reared him as a Dakota. Late in 1853, the band moved to the reservation on the upper Minnesota River. Slowly his family adopted a few white customs.

Wowinape's role in the war is not known. Evidence suggests that he accompanied his father at the second battles at Fort Ridgely and New Ulm and on the expedition to the Big Woods. After the battle at

Wood Lake he fled with his family to the Dakota plains. The follow-
ing summer Wowinape returned to Minnesota with Little Crow, who
was killed on July 3. Wowinape escaped toward Devils Lake but was
captured by army scouts on July 29, 1863. The statement he gave to
the army was translated by Joseph De Marais, Jr., and printed in the
St. Paul and St. Peter newspapers.

He was tried for his part in the war by a military commission at
Fort Abercrombie, convicted, and sentenced to be hanged. Receiving
a reprieve, he was sent to prison at Davenport, Iowa. There, he be-
came literate in Dakota and converted to Christianity. In the spring
of 1866 he was pardoned and taken to the Santee Reservation. Thom-
as Wakeman, as he was now known, married Judith Minnetonka in
1874, and they moved to the vicinity of Flandreau, Dakota Territory.
He was active in the local Presbyterian church and conceived the con-
cept of a Dakota Indian Y.M.C.A., to which he devoted the rest of
his life. He died at Redwood Falls on January 13, 1886.[10]

Narrative Source: "Statement of Wo-wi-nap-a," translated by Joseph De
Marais, Jr., *St. Paul Pioneer*, August 13, 1863.

FATHER [Little Crow] went to St. Joseph last spring [1863]. When
we were coming back he said he could not fight the white men, but
would go below and steal horses from them, and give them to his
children, so that they could be comfortable, and then he would go
away off.

Father also told me he was getting old, and wanted me to go with
him to carry his [medicine] bundles. He left his wives and other children behind. There were sixteen men and one squaw in the party that
went below with us. We had no horses, but walked all the way down
to the settlements, Father and I were picking red berries near Scattered Lake at the time he was shot [July 3]. It was near night. He was
hit the first time in the side, just above the hip. His gun and mine were
lying on the ground. He took up my gun and fired it first, and then
fired his own. He was shot the second time when he was firing his own
gun. The ball struck the stock of his gun, and then hit him in the side,
near the shoulders. This was the shot that killed him. He told me that
he was killed, and asked me for water, which I gave him. He died immediately after. When I heard the first shot fired, I laid down, and
the man did not see me before father was killed.

A short time before father was killed, an Indian named Hi-u-ka,
who married the daughter of my father's second wife, came to him.

WOWINAPE
in 1863

He had a horse with him — also a gray colored coat that he had taken from a man that he had killed to the north of where father was killed. He gave the coat to father, telling him he might need it when it rained, as he had no coat with him. Hi-u-ka said he had a horse now, and he was going back to the Indian country.

The Indians that went down with us separated, eight of them, and the squaw went north, the other eight went farther down. I have not seen them since after father was killed. I took both guns and the ammunition, and started to go to Devil's Lake, where I expected to find some of my friends. When I got to Beaver Creek, I saw the tracks of two Indians, and at Standing Buffalo's village saw where the eight Indians [who] had gone north had crossed.

I carried both guns as far as the Sheyenne river, where I saw two men. I was scared and threw my gun and the ammunition down. After that I travelled only in the night, and as I had no ammunition to kill anything to eat, I had not strength enough to travel fast. I went on until I arrived at Devil's Lake, when I staid in one place three days, being so weak and hungry that I could go no further. I had picked up a cartridge near Big Stone Lake, which I still had with me, and loaded father's gun with it, cutting the ball into slugs; with this charge I shot a wolf, ate some of it, which gave me strength to travel, and I went on up [to] the Lake until the day I was captured which was twenty-six days from the day my father was killed.

Narrative 7
IRON HOOP'S TESTIMONY

IRON HOOP or Canhdixkamaza was born in 1847. He was a member of Sweet Corn's band of Sissetons in August 1862. They lived with Wanata's band near the southwest shore of Lake Traverse. In the fall, they buried their dried corn stores and went to Devils Lake, Dakota Territory, for the winter. Iron Hoop was present at the battle of Big Mound on July 24, 1863. On August 29, 1901, at Devils Lake he testified for the claimants before a U.S. Court of Claims commission. Thomas A. Robertson was the interpreter. The date of Iron Hoop's death is not known.

Narrative Source: Iron Hoop, "Evidence for the Claimants," *The Sisseton and Wahpeton Bands of Dakota or Sioux Indians v. the United States*, 1901–07, U.S. Court of Claims no. 22524, part 1, p. 211–13.

AT THAT TIME [July 1863] the Sissetons and Wahpetons were hunting buffalo north of here [Devils Lake], this side of the Missouri River, following the buffalo down this way. About that time news came in that Inkpaduta and his followers were down this way, near Long Lake, and that they were hunting buffalo, and also that the Tetons, following the buffalo, had crossed the Missouri River and come on to

IRON HOOP
at Devils Lake
in 1913

this side, and shortly after that the three different tribes, or bands, came near together, and, in hunting the buffalo, met one another, and, while camped near together, General Sibley came, and there is where they met. . . .

The day after the buffalo hunt, in which we and others met, that I spoke of, early in the morning, it was reported that there was buffalo east of us, and we got together and started in that direction to hunt buffalo. One man on horseback went quite aways ahead and got up on top of a hill and immediately turned around and came back towards where we were, and said that all the Americans in the land were close onto us. It was afterwards reported that some of those on our side, who had gone ahead of the main body, had met scouts from Sibley's command and had had talks with them. I immediately turned back and came back to camp, and shortly afterwards it was reported that it was General Sibley that was coming, and that he wanted to have a talk with Standing Buffalo; that General Sibley had sent word to Standing Buffalo that he had brought him his goods, and that he wanted him to be sure and separate himself from the Medawakantons. I saw quite a number gathered about Standing Buffalo's lodge and I went over there and saw him and all of the old men sitting together and talking. There was a crowd standing around them on the outside. The understanding there was that Sibley and Standing Buffalo were to meet on friendly terms. Shortly afterwards they all got up and started towards Sibley's command, but, before they got there this man [Dr. Weiser] was shot. In the meantime, scouts on one side, and young men on the Indian's [sic] side, had been meeting and shaking hands and talking together. . . .

The Indians started to run away. There was not much fighting going on. Sibley immediately followed up; after the killing of Dr. Weiser, the Indians on the other side commenced to run and a few old men that had gone to the front, expecting to have a talk, were caught by the soldiers and killed. . . .

As soon as it got dark the Wahpetons and Sissetons struck off north. Among them was Iron Heart, my uncle, with whom I was at that time. Inkpaduta and his followers went toward the Missouri and met the Tetons who had crossed the Missouri on to this side and were coming this way, hunting buffalo. . . .

It was reported that the Medawakantons went over west of here to a place called "Where they painted the wood," and the Tetons belonged over there [across the Missouri River]; they went back there.

Narrative 8
LITTLE FISH'S TESTIMONY

LITTLE FISH, also called Pretty Lodge or Tiowaste, was born in about 1827 and was probably of Sisseton and French descent. In the early 1860s when his band was leaderless and suffering from famine, a United States Army officer selected him as its leader because of his personal qualities. By 1862 he was affiliated with Standing Buffalo's band of Sissetons.

In August 1867 he led his band to Fort Totten, Dakota Territory, and settled down to live there for the remainder of his life. He was married twice and was the father of many children, but only one of them survived in 1909. A popular local figure, he led an annual parade of Dakota Indians to the Chautauqua at Fort Totten from 1893 well into the new century. He was also famed for his oratory and spoke annually to thousands at this event. In 1893 he was a judge of the Court of Indian Offenses. On August 28, 1901, he testified for the claimants concerning the movements of Standing Buffalo's band and about events at the battle of Big Mound before the U.S. Court of Claims. Thomas A. Robertson was the interpreter. Little Fish died at his home on December 8, 1919.[11]

Narrative Source: Little Fish, "Evidence for the Claimants," *The Sisseton and Wahpeton Bands of Dakota or Sioux Indians v. the United States,* 1901–07, U.S. Court of Claims no. 22524, part 1, p. 191–208.

LITTLE FISH at Devils Lake in 1913

GENERAL SIBLEY was camped on one side of this Big Mound and the Indians on the other side, and scouts had come from Sibley's camp and the Indians came, saying that Sibley wanted to see Standing Buffalo and to have a talk with him, and that any other Indians who had been hostile to the whites or had killed whites were the ones he had come to fight, but not Standing Buffalo; and then some of the young men from the Indians' camp went over to Sibley's line and shook hands with them over there and they gave them crackers and they had something to eat; and while Standing Buffalo was getting ready to go over there one of those young men who had gone over there, hearing that Sibley had come to kill or to fight such as he, he concluded to keep up the fighting, and shot this doctor [Dr. Weiser] before Standing Buffalo got there, and caused them to fall back, because after the fight commenced they were afraid to go in. . . .

We, and Inkpaduta and his party that were with him, and also the Tetons, were all following the buffalo, and, for that reason, a large party of the Tetons had crossed over on this side of the Missouri, following the buffalo, and Inkpaduta's band were in between us and the Tetons, but we were all following the buffalo, and that is how we came to be there together at that time. . . .

We were there the first day when Sibley had the first fight, and, as I stated before, that night we, the Sissetons, hid and got away from there — went off in another direction. Inkpaduta's band and those that were with him were the ones that General Sibley followed until the next day. In the meantime the Tetons had crossed over from the west side of the Missouri to this side and were camped there. Inkpaduta and his party met them the next day, and they and the Tetons was — I have been told were the ones that had the fight with General Sibley the next day, and I have been told that there was not any very heavy fighting going on. The Indians were moving toward the Missouri River with their families, but Sibley was following them up until they got to the Missouri River; then the Indians camped on the other side and Sibley camped on this side.

Narrative 9
ANTOINE J. CAMPBELL'S TESTIMONY

ANTOINE J. CAMPBELL was born at Mendota on November 25, 1825. His parents, Scott Campbell and Margaret Menanger, were both mixed-bloods. In about 1840 he began to trade with the Indians and later clerked in a St. Paul store. He and Mary Ann Dalton were married in October 1845 at St. Paul. In 1851 they moved to Traverse des Sioux on the Minnesota River and four years later to the Redwood Agency where he was the government interpreter.

During the war he was protected by Dakota relatives. He was forced to drive Little Crow to battles and to act as his secretary for correspondence with Colonel Sibley. After the battle of Wood Lake he persuaded Little Crow to give him forty-six white captives whom he surrendered at Camp Release. He testified before the military commission at the trials of participants in the war.

He served as a scout on the Sibley expedition of 1863 into northern Dakota Territory. Afterward he lived with his family in St. Paul until 1870 when they moved to the Santee Reservation in Nebraska. On September 28, 1901, at Santee Agency, Nebraska, he testified before a U.S. Court of Claims commission investigating the Sisseton and Wahpeton claims resulting from the war. He spoke in English. By 1908 he was living with his daughter, Cecelia Campbell Stay, near Montevideo, where he died on January 9, 1913.[12]

Narrative Source: Antoine J. Campbell, "Evidence for the Claimants," The Sisseton and Wahpeton Bands of Dakota or Sioux Indians v. the United States, 1901–07, U.S. Court of Claims no. 22524, part 2, p. 255–65.

ME AND Joe La Framboise and three white men were sent out on the frontier as scouts ahead of the army, and we discovered this camp and they chased us, and I told General Sibley all the time that I didn't want no white man to go around with me, because, if they happened to be killed by the Indians and [the Indians] let me go, they [the whites] would blame us for it. "Well," he says, "let them go and be killed, if they want to." So we started, us five, and while passing along a lake all at once I discovered that camp. I tell you them fellows they made tracks — them white men; they wished they never had come. They saw the Indians coming down over the hill and I tell you they made tracks, and our horses couldn't run as fast as theirs, but I kept with Joe, all the time together. I kept courage and says I, "We will do something." They were trying to cut us off at the end of the lake and capture us, or drive us into the lake, but they couldn't. We got past first. So we brought the news to General Sibley, and we come there, and by that time there was another party went to the left of the soldiers, and there was an officer got killed [Lieutenant Ambrose Freeman]. . . . [13]

We came and camped right there at the lake, and the next thing was old Joe Brown wanted to send more scouts — wanted to send Gabriel [Renville] to go and see them Indians there at that camp, and he wouldn't go, and General Sibley came up and he says, "Where is Joe Campbell?" He says, "My good fellow, can you go and see what camp it is there?" I says, "Yes, sir; that is what I am here for." So I went toward the camp, but before I got there there was a crowd, I

ANTOINE J. CAMPBELL in 1858 in Washington, D.C.

suppose. I suppose they had scouts, and they came and met us. They asked me what I wanted, and I told them I was sent there by the orders of General Sibley; that he didn't come there to fight them; he came there to make peace by the orders of the Great Father. Well, they didn't want no peace at all, and they told me it was best for me to leave them. I told them I would leave by and by. I had a good many friends there, talking with them. Some of them asked me for a little tobacco, and I said, "If the general sends me back again, I will bring you some tobacco," and I did, too. At that time there was an Indian we got somewhere on the prairie; he followed me from our camp, and when I gave him a little tobacco they said the decision was they were going to have no peace at all. . . .

After I came back I told the general that he had to look out, them Indians say they are going to fight, and they are going to. So this Dr. Weiser and some of the scouts they went up on that Big Mound. He went up there, and just as I was sitting there to eat, in the camp, he was shot; right on the hill there.

Narrative 10
LITTLE WHEAT'S LETTER

LITTLE WHEAT was a Sisseton who had married Standing Buffalo's sister. He took no active part in the war itself. Instead he followed Standing Buffalo's lead in seeking peace after the war. He almost certainly accompanied Standing Buffalo to Manitoba and Montana, 1864–71. The date of his death is not known.

Narrative Source: Little Wheat to Wasothiyapa [Sibley] and Other Military Officers, January 4, 1864, recorded [in French?] by Father A[lexis] André, transcription in English, Letters Received, Northwest Department, National Archives Record Group 393.

I GIVE strongly the hand to all Americans because our father the English as well as the Blackrobe [Father Alexis André?] our father counsels us to do so. I have at heart to accomplish it. All the half-breeds Wilkie [?] at the head tells us that we shall have life.[14] I believe them all; I have in the words of the Blackrobe the same faith that I have in the word of God, and I know that neither one nor the other is capable of deceiving us. Weary and abandoned to myself I could not have found those good words to send you; it is the presence of the Blackrobe our father that brings those thoughts from the bottom of my heart[;] it is a long time that I have found hid in the bottom of my heart the desire to make peace with the Americans, but the words of my father the Blackrobe has rendered more quick this desire.

I had promised myself this winter to render myself up at the fort of the Americans, but the news that has come to us by our father makes me defer my design. This letter that I get written this night by my father[,] I would like my mother, my cousin, Joseph Desmarais [De Marais, Jr.] and my nephews to have a knowledge of. This spring when the snow has disappeared I calculated to go to Fort Abercrombie. The massacre of the Americans by our people have affected me as truly [in] the heart that [as] the death of my father[.] When I return I desire that they permit me to go and sow [corn] on the ground where my father died[.] I declare here to the American authorities that our father searches the good of my people in the affair he has been charged with by the government. Me also. I'll try to second his efforts if, nevertheless, it happens that he does not succeed and that the Sioux do not understand his charitable intentions, I separate myself from them and will render myself with my family when the time comes this spring when I shall start to give myself up to the Americans.

I would like you to furnish me a little powder to kill ducks on the road. The Sioux begs me to join my request to his to obtain with the powder a little flour and other provisions, and so permit him to surrender himself at Fort Abercrombie. This letter that I send through my father I send as a mark of my submission to the government. I have learned that my mother was with the Americans that they took good care of her and that she wants for nothing. This news has caused me as much pleasure as if I had been transported to heaven with the good God[.] I could not have been better pleased.

My heart approves the same affection for the Americans as for the English. I like them both. When I meet with Wilkie and the half-breeds I approve [sic] as much pleasure as I do when I meet my near relations. I give them all my hand with a good heart. When my father will see our Great Father the President, the Americans will confer on him the place of chief and will remit to me the title this position gives him. He'll tell me here is what your friends the Americans send you in effect from this time I regard the Americans as my friends, and they on their side will treat me as their child. Every time I went to their houses they received me with cordiality doing every thing to receive me well and gave me flour, pork, and everything that was good to eat, but Little Crow destroyed our happiness, and by his malice he has plunged us into misfortune.

This spring when I surrender you will know me by the flag that I shall have floating before me. I give strongly my hand to our father who writes this letter and I regard him as my best friend. I give anew my hand to all the Americans.

Narrative 11
STANDING BUFFALO'S LETTER

STANDING BUFFALO was born in about 1833 near the headwaters of the Minnesota River. His father was Star Face or Wicanrpihiteton (later called The Orphan or Wamdenica); he was the leader of a Sisseton band. Standing Buffalo was given a Dakota education. In 1858 his father passed his symbols of leadership to his favorite son.

Standing Buffalo's band was hunting buffalo on the Sheyenne River when the war began. In about mid-September 1862 he and other Sisseton leaders visited Little Crow and spoke against the conflict. Standing Buffalo then sent a letter to General Sibley in which he stated a desire for peace.

After the battle at Big Mound the Sissetons fled northwest and by 1864 were in Manitoba. The United States government used Father Alexis André and Joseph R. Brown as its agents to negotiate their surrender. Gradually the band moved westward to Montana. Repeated attempts were made to have them surrender, but Standing Buffalo could not make this decision. Finally he was killed in battle with the Gros Ventres and Assiniboine Indians on June 5, 1871.[15]

Narrative Source: "Discourse of Standing Buffalo," recorded [in French?] by Father Alexis André, [1864?], transcription in English, Letters Received, Northwest Department, National Archives Record Group 393.

THE WORDS that you [Father Alexis André?] have just addressed to us has made my heart glad. When I learned you were here I feared not to brave the cold the most vigorous to come and listen to your words. On arriving in the camp, [with] my brother-in-law Little Wheat, I had heard a little about this grand affair for which you have

*STANDING
BUFFALO
in 1862*

come and which occupies the minds of all the Sioux, but I was far
from expecting to hear such grand revelations as you have just made.
Yes, as you have just been telling us the Sioux are all in a very sad position; the numerous massacres that the wicked have perpetrated on the
whites and the war that has followed has all rendered us unhappy, but
what consoles me is to see that neither I nor my people took any part
in all those massacres, me, I always loved the Americans. I always
regarded the President as my great father the agents as my father and

all the Americans as my brothers and my friends that is why I always recommended to my people to do nothing wrong. When my father became old and wanted to retire and remitted me his charge he recommended me to love the whites. He told me that as long as I loved the whites I would be well; and that they would protect me. His words are always present to my mind and I never forget them. From that moment I regarded all the whites as my brothers, and the thing which I most dreaded was to cause the least wrong to the whites.

I loved my lands, it was on them that I had been raised and fed, it was the land of my fathers. I therefore had reason to love it. In the meantime the Americans came and demanded my lands[.] I at once acceded for I loved the Americans[.] I sold my lands for fifty years.[16] My great father was to give me money and goods, I know that my great father is good and that he wishes only my good, but some of his children are not all as good as him, they are traitors[.] I was to receive a great quantity of money every year[;] the money left the hands of my great father but in passing from hand to hand each one taking his part nothing reached my hand more than a dollar[;] my heart was sad in seeing that but I never said to my people to do harm to the Americans. Why not? because I loved my great father, my fathers and my brothers; I was to receive a great quantity of goods in blankets, in cottons, and all kinds of effects. My great father did send me all these merchandize, but on the road each one appropriated his morsel and I often got but a small piece of cotton. My heart was sad on seeing that, but I never told my people to do any harm to the Americans. Why not? because I loved my great father, my father[s] and my brothers.

I was to receive also a great deal of flour. My great father sent me what was my due, but in passing from hand to hand it diminished by half and I received nothing more than a barrel of flour. All this made my heart sad but I never told my people to harm the Americans. Why not? because I loved my great father, my fathers, and my brothers.

When my young men committed any wrong on the whites either on any goods or on their persons, I at once punished them according to the extent of their faults. I loved my people but why did I punish them? Because I loved the Americans. When the massacres commenced I was not on the spot where they where [were] committed. All those horrors[,] which has irritated, with reason, the heart of my great father, the Americans all know that I was on the prairies occupied in hunting and when the news of all the wrongs that had been committed by my nation reached my ears anguish took possession of my heart; it was as if I had been thrown into the fire; it was as if a sharp poigniard had transfixed my heart. There again I ordered my people to do no harm to the whites and those who did take part in the massacres, being orphans, having neither father nor mother to give them good counsels.

I them [then] wrote to Gen. Sibley telling him I abandoned my lands till I could make another arrangement that I did not want to animate the fire that was lit on my lands and I withdrew towards the north. The grand affair you have undertaken in coming here is grand and serious. We cannot in the meanwhile terminate in one day; it will require maybe one year to terminate. . . . First, on account of the Yanktons, who has been attacked on their own lands and without having done any wrong. The great road that was made on their lands and the noise of the cannon that we have heard have chased the buffalo from their grounds and they are to-day reduced also to as great misery as the culpable ones; that is the reason why although I kindly received your words I cannot give you an answer before knowing the sentiments of the Yanktons, but I will be with them in anything they may decide.

The second thing is what has just happened at St. Joseph. The news that the Americans had massacred women and children has very much troubled our minds.[17] The third thing is that army which came and attacked the Tatons [Tetons] who lived tranquil without ever having done any harm to the whites and where the [U.S. Army] came also and attacked them [probably a reference to General Alfred Sully's attack at Whitestone Hill on September 3, 1863].[18] They would say that our great father wanted to destroy all his children the Indians.

Take courage if you and all the Blackrobes will pray to the Great Spirit, you will bring about this grand affair. Beg our great father to take pity on his children the Indians let him give us the time to see each other & consult one another and the words that you have come to announce to us will overrun the prairie and be carried into all the camps.

But in learning the Black robe had arrived I understood at once he came to bring us life for I know that the man of God travels not for evil and that lies stain not his lips. Yes I have the confidence the American wants sincerely [sic] to give us peace because he sends to us the Blackrobe he knows that he cannot deceive us.

I receive therefore my father your words. I put them in my two ears and in my heart. I belong to the father and if [I] did not suffer in the legs I would march myself to go and carry your words to my friends but my friend who is here present (pointing to the deputy of the Yanktons) will carry my words to my friends and I know they will listen[;] have courage my father take pity on us and work for to get us life[.] I will help you according to my feeble efforts. There are amongst us some hard ears and some bad hearts but the greatest number desire the good. Take pity on them and you will see you will succeed.

NOTES

1. For an account of Little Crow's death, see Anderson, *Little Crow*, 7–8, 178.

2. Isaac Renville was the son of Antoine Renville, a trader, and Winona, a Dakota full-blood, and was Nancy McClure's half brother. He was born at Lac qui Parle in about 1840 and attended mission schools there and at Hazelwood. In August 1862 he belonged to a Wahpeton farmer band headed by Paul Mazakutemani. He was active in the peace party during the war and was chosen to be a scout in February 1863. In 1867 he settled on the Sisseton Reservation and was allotted land there in 1875. Licensed to preach by the Dakota Presbytery in 1878, he was ordained in 1879 and served as pastor for Dakota churches. He died in 1919. See Adams, Williamson, and Renville, *First Fifty Years*, Appendix, xiv; Chilson, "Dakota Indian Scout Roster"; U.S. Congress, *Sisseton and Wahpeton Sioux Indians*, 44th Cong., 1st sess., 1875, H. Doc. 42, p. 5.

Michael Renville, a son of Mary and Joseph Renville, Sr., was born at Big Stone Lake in 1822 or 1823 and educated at the Lac qui Parle mission school. He married in about 1848 and settled on the reservation in the 1850s. After serving as a scout, he moved to the Sisseton Reservation in 1867 and received land in 1875. He was one of the signers of the Treaty of 1873. In the early 1880s he translated many Dakota legends into English, which were published in *Iapi Oaye (The Word Carrier)* and later reprinted in "Dakota Grammar, Texts, and Ethnography" by Stephen R. Riggs (1893). He died at the Sisseton Agency in February 1899; Kappler, comp. and ed., *Indian Treaties*, 2:1062; U.S. Congress, *Sisseton and Wahpeton Sioux Indians*, 44th Cong., 1st sess., 1875, H. Doc. 42, p. 5; Alfred L. Riggs, "Michael Renville," *Iapi Oaye (The Word Carrier)* 23 (March 1899): 1.

3. Hanyokeyan or Flying at Night was a scout and courier, 1863–65; Chilson, "Dakota Indian Scout Roster."

4. Owineku or Owanku or Put Blanket on the Ground was either a Sisseton or a Wahpeton. He served as a scout on the James River and at Skunk Lake on the northern Coteau des Prairies in 1864. In 1865 he was at Bears Den and the head of the Coteau. By 1867 he had settled on the Sisseton Reservation; Chilson, "Dakota Indian Scout Roster"; Crawford and Brown, Census of the Lake Traverse Reservation, 1867, p. 7, Brown Papers; Paul M. Edwards, "The Development of the Frontier Post of Fort Wadsworth," *South Dakota Historical Collections* 31 (1962): 120.

5. John Pope was the commanding officer of the Department of the Northwest, which was organized in 1862. For information on Pope's career and the organization of the command, see Jones, *Civil War in the Northwest*, 1–13.

6. Ekanazinka or Stands Firmly settled on the Sisseton Reservation in 1867, signed the Treaty of 1872, but was not there in 1875 when land allotments were made. He was at the Devils Lake Reservation by 1891; Kappler, comp. and ed., *Indian Treaties*, 2:1059; Chilson, "Dakota Indian Scout Roster"; U.S. Congress, *Sisseton and Wahpeton Sioux Indians*, 44th Cong., 1st sess., 1875, H. Doc. 42; Census of 1891, Devil's Lake, North Dakota, Santee Sioux Annuity Rolls, 1892–1899, Records of the Bureau of Indian Affairs, NARG 75.

7. Sets Fire to Hail or Wasudeya or Hailfire was a Sisseton or Wahpeton. He settled on the Sisseton Reservation in 1867 and was killed by a war party of Leech Lake Ojibway; Chilson, "Dakota Indian Scout Roster."

8. Joseph De Marais, Jr., was living at Big Stone Lake in 1856 and claimed to be thirty-nine years old. He served as a scout at many locations along the James River, 1864–65. He received an allotment of land on the Sisseton Reservation in 1875 and appears to have lived there the rest of his life; Chilson, "Dakota Indian Scout Roster"; U.S. Congress, *Sisseton and Wahpeton Sioux Indians*, 44th Cong., 1st sess., 1875, H. Doc. 42, p. 19; Roll of Mixed-Blood Claimants, 1856, Records of the Bureau of Indian Affairs, NARG 75.

9. Wasukiye or Blue Hail, a Sisseton leader, was a scout on the James and Elm rivers, 1864–66. He moved to the Sisseton Reservation in 1867 and appears to have lived there the rest of his life. He signed the Treaties of 1867, 1872, (as "chief councilor, Sissetons"), and 1873. Wasuiciyapa or Rattling Hail served as a scout at Dry Wood Lake and Elm River in 1865–66 and then settled on the Sisseton Reservation. He signed the Treaty of 1872 as "Wasuiciyapi, chief Sisseton band Swantain." Isakiye may have been a headman in White Eagle's band of Sissetons. He served as a scout at the James River in 1864 and scouted at Dry Wood Lake and Bears Den in 1865–66. He moved to the Sisseton Reservation in 1867 where he received an allotment of land in 1875. Hupacokamaza or Rupacokamaza or Iron Wing or Iron on the inside of his Wing was a scout on the James and Elm rivers in 1864–66 and settled on the Sisseton Reservation in 1867. He signed the Treaty of 1872 as "Rupacokamaza, Wahpeton Soldier." He was allotted land there in 1875 and appears to have lived there the rest of his life. See Chilson, "Dakota Indian Scout Roster"; Crawford and Brown, Census of Lake Traverse Indians, 1867, p. 3, Brown Papers; U.S. Congress, *Sisseton and Wahpeton Sioux Indians*, 44th Cong., 1st sess., 1875, H. Doc. 42, p. 13, 25; Kappler, comp. and ed., *Indian Treaties*, 2:959, 1058, 1059, 1062. The editors have found no further information on Wamnahize.

10. Gordon, *Indian Legends and Other Poems*, 380–83, and *Feast of the Virgins*, 343–44; "Proceedings of a Military Commission which convened at Fort Abercrombie D.T. by virtue of the following Special Order," August 23, 1863, typescript, Division of Libraries and Archives, Minnesota Historical Society; *St. Paul Pioneer Press*, April 29, 1894, p. 14; *Iapi Oaye (The Word Carrier)* 15 (January 1886): 3.

11. *History of the Red River Valley*, 1:274–79.

12. *Mankato Weekly Record*, February 27, 1863, p. 2, 3; *Montevideo Leader*, January 17, 1913, p. 3.

13. Ambrose Freeman was born in Virginia in 1823 and moved to Minnesota in 1857, settling near St. Cloud. In 1862 he organized and led the Northern Rangers. He accompanied the Sibley expedition of 1863 to northern Dakota Territory and was killed on July 24, 1863; Upham and Dunlap, *Minnesota Biographies*, 238.

14. Jean Baptiste Wilke was born in 1801 and settled in St. Joseph, Dakota Territory, in about 1847. His house was a meeting place for both Sioux and Ojibway Indians. He died in 1886; "Gazetteer of Pioneers and Others in North Dakota Previous to 1862," *Collections of the State Historical Society of North Dakota* 1 (1906): 380.

15. Stephen R. Riggs, "Dakota Grammar, Texts, and Ethnography," in *Contributions to North American Ethnology*, ed. James Owen Dorsey (Washington, D.C.:

Government Printing Office, 1893), 196–200; *St. Paul Daily Press*, August 9, 1871, p. 2.

16. The Treaties of 1851 and 1858 relinquished title to Dakota lands in Minnesota forever, not just for fifty years.

17. In mid-December 1863 a detachment of about twenty men from Major Edwin A. C. Hatch's Independent Battalion of Cavalry attacked an Indian camp near St. Joseph, Dakota Territory, at three in the morning. Several Indians were killed and the rest captured. See Board of Commissioners, *Minnesota in the Civil and Indian Wars*, 1:597–99.

18. Sully attacked an Indian camp northwest of present-day Ellendale, No.Dak., killing 150 to 200 men, women, and children. Samuel J. Brown wrote to his father that the battle was a slaughter and that the Indians "had no hostile intention whatever"; quoted in Carley, *Sioux Uprising*, 90–91.

Appendix

THIS LIST includes narratives from the sixty-three Dakota full- and mixed-bloods who are known to have produced accounts of the war and its immediate aftermath. Where multiple versions of a narrative are known to exist, they are listed.

The following abbreviations have been used:

The Sisseton and Wahpeton Bands of Dakota or Sioux Indians v. the United States, 1901–07, U.S. Court of Claims no. 22524 (bound testimony in the Minnesota Historical Society reference library) — *Sisseton and Wahpeton Bands v. the United States*

Collections of the Minnesota Historical Society — *Minnesota Collections*

Division of Libraries and Archives, Minnesota Historical Society — DLA, MHS

Record Group, National Archives, Washington, D.C. — NARG

Big Eagle (or Wamditanka or Jerome Big Eagle). "A Sioux Story of the War," recorded in the *St. Paul Pioneer Press*, July 1, 1894, reprinted in *Minnesota Collections* 6 (1894): 382–400 and as "Chief Big Eagle's Story," *Minnesota History* 38 (September 1962): 129–43; "Testimony, June 15, 1868," *Papers Relating to Talks and Councils Held with the Indians in Dakota and Montana Territories in the Years 1866–1869* (Washington, D.C.: Government Printing Office, 1910), 93–94.

Brown, Samuel Jerome. "In Captivity: The Experience, Privations and Dangers of Sam'l J. Brown, and Others, while Prisoners of the Hostile Sioux, during the Massacre and War of 1862," recorded in the *Mankato Weekly Review*, April 6, 13, 20, 27, May 4, 11, 1897, reprinted as a pamphlet by the *Mankato Review* and by the U.S. Senate, *In Captivity: The Experience, Privations, and Dangers of Samuel J. Brown . . . ,*" 56th Cong., 2d sess., 1900, S. Doc. 23 (Serial 4029); an early version appeared as "Captivity of the Family of Joseph R. Brown," in Isaac V. D. Heard, *History of the Sioux War and Massacres of 1862 and 1863* (New York: Harper & Brothers, 1864), 202–8; "Evidence for the Claimants," *Sisseton and Wahpeton Bands v. the United States*, part 1, p. 25–74; "Little Crow's Famous Trip to the Missouri River," told to Marion P. Satterlee, undated typescript, Marion P. Satterlee Papers, DLA, MHS.

Campbell, Antoine Joseph. "The Indian War," recorded in the *Mankato*

Weekly Record, February 21, 1863; "Evidence for the Claimants," *Sisseton and Wahpeton Bands v. the United States,* part 2, p. 255–65.

Cetanxan (or Yellow Pigeon Hawk). "Testimony of Ce-tan-xan," Proceedings of Military Commission for the 1863–64 Trial of Little Six [Shakopee], handwritten transcript, United States Army Military Commission, Sioux War Trials, 1862–65, United States Senate Records, NARG 46.

Cloud Man (or Marpiyawechasta or L. O. Skyman). "Indian Tells of Outbreak," recorded in the *Granite Falls Tribune,* November 8, 1910.

Cloud Woman (or Marpeehederawin). "Testimony of Mar-pee-he-de-ra-win," Proceedings of Military Commission for the 1863–64 Trial of Little Six [Shakopee], handwritten transcript, United States Army Military Commission, Sioux War Trials, 1862–65, United States Senate Records, NARG 46.

Coursolle, Joseph (or Hinhankaga or The Owl). "The Ordeal of Hinhankaga," as told by Clem Felix to F. J. Patten, ca. 1962, typescript, DLA, MHS.

Crawford, Charles Renville (or Wakanhinape or Appearing Sacred). "Evidence for the Claimants," *Sisseton and Wahpeton Bands v. the United States,* part 1, p. 159–79.

Crooks, George (or Wakanajaja or Holy Lightning). "Grievance of an Indian," *Hector Mirror,* February 12, 1909, and "Geo. Crooks Not the Man," *Redwood Gazette,* February 24, 1909, p. 1; "Reminiscences," 1937, typescript, DLA, MHS.

Du Marces, Alexis (or Alexis De Marais). "Evidence for the Claimants," *Sisseton and Wahpeton Bands v. the United States,* part 1, p. 217–23.

Ecetukiya (or He Who Brings What He Wants or Big Amos). "Evidence for the Claimants," *Sisseton and Wahpeton Bands v. the United States,* part 1, p. 120–29.

Godfrey (or Joseph Godfrey or Otakle or Many Kills). "Godfrey's Story," in Isaac V. D. Heard, *History of the Sioux War and Massacres of 1862 and 1863* (New York: Harper & Brothers, 1864), 191–201, 251–54.

Good Singer (or Tantanyandowan). "Evidence for the Claimants," *Sisseton and Wahpeton Bands v. the United States,* part 1, p. 230–34.

Good Star Woman (Wicahpewastewin). " A Sioux Woman's Account of the Uprising in Minnesota," recorded by Frances Densmore, 1934, typescript, Frances Densmore Papers, DLA, MHS.

Good Thunder (or Andrew Good Thunder or Wakinyanwaste). "Testimony of Good Thunder," Proceedings of Military Commission for the 1863–64 Trial of Little Six [Shakopee], handwritten transcript, United States Army Military Commission, Sioux War Trials, 1862–65, United States Senate Records, NARG 46; "Statement of Andrew Good Thunder," in Henry B. Whipple,

Lights and Shadows of a Long Episcopate (New York: Macmillan, 1912), 114.

Hakewaste, Robert (or Good Fifth Son). "Evidence for the Defendants," *Sisseton and Wahpeton Bands v. the United States*, part 2, p. 358–59.

Hopkins, James (or Akicitamaza or Iron Soldier). "Evidence for the Defendants," *Sisseton and Wahpeton Bands v. the United States*, part 2, p. 343–46.

Huggan, Nancy McClure Faribault. "Reminiscences," 1894, DLA, MHS, printed as "The Story of Nancy McClure," in *Minnesota Collections* 6 (1894): 438–60, and in the *St. Paul Pioneer Press*, June 3, 1894.

Huntka, Andrew (or Andrew Cormorant). "Evidence for the Defendants," *Sisseton and Wahpeton Bands v. the United States*, part 2, p. 388–90.

Iron Hoop (or Canhdixkamaza). "Evidence for the Claimants," *Sisseton and Wahpeton Bands v. the United States*, part 1, p. 211–13.

Jetty, Frank (or Frank Shetais). "Frank Jetty's Life — Related by Himself to the Grey Nuns at St. Michael's Mission, St. Michael, North Dakota," ca. 1952, typescript, Cecelia Campbell Stay Papers, Provincial Archives of Manitoba, Winnipeg, Manitoba.

Kitto, Joseph H. (or Hoksidamnimani or Boy That Walks on Water). "Evidence for the Defendants," *Sisseton and Wahpeton Bands v. the United States*, part 2, p. 346–50.

La Framboise, Joseph, Jr. "Evidence for the Claimants," *Sisseton and Wahpeton Bands v. the United States*, part 1, p. 144–57.

Lawrence, Lorenzo (or Towanetaton or Face of the Village). "Story of Lorenzo Lawrence," 1894, Lorenzo Lawrence Papers, DLA, MHS; "Statement of Lorenzo Lawrence," in Henry B. Whipple, *Lights and Shadows of a Long Episcopate* (New York: Macmillan, 1912), 114–18.

Light Face (or Lotitojanjan). "Evidence for the Claimants," *Sisseton and Wahpeton Bands v. the United States*, part 1, p. 94–101.

Lightning Blanket (or Hachinwakanda or Wichunkpeduta or Red Star or David Wells). "Story of the Battles of Fort Ridgely, August 20 and 22, 1862," recorded in the *Morton Enterprise*, August 28, 1908.

Little Crow (or Taoyateduta or His Red Nation). "Taoyateduta Is Not a Coward," in Hanford L. Gordon, *The Feast of the Virgins and Other Poems* (Chicago: Laird & Lee, 1891), 343–44, and *Indian Legends and Other Poems* (Salem, Mass.: Salem Press Co., 1910), 381–83, reprinted in *Minnesota History* 38 (September 1962): 115.

Little Fish (or Tiowaste or Pretty Lodge). "Evidence for the Claimants," *Sisseton and Wahpeton Bands v. the United States*, part 1, p. 191–208.

Little Iron Thunder (or Louis Mazawakinyana). "Evidence for the Claimants," *Sisseton and Wahpeton Bands v. the United States*, part 1, p. 179–83.

Little Paul (or Wahnaxjuya). "Evidence for the Claimants," *Sisseton and Wahpeton Bands v. the United States*, part 1, p. 105–12.

Little Soldier (or Akicitaciqa). "Evidence for the Claimants," *Sisseton and Wahpeton Bands v. the United States*, part 1, p. 223–29.

Little Wheat. "Little Wheat to Wasothiyapa [General Sibley] and Other Military Officers," January 4, 1864, recorded [in French?] by Father A[lexis] André, transcription in English, Letters Received, Northwest Department, NARG 393.

Mazakutemani, Paul (or He Who Shoots as He Walks or Little Paul). "Reminiscences," in Dakota, 1869, DLA, MHS, printed as "Narrative of Paul Mazakootemane," *Minnesota Collections* 3 (1880): 82–90.

Medicine Bottle (or Tahtayechasenemahne). "Statement of 'Tah-tay-e-chah-se-ne-mah-ne,' Chief of 'Black Dog' Band of Mde-wah-kon-ton Sioux," recorded in the *St. Paul Pioneer*, February 19, 1864.

Otherday, John (or Ampatutokacha). "Highly Interesting Narrative of the Outbreak of Indian Hostilities," recorded in the *St. Paul Press*, August 28, 1862, p. 2; "Statement of John Other Day," in Henry B. Whipple, *Lights and Shadows of a Long Episcopate* (New York: Macmillan, 1912), 119–21.

Paul, Daniel. "Evidence for the Claimants," *Sisseton and Wahpeton Bands v. the United States*, part 1, p. 234–45.

Quinn, George (or George Ortley or Wakankdayamanee or Spirit That Rattles as It Walks). "Statement of George Quinn," 1898, Minnesota Historical Society Archives, DLA, MHS, printed as "Account of George Quinn," ed. Kenneth Carley, *Minnesota History* 38 (September 1962): 147–49.

Redowl, Johnson (or Hinhanduta or Anpetuwaste or Good Day). "Evidence for the Defendants," *Sisseton and Wahpeton Bands v. the United States*, part 2, p. 350–57.

Renville, Gabriel (or Tewakan). "Narrative," undated, Joseph R. and Samuel J. Brown Papers, DLA, MHS, printed as "A Sioux Narrative of the Outbreak of 1862, and Sibley's Expedition of 1863," *Minnesota Collections* 10 (1905): 595–613.

Renville, Isaac. "Evidence for the Claimants," *Sisseton and Wahpeton Bands v. the United States*, part 1, p. 112–29.

Renville, John B. "Evidence for the Claimants," *Sisseton and Wahpeton Bands v. the United States*, part 1, p. 129–33.

Renville, Victor. "A Sketch of the Minnesota Massacre," *Collections of the State Historical Society of North Dakota* 5 (1923): 251–72.

Robertson, Thomas A. "Evidence for the Claimants," *Sisseton and Wahpeton Bands v. the United States*, part 1, p. 133–44; "Reminiscences," 1918, typescript, DLA, MHS, printed as "Reminiscence of Thomas A. Robertson," *South Dakota Historical Collections* 20 (1940): 568–601.

Robinson, Peter (or Tasunkemaza or His Iron Horse). "Evidence for the Defendants," *Sisseton and Wahpeton Bands v. the United States*, part 2, p. 326–38.

Scarlet (Red) Eagle (or Wamdiduta). "Evidence for the Claimants," *Sisseton and Wahpeton Bands v. the United States*, part 1, p. 184–88.

Snana (or Tinkling or Maggie Brass). "Narration of a Friendly Sioux," [1900?], Minnesota Historical Society Archives, DLA, MHS, printed in *Minnesota Collections* 9 (1901): 426–30; "Evidence for the Defendants," *Sisseton and Wahpeton Bands v. the United States*, part 2, p. 379–85.

Standing Buffalo (or Tatankanajin). "Discourse of Standing Buffalo," [1864?], recorded [in French?] by Father Alexis André, transcription in English, Letters Received, Northwest Department, NARG 393.

Star (or Wicanrpi or Adam Magaiyahe or Lightning Goose). "Evidence for the Claimants," *Sisseton and Wahpeton Bands v. the United States*, part 1, p. 101–5.

Stay, Cecelia Campbell. "The Massacre at the Lower Sioux Agency, August 18, 1862," 1882, typescript, Provincial Archives of Manitoba, Winnipeg, Manitoba; Interview, in Alexander Seifert, "Notes of Committee Selecting Historical Data from New Ulm, Minn.," August 5–6, 1924, typescript, Sioux Uprising Collection, DLA, MHS; "Camp Relief [Release] in 1862," [1924?], typescript, Sioux Uprising Collection, DLA, MHS; "Interesting Experiences in Sioux Indian Uprising in '62," recorded in the *Madison Independent Press*, June 15, 1923.

Taopi (or Wounded Man). "Testimony of Taopi," Proceedings of Military Commission for the 1863–64 Trial of Little Six [Shakopee], handwritten transcript, United States Army Military Commission, Sioux War Trials, 1862–65, United States Senate Records, NARG 46; "Statement of Taopi, Chief of the Farmer Indians," in Henry B. Whipple, *Lights and Shadows of a Long Episcopate* (New York: Macmillan, 1912), 111–13.

Tati (or Her Lodge). "Testimony of Ta-ti," Proceedings of Military Commission for the 1863–64 Trial of Little Six [Shakopee], handwritten transcript, United States Army Military Commission, Sioux War Trials, 1862–65, United States Senate Records, NARG 46.

Thompson, John (or Mazaiciyapa or Striking Irons Together). "Evidence for the Defendants," *Sisseton and Wahpeton Bands v. the United States*, part 2, p. 321–26.

Two Stars, Solomon (or Wicanrpinonpa). "Evidence for the Claimants," *Sisseton and Wahpeton Bands v. the United States*, part 1, p. 75–93.

Waachankaa (or Shield). "Testimony of Wa-a-chan-ka-a," Proceedings of Military Commission for the 1863–64 Trial of Little Six [Shakopee], handwritten transcript, United States Army Military Commission, Sioux War Trials, 1862–65, United States Senate Records, NARG 46.

Wabasha (or Red Standard). "Testimony, June 15, 1868," *Papers Relating to Talks and Councils Held with the Indians in Dakota and Montana Territories in the Years 1866–1869* (Washington, D.C.: Government Printing Office, 1910), 90–91.

Wakute (or The Shooter). "Testimony, June 15, 1868," *Papers Relating to Talks and Councils Held with the Indians in Dakota and Montana Territories in the Years 1866–1869* (Washington, D.C.: Government Printing Office, 1910), 94.

Wakeman, Esther (or Mahpiyatowin or Blue Sky Woman). "Narrative," in Mr. and Mrs. Harry Lawrence, "The Indian Nations of Minnesota: The Sioux Uprising," in *Minnesota Heritage: A Panoramic Narrative of the Historical Development of the North Star State*, ed. Lawrence M. Brings (Minneapolis: T. S. Denison and Co., 1960), 80–82; Mrs. Harry Lawrence, Interview, April 27, 1965, typescript, DLA, MHS.

Wakeman, John C. (or Unktomiska or White Spider). "The Story of the Sioux Outbreak," recorded in the *Minneapolis Sunday Times*, August 15, 1897.

Weston, David (or Tunkanwanyakapi or Seeing Stone). "Evidence for the Defendants," *Sisseton and Wahpeton Bands v. the United States*, part 2, p. 304–21.

Whale, David (or Hmuyanka or Whirring Sound). "Evidence for the Defendants," *Sisseton and Wahpeton Bands v. the United States*, part 2, p. 338–43.

Williamson, Thomas (or Mahpiyasotodan or Smoky Cloud). "Evidence for the Defendants," *Sisseton and Wahpeton Bands v. the United States*, part 2, p. 287–303.

Wowinape (or The Appearing One or Thomas Wakeman). "Statement of Wo-wi-nap-a," recorded in *St. Paul Pioneer*, August 13, 1863.

Young, Benjamin. "Evidence for the Defendants," *Sisseton and Wahpeton Bands v. the United States*, part 2, p. 385–87.

Index

Picture Credits

The photographs and other images used in this book appear through the courtesy of the institutions listed below. The names of the photographers, when known, are in parentheses.

Pages 22, 28, 37 (courtesy of Amos Owen), 61 (Benjamin Upton), 64 (Martin's Gallery of St. Paul), 86, 101, 106 (courtesy of Joseph J. Martin), 110, 114, 121 (J. E. Whitney), 142, 155, 178, 195 (Isaac V. D. Heard, *History of the Sioux War*), 246, 257, 260, 262, 281 (J. E. Whitney), 292 (J. E. Whitney) — Minnesota Historical Society

Pages 41 and 81 — Edward E. Ayer Collection, The Newberry Library, Chicago, Illinois

Pages 46 and 288 — Chippewa County Historical Society, Montevideo, Minnesota

Page 71 — Browns Valley Historical Society, Browns Valley, Minnesota

Pages 148 and 242 (Gill) — National Anthropological Archives, Smithsonian Institution, Washington, D.C.

Pages 283 and 285 — Wanamaker Collection, William Hammond Mathers Museum, Indiana University, Bloomington, Indiana